One Thousand Years

EDITED BY RICHARD L. DEMOLEN

ESSAYS BY

David Herlihy

David Nicholas

Donald E. Queller

Robert E. Lerner

Jeffrey Burton Russell

One Thousand Years

WESTERN EUROPE IN THE
MIDDLE AGES

Houghton Mifflin Company · Boston

Atlanta · Dallas · Geneva, Illinois · Hopewell, New Jersey

Palo Alto · London

For the American Philosophical Society

CB
351
.D47

Printed in the U.S.A.

Library of Congress Catalog Card Number: 73-5246

ISBN: 0-395-14032-3

Contents

v

Preface

One Thousand Years: Western Europe in the Middle Ages is a collection of original essays in which five medievalists interpret the multifaceted world of western Europe between the collapse of the Roman Empire and the dawn of the modern era. The writers explore economic, social, political, intellectual, and religious developments during this large segment of our past. This book is an alternative to the chronological, single-author approach of most college textbooks. Concentrating on a unifying theme or themes, each author considers a major aspect of the Middle Ages in western Europe. The result is a thematic presentation of one thousand years of history, designed specifically for the undergraduate.

In "Ecological Conditions and Demographic Change" David Herlihy examines the effects of environment on medieval society. He analyzes the staggering consequences of the fall of the Roman Empire on population growth, the size of cities, and the deterioration of the environment. He also discusses the effects of desiccation, denudation, erosion, and demographic decline on the collapse of the Roman Empire. He describes the ominous effects of climate, settlement, communication, forests, agriculture, the manor, and internal constraints on the economy and ecology of the early Middle Ages. Acute population pressure, but little real population growth, and overcrowding in the midst of open spaces characterized the period between A.D. 500 and 1000. In his discussion of the age of expansion (ca. 1000–1350), he relates how internal colonization and the extension of Europe's frontiers enlarged the areas of settlement. The advance failed to stabilize, however, and by the time of the late Middle Ages (ca. 1350–1500), "war, plague, famine, and death . . . dominate the annals of the epoch, as they decimated the people." Herlihy concludes that ecological pressures are the products of social, institutional, technological, and physical and biological factors. Such pressures have led to disastrous social consequences as well as to major technological improvements.

David Nicholas, in "Patterns of Social Mobility," contends that social status in medieval society was not unchangeable. On the basis of his investigation of the nobility, the peasantry, and the bourgeoisie, he writes that "economic change and the physical necessity of contact among persons and groups made a static society impossible." In the early Middle Ages, physical power was the principal catalyst of social mobility. The process changed slowly in the intervening years, until in the fourteenth century economic power surpassed physical force as the primary means to effect upward mobility.

In the third essay, Donald E. Queller sees a "healthy" society as a configuration of coherent elements. Politics, religion, culture, society, and economics define it and promote its harmony. Queller applies this view in "Political Institutions," perceiving three major periods of change in the Middle Ages. He considers the efforts of western Europeans to devise an effective system of government—namely feudalism—after the collapse of the Roman Empire. In addition, he traces the origin and development of national monarchies in Sicily, France, and England during the High Middle Ages and the appearance of representative bodies such as the parliament in England and the cortes in Spain. Queller also relates how political institutions in the fourteenth and fifteenth centuries lost their idealism and degenerated into despotism amid chaos and depression.

Robert E. Lerner traces the demise of early Christianity's anti-intellectual strain and the rise of an intellectual tradition. In "Literacy and Learning," he examines "what men in the Middle Ages thought about learning, and how and to what extent they became learned." He explains how Saint Augustine engaged the problem of how a Christian should deal with classical education and culture and greatly affected the course of medieval education by not wholly rejecting the classical tradition. Augustine developed an attitude of compromise—"liberal education for an elite leading to biblical studies, technical education for some others, and the catechizing of the unlearned." Roman education and culture were replaced gradually with parochial pedagogy. The Carolingian Renaissance (ca. 750–850) ushered in a new age and a new perspective. It promoted an improvement in handwriting, a clarification of grammar, and a system of textual editing, in an effort to improve communication. Although late-ninth-century invasions blurred earlier advances, economic prosperity and population growth helped to produce the Renaissance of the Twelfth Century. Man turned to educational institutions as the means to economic advancement. Twelfth-century schools were clerically run but secularly oriented. In the thirteenth century, with the development of professional studies at the university level and lay primary schools, education became a reality for the layman. Despite setbacks in the fourteenth century, education managed to survive. Even in the face of anti-intellectual sentiment, the late Middle Ages saw the emergence of vernacular instruction, the education of lower classes, and the continued secularization of learning.

Jeffrey Burton Russell concludes the volume with "Varieties of Christian Experience." Going beyond R. W. Southern's social view of medieval Christianity, he argues persuasively that in the Middle Ages Christianity served as a radical witness to the Kingdom of God. Russell describes it in terms of two traditions—prophecy and order. The tradition of prophecy urged man to seek truth outside a transitory world; the tradition of order urged him to build a New Jerusalem in accordance with God's Ten Commandments. Russell develops his theme through biographical sketches of eight medieval Christians: Saint Benedict of Nursia (founder of Western monasticism), Saint Boniface

(Benedictine missionary), Gregory VII (pope), Saint Bernard of Clairvaux (Cisterican reformer), Valdes (lay heretic), Saint Louis (king of France), Saint Thomas Aquinas (Dominican theologian), and Julian of Norwich (anchoress).

In selecting the contributors, I relied upon the advice of my colleagues and deliberately chose medievalists who shared a common view of the past and who could work together compatibly. I wish to take this opportunity to thank them for their cooperation during the three-year period of the preparation of the manuscript. While writing their individual essays, the contributors read and criticized each other's work. Thus this book is in one sense a group project, and much of its strength and originality derives from the combined expertise of all the participants.

R.L.D.

One Thousand Years

"Good democracy" in the country, a late-fourteenth-century representation of the harmony resulting from sharing responsibility. Some of the men holding tools wear cowls; the others, probably peasants, are bareheaded.

I.

Ecological Conditions
and Demographic Change

DAVID HERLIHY

A SALIENT characteristic of recent trends in historical study has been a concern for ordinary men, who constitute the vast majority of all past generations but who have traditionally earned scant attention in historical literature. This concern has engendered an interest in the total society of past epochs, its numbers, its demographic characteristics, and the physical setting in which its members lived. New trends have thus carried the historian into the fields of historical demography and human ecology. The latter science in its most literal meaning is the study of the human community in relation to its environment, and it takes from demography part of its fundamental data. Doubtlessly, the present concern with questions of population and the environment has helped remind historians that ecological factors and ecological problems have played a role in all societies. Ecologists and demographers are also gaining from history a better sense of the subtle, complex, and at times paradoxical ways in which human communities have interacted with their physical surroundings.

In this essay we shall consider some demographic and ecological factors that seem to have influenced the history of the peoples of western Europe during the period traditionally called the Middle Ages. Our purpose is two-fold. For readers primarily interested in the Middle Ages, we hope to provide an introduction to factors, largely overlooked in older studies, that according to recent interpretations helped shape the civilization of the medieval world. For those concerned with the historical dimensions of demography or ecology, the essay is intended to illustrate the considerable interest of this lengthy chapter of Western history. It is of course true that deficiencies in the data limit what we can know about medieval society and its environment; it is also true that important tools of this inquiry, such as paleoclimatology and historical demography, are still so new that we are far from realizing their full potential. But enough can be known of the inter-actions of the medieval community and its surroundings to provide a grossly accurate picture. For ecological studies, the great interest of the Middle Ages, now and in the future, is that the period represents more than a millennium of fairly well documented human experience; it offers time, which brings in turn the opportunity, to observe how human communities acted under quite different ecological and demographic conditions.

The Birth of the Middle Ages

The origins of the Middle Ages were one with the decline and fall of the Roman Empire. In a strictly technical sense the Roman Empire fell only in the West, but even in the East, in spite of the continuation of imperial authority in the East Roman or Byzantine state, the transformations of antique civilization were so profound that we must recognize the appear-ance of a new culture and society.

The crisis of the ancient world was accompanied by both demographic and ecological changes, which helped make the society of the Middle Ages much different from its classical parent. Although no precise figures can be offered, a considerable contrast in the size of populations certainly distin-guished the two epochs. The settlements of the early Middle Ages seem to have been substantially smaller, at least in the West, than they had been at the height of the Roman Empire.

Occasionally, the demographic plunge dividing the ancient and medieval worlds is dramatically apparent. Most classical scholars, for example, con-sider that the city of Rome in the third century A.D. possessed at least 500,000 persons. It was huge; the walls constructed by Emperor Aurelian enclosed 1,230 hectares (about 3,075 acres). In the early Middle Ages (ca. A.D. 500 to 1000) probably no city in western Europe had as many as 20,000 inhabi-tants. Before 1500, the largest European cities (Paris, Milan, Venice, Naples) counted only between 100,000 and 150,000 citizens. Not until the middle of the seventeenth century, fifteen hundred years later, did European cities (London and Paris) finally reach and surpass the population apparently claimed by imperial Rome.

In rural areas of the empire, the most telling (though still indirect) evi-dence of declining numbers is the spread of *agri deserti,* "abandoned fields," which had begun before the end of Roman political rule in the West (A.D.

476). The distinguished British classicist A. H. M. Jones, a scholar not given to rash speculations, accepts as reasonable the estimate that one-sixth of the land in the East and one-third to one-half of the land in North Africa were lost to cultivation in the period of the late empire.

The population fall was accompanied by a visible deterioration of the physical environment, considered in human terms. As the cultivated area contracted, forests, moors, marshes, and deserts grew commensurably. In North Africa, for example, the Romans, aided perhaps by better weather or by an ingenious system of dams and aqueducts, had been able to maintain a settled agriculture in numerous locales that today are desert. By the fourth century, swamps were spreading in the Campagna south of Rome and in other lowland areas; mosquitoes from these Pontine swamps were to plague the Eternal City in the summertime until the twentieth century. Ravenna, Ostia, and other cities, major ports in the classical age, are today miles from the sea.

As the numbers of men decreased, their control over their surroundings seems to have weakened, and the environment rapidly lost the traces of human discipline. The literary sources of early medieval history leave the impression of extensive forests and wastelands. Saints' lives of the early Middle Ages frequently describe how holy men fled from communities to the nearby wilderness—even in such old-settled areas as central Italy. Frequently too they mention the ruins of a pagan temple or villa in the midst of this desolation.

Declining numbers of men and a weakening control over the physical surroundings plagued the Roman government from the second century A.D. and reached critical proportions during the last centuries of Roman rule in the West. The emperors encouraged the settlement of barbarians and prisoners of war upon the deserted fields and enlisted barbarian contingents into the army. To slow or halt the flight from the land, Diocletian, Constantine, and other emperors of the fourth century decreed that the cultivators known as *coloni,* even though technically freemen, had to remain permanently bound to the soil, and their children after them. The institution of the Roman "colonate" is often viewed as a principal source of medieval serfdom. The emperors similarly sought to bind to their station in life urban artisans, soldiers, even some government officials, in order to assure the performance of essential tasks. Such obligatory services were made hereditary as well. With dwindling human resources, only a totally regimented society seemed able to give to Rome any hope of survival.

But demographic and ecological trends could not be permanently reversed. They worked effectively to transform the ancient economy, society, and culture and to prepare the Middle Ages. Ancient civilization in all its aspects had been based upon cities—the Greek *poleis* and the Roman *civitates.* A great classical historian once described the empire as primarily a confederation of city-states. Large urban markets stimulated exchange between the cities and countryside, favored the growth of urban industries and the development of a commercially oriented agriculture. Besides merchants and artisans, the urban population included administrators, lawyers, and other professional men, who were usually literate and provided a sophisticated audience for the writers and thinkers of antiquity. Declining population weakened the cities and undermined their economic and cultural influence. Trade diminished, money transactions rarefied, and an agricultural economy aiming at local self-sufficiency came to dominate the western provinces. The literate classes, urban and lay, all but disappeared; only the clergy of the Christian Church preserved a mastery of letters. By the ninth century, to say "illiterate" was to signify "layman."

Decline in human numbers and visible environmental deterioration thus marked the transition from the ancient to the medieval worlds. How are these two phenomena related, and what other factors contributed to them? Scholars have proposed many theories to explain the crisis of the ancient world, and three of them have a special interest for ecologists and demographers. These theories would locate the principal reason for Rome's crisis in the following factors, respectively: environmental deterioration resulting from changes in climate, environmental deterioration resulting from human action, demographic decline provoked by certain social institutions and practices of ancient society.

Since the eighteenth century, scientists have been aware that the weather of the world changed greatly in the past. Since the late nineteenth century, they have known that the weather has also fluctuated during the brief span of historical time, the approximately five millennia in which men have known how to produce and preserve written records. (These five thousand years are of course a nearly infinitesimal interval on the scale of geological time.) At the turn of the nineteenth century, a young Russian naturalist, Prince Kropotkin, who later gained fame as a leader of the anarchist movement in Europe, was impressed by the desiccated and calcified remains of extensive forests on the arid steppes of Turkestan. He proposed the then daring hypothesis that the weather of Turkestan and the south Russian steppes had grown much drier in fairly recent times. In 1903 a team of American geographers and naturalists, under the auspices of the Carnegie Foundation, explored the steppes in search of evidence of climatic change. With them was a young student named Ellsworth Huntington, who thereafter devoted his life (for many years he was a professor at Yale University) to a study of weather and human civilization. The mature expression of his views is the third edition of his *Civilization and Climate,* published in 1924.

Huntington argued that cyclical waves of desiccation have struck large areas of the Northern Hemisphere and were most noticeable in the Mediterranean regions and the steppe lands of comparable latitudes stretching across central Asia. The chief source of moisture for the lands of the Northern Hemisphere is cyclonic weather systems, the depressions or "lows" familiar from weather reports, which move from west to east and carry moisture from the seas to the inland areas. The greater the frequency with which such depressions pass over a region, the more moisture it will receive. Today, the main depression track in Europe swings just north of the Cantabrian mountains in northwest Spain and the Pyrenees, concentrating rainfall in the northern parts of the Eurasian continent.

According to Huntington, the main track was subject to cyclical shifts, thus redistributing rainfall in the Northern Hemisphere. At certain epochs it followed a more southerly path, entering the Mediterranean region through the gap in the coastal mountains afforded by the Strait of Gibraltar and moving across the Mediterranean, Black, and Caspian seas into the steppes of central Asia. This route assured abundant precipitation for now relatively arid areas of the world, but the regions remained subject to recurring periods of desiccation.

Periodic shifts in the main depression track and resulting waves of desiccation explain what Huntington called the "pulse of Asia," the recurrent eruptions of the steppe peoples out of their homes in search of water and pastures. During the great age of classical antiquity, from about 2000 B.C. to A.D. 200, the depressions followed the southern track and favored the Mediterranean area and the central Asian steppes with relatively abundant rain. But from approximately the third century A.D. the main depression track once more bent to the north, with catastrophic effects in the Mediterranean regions and the central Asian steppes.

Rain diminished, and the resulting desiccation had a double impact. Within the empire, the diminution of rainfall hampered reforestation and provoked erosion. The good soil was lost, and lowland areas turned into swamps. Outside the empire, the desiccation of the steppes forced the nomadic peoples, notably the Huns, to migrate outside their ancestral homes to find pasture for their animals. The pressure from the steppes set in motion a vast migration of peoples. The Germans and other barbarians pressed across the borders of the Roman Empire and eventually ended its rule in the western provinces. A Spanish historian, Ignazio Olagüe, affirmed as recently as 1963, "the progress of aridity in the Mediterranean regions dislocated and ruined the great civilizations of antiquity."

Today, however, most scholars, both meteorologists and historians, express doubts about Huntington's grand exposition of the pulse of history. Virtually all paleoclimatologists admit that the weather of the world has fluctuated in historical times, but in spite of intensive efforts, no one has successfully proved the existence of weather cycles, whether short-term (as, for example, linked with the sun-spot cycle) or long-term. The analysis of tree rings, carried on principally in the southwest United States, has afforded an indirect insight into the weather of the past. The rings, formed yearly by the tree, indicate how favorable the weather of a given year was to growth. The studies have revealed fluctuations but not cycles, and the results are perhaps most impressive for showing the overall stability of weather conditions in this area of the world over the past millennium and more. Historians have been even more skeptical than climatologists about Huntington's theory. They have argued that in the absence of statistics concerning rainfall in antiquity the theory is beyond critical evaluation. They have further noted that the characteristic flora of the Mediterranean world—the palm, olive, and grape —seems to have remained the same throughout antiquity and is the same today. More trenchantly, Huntington's methods have been called too anthropocentric, too much based on human behavior, for which a variety of factors other than climate might have been responsible. In order to date the recurrent dry periods and to establish the "pulse of Asia," he seems to resort to a circular argument. Dry periods are dated by nomadic migrations. The nomads were allegedly driven from the steppes because their pastures were becoming desiccated; we know that their pastures were becoming desiccated primarily because they emerged from the steppes. In brief, in the absence of hard and certain evidence, Huntington's theory of the periodic desiccation of the Mediterranean region and the steppes remains an ingenious but unproved and perhaps unprovable hypothesis.

Still, the theory has had a lasting influence, and although the notion of cyclical recurrence of dry periods seems untenable, the fundamental assumption that the weather of central Asia especially has changed in historic time is better founded. Still today, paleoclimatologists, notably in the Soviet Union, continue to accumulate considerable evidence that a different climatic regime prevailed in central Asia within the bounds of historic time. Perhaps the last word on the theory of desiccation is yet to be stated. Moreover, Huntington forced historians to consider a factor, the physical environment of the classical world, which they had hitherto ignored. The continuing and now heightening interest in the role of water, weather, and soil in history undoubtedly owes much to Huntington's stimulating ideas.

Although the classical writers did not leave us statistics concerning rainfall, they left a rather abundant comment on agriculture and the quality of the soil. In 1916 a Russian scholar who was something of a polymath, Vladimir G. Simkhovitch, developed from those comments a thesis that has continued to intrigue historians. The Roman Republic had risen to dominance in the Mediterranean area principally through the efforts of peasant soldiers, who fed the community and filled the legions; they both fought and farmed with efficiency and often spectacular success. Then, in the first century B.C. as the republic was being transformed into the empire, the small farm and the social class of peasant fighters were all but swept from the Italian countryside by the inexorable advance of the latifundia (great estates). The Roman author Pliny the Elder in the first century A.D. affirmed that "the large estates have destroyed Italy and already too the provinces." The triumph of the latifundia brought numerous social, economic, and moral ills in its wake. The dispossessed small peasants flocked to the cities and swelled the ranks of an unemployed, parasitic proletariat, supported by doles of bread and entertained by circuses. Italy itself could not feed its own inhabitants but became critically dependent upon imports of grain from distant provinces, notably Egypt. The *agri deserti* spread across the country-side. The population declined, morals and morale decayed, and Rome could not find the fighters and the taxpayers needed to meet the growing barbarian menace.

The key to Rome's decline was thus the destruction of the small farms worked by peasant soldiers. Why could they not meet the competition of the great estates? Simkhovitch argued that soil exhaustion on a massive scale was ruining the empire and forcing the adoption of the more extensive agricultural techniques characteristic of the latifundia. The Roman poet Lucretius (d. 55 B.C.) and later Pliny affirmed that the soil no longer yielded its former abundance. The agricultural writer Columella, writing about A.D. 60, mentioned that many of his contemporaries believed that the land had grown old. Though he did not think that the soil was aging like a living organism, he did recognize that traditional yields had drastically declined. He therefore recommended that vines be raised instead of wheat, for no one could remember when in Italy a harvest of grain returned as much as four to one of the seed. Even under relatively primitive methods of agriculture, a fourfold yield must be considered a miserable return. Among the provinces, only Egypt, where the yearly flooding of the Nile restored the topsoil, escaped the blight of sterile fields. The small farmer, practicing intensive cultivation, could not gain enough produce from his modest and exhausted holding to survive. The owners of the latifundia concentrated their efforts on raising animals, thus favoring an extensive use of the sterile land. According to Cicero, Cato the Censor, who was for the Romans a patriarchal sage, ranked the most profitable characteristics of an estate in the following order: (1) good pasturage, (2) fairly good pasturage, (3) bad pasturage, and (4) tillable soil. The low value he gave to plowland clearly indicates, according to Simkhovitch, the exhaustion of the soil. "One single, major and strikingly variable productivity factor," concluded Simkhovitch, "suffices to solve the problem [of Rome's decline]. That factor—the exhaustion of Roman soil and the devastation of Roman provinces—sheds enough light for us to behold the dread outlines of its doom."

Simkhovitch did not anticipate one objection that was quickly raised against his theory: Is not soil exhaustion an abuse that is in large measure self-corrective? Will not a sterile and abandoned field rather quickly recover its fertility if allowed to lie fallow for relatively few years? But other scholars, continuing his line of inquiry, have affirmed that the agricultural methods of antiquity not only exhausted the soil but dealt it a long-lasting injury. The terrain and climate of the Mediterranean area make erosion of topsoil a permanent menace. The surface is formed predominantly of hills and mountains. Streams tend to be short and, in the rainy season, torrential. The rains come predominantly in the winter; the long and arid summers do not favor a rapid growth of trees, and forests once lost are with difficulty restored. Without trees to hold the soil, the hard rains of autumn and winter quickly erode the land. Rapid runoffs from the hills can injure agriculture on the plain by floods, impalustration (the formation of swamps), and the deposition of stones and other debris from the mountains.

Under such conditions, two characteristics of the ancient economy seem to have promoted denudation and erosion. The ancient economy undoubtedly consumed large quantities of wood. Although the Romans preferred bricks for their buildings, wood was needed to roof the many basilicas (courthouses) and, from the fourth century, the Christian churches modeled after them. Wood was the chief fuel for heating not only houses but the enormous Roman baths; it was essential too for the smelting of metals. The large mines of Spain probably could not have functioned in the absence of extensive, nearby forests. Finally, from wood were constructed the ships upon which essential communications depended.

Moreover, the extensive land use characteristic of the latifundia obstructed reforestation once the wood had been taken. Concentrating on raising animals, the owners of great estates owned huge herds of cattle and still larger flocks of sheep and goats. Pliny mentions an Italian landlord, Claudius Isidorus, who in his will disposed of 4,111 slaves, 3,600 teams of oxen, and 257,000 sheep and goats. The grazing habits of goats are particularly destructive; they readily consume young saplings and do not allow the land to regain its natural cover of trees. Even in the absence of a modern industrial plant, the Roman economy based upon the latifundia seems to have been powerful enough to do its environment major damage.

How extensive was erosion, and what was its role in Rome's decline? Recently, geographers and geologists have been studying the river valleys of the Mediterranean regions with remarkable if still inconclusive results. Erosion, impalustration, and aggradation (the building up of river valleys) are widely evident and seem to have been particularly rapid in the period of late antiquity and the early Middle Ages. It is not unusual to find as much as eight meters (twenty-six feet) of sediment in Mediterranean valleys deposited since Roman times. But geographers and geologists have been reluctant to speculate on the causes or the human impact of this considerable erosion. Distinctive climate or the destructive intervention of man may have been factors, but erosion of this sort must also be considered in some sense normal for the regions of the Mediterranean basin. Erosion to this extent certainly disturbed the agricultural economy of the valleys and in many lowland areas built up malarial swamps. On the other hand, by extending deltas and providing deep alluvial fill, the same erosion may have benefited the agriculture of future generations—or future civilizations. In spite of their cautious analysis, geographers and geologists have at least shown that the traditional "historian's faith in the permanence of the landscape," as one of them has phrased it, cannot now be justified. Either through climate or the work of men, the physical surroundings of classical settlements were often much different from what they are today, and even from what they were in the Middle Ages.

Roman institutions and practices—the latifundia, destructive tendencies of agriculture, the ill-considered use of limited supplies of wood—thus stand accused in the eyes of some scholars of accelerating if not precipitating the crisis of the ancient world. Still other scholars read the same data in a slightly different fashion. In their estimation, certain fundamental social and political institutions of the classical world worked to depress the birth rate, encouraged depopulation, and thus deprived the empire of the manpower it needed both to defend itself against its foreign enemies and to maintain a productive economy.

This analysis has been applied with particular rigor to the institution of ancient slavery. One of the best succinct examples of it is contained in an article by a French medievalist, Marc Bloch, which was published in 1948, four years after the author's death. Slaves were everywhere in the ancient world, Bloch reminds us; ancient civilization would be inconceivable without them. Under harsh conditions of life, the slaves of antiquity had little will or incentive to bring children into the world, to care for them, and thus to pass on to them their own misery. To replenish this essential working force, the Romans depended upon constant large additions to the ranks of the unfree. These were principally obtained in the course of Rome's successful conquests. But after the first century A.D. the Roman frontiers stabilized, conquests ceased, and the external sources of new slaves dried up. The slaves within the empire, failing to maintain their own numbers through natural reproduction, declined in numbers, and the Roman economy had to function even while its capacity to do work was falling. It was as if a modern industrial economy had to face each new year with a diminished number of machines. Eventually, the economy could not meet the heavy demands placed upon it, both military and civilian. The empire entered into a state of crisis from which it could not recover, at least in the West. The ancient slaves thus overturned the system that oppressed them, not by violently revolting but by quietly dying.

Further, slavery demeaned the dignity of labor and helped paralyze the technological development of antiquity. Why design and invest in better machines when only despicable bondsmen would benefit from them?

Other scholars have seen an analogous situation in the relations between the Roman government and the poor but free classes and would locate the root cause of Rome's crisis in a *penuria hominum,* a growing lack of workers and warriors, whether slave or free. There is little doubt that the emperors were imposing heavy burdens in taxes upon their subjects, which particularly oppressed the poor. A fourth-century Christian moralist, Salvian of Marseille, has left a vivid (if perhaps exaggerated) picture of the plight of the poor. Pursued by the tax collector, they either fled to the barbarians or sought out the protection and patronage of some local lord, giving up their properties and assuming a quasi-servile status. These harassed and oppressed persons, it is argued, refused to or could not marry and raise enough children to maintain their own numbers. Fiscal and social oppression, abandonment of the land, and depopulation are thus taken to be closely linked phenomena marking out the course of Rome's decline. The ultimate solution had to be a different fiscal and social system, somewhat less oppressive for the humble, somewhat fairer in its distribution of social burdens and benefits. Inequities of this kind were thus a major factor in generating depopulation, but the hard-pressed Roman state had no time to implement the needed reforms.

Inevitably, this view also has its critics. A fundamental assumption is that the oppressed do not reproduce well; there are suggestions, but unfortunately no conclusive evidence, that this accurately describes the demographic behavior of the ancient slaves and poorer freemen. The argument seems plausible, but it is not yet scientifically established.

Doubtlessly, historians will continue to interpret the interactions of ecological deterioration and demographic decline in different ways in their efforts to understand the transition from ancient civilization to the medieval world. We can still hope for fresher and firmer evidence, especially from archaeological investigations, which can cast much light upon both ancient society and its physical surroundings. Finally, one additional comment may be offered concerning the ecological and demographic transition from antiquity to the Middle Ages. Environmental deterioration was occurring against a background not of a growing population, as in our own time, but of one almost certainly declining. The extensive agricultural methods, denudation of the land, erosion, were closely linked, whether as effect or cause, with a contracting human community. The disappearance of men, as well as their rapid increase, seems capable of upsetting the delicate ecological balance.

Economy and Ecology in the Early Middle Ages, ca. 500–1000

The crisis of antique civilization helped implant a new ecological system in western Europe, a new set of relationships between human communities and their physical environment. We have already reviewed its chief characteristics: a thin population; a vast extent of forests, moors, meadows, and wastelands; a dearth of towns; and an economy based primarily upon agriculture and herding; in sum, a preponderantly peasant society.

Another factor influencing human life in the early Middle Ages was climate. For this period, as for all periods before the survival of accurate records, climate remains an elusive but obviously important subject. One way paleoclimatologists study the weather of the past is by investigating the advances and retreats of glaciers. In expanding, almost certainly in response to a protracted decline in annual mean temperatures, glaciers frequently uproot and bury trees or shrubs, which are then exposed in subsequent glacial retreats. Through analysis of the radioactivity of carbon-14, an isotope of carbon, contained in the wood, it is possible to estimate within one or two centuries when the tree or shrub was growing. This information indicates when the glacier advanced, killing the tree, and indirectly signifies when the weather became cooler.

Studies of the glacier of Fernau in the Tyrolean Alps between Austria and Italy have indicated, for example, that a maximum advance of the glacier occurred between A.D. 400 and 750; this suggests that the climate of the early Middle Ages was distinctly colder than it is today—at least in the Tyrolean Alps. But the climate was growing warmer from approximately A.D. 750, and this warming phase reached its peak probably between the years 1000 and 1200. Paleoclimatologists now speak with confidence of an "early medieval warm epoch," or a "little optimum" of the early Middle Ages. But there are no clear and certain indications of how this favorable climate affected European settlement, at least within its older centers.

Favorable weather did seem to allow European settlement to push into new areas—Iceland, Greenland, and other islands of the North Atlantic, and probably into the higher latitudes and higher slopes of hills and mountains across the continent. Grapevines, for example, were common, though not exactly numerous, in England between the eleventh and thirteenth centuries; elsewhere too they were being cultivated at altitudes and latitudes that are too high or too far north for grapes to survive today. In the North Atlantic, drift ice seems to have offered no hazard to navigation, even in the waters off the northern coast of Iceland, where such ice is now common. The climatic optimum thus seems to have encouraged the Viking explorations and settlements in Iceland and Greenland and the discovery of "Vinland" somewhere on the North American continent. Even the name Vinland gives some suggestion of a mild climate in the North Atlantic at about the year 1000. The most visible, though surely not the only and perhaps not the most important, effect of the "early medieval warm epoch" was the enlarging of the areas of possible human settlement within Europe and at its margins.

The population of early medieval Europe, though small, was not distributed evenly across the countryside. The people tended to cluster into relatively large, often quite densely settled communities or villages, which remained separated by extensive tracts of nearly deserted land. For example, in the first quarter of the ninth century, probably during the reign of the great Frankish emperor Charlemagne (768–814) or of his successor Louis the Pious (814–840), the monastery of Saint-Germain-des-Prés, located in what is now the Latin quarter of Paris, drew up a list of its serfs, who were settled on some twenty estates in the environs of Paris. The survey probably did not include all the inhabitants of the villages, since freemen or the serfs of other lords presumably were not included in it. Still, the document enumerates about ten thousand persons, which represents an approximate density of settlement in the range between twenty-six and twenty-nine persons per square kilometer.

The figure seems extraordinarily high. Fifty years ago, a perceptive French medievalist, Ferdinand Lot, pointed out that one well-documented village named Palaiseau, now a Parisian suburb, probably possessed under Charlemagne the same number of inhabitants as it claimed in the early eighteenth century. On the basis of this density of settlement, with the assumption that all Carolingian France might have shared it, Lot and other scholars estimated that the population of France in the Carolingian period was between 14 million and 26 million. If such calculations were at all close to the truth, France under Charlemagne would have contained as many inhabitants as France on the eve of the Black Death of 1348, and even as many as the France of the "sun king," Louis XIV (1643–1715).

The fallacy in this reasoning, as critics subsequently pointed out, was the assumption that all France shared the density of settlement characteristic of these estates, mostly located near Paris. The most recent interpretations of the importance of these figures stress not the size of Carolingian France but the remarkably uneven geographic distribution of its people, the sharp contrasts between densely settled "population islands" and the vast expanse of surrounding forests and wastelands.

Besides highly clustered settlement, a second factor profoundly influenced the society of the early Middle Ages: sporadic and unreliable communications. The Carolingian emperors, to be sure, made strenuous efforts to maintain contact through *missi dominici,* "messengers of the lord," with the far-flung lands of their empire. Monasteries, churches, and important laymen often imposed upon their subjects and dependents an obligation to maintain horses and to carry messages when so ordered. News, rumors, legends, administrative decrees, letters, and books often traveled remarkably well over great distances. The German chronicler Thietmar of Merseburg (d. 1018) shows an accurate knowledge of events in distant Kiev. But given the sporadic character of much of this contact, writers of the early Middle Ages could also be remarkably ignorant of events occurring much closer to home. Fulbert, bishop of Chartres in northern France, was surprised to learn that the neighboring ruler, Canute the Great (1014–1035), king of Denmark and of England, whom he thought to be a pagan, had been baptized at birth.

Trade too continued. The Christian liturgy required wine, and many regions could not produce their own, even in this period of climatic optimum. Salt and iron were similarly essential and not everywhere available. The great men of the age still appreciated spices in their food and delighted in the luxurious cloths from the lands of the eastern Mediterranean. Although trade never ceased, it remained unreliable; communities could not depend on commerce regularly to supply a substantial part of their basic needs. Bulky commodities such as cereals were especially difficult to transport, and famine could frequently strike one place while plenty prevailed in a neighboring locale.

Under such conditions, communities sought to achieve economic self-sufficiency, to meet as many local needs as possible through local production. Charlemagne's capitulary *De Villis (Concerning Estates)*—an administrative directive dispatched to his local officials and stewards—gives an excellent expression of this policy. Although the stewards were to deliver provisions for the court and army, there is no suggestion that they were regularly selling produce at an external market. The stewards were also to maintain their own brewers, smiths, carpenters, soap makers, weavers, and other artisans, so that purchases would not have to be made outside the estates. The great emperor even listed seventy-five plants and about twenty types of tree that were to be planted on his lands to assure self-sufficiency in fruits and herbs. The ideal of local self-sufficiency, even if only partially achieved, meant that the estates had to carry on a range of economic activities, both agricultural and industrial, even if their lands or resources were not suited for them.

In the economic life of these scattered settlements, the surrounding forests, moors, and wastelands had a particular importance. Wood was the basic building material in the early Middle Ages. The forests provided not only the wattle characteristically used for constructing the peasants' hovels but also the lumber needed for erecting the churches, fortresses, and palaces of the aristocracy. Not until the twelfth and still more in the thirteenth century was stone widely applied in building, its appearance indicating improved technical skills, a higher living standard, and perhaps also an expanding area of settlement and a declining extent of woodland. Wood was used in making boats, barrels (Charlemagne insisted that they rather than skins be used for carrying his wine), fences, shingles, and most tools. It was the essential fuel. The forest also yielded the resin used in torches, bark for making rope, charcoal for smelting metal, wax for candles, and honey, which, in the absence of sugar, was the only sweetener in the diet.

Horses, cattle, and pigs were permitted to roam freely through the woods and wastes, feeding upon grasses, nuts, leaves, and bark. Pigs, the most efficient foragers, were also the most numerous animals, and consequently pork was the meat usually consumed. Medieval men, especially the leaders of society, eagerly hunted wild animals in the forest—deer, boars, rabbits, foxes, and wolves. The hunt was far more than a diverting sport; it was an exercise for war, a means of protecting domesticated herds and flocks from wild predators, and an important source of meat.

Nevertheless, forests were a principal obstacle to the economic and social advance of early medieval society. Growth in population inevitably made essential the clearing of new lands, but for long the medieval community seems to have been too poor or too disorganized to launch a vigorous attack upon the wastelands. The population seems also to have retained a deep fear of the wilderness. The best expression of this is probably in the Anglo-Saxon epic *Beowulf,* which presents the uninhabited wilderness as the abode of dark and fearsome monsters that constantly make war upon the society of men. Only heroes like Beowulf himself dared venture into their hostile domains. Terror of the wilderness seems to have been a principal factor in keeping the men of the early Middle Ages huddled together in their small but frequently crowded and harassed communities.

The peasants, timidly exploiting the resources of the forest, depended for their sustenance primarily upon settled agriculture. The period witnessed several changes and improvements in the routines of cultivation and in the tools by which the peasants, especially in northern Europe, worked the soil.

Nitrates or nitrogen compounds are essential to the growing plant; cereals in particular rapidly deplete the soil of the nitrates naturally found within it. The restoration of nitrates to the land is therefore a central problem in any agricultural system. One rich source of nitrates is the manure from farm animals. Where those animals are many, the nitrogen exchange between plants and animals can be quite vigorous, and the fertility of the soil can be efficiently maintained. However, under systems of primitive agriculture, farms and estates were not productive enough to support many animals, and the supply of manure was inadequate to maintain fertility. It was therefore necessary to allow the fields periodically to lie fallow; in this period of rest, bacteria found naturally in the soil could replenish the needed nitrates by fixing nitrogen directly from the air.

In classical antiquity, the most common practice was to sow a field with cereals for one year and then rest it the next. This was the two-field system. The cereal was usually winter wheat, planted in the fall; its growth was aided by the rains of autumn, winter, and early spring, characteristic of Mediterranean areas. But the rotation meant that only 50 per cent of the land was under cultivation in any given year.

North of the Alps and Pyrenees, sources from the late eighth century show the practice of a new system of crop rotation, which was better suited to the distinctive conditions of soil and climate characteristic of northern Europe.

This three-field system differed from the older two-field system primarily in the introduction of a spring planting into the cycle. A field, in other words, was planted first with winter wheat, then with a spring crop (fast-growing cereals such as oats and barley or legumes such as beans and peas), and then allowed to lie fallow. Spring crops were difficult to raise in Mediterranean regions because of the scant rains of late spring and early summer, but northern Europe was favored with a plentiful rainfall in all seasons. The three-field system possessed several advantages. Two-thirds of the land was kept under cultivation. The alternation of a winter crop with a spring crop was good for the soil; legumes in particular aided the restoration of fertility. The risk of famine lessened, for the food supply was not dependent upon a single harvest. The peasant's labors were better distributed throughout the year. Finally, one important use of the spring planting was fodder for animals. Larger herds intensified the nitrogen exchange between plants and animals and thus raised the level of fertility and productivity.

The alluvial soils of the north European plain tend to be much heavier and wetter than those characteristic of most southern regions, where hills and high plateaus dominate the landscape. The cultivator of the classical Mediterranean world had worked with the *aratrum,* a light scratch plow; because of the risk of erosion, he did not attempt to cut the land deeply or to turn a furrow. The light plow, however, was not suited for the heavy soils of the North. There, the fields were better prepared for planting by cutting the soil deeply and turning a furrow. The resulting ridge and furrow pattern allowed excess moisture to be drained, and the deep plowing improved the circulation of minerals and plant nutrients within the ground. At an unknown time and place, but probably during the sixth century in north-central Europe, a heavy plow called the *carruca* or *charrue* came into extensive use and was subsequently adopted in surrounding regions. A more complex instrument than the older scratch plow, the *carruca* consisted of three basic parts: a colter or long knife set at its front to cut the soil deeply, a plowshare to widen the breach, and a moldboard to turn the furrow. For the first time, the heavy plow made possible the efficient cultivation of Europe's most fertile area, the great plain of the North.

However, the heavy plow was difficult to move. The peasants sought greater traction by hitching as many as eight oxen to it. Horses too were harnessed. Surprisingly, the men of the ancient world joined the horse to his burden only with pliant straps, which cut off his wind as he labored. The horse was also hitched too high on his withers and thus prevented from throwing his full weight into pulling his load. The firm, "modern" horse collar first appears in illuminated manuscripts of the Carolingian age; it permitted the horse to work without cutting off his air and also (since he was harnessed lower on his withers) to take full advantage of his weight to develop traction. This deceptively simple invention seems to have increased the efficiency of the horse's traction by a factor of four. Other inventions enhanced the role of the horse in medieval economic life. The horseshoe, known but apparently little used in the ancient world, protected his sensitive hoofs, allowing him to work with diminished risk of injury. The tandem harness permitted horses to be hitched one behind the other as well as side by side; the stirrup kept the rider firmly in the saddle, even when wielding a heavy ax or lance. Without the stirrup, the heavily armed mounted warrior—the knight—would probably never have acquired his prominent position in medieval armies and consequently in medieval society.

From about 750, the new agricultural methods and tools appear in our sources, and we also learn of the existence of a fundamental institution of medieval agrarian society. The manor was a highly disciplined community of peasants who owed rents and services to a lay or ecclesiastical lord. At no point in its history did the manor dominate all regions of Europe; it was characteristically found only in areas of good soil and intensive agriculture, in the great plain of the North and the river valleys of the South. We do not know when manors were first organized. Some historians believe they were the direct descendants of the villas of the ancient world, and others maintain that they were formed sometime in the early Middle Ages, perhaps as late as the eighth century. All that can be said with certainty is that the sources do not give us a good picture of manors until after 750, until the Carolingian age of European history.

Most residents of the manors were serfs, who could not, nor could their children after them, leave the estate without the lord's consent. Still, the social position of the medieval serf was distinctly better than that of the slave of the ancient world. He retained a moral right to his family farm, called in its usual Latin name the *mansus*, which he could pass on to his descendants. The lord could not take the farm from the serf or the serf from his farm without committing a grave ethical and religious offense. The dues to which the serf was subject, though heavy, were considered fixed by a timeless tradition that even the lord had to respect. Manorial discipline, in other words, defined by tradition, in important ways bound the master as well as his dependents.

Perhaps the most distinctive feature of the manor is that at one and the same time it was the basic economic, social, and political unit of early medieval society. As an economic unit, it was primarily organized for agricultural production. Physically, the manor was divided into two approximately equal parts—the area taken up by the separate farms of the servile families, and the lord's own reserve or demesne, from which he took the total harvest. To work his demesne, the lord required that his serfs spend usually half their time (three days per week) tilling his lands, and he imposed even heavier services at busy times of the year such as fall planting and summer harvest. The serfs were subject to a variety of other payments or dues. They often paid a head tax, made gifts to their lord of eggs in the spring or a capon in the fall, and were liable to extraordinary payments at times of special need. In keeping with the ideal of local self-sufficiency, the manor was the basic unit for the production of goods, notably cloth and clothing. The wives of the serfs often had to labor in a special workshop to produce the garments needed by the community.

The manor was also a social unit; most of its residents lived out their lives within the physical and social space it defined. Even to marry outside the manor required the lord's permission. Kinship ties, as well as common service to the lord, thus helped hold together the manorial community. The lord, moreover, was not only the owner of the manorial lands but also the political chief of the community. He presided over a court that heard most of the disputes involving his dependents. He imposed taxes and recruited and organized the military contingents that the distant king or emperor might require from him. His "banal rights" (that is, rights from the ban, meaning governmental authority) gave him a monopoly over milling, baking, brewing, the sale of salt, and other economic activities. The manorial community, bound tightly together by economic, social, and political ties, fully reflects the intense localism and local self-sufficiency characteristic of Western society in the early Middle Ages.

The development of new agricultural techniques and tools and the appearance of the manor did not, however, result in immediate and permanent improvements in the material levels of European life. The population does seem to have expanded, and perhaps production likewise, during the early Carolingian age, and this may have assisted Charlemagne, who reigned from 768 to 814, in establishing his enormous empire.

But the successes and apparent prosperity of Charlemagne's reign were remarkably short-lived. Particularly after 850, a new dark age descended over Europe, and the shadows persisted until the eleventh century. New waves of invaders—Vikings from the north, Hungarians or Magyars from the east, and Saracens from the south—swept into Europe; the later Carolingians and their successors for long seemed incapable of mounting an effective defense. The church as well as the state fell upon dark days; the two ills of simony (the buying and selling of church offices) and sexual incontinence ran rampant through the clergy, provoking a near breakdown in ecclesiastical discipline and morality. Severe famines struck Europe in appalling numbers and seem to have been especially severe about the year 1000, when, in the eyes of several chroniclers, they portended the end of all mankind.

There is considerable evidence that an underlying economic crisis was contributing to this chaos. One principal obstacle to achieving or maintaining a satisfactorily productive economy in Europe was the uneven distribution of settlement, the clustering of the population into densely settled communities, isolated from one another and seeking to solve their problems with local resources. Within their restricted geographic space, these communities could not effectively cope with the problems thrust upon them—problems of security, of supplying essential needs, and of maintaining adequate balance between their numbers and their land. They were especially vulnerable to population pressures. Rather than directing their crowded residents toward an attack upon the surrounding wilderness, these communities sought support for them through allowing established farms and estates to be divided into ever smaller and ever less efficient parcels. Both peasants and lords tried to compensate for the inadequacies of their holdings by constantly trading land in an effort to put together reasonably efficient farms and estates. But the pernicious practice of subdividing properties continued. In other words, population pressures were turned inward, and they worked to undermine the efficiency of agricultural production, deepen the poverty of the people, and increase the risks of famine.

Why were these communities so much turned inward? Some historians now point to certain powerful "internal constraints" that kept people huddled together in their crowded settlements set in the midst of emptiness. These were the sense of safety afforded by numbers in an age often disturbed by invasions and wars; the strength of family and kinship ties in villages where for generations intermarriage had linked neighbors; manorial discipline, or the interest of lords in maintaining close supervision over their serfs; low productivity, which could not easily support without extraordinary effort the expensive work of felling trees, clearing land, and feeding colonists until their first harvests; and finally, a deeply rooted fear of the wilderness.

European economic life in the early Middle Ages was thus rife with paradoxes, which became especially pronounced between 850 and 1000. Poverty and starvation were widespread in the midst of apparently abundant resources and in spite of a satisfactory technology. After 850 in particular the communities were gripped by acute population pressures but seem to have achieved little real population expansion. By about the year 1000, Europe desperately needed an integration of efforts on a broad geographic scale if it was to achieve an acceptable balance between its people and its lands.

The Age of Expansion, ca. 1000–1350

The economic history of the early Middle Ages is a record of significant achievements and some stunning reversals. The extension of new forms of settlement—most notably, the family farm—and the development of technologies and tools appropriate for agriculture in northern Europe helped establish a new ecological system in the West. But that system still possessed some critical weaknesses, especially in the clustering of its population into packed communities and the strength of the constraints that kept those communities turned in upon themselves. Acute population pressure, but little real population growth; overcrowding in the midst of still abundant open spaces—this was the paradoxical state of many European communities in the tenth century.

In contrast, the period from early in the eleventh to the middle of the fourteenth century was one of sustained expansion, discernible in the size of the cultivated area, the number of peoples, and the productivity of the economy. Internal colonization and the expansion of Europe's frontiers considerably and quite visibly enlarged the area of settlement. Although the evidence is nearly all indirect, it remains incontrovertible that the number of Europeans was also growing. Figures describing the performance of the economy are nearly nonexistent, but new forms of economic endeavor associated with commerce and town industries, which had all but disappeared in the early Middle Ages, once again achieved prominence. The qualitative change, the appearance of a more varied and complex economy, certainly indicates a quantitative expansion in output. This remarkable growth in turn sustained the brilliant flowering of medieval culture in the central span of its history.

Here we shall examine the forces that initially helped transform the beleaguered Europe of the tenth century into the growing Europe of the eleventh, twelfth, and thirteenth centuries. We must also examine in greater detail the economic expansion.

A variety of factors were working from about the year 1000 to break down local obstacles to the movement of men and goods and thus to readjust the balance between men and land in medieval Europe. We know what some of the factors were, but it is still not possible to rank them in order of importance or to explore satisfactorily their complex interrelationships. These problems will undoubtedly attract the close attention of historians in the years to come.

On the local level, one powerful force turning communities inward was the discipline characteristic of manorial organization, the reluctance of lords to permit the departure of men who owed them services. Manorial discipline seems to have weakened considerably in Europe amid the chaos of the tenth century. Lords sometimes lost track of who their serfs were, or they were unable to extract the dues and services owed them. In a world dominated by tradition, once obligations were allowed to lapse, they were with difficulty restored. Some historians believe that the bonds of kinship, which had also helped knit together the local community, were weakening. New forms of association, based upon common economic interests or upon the feudal relationship of lord and followers, began to compete with ties of blood for the loyalty of men and frequently prevailed over them. The blows suffered by Europe in the post-Carolingian chaos were, in other words, not without a positive value, for they loosened the grip of older and sometimes obstructive institutions. Then too, the revival of commerce from the early eleventh century reduced the need for local self-sufficiency. Lords and peasants could concentrate their efforts on what their lands could best produce and trade for their other needs at market.

This, however, required the establishment of fairly secure social and political conditions over entire regions. The need for personal protection in a tumultuous age had also been among the most effective forces in keeping the population of the early Middle Ages huddled together in overcrowded communities. From the middle of the tenth century, the incursions of Vikings, Hungarians, and Saracens significantly abated. Probably more important was the growth of effectively governed feudal principalities from the eleventh century. Counties, duchies, and kingdoms in the North and West of Europe and city republics in Italy sought with ever greater success to limit brigandage and private warfare and to develop systems of law and courts to effectively limit recourse to violence.

The church too, which claimed a large share of the resources and talent of Europe, joined in the quest for security. The church had been a principal victim of the chaos and disorders. From the tenth century, and still more vigorously in the eleventh, a group of reformers within the church tried to suppress simony and sexual incontinence, which had disturbed clerical life in the West. This movement is usually called the Gregorian reform, after its principal leader, Pope Gregory VII (1073–1085). To support the new celibate clergy and to free them from temptations to simony, the principal goal of the reformers became the restoration of the landed endowment of the church, a large part of which had fallen into the hands of laymen in the tenth century. Through movements known as the Truce of God and the Peace of God, the reformers sought to limit fighting to certain periods of the year and to win for certain persons (clerics, women, peasants, merchants) and places (churches and consecrated ground) immunity from violence. To direct the energies and the ambitions of the troublesome warriors into socially acceptable outlets, the reformers urged that they fight for the cause of Christianity in Spain, southern Italy, or Germany, or that they undertake crusades to Palestine. In summoning the first crusade at Clermont in southern France in 1095, Pope Urban II is reported to have told the assembled knights that because they were too many for their narrow land, shut in between the mountains and the sea, they murdered and devoured one another and therefore should betake themselves to Jerusalem, the navel of the world, and not allow concern for their families or possessions to detain them. The church too was working to turn the gaze of these warriors toward the outer world.

The loosening of internal constraints permitted Europeans to flow out of the old centers of settlement and to launch a vigorous attack upon the continent's extensive forests and wastelands. All segments of society participated in this massive reclamation of land. Great lords, lay and ecclesiastical, established "new villages" (*ville nove, villes neuves*) or free villages upon their lands and offered favorable terms to colonists willing to settle in them. Typically, the new settlers were obligated to pay a moderate yearly rent but not to render labor services; they could pass on to their heirs the land they cleared or sell it and move on. A serf who remained in such a village a year and a day without being reclaimed by his lord was guaranteed his freedom. A new religious congregation, the Cistercians (founded in 1098), consciously sought out wild and isolated locales to establish their houses. Aided by lay brothers known as *conversi,* Cistercians developed excellent methods of "high farming." Their estates in northern and western England, for example, were principal suppliers of raw wool not only for the textile towns of Flanders but for distant Italy.

Within France, these *grands défrichements,* "great clearances," progressed so rapidly that by 1300 a larger area of France was under the plow than is cultivated today. The sea was pushed back along the North Sea coast in the Low Countries and along the shores of the Bay of Biscay in France. River valleys too were being drained of the swamps that frequently had limited cultivation in the early Middle Ages.

The internal expansion of the area of cultivation was matched by an equally vigorous expansion of Europe's external frontiers. On the Iberian Peninsula, the borders of the Carolingian Empire had not extended much beyond the southern slopes of the Cantabrian and Pyrenees mountains; the southern limit of Charlemagne's "March of Spain" had been the Ebro River, which flows into the Mediterranean close to Barcelona. But in the eleventh and twelfth centuries, the small Christian states formed in the north of the peninsula, led by Aragon in the east and Castile in the west, pushed relentlessly against the Muslim principalities in the south. This *Reconquista,* "reconquest," gained its greatest single victory in 1212 at the battle of Las Navas de Tolosa in southern Spain, where the Christian forces defeated a Muslim army from North Africa. The victory enabled the Christian states to establish dominion over virtually all the peninsula, with the exception only of the small principality of Granada.

To the east, warriors and peasants, chiefly recruited from German lands and the Low Countries, were penetrating beyond the Elbe River, which had marked the effective eastern limit of the Carolingian Empire. Their movement, known to history as the *Drang nach Osten,* "Push to the East," took two principal directions, the one following the shores of the Baltic Sea in the north and the other moving down the Danube valley in the south. By the time the German expansion lost momentum in the fourteenth century, it had succeeded in tripling the area of Germanic settlement over what it had been in Carolingian times. The two states of Austria and Brandenburg-Prussia, destined for major roles in subsequent European history, were formed mostly as a result of this successful push to the east.

In the Mediterranean regions, knights from the French duchy of Normandy, invited into southern Italy as mercenaries from approximately 1036, dislodged both the Byzantines and the Muslims who had been contending for domination over the area. Under Robert Guiscard (1057–1085), they set up a Norman duchy in southern Italy. Robert's brother Roger I (1085–1101) conquered Sicily, and his son Roger II united all the Norman principalities of southern Italy and Sicily and secured recognition as king from Pope Innocent II. At the same time, Christian fleets, from Pisa and Genoa in particular, were freeing Sardinia, Corsica, the Balearics, and other islands of the western Mediterranean from Muslim rule. The most dramatic example of European resurgence in this epoch was the series of armed expeditions to Palestine, initiated in 1095, the crusades. Although they are the best known of Europe's medieval excursions, the impact they had on the boundaries of Christendom was the least lasting.

The new mobility of the population evident from the eleventh century was accompanied by changes in the rural institutions, particularly in the organization of the manor, or great property. In fact, in the tumultuous tenth century it is frequently difficult to discern how agricultural production was being carried on and thus to trace how the manor was changing in most parts of Europe. In Italy, for example, when our records provide us a new view of the countryside from the eleventh and twelfth centuries, lords were no longer actively engaged in the direct cultivation of extensive demesnes; the great property had largely come to rest on long-term leases to free cultivators, set for high rents usually in kind. In other words, the labor obligation imposed upon serfs, which had been the cornerstone of the Carolingian manor even in Italy, had faded in importance. North of the Alps, the decline of direct cultivation of the lord's demesne came more slowly, but there too the trend away from farming through forced labor was unmistakable.

Several factors contributed to the transformation of the great property. In an age of expansion, lords in old centers of settlement had little hope of holding their peasants, even their serfs, to the soil, unless they offered terms of tenure comparable to those prevailing in the new villages and along the frontiers. Moreover, the growth of a strong market for agricultural products stimulated and encouraged a reorganization of cultivation in the interests of greater flexibility and efficiency. The traditional requirement that the peasant divide his efforts between working his own farm and his lord's demesne was wasteful; much time and energy were lost as the serf moved back and forth between his land and the often distant fields of his lord. Moreover, he was likely to cultivate his lord's land with minimal care and zeal. The lease of a fairly compact farm to a free cultivator increased the efficiency of the tenant's efforts and his incentive to work the land well. Although rents were high, he could still hope to produce a surplus, which could be converted at the market into money or exchanged for desired goods. If he worked the land poorly, he might lose it when his lease expired. In sum, the old manorial structure was too rigid and could not easily adapt to the needs of an expanding society. Manorial custom bound the lord as well as the serf, and he was not free to alter the traditional ways by which the land was worked. The lord frequently found serfdom a principal obstacle to changing his own managerial policies or use of the land. Emancipation, in other words, and the new reliance upon free tenants, liberated the lord as well as the cultivator.

In England, the movement away from cultivation through forced labor followed a distinctive path. The labor obligation seems to have been declining in the late twelfth century. However, the development of a strong market for cereals in northern Europe, generated by the needs of the growing Flemish textile towns, seems to have given the English lords a powerful incentive to continue, and perhaps to enlarge, the direct cultivation of their lands, and thus to preserve or even to restore the labor obligation upon their dependents. The "classical" manor thus lasted in England considerably longer than it did on the continent; not until after 1300 does the characteristic conversion to long-term, high-rent leases triumph. But even in the thirteenth century, the English manor, producing for a commercial market, differed fundamentally from the Carolingian estate, governed as it was by the ideal of self-sufficiency and serving the needs of closed communities.

Of no less importance for the society of the central Middle Ages were the revival of commercial exchange and the considerable growth of artisan industries in European towns. This too reflects the breakdown of the isolation and local self-sufficiency characteristic of communities in the early Middle Ages. The lands touching on the Mediterranean, especially Italy, were early participants in what many historians now term the commercial revolution of the Middle Ages. Again, especially from the year 1000, Venice, Amalfi, Pisa, and Genoa were taking advantage of new contacts with the East to bring silks and other fine cloths, spices (including condiments, medicinal herbs, and dyes), jewels, relics of saints, and other small and precious objects into Europe. The mass pilgrimages and crusades to the Holy Land introduced thousands of Westerners to Eastern commodities and thus helped create a strong market for them after the pilgrims and crusaders returned home. In turn, the Western merchants carried materials that were expensive or difficult to find in the East—lumber, iron and iron products, wine, oil, grain, and slaves. From about 1200, wool cloth, often woven in Flanders and finished in Italy, assumed chief place among the products Western merchants sold or bartered in Byzantium, the Levant, and Egypt. We know little of the flow of precious metals in and out of Europe or the balance of monetary payments generated by this commercial exchange. The renewed minting of gold coins in the West in the thirteenth century, which had halted after the reign of Charlemagne, indicates that Europe was achieving a favorable balance, at least in gold payments, in its relations with the East and with North

Africa. The most successful of the new gold coins, destined to serve for centuries as a principal means of settling international accounts, was the florin, which the commune of Florence minted for the first time in 1252.

A second major trading area linked the peoples settled along the shores of the Baltic Sea in northern Europe. To this trade, the cities of Flanders contributed their excellent wool cloth; the Scandinavian countries provided fish and lumber; England delivered grain and raw wool; and furs, honey, wax, lumber, and other forest products were exported from the eastern Baltic regions, where the Russian city of Novgorod was the principal commercial entrepôt. By the late thirteenth century, strong links were also tying this trading zone with the English duchy of Gascony in southwest France. Gascony exported wine in ever larger quantities to northern Europe, especially to England, and received in turn cloth and cereals, which its own lands, increasingly given to viticulture, could not sufficiently provide. It has been estimated that the average annual exportation of wine from Gascony to England in the early fourteenth century reached 450,000 hectoliters, a quantity larger than that exported by the same region today. The "average" Englishman (although most of the wine was doubtlessly consumed by the aristocracy), it has further been estimated, drank three or four times more wine than does his descendant of the twentieth century.

Across the continent of Europe, from late in the eleventh century, routes of overland commerce were springing to life and linking the great trading zones of the Baltic and the Mediterranean seas. Pope Gregory VII refers for the first time to Italian merchants in France. By the early twelfth century, merchants from southern Europe were coming in considerable numbers to fairs held in the French county of Champagne, at the towns of Troyes, Provins, Lagny, and Bar-sur-Aube. The calendar of the fairs was arranged so that at least one would be open at all months of the year. The counts of Champagne offered special protection and favorable tolls to the merchants who frequented the fairs, and special judicial procedures were established, allowing the quick and equitable transaction of business. At their height, from approximately 1100 to 1300, the great fairs were the principal entrepôts where goods from northern Europe, wool cloth in particular, were exchanged for the spices and other valued products of the South.

The volume of goods involved in medieval trade was paltry by modern standards. Before the early fourteenth century, there were no regular maritime communications between northern Europe and the Mediterranean ports, and no road passable for carts crossed the Alps. Nevertheless, trade had become essential for the welfare, the standard of living, and perhaps even the survival of many European cities and regions. By the early fourteenth century, the city of Florence could feed its population from the produce of its own countryside for only five months a year. To pay for food imported from distant regions, it had to maintain productive industries. The manufacture of wool cloth alone supported a third of the Florentine population and required a massive importation of raw materials and an equally large exportation of finished cloth. The large export of wine from Gascony to northern Europe and to England led to agricultural specialization in southwest France. Without this trade, Gascony would have been much poorer, and the ports of Bordeaux and Bayonne probably would have been villages. The standard of living—or at least the drinking habits—of numerous Englishmen would also have been much different. Other examples of regional specialization in agriculture could be given—the concentration on sheep raising on the Cistercian estates of northern England, grain production in Prussia and the eastern Baltic. However small the volume of medieval commerce, commercial exchange deeply affected the economic activities and the style of life of many Europeans.

Rural estates and monasteries had been the centers of European economic, social, and cultural life in the early Middle Ages. But from the eleventh century, in close association with the commercial revolution, towns once more began to assume economic, cultural, and political importance. Towns of course had never disappeared from Europe, even during the disturbed centuries of the early Middle Ages. They had continued to function as centers of administration; in particular, bishops, by residing in towns, assured them a continued though precarious existence. Moreover, towns were often fortified and could offer protection to the surrounding population. They were *refugia,* to which peasants could flee in times of attack; the root sense of the English *borough* and the German *Burg* is "fortress." But the towns in the early Middle Ages were primarily centers of consumption, not of commercial exchange or industrial production.

The commercial revolution, without destroying the administrative function of towns, made many of them centers of exchange. Merchants clearly needed a secure locale in which they could live and store their goods and in which their transactions could be carried on. In northern Europe, merchant quarters often grew up near the central fortress or *burgus,* and they came to be known in some places as *faubourgs* (from *foris burgi,* "outside the burg"). In Italian towns, reflecting the greater complexity and social intermixture of the population, specifically mercantile quarters are not easily discernible, but there is no doubt that in Italy too the revival of commerce was bringing about a steady increase in urban size.

By the thirteenth century, many towns were becoming important centers for the production as well as for the exchange of goods. Large numbers of artisans collected in them, finding employment in many trades but especially in manufacturing wool cloth. Typically, the medieval artisan worked in his own home; there were no factories and even large shops were rare. Usually, a great merchant, called draper in the North and *lanaio* in Italy, supervised and coordinated the manufacture of wool cloth. He procured the raw wool, often from distant areas, and then allocated it successively to washers and beaters, carders and combers, spinners, weavers, fullers, dyers, and finishers. He then took responsibility for selling the finished cloth. Each artisan worked with his own tools but frequently was dependent upon loans or advances in wages from the draper. This so-called putting-out system remained the fundamental form of European manufacture until the Industrial Revolution in the eighteenth century.

Urban institutions were changing and developing even as the city was growing. The merchants gathered around the *burgus* often resented the authority of the traditional lord of the fortress, usually the bishop in northern Europe, who was prone to tax them at will, impose military services upon them, or require them to settle their juridical disputes according to local custom in his own court. The bishop usually had little comprehension of the special needs of merchants, and characteristically his justice was slow and expensive. Very early in the economic revival, from about 1080 in both Flanders and Italy, town dwellers were organizing themselves into communes, associations bound together by a common oath taken by the members. Simultaneously, through petition, purchase, or on occasion through violence, the communes were winning charters of liberties from the town lords. One of the most influential of these charters, used as a model for many such concessions in the North, was granted by William of Normandy, then count of Flanders, in 1127 to the commune of St. Omer. In the charters the lords typically promised not to impose arbitrary taxes, tolls, or services upon the townsmen, and to allow the merchants to judge their own disputes according to their own customs.

The commune governed itself through officials called consuls in Italy and aldermen (*échevins*) in the North. There were almost always several of them, and they were elected yearly. The consuls judged the disputes of the citizens, administered communal properties, and negotiated with outside authorities. The early communes were narrow aristocratic associations, dominated by a few patrician families. Urban expansion, especially in the thirteenth century, brought to the towns many newcomers who contended with the old patrician houses for power over the government. Social tensions in medieval towns increased, and conflicts were frequent and violent. Some cities, such as Florence from 1282, became true guild republics, in which power rested with the middle ranges of urban society. The medieval commune was never a true democracy, and the very poor were almost always effectively disfranchised. Nevertheless, the commune extended participation in political affairs to a much larger segment of society than did any other form of medieval government.

Like the commune, the guild was an association created by oath. It differed from the town government in that it included as its members only those pursuing a particular trade or profession. Both barbarian and Roman societies had had associations organized for the social or religious welfare of members. The word *guild* is of Germanic origin, probably meaning "payment," perhaps in the sense of a religious offering. However, not until approximately the year 1000, when the commercial revolution was just getting under way, did guilds have a specific relationship to economic life. By the twelfth century, guilds formed of merchants had appeared in most of the principal European cities. Initially, each town had only a single "guild merchant," but unity could not be preserved as the economy grew more complex. By the middle of the thirteenth century, specialized groups of merchants—dealers in woolens, silks, and spices, bankers and money changers, and many others—and the principal artisan crafts had separate and autonomous associations.

The guild aimed primarily at advancing the professional, social, and religious interests of its members; it also sought to assure the survival of its particular "art" by supervising the training of new masters. Professionally, the guild protected its members from what was considered unfair competition. Foreigners who wished to practice the trade within the town had to secure the guild's permission, and its own members were restricted in the hours they could work and even in the methods they could use to call attention to their wares. The guild also functioned as a court, in which litigation involving the members could be settled and the peace of the profession maintained. Because the prosperity of the profession so much depended on the reputation of its products in international markets, the guild, to maintain quality, determined the raw materials that could be used and the processes of manufacture that could be followed. Socially, the guild assisted a member who was sick or disabled or who may have suffered some calamity—fire or theft— in the practice of his trade. After a member's death, it helped support the widow or train young children. A major interest of the association was religion. All guilds prayed together, at stated times in the year, for the souls of deceased members; solemn religious services were held to celebrate the feast of the guild's patron saint. Guilds usually had their own church or at least a chapel in the town cathedral, and they often supported hospitals or other charitable and religious activities for the benefit of the entire community. At Florence, the guild of wool merchants had responsibility for the construction and maintenance of the principal church of the city, the cathedral of Santa Maria del Fiore.

To ensure the survival of the art over generations, the guilds maintained the quality of the training received by new masters. This apprenticeship system required that the young novice spend several years living at the home of an established master; he received room, board, and at times a small salary, assisted the master in his work, and thus learned the skills of the trade. After this term of service and study, the apprentice had to offer proof to all the established masters that he had indeed suitably learned the art. He might have to pass some form of examination or produce a "masterpiece," which would give visible proof of his skill. Often too he had to entertain the masters at an initiation banquet. Once he had secured the approval of the guild, he was free to open his own shop. However, the young man often had to labor for several years as a journeyman (literally, one who is paid by the day) in the shop of an older master, until he accumulated enough capital to go into business for himself. Particularly in the late Middle Ages, many artisans worked as journeymen for their entire lives. Only when he opened his own shop and accepted his own apprentices was he considered truly a master. The guild supervised all phases and all aspects of this educational process, determining the number of apprentices a master could accept, the number of years they had to serve, and the prerequisites they had to fulfill to secure the guild's approval. In distinguishing levels of skill (apprentice, journeyman, master) and in certifying proven accomplishment, the guild gave structure and rigor to the training of new masters and helped maintain the quality of its product.

In minutely supervising the work and training of their members and the quality of their manufactures, the guilds could also—particularly in the late Middle Ages and early in the modern epoch—exert a baneful influence upon the economy. Their tight regulations frequently discouraged beneficial competition, vigorous entrepreneurship, and technological innovation. But in spite of the obstructions the guilds later presented to economic development, their contribution to the early phases of the medieval economic advance was fundamental. New trades and professions were growing up in a hostile world dominated by military and clerical aristocracies having little comprehension of the interests of merchants and artisans and little sympathy with their needs. Without the self-help made possible by guilds, without the protection and aid they extended to their members, the growth of the commercial and industrial sectors of the medieval economy would have been much slower, if indeed it would have occurred at all.

Europe in the Middle Ages remained an overwhelmingly agricultural society. The population of the largest medieval towns—Milan, Venice, Paris—probably never surpassed 150,000 persons. In the most heavily urbanized areas of Europe—northern Italy and Flanders—probably three out of four people continued to live in the countryside; in most regions only one out of ten Europeans lived in a city. But in spite of the relatively small size of the urban sector of the economy and society, the appearance of towns influenced the medieval world in almost all its aspects. The commercial revival permitted certain families to accumulate large amounts of capital, which could be tapped for uses other than trade. War, politics, and artistic patronage were all touched by the availability of large sums of money. The changes in medieval government—the growth of a paid bureaucracy, the increasing reliance on mercenaries, the development of more expensive weapons—reflect the new sources of credit that towns made available to rulers. English participation in the early phases of the Hundred Years' War would have been inconceivable without the financial support of Florentine bankers. The uses to which capital was turned seem more often than not extraordinarily wasteful, but there is no discounting its influence. Moreover, the mechanism developed in the towns for recruiting capital continued to play a major role—military, political, and cultural as well as economic—in European history in subsequent centuries.

The towns also introduced into medieval society a pool of trained laymen, many of whom had to be literate. Hitherto, the church had exercised a near-monopoly over literacy in medieval society, and this was a principal reason for its pervasive influence early in the Middle Ages. Secular governments could now recruit administrators and bureaucrats from the trained men of the cities. Many historians speak of a growing "lay spirit" in medieval political and cultural life from the thirteenth century, and there is no doubt that the towns contributed to it.

It would, however, be a gross error to imply that the bourgeoisie was in any sense anti-religious; it could on the contrary be argued that the piety characteristic of cities was more sensitive, even more mystically inclined, than was the religion of the countryside. But there seems little doubt that the townsmen manifested a new psychology, a new approach to the world and to their fellow men. They brought with them a rigorous sense of precision, a desire to know exactly the factors upon which decisions had to be made. Their affairs brought them into close and complex relationships with their fellows, and they recognized the social value of urbane manners and social graces. Cities added a new refinement, with all that the word implies, to the hitherto rustic culture of the Middle Ages. The appearance of towns did not revolutionize medieval values, but it did give cultural development in Europe new directions, which the following centuries would emphasize.

The historian who compares the Europe of 1300 with the Europe of 800, during the reign of Charlemagne, must be impressed by evidence of enormous growth. A small, harassed, impoverished, and overwhelmingly agrarian world had become much larger, both in the space it occupied and in the population it included. Its economy, with a small but important and dynamic urban sector, was considerably more varied, its governments more effective, and its culture more creative.

In this great age of growth, medieval Europe had been aided by certain environmental factors. The weather in the period of the "little optimum" seems to have been especially favorable, although to evaluate its true influence remains impossible. Much more evident was the favorable balance between population and resources prevailing in the early phases of the expansion. Once the internal restraints that had kept the local communities of the early Middle Ages turned in upon themselves had been loosened, from approximately the eleventh century, the newly mobile settlers found readily accessible an abundance of good land that could be brought under cultivation with minimal expenditures of capital and effort. These favorable conditions assured that production would initially grow faster than population. The economy, in other words, could deliver surpluses, which could be turned to the creation or support of larger towns, stronger governments, greater schools, and bigger churches.

Medieval expansion, however, never achieved a true breakthrough, never reached what some economists today term the stage of "takeoff," in which a built-in capacity for continuing growth is developed. By around 1300, certain obstacles were beginning to hinder economic expansion. One was the relative stagnation of technology. In spite of important technological discoveries that introduced the Middle Ages, peasants in 1300 were working the land much as their ancestors had several centuries before. However, technological stagnation alone does not seem to have imposed a rigid ceiling on growth. Paradoxically, many peasants in the late thirteenth century were not working the soil according to the best known and available methods. Their chief handicap was not lack of knowledge but lack of capital, for the best methods were based upon the effective use of cattle to supply both labor and manure. Insofar as we can judge, many small cultivators of the thirteenth century could not afford cattle and had to work their plots with their own unaided and inefficient efforts.

A second limitation upon expansion was the failure to develop institutions and values that would maintain appropriate levels of investment, especially in agriculture. In spite of the growth of cities, a large part of Europe's lands was controlled by military and clerical aristocracies, which were not likely to reinvest their profits received in rent. The great landlords were rather prone to spend their rents on conspicuous but economically barren forms of consumption such as manor houses, castles, churches, wars, the maintenance of a lavish style of living. They were also likely to demand from the towns money in loans for such unproductive expenditures.

A third limiting factor seems to have been the growing scarcity of resources, especially good land. As the best soils were taken under cultivation, the still growing population had to rely increasingly upon poorer, marginal lands, which required more effort and capital to assure a good return. The European economy was burdened by a growing saturation in the use of its readily available resources, and it had neither the technology nor the capital to improve its returns from what it possessed. In the opinion of many historians today, this saturation in the use of resources not only ended the economic advance of the central Middle Ages but precipitated a profound demographic and economic crisis in the fourteenth century. Had Europe become overpopulated by the early fourteenth century? Do the terrible disasters of the late Middle Ages reflect the outlines of a classical Malthusian crisis? These questions have become the central issues in the economic and ecological history of Europe in the late Middle Ages.

Crisis and Recovery, ca. 1350–1500

Probably never in the entire Western experience has Europe endured such ferocious blows and suffered such tremendous human losses as in the fourteenth century. War, plague, famine, and death—the dread four horsemen of the Book of the Apocalypse—savagely attacked and reduced the population. Historians formerly estimated that the number of European inhabitants fell by about a third during the second half of the fourteenth century, but more recent and more thorough research has pushed that estimate ever higher. In Provence in southern France, the population in 1310 numbered between 350,000 and 400,000 persons. By 1410, it had sunk to somewhere between a third or a half of these figures. It then stabilized, but not until after 1470 is there evidence of renewed growth. In some rural areas of Italy —the countrysides of San Gimignano and Pistoia in Tuscany, for example— the population fall was more than 70 per cent. In other words, for every three persons who inhabited those regions in the late thirteenth century, there was only one to be found a century later. The English population was 2.2 million in 1377, down from a height of 3.7 million, although many scholars now hold that the latter estimate is much too low. In Germany, evidence of population decline comes chiefly from the extension of *Wüstungen,* waste or deserted lands, which can be discerned by the disappearance of place names from the documentary record. Of some 170,000 localities mentioned before 1300, 23 per cent disappear in the late Middle Ages. These are the totally deserted and forgotten villages and localities; the villages that survived were shrinking.

The most evident reason for the decrease in population was the toll taken by the rampant killers of the late Middle Ages—famines, wars, and plagues. Famine not only claimed a huge number of lives, but in weakening the population it often prepared the way for still more devastating plagues. Moreover, the periods of hunger often continued for more than a single year. The population, in order to feed itself, tended to consume the seed needed for planting, and inadequate harvests in the following year could not loosen the grip of hunger. Only an extraordinarily good harvest was likely to break this vicious cycle. In northern Europe, acute hunger prevailed from 1315 to 1317 and was especially severe in Flanders and the Low Countries, where the chroniclers record grisly stories of how the living were prone to devour the dead in their desperate need. The Black Death in 1348 struck after two consecutive years of dearth in southern Europe.

The age was also one of frequent war, the most famous being the Hundred Years' War, intermittently fought from 1338 to 1453. Some areas of France —the principal battlefield—were so devastated that according to contemporary accounts travelers could go for miles without hearing a cock crow. In other areas of Europe, war was a frequent occurrence and was brutally waged. Even in periods of truce, bands of unemployed mercenaries roamed over the countryside, pillaging, robbing, and adding to the plight of the population.

Of all the late medieval killers, the most stupendous in its impact was plague, and the most notorious of many plague onslaughts was the Black Death of 1348 and 1349. The disease seems to have appeared first in Tana, a Genoese colony in the Crimea on the Black Sea. A Mongol khan, besieging the town, catapulted bodies of plague victims over the walls in an early and successful effort at germ warfare. From Tana the infection followed the trade routes to Sicily in 1347, and in the following year it struck many of the principal cities of southern Europe. Giovanni Boccaccio in the preface to his *Decameron* has left a lengthy description of the plague at Florence, which in his estimation took 100,000 lives. By 1349, it had swept to the north, striking England, Flanders, Germany, and the Scandinavian countries. It followed the trade routes of the Baltic Sea, penetrated through Novgorod into Russia, and struck Moscow itself in 1352. This pandemic thus all but completed a circular sweep around and across the European continent. It probably claimed a third of the population of the regions it struck, and it was only the first of a series of plague visitations in the fourteenth century. Most regions seem to have suffered a plague attack on the average of once every ten years, and in all years, in some part of Europe, plague was raging.

From contemporary descriptions of the victims, medical historians identify the disease as bubonic plague, so named because of the buboes or swellings that develop in the lymph glands of the infected. Medical reasons alone do not satisfactorily account for its highly contagious and lethal character. Bubonic plague is more truly a disease of small mammals, notably rats, than of men. The plague bacilli are carried by fleas from the sick rat to its human victim. The disease cannot be passed directly from man to man, and this considerably reduces its contagion. Nevertheless, numerous contemporary descriptions of the plague give the impression of extraordinary contagion, of people falling sick from the slightest contact with an infected person. Bubonic plague is by no means a highly lethal infection, and an otherwise healthy person struck by it has a fairly good chance of recovering. But this characteristic too is at odds with medieval descriptions, which stress how deadly the illness was.

To reconcile the medical characteristics and the contemporary descriptions of the plague, medical historians postulate that the most vicious killer was not bubonic plague but a pneumonic plague triggered by it. The infection among the early victims in a plague attack reached the lungs and there induced a form of pneumonia, which could spread directly through the air from one person to another. In a society without the protection of antibiotics it was almost always fatal.

Even if this reconstruction of the character of the pneumonic plague is correct, medical reasons alone still seem insufficient explanations of the great carnage. The plague characteristically struck in the summer months, but pneumonia is a wintertime disease, spreading most easily when people are living in close quarters and are exposed to chills. Most puzzling, the plague was endemic to the regions of the eastern Mediterranean, with which west Europeans had been in close contact since at least the eleventh century. But in spite of repeated exposure, Europe in the central Middle Ages experienced nothing approaching the pandemic of 1348 and 1349. Why were Europeans relatively immune to the pestilence in the eleventh, twelfth, and thirteenth centuries and so susceptible in the fourteenth? Finally, medical reasons do not explain the great famines of the epoch, which, in weakening the population, undoubtedly contributed to the number of plague victims.

Historians have wondered if a changing climate was responsible for the increased frequency of failed harvests. Did climate also somehow facilitate the spread of disease? The weather does seem to have changed in the late Middle Ages. The "little optimum" came to an end in the thirteenth century and was followed by cooler, wetter weather in the fourteenth century. Some paleoclimatologists speak of a partial return to warmer temperatures from 1400 to 1550, but the long-term trend was toward colder climate, culminating in the "little ice age," which persisted from 1550 to 1850. Evidence for this little ice age, coming from the recorded advances and retreats of Alpine glaciers, is particularly convincing. We know that the great famine of 1315–1317 in northern Europe was attributed to excessive rainfall, which did not allow the wheat to ripen. The late Middle Ages, in other words, probably did experience harsher climatic conditions in Europe. However, it remains difficult to determine how harsh the climate became or what its role might have been in precipitating the great disasters of the fourteenth century.

For want of conclusive answers to these problems, historians have tended to discount the impact of climate and to concentrate upon investigating human or social factors at work in the late medieval crises. One issue in particular has gained the close attention of scholars: Had the European community by the fourteenth century grown so large that it could not adequately nourish its people? Were the famines, plagues, and wars manifestations of Malthusian checks, operating to bring a swollen population back into balance with its limited resources?

Certain incontrovertible facts strongly indicate that the crisis of the fourteenth century was fundamentally Mathusian. Time and again, the surviving demographic sources reveal populations of extraordinary size on the eve of the Black Death. One scholar has recently estimated that the population of the province of Tuscany in the late thirteenth century was no fewer than 2 million people—a figure it was not again to attain until 1850. Some regions of the province, such as the rural areas around San Gimignano, were more densely settled in the late thirteenth century than they are today. How could so many persons have been supported without the aid of steamships, trains and trucks, chemical fertilizers, and the other essential supports of a modern economy?

The Malthusian interpreters would reconstruct the economic and ecological history of medieval Europe in the following way. In the early phases of the growth cycle, in the eleventh and twelfth centuries, a small population had easy access to abundant resources, especially good land. It successfully exploited them, and its own size began to expand vigorously. With time, however, as resources diminished, the population inevitably reached a Malthusian ceiling. It challenged that ceiling in the fourteenth century and was violently repulsed and reduced. Some scholars have integrated this view of medieval development within a larger picture of European history before the Industrial Revolution in which the most powerful factors remain Malthusian. From the late Middle Ages, the cycle of growth began again, for the much smaller population could take advantage of plentiful resources. But continuing growth once more called into play Malthusian restrictions on advance, in the seventeenth century—another time of troubles for Europe. Again the cycle was renewed, the ceiling challenged, but this time the wave of expansion, blending into the Industrial Revolution, was able to break through the historical Malthusian ceiling, or at least displace it to a considerably higher level.

The medieval experience is thus seen as one cycle in a sequence of essentially Malthusian cycles that has marked the history of traditional Europe. However, some aspects of the fourteenth-century crisis are not well explained by the classical Malthusian model. Was Europe truly overpopulated by 1300? The question is difficult to answer, because the shortage or misuse of capital and poorly implemented technology certainly added to Europe's woes. But the chief reason for questioning a purely Malthusian interpretation derives from the movement, insofar as we can reconstruct it, of the population curve itself. The peak population size seems to have been attained not immediately before the Black Death but several decades before, late in the thirteenth or early in the fourteenth century. The external checks of plague, famine, and war, in other words, struck not against a rapidly expanding population but against one that had already stabilized and in some areas had even slightly declined. This suggests that external checks were not the sole factors determining the population movements of the late Middle Ages. Moreover, the plunge, once under way in the middle of the fourteenth century, continued into the fifteenth, well beyond the point when one can reasonably speak of inadequate resources. Population movements are of course determined by births as well as by deaths, and perhaps the chief theoretical weakness with the Malthusian model is that it assumes that the birth rate remains high and constant, even in the face of social disaster. Recent research in historical demography suggests, on the contrary, that even in traditional societies the birth rate can be extremely sensitive to social conditions.

Unfortunately, our knowledge of European birth rates in this critical period is scanty, for want both of suitable documents and of suitably intensive research. We do know that even among the serfs of Carolingian Europe, a family's ability to rear children was strongly influenced by its social circumstances. Characteristically, the families that supported the heaviest burdens —that were, in other words, the most oppressed socially—also appear with the fewest children. Poverty could reduce family size in several ways. Marriages usually involved an exchange of property, and at least by the late thirteenth century poor fathers often could not afford the high dowries required to marry their daughters. Hard times seem to have forced married couples to practice restraint in the procreation of children and even to adopt primitive methods of birth control, which the preachers and moralists of the epoch mention and condemn. The poor household probably suffered the most in periods of famine, for it did not have the resources to sustain its members. The poor and socially disadvantaged segments of the community were therefore the least efficient producers of children.

It seems, in sum, that diminishing resources available to the thirteenth-century community led to worsening social conditions for its poorest members and to an enlargement of their numbers. As land came to be in short supply, workers found their bargaining position deteriorating and had no choice but to lease the land under onerous terms. Not only could the landlords win high rents, they had little incentive to return part of their profits to the land in the form of improvements, because tenants could easily be found even for the worst plots. Forced to pay high rents and to farm with the aid of little capital, the cultivators were prone to exhaust the soil through repeated croppings of cereals. Extensive exhaustion of the soil may have been a major factor in precipitating the famines of the late Middle Ages.

In a manner which may be analogous to the fate of the slaves of antiquity, the growing numbers of oppressed poor of the thirteenth century seem to have reacted to their plight by not reproducing. The lowered birth rate was sufficiently important to halt the expansion of the entire community by around 1300, and it hampered recovery from the plague onslaughts in the middle of the fourteenth century. If this analysis is correct (more research is needed to support or refute it), it seems that only improved treatment for the poor could halt the horrendous population fall of the late Middle Ages and prepare the way for recovery.

The most immediate impact of the population collapse of the fourteenth century was shock and disruption. With the numbers of both workers and consumers rapidly and radically falling, the economy had to adjust to vastly different conditions, and adjustment was slow and difficult. Few figures reflecting output have survived, so our best indication of what was happening in the economy comes from price movements. Prices and wages rose in the decades immediately following the Black Death (grain prices in the North, for example, seem to have peaked at about 1370) and remained at high levels through the closing decades of the fourteenth century. High prices for virtually all goods indicate that production was falling even more rapidly than the number of consumers. The late fourteenth century, in other words, witnessed the darkest hours of what some scholars now term the economic depression of the Renaissance.

By approximately 1400, the prices of various goods had begun to move in different directions, creating a scissors pattern with important repercussions. Cereals and the cheapest grains decline, clearly responding to a restricted market. The more expensive agricultural products—meat, cheese, wine, oil, beer—while declining slightly still hold their value better than does wheat. This price structure indicates that Europeans were beginning to eat a more varied and presumably a healthier diet in the fifteenth century than in the thirteenth and that European agriculture was becoming more varied too. Industrial prices show a similar movement, with the cheapest cloths declining but more expensive woolens and silks retaining their value. Luxury goods, in other words, did well in late medieval markets, in spite of repeated efforts by governments to control tastes through sumptuary laws.

Rents too show a strong tendency to decline immediately after the Black Death. The fewer laborers, in other words, could win from landlords more advantageous terms. Wages climbed steeply. Governments, controlled by the propertied classes, often tried to dampen such movements. In the Statute of Laborers (1351), the English Parliament, for example, tried to freeze wages and prices and to force workers to accept employment offered them at pre-plague salaries or terms. These governmental interventions were more successful in heightening social tensions than in controlling prices and wages, and the decades immediately following the Black Death were a period of acute unrest. The uprising of the wool workers at Florence, called Ciompi, in 1378, and the English Peasants' Revolt of 1381 are the best examples of many such protests. But by the early fifteenth century, society was gaining a new equilibrium, and the poor segments of the community had gained a larger share of social benefits. Perhaps an improved standard of living and a healthier diet enjoyed by the formerly oppressed classes helped reduce the high mortality claimed by the plague and added to the physical and psychological energies of the population.

As wages climbed to and remained at high levels in the fourteenth and fifteenth centuries, employers were given a powerful inducement to make more efficient use of their workers. In agriculture, this led to a clear increase in the number of animals on the farms. Not only did cattle perform work, but animal products commanded a strong price in the marketplace. Sheep raising also gained enormously in importance, because a few shepherds could guard flocks of thousands and because wool, cheese, and mutton were again valued products. Systems of transhumance, involving summer grazing in the mountains and winter grazing on lowland plains, developed rapidly in many Mediterranean areas—Italy, Provence, and Spain. Similar circumstances induced English landlords to enclose their lands—that is, to rearrange their fields into large blocks that could be converted into fenced meadows for the grazing of sheep. From slow beginnings in the fourteenth and fifteenth centuries, the enclosure movement created a major social problem for the English government of the sixteenth century, as it dislodged many small cultivators. The emphasis on sheep raising, continuing into the sixteenth century, may also have damaged the environment in some European areas, notably the Iberian plateau, through overgrazing, deforestation, and erosion. Here again we encounter the paradoxical situation of depopulation and a shift to less intensive use of the land bringing about damage to the soil.

The high cost of labor helped make the late Middle Ages a period of numerous technological innovations, and improved tools enabled workers to produce more efficiently and more cheaply. Important developments occurred in navigation. Large ships were constructed or, like the Portuguese caravel, were significantly improved in design. The bigger ship could challenge the open sea, undertake longer voyages, sail directly from port to port, and thus carry more goods more rapidly. To sail big ships for long distances demanded an efficient utilization of the wind. The Mediterranean galley, carrying oarsmen for propulsion (although it cruised with sail when winds were favorable), continued to be used for wars and ceremonial voyages but declined rapidly in commercial importance. The stern rudder was perfected to steer the big ship better and to allow it to hold a firm course when tacking against the wind. Improved navigational aids—the compass, astrolabe, astronomical tables, maps, port descriptions—gave captains new confidence when undertaking long voyages out of sight of land.

Still other technological changes affected the writing of books. Many Europeans were experimenting with cheap ways of reproducing books in the fourteenth and fifteenth centuries. Probably in 1453, Johann Gutenberg of Mainz in Germany perfected the method of printing with movable metal type, and the art diffused with extraordinary rapidity through Europe, to become a major industry by 1500.

War too was affected. The development of firearms, to which the wars of the late Middle Ages gave a powerful incentive, could be considered a substitution of capital for labor. Troops armed with cannon could fight with efficiency. Firearms in turn stimulated the arts associated with metallurgy and milling, for the powder itself had to be ground and properly granulated. Mining and metallurgy represented one of the most rapidly growing economic sectors in the late Middle Ages. With better pumps and better means of extracting metal, miners were working at depths never before reached. The silver mines of Tyrol and Hungary by the late fifteenth century were finally relieving Europe's chronic shortage of precious metal.

The uncertainties of late medieval economic life affected business organization. Companies formed after the Black Death tended to be smaller and more specialized in their interests than the great commercial houses of the early fourteenth century had been. If one compares the Medici bank of Florence in the fifteenth century with the companies of the Bardi and Peruzzi of the same city, which went bankrupt in 1343, the Medici bank is seen to be based on less capital but to possess a more complex inner structure, founded on interlocking partnerships. The senior partner at Florence entered into separate partnerships with the managers of the various branch banks at Rome, Venice, Avignon, Bruges, London, and elsewhere. If one branch failed, there was less likelihood that the entire structure would collapse.

Of all business institutions, maritime insurance probably grew most rapidly in the late Middle Ages. Ships were growing larger and more expensive, and without a means of offsetting high risks, capital for their construction would have been difficult to find. The earliest insurance contracts date from approximately 1300 in Italy and were initially conditional sales. The insurance broker would buy the ship and cargo from the shipper during its voyage and agree to sell it back at an enhanced price when it arrived safely at port. If it sank en route, the broker absorbed the loss, and the differences in prices paid and received represented his premium. This crude arrangement gave way in the fourteenth century to forms of insurance underwriting not essentially different from those practiced today. Insurance for land shipments, where risk was not so great, was about half a century behind maritime insurance in its development. Life insurance, though occasionally practiced, had to await the preparation of accurate actuarial tables before being widely utilized. The protection offered by these new arrangements encouraged investors to make substantial investments, in spite of the uncertain times.

After the great disasters of the fourteenth century, Europe was a much smaller community in 1500 than it had been in 1300. But, by measure of its per capita productivity, it seems almost certainly to have been a richer community. Its people could concentrate their efforts on the better land and were working with an improved technology and with the assistance of bigger capital investments. Probably too their diet was improved. Europeans, in other words, were well equipped to embark on the remarkable worldwide expansion, initiated by the geographic revolution, that as much as any single movement or event separates the Middle Ages from the modern era.

Retrospect and Conclusion

At all periods, ecological pressures have significantly affected European history. They are the products of complex factors—social, institutional, and technological as well as physical and biological. Social factors and institutions—population decline, oppression, the character of antique slavery—seem to have played a major role in the deterioration of the ancient environment and the collapse of the classical world. Similarly, internal constraints operating on the communities of the early Middle Ages created conditions of severe overpopulation, even though space, land, and resources remained abundant. The great expansion of the Middle Ages ended in a disaster with strong Malthusian overtones, although this disaster should not be read as a purely Malthusian crisis in which population size and resources were the only operative factors. The much lowered and for long stable population of the late Middle Ages did not assure ecological stability. The high cost of labor encouraged investments with a considerable ecological impact, such as the maintenance of large flocks of sheep. It also created incentives for the development of a more powerful technology. The technological improvements of the late Middle Ages—firearms, printing, bigger ships suitable for longer voyages—already pointed to, if they were not already part of, the technological revolution that still aids and threatens our own society.

If ecological pressures are not the exclusive product of natural conditions and human numbers, then the thesis sometimes advanced today that population stability will assure ecological stability seems at odds with historical experience. Moreover, the goal of stability contains within it a risk of social stagnation. Our present age does not represent the first time that Western society has lived under acute ecological pressures. Had it been possible in the past for Western society to relieve those pressures by stabilizing its growth, it is likely that we would be living as if in the Middle Ages. Few advocates of stability would really want that, and who among us today truly can predict the future possibilities of mankind?

A Critical Bibliography

The classical statement of the theory that weather cycles established a pulse of history is Ellsworth Huntington, *Civilization and Climate,* 3d. ed. (New Haven, 1924). For the thesis that soil erosion explains the fall of Rome, see especially Vladimir G. Simkhovitch, *Toward the Understanding of Jesus and Two Additional Historical Studies: Rome's Fall Reconsidered. Hay and History* (New York, 1937). The most recent study of population in ancient Italy, which carries the analysis only as far as A.D. 14, is P. A. Brunt, *Italian Manpower, 225 B.C.–A.D. 14* (Oxford, 1971). For a short and forceful exposition of the thesis that a declining population fatally weakened the empire, see Arthur E. R. Boak, *Manpower Shortage and the Fall of the Roman Empire in the West* (Ann Arbor, 1955). A recent, reasoned assessment of the extent of erosion in the ancient Mediterranean regions may be found in Claudio Vita-Finzi, *The Mediterranean Valleys: Geological Change in Historical Times* (Cambridge, 1969).

The best assessment of the role of weather in European history, rich in information and cautious in conclusions, is Emmanuel Le Roy Ladurie, *Times of Feast, Times of Famine: A History of Climate Since the Year 1000,* trans. Barbara Bray (New York, 1971). Much information on the weather of the past can also be gained from H. H. Lamb, *The Changing Climate: Selected Papers* (London, 1966).

On the history of European populations in the medieval period, the basic survey is J. C. Russell, *Late Ancient and Medieval Population,* Transactions of the American Philosophical Society, 43, no. 3 (Philadelphia, 1948). More recent and much briefer is the same author's chapter "Population in Europe, 500–1500," in *Fontana Economic History of Europe,* vol. 1, ed. Carlo M. Cipolla (London, 1969). Although restricted to cities and to a later period, R. J. Mols, S.J., *Introduction à la démographie historique des villes d'Europe du XIVe au XVIIIe siècle,* 3 vols. (Gembloux, 1954–1956), is a mine of information.

The fundamental survey of the English medieval population remains J. C. Russell, *British Medieval Population* (Albuquerque, 1948). For Italy, Julius Beloch, *Bevölkerungsgeschichte Italiens,* 3 vols. (Berlin, 1937–1961), though based on research accomplished long before its publication, is still the standard introduction. The student who wishes to keep abreast of the most recent advances in the historical demography of the Middle Ages must consult numerous regional studies. French scholars have been especially prolific in publishing such studies. One of the best examples of the genre is Robert Fossier, *La terre et les hommes en Picardie jusqu'à la fin du XIIIe siècle,* 2 vols. (Louvain, 1968). More exclusively demographic and concerned with a later period is Edouard Baratier, *La démographie provençale du XIIIe au XVIe siècle, avec chiffres de comparaison pour le XVIIIe siècle* (Paris, 1961). Italian archives are especially rich in demographic records. For representative studies based upon them, see the following: E. Fiumi, *Demografia, movimento urbanistico e classi sociali in Prato dall' età comunale ai tempi moderni,* Biblioteca storica toscana, 14 (Florence, 1968); Fiumi, *Storia economica e sociale di San Gimignano,* Biblioteca storica toscana, 11 (Florence, 1961); David Herlihy, *Medieval and Renaissance Pistoia: The Social History of an Italian Town* (New Haven, 1968); J. K. Hyde, *Padua in the Age of Dante*

(New York, 1966) ; Elisabeth Carpentier, *Une ville devant la peste: Orvieto et la Peste noire de 1348,* Collection "Démographie et Sociétés," 7 (Paris, 1962). German scholars have been particularly active in studying the agricultural desertions *(Wüstungen)* of the late Middle Ages. For a summary of the recent results of this research, see Wilhelm Abel, "Désertions rurales: bilan de la recherche allemande," *Villages désertés et histoire économique, XIe–XVIIIe siècle,* Collection "Les hommes et la terre," 11 (Paris, 1965), pp. 515–32.

On the question of overpopulation in the late Middle Ages, see Norman J. G. Pounds, "Overpopulation in France and the Low Countries in the Later Middle Ages," *Journal of Social History* 3 (1970) : 225–47. Many of the regional studies cited above also discuss the problem.

For nearly all topics in medieval economic history, the *Cambridge Economic History of Europe,* vols. 1–3 (Cambridge, 1941–1966; vol. 1 revised, 1966), offers substantial essays and large bibliographies. Henri Pirenne, *Economic and Social History of Medieval Europe* (New York, 1937), is a short survey, now considered a classic, but with an exaggerated emphasis on the importance of long-distance trade in medieval economic development. Less stimulating, but more balanced and more recent, is Robert-Henri Bautier, *Economic Development of Medieval Europe,* History of European Civilization Library, ed. Geoffrey Barraclough (New York, 1971). Still more recent are Robert S. Lopez, *The Commercial Revolution of the Middle Ages, 950–1350* (Englewood Cliffs, 1971), which concentrates on commercial history, and Harry A. Miskimin, *The Economy of Early Renaissance Europe, 1300–1460* (Englewood Cliffs, 1969). Currently being published is the *Fontana Economic History of Europe,* ed. Carlo M. Cipolla; one of its projected four volumes concerns Europe before 1500. Each chapter is written by a specialist, and the chapters are being published in pamphlet form as they are finished. When the volumes are completed, library editions will be available. The contributors include prominent scholars such as J. C. Russell, Georges Duby, Lynn T. White, Jr., Jacques Le Goff, and Sylvia L. Thrupp.

For medieval agrarian history, the fundamental work is Georges Duby, *Rural Economy and Country Life in the Medieval West* (Columbia, 1968). Also valuable are the medieval sections of B. H. Slicher van Bath, *The Agrarian History of Western Europe, 500–1850,* trans. Olive Ordish (London, 1963). Technological aspects of medieval times are considered by Lynn T. White, Jr., *Medieval Technology and Social Change* (Oxford, 1962). On the medieval town there is no satisfactory survey. Henri Pirenne, *Medieval Cities* (Princeton, 1925), is a classic but very dated in many of its affirmations. Fritz Rörig, *The Medieval Town* (Berkeley, 1967), concentrates on German cities.

For additional bibliographical guidance, see David Herlihy, "The Economy of Traditional Europe," *Journal of Economic History* 31 (1971) : 153–64.

Two twelfth-century miniatures from the Chronicle of John of Worcester *showing a nightmare of Henry I of England. The king sees peasants (top) and knights (below) threatening to kill him.*

We shall argue not that the Middle Ages exhibited a great deal of social mobility, but that mobility did occur and was significant. As historians have investigated economic conditions, migration patterns, mortality ratios, and the like, they have found that even the early Middle Ages did not know as highly stratified and physically immobile a society as an earlier generation of scholars believed.

The three main divisions of society in the Middle Ages were the nobility, the peasantry, and the bourgeoisie. The clergy were drawn from all social classes. For purposes of convenience, we shall deal with each group separately within the three chronological periods into which the Middle Ages are customarily divided.

The Early Middle Ages: Barbarism and Social Change

THE ARISTOCRACY

The aristocratic or noble classes have a much stronger group social consciousness today than do the middle and lower classes, and the same was true in the Middle Ages. Accordingly, throughout the medieval period there was less vertical mobility within and into the upper classes than among the peasants and townsmen, but more horizontal mobility. At the same time, the attitudes of the nobles to a certain extent conditioned the social values of other groups. Furthermore, the aristocracy held political power and hence helped determine the degree of both horizontal and vertical mobility of the lower classes, though the physical environment played a more important role.

Historians have long debated whether the upper classes were an aristocracy or a nobility in the early Middle Ages. The question will never be answered satisfactorily. A nobility is a juridical class whose membership is determined by ties of blood. This was generally combined in the Middle Ages with the exercise of some public legal authority. Until the eleventh century the word *nobilis* was never used in the sources to mean a social class; earlier it had denoted a moral quality. *Aristocracy* is a general term indicating those who have more authority, power, wealth, and social prestige than their fellows. The blood tie is important in questions of inheritance and in the maintenance of kinship bonds, but greater social mobility is possible within an aristocracy, where power and influence are the essential membership criteria, than in a nobility, where the essential criterion is the blood tie. In any case, a totally closed caste cannot maintain itself biologically. Replenishment of the stock is needed, for not only is part of the population infertile, but constant inbreeding leads to exaggeration of the weaker aspects of the parent stock over a period of years, as the men of the Middle Ages were aware. Even so, the extent of inbreeding is quite striking, both within social classes and within geographical areas.

We may say, then, that the early Middle Ages, the period of the great migrations, was a time of aristocracy with overtones of nobility. The aristocracy originally created its position by brute force, economic power, and service to a powerful chieftain. By the ninth century, the period of the breakup of the Carolingian Empire, the upper classes were attempting, not wholly successfully, to close themselves off to newcomers. Finally, in the twelfth and thirteenth centuries, the nobility did become a formalized legal grouping in most regions of western Europe. It was never totally closed, however, for the lesser nobility continued to be infiltrated by prosperous peasants and especially by wealthy townsmen, who rose through service to a prince just as the forebears of their social "betters" had done. Once noble status was recognized for these persons, it was perpetuated by a blood tie. In short, we have an extremely diverse social picture among the upper classes throughout the entire medieval period.

The Italian or Gallo-Roman upper class of the late Roman Empire had been in no sense a nobility. "Equestrian" rank, corresponding roughly to the upper middle class, was by law a matter of appointment, in fact a question of wealth. When the emperor wished to weaken the Senate, he relied largely on equestrians for his bureaucracy. But by the middle of the fourth century the Senate was so impotent that the emperors no longer feared that its political power might rival their own, whereupon they drastically increased the number of persons in the Senate and used them in the imperial bureaucracy.

Although elevation to senatorial rank was by appointment, it was transmitted by blood. The essential ingredient of the wealth of most senators was land. Roman landholders had obtained governmental authority over their peasant dependents by the fourth century. During the Germanic invasions Gallo-Roman aristocrats such as Sidonius Apollinaris, whose surviving letters portray an almost luxuriant country life in gentlemanly style in fifth-century Gaul, were in effect waiting for the end.

It was not long in coming. Germans occupied Roman estates and soon displaced the lords. The Romance population declined in numbers and importance. Statutes of the fourth and fifth centuries repeatedly prohibit marriages between Roman and German. As with most statutes of late Rome, this simply means that the practice was occurring on a large scale and was impossible to stop. The church is particularly important in the decline of the authority of the Gallo-Roman aristocracy. Although clerical celibacy was not an absolute rule until early in the twelfth century, marriage and concubinage were frowned upon. The safest place for a Roman aristocrat seemed to be a monastery or, more often, a bishopric. Sidonius Apollinaris became bishop of

Auvergne, an office that eventually brought him into more physical danger than landlordship had done. The new German rulers needed educated bureaucrats to maintain some semblance of a tax structure and chancery and usually found them among the Gallo-Roman clergy. Roman taught German, and by the seventh century the Germans were the major ethnic group within the episcopate of northern Europe.

The extent to which the Roman upper classes persisted in southern Gaul is problematical. The Germans settled in large numbers only as far south as the Loire, the area of northern France where the Romans had been least numerous and where they could most easily be displaced. The Visigoths and the Burgundians, who occupied southwestern and southeastern France respectively in the fifth century, were small tribes and took care in their laws to protect the rights of the Romans, among whom they lived as a conquering minority. Both allowed the use of Roman law, and there was no thorough Germanic penetration of southern France even after the Franks conquered it in the sixth century. Accordingly, while Merovingian and Carolingian sources show that the greatest men of this area were Germans, a substantial class of mixed Romance and Germanic origin remained. This circumstance, together with the fact that practically all peasants were Gallo-Roman, gave a neo-Roman cast to many institutional forms in the region.

A similar situation is found in Italy. The Lombards tried to displace Roman nobles and farmers in the north and were moderately successful, but their own occupation of the land was uneven. We find the creation not of a great Lombard nobility but rather of an extremely weak group of petty nobles that was to characterize all Italy in the Middle Ages. In central and southern Italy the old Roman aristocracy more or less perpetuated itself. The Byzantine conquest of part of Italy had even less effect on the Roman aristocracy than did the Lombard invasion.

The Gallo-Roman aristocracy thus was a significant force in the creation of the early medieval nobility in southern Europe, but generally only after thorough social contact and intermarriage with the Germans. The sources unfortunately tell us little of the Romance populations until Roman and German had for practical purposes merged. But we know more about the Germanic aristocracy. Although most surviving sources were written by Romans or Gallo-Romans, only the deeds of the governing classes, the Germans, were considered worth the chroniclers' attention.

Earliest Germanic society was extremely mobile on all levels. Service to a person of more elevated status than oneself was an important means of social advancement. The importance of the chieftain's war band must be seen in this context. It was a fluctuating group of private retainers who were bound to defend their leader to the death. The primary characteristic of the Germanic warriors was prowess. There is little evidence of hereditary status, but as the Germans became settled agriculturalists, the great warriors acquired lands and dependents of their own. They still were bound to serve the king during the annual campaigning season, but this obligation fell also on all other freemen of the tribe.

Hence the original members of the war band were no longer in the royal household at all times, and the monarch added new members to his entourage. They were called by various names—the "trusted ones," "the king's boys," and the like. It is significant that the wergeld system—according to which "worth money" had to be paid, according to social rank, to the family of a person who was killed—was based upon distinctions of wealth among the Franks, but in other tribes upon more abstract criteria of social status. This difference undoubtedly is due to the fact that only the Franks developed a significant service aristocracy after the migrations, for they held most of the important positions throughout Gaul following their conquest of other tribes.

Many of the new retainers were of servile origin. The Latin *vassus* ("vassal") originally indicated a servant, but it lost its servile connotation as more vassals elevated themselves into the aristocracy through service to a powerful lord. Other terms came to be used for the unfree. Mobility into the aristocracy from the peasantry could be meteoric, but so could a fall from favor, for the peasant once elevated was entirely at his lord's mercy. Gregory of Tours tells of Marileif, son of a serf overseer on the estates of the Merovingian king Chilperic (561–584). He became head of the royal medical staff while his relatives still tilled their fields, but he fell out of Chilperic's favor and was forced back into serfdom.

The Frankish aristocracy thus was derived from a wide variety of backgrounds. Once the Merovingian retainer received lands as reward for his services, he began living on them and lost personal contact with the king, just as the earlier generation of aristocrats had done. He could not easily be displaced except by military action and was a powerful man in his own right. Meanwhile the kings acquired new personal retainers from lower social groups.

By no means did all royal retainers at any time receive lands. We know little of the "household knight," the vassal without fief who was in constant attendance upon his lord. Most charter evidence from the early Middle Ages concerns transfer of lands, and he had none. But he was important in royal military calculations. He owed his position totally to his lord, who often had raised him from among the peasants on his estates.

The Frankish aristocracy was profoundly changed in the eighth and ninth centuries. The great men took on more governmental power than before. The Germans had only a primitive concept of the state. Their primary social and political bond was the personal tie of man to man. Hence even kings encouraged the growth of feudal ties between men of theoretically equal status. Feudal relationships involved vassalage and fiefholding, and the counts, dukes, and others who held offices of the state were also vassals of the king.

The growth of feudal ties is more properly an aspect of political and military history than of social history, but it is important for questions of social mobility. Whereas the nobles had concentrated earlier on acquiring land, they now assumed governmental functions, generally in the area where most of their lands were located. Plurality of vassalage and fiefholding soon gave opportunity for economic mobility. One might accumulate fiefs from several lords, then choose among them in case of conflict. In the twelfth century the count of Champagne held twenty-six fiefs from nine lords; he had subinfeudated most of the land and was owed the service of over two thousand knights as a result. Economic and social stagnation was prevented even as the feudal relationship lost its most essential aspect, the tie of man to man. We thus find seeds of mobility more in the corruption of the purely personal tie than in vassalage per se. Most of the great territorial principalities of northern Europe were founded late in the ninth and early in the tenth centuries, but they became subject to the internal dissolution that had affected the united realm of Charlemagne a generation earlier. Those taking control of local territories were aristocrats in their own right, capable of exercising governmental functions.

A classic example of many of these trends—personal service and contact, blood ties, landholding, removal from direct royal control—is the story of Baldwin I, called the Iron-Arm, the founder of the county of Flanders. His family originated in Lorraine and was related to another Frankish house whose members were counts of Laon, in northern France. In 862 he ran away with the daughter of King Charles the Bald, who after some pursuit restored him to favor and sent him as count to Flanders. He and his son Baldwin II drove the Norman invaders away in the 870s and 880s. Baldwin II added other counties to his father's original territory around Ghent and Aardenburg. The inheritance was totally free of royal interference by 900, but shortly thereafter the new principality was divided when two sons survived Baldwin II in 918. Subsequent generations reunited and again dismembered the original patrimony while expanding Flanders on its southern border. Only in the eleventh century was Flanders to take the form that it held into the late Middle Ages.

KINSHIP AND THE FORMATION OF A NOBLE CLASS

To the primitive German, the tie of kinship was paramount. In the age of migrations he looked to his kindred to avenge wrongs and protect him from injustice. The early Germans apparently had a very extended notion of who their kin were. Yet recent studies have shown that by the time they became settled agriculturalists and their family structure can be studied at all scientifically, kinship ties actually bound only the immediate conjugal family and those most closely associated with it. Various explanations have been offered for the change. The dislocation involved in the migrations may have loosened the ties. Once the Germans had settled, lordship replaced kinship as a peacekeeping force. Vassalage, the tie of man to man regardless of blood relationship, has been seen as the chief force in the dissolution of the role of kinship, only to be replaced by the tie of the individual to the state.

Yet kinship always was recognized as a legitimate social bond; blood feuds between sets of kinsmen began to reappear in the central and late Middle Ages. Furthermore, the blood tie was the most important feature separating nobles from lesser mortals in the creation of a noble class and class consciousness. Tenth-century nobles were not simply persons who usurped governmental functions but rather those who exercised them legitimately by blood right. Legitimacy and usurpation amounted to the same thing in practice—power —but in the post-Carolingian period only those of proper blood were seizing power; in the Merovingian age it had been every man for himself. As aristocracy passed toward nobility, social relationships stabilized and mobility was slowed.

A greater nobility had been created from the aristocracy of the Carolingian Empire by the tenth century, but still there was mobility among the lesser nobles. Fixed traditions of inheritance were few. The great Frankish aristocrats ordinarily passed their fiefs down to their sons, but heredity took longer to reach the lesser nobility. Outright inheritance of fiefs was unusual in Italy and Germany until the eleventh and twelfth centuries. Cadet lines (those descended from younger sons) developed, and they were as noble as the parent branches. In addition, however, there continued to be mobility among those whom the king chose to favor. The *missi dominici* ("messengers of the lord") of Charlemagne and his successors, an extremely varied social group, moved into the lower aristocracy as holders of small territories and castles. The growth of the lesser nobility was to prevent many of the great barons from forming governable territorial principalities in the tenth and eleventh centuries; we have noted the problems of the family of the counts of Flanders with younger sons.

The idea of a nobility of birth was carried by bonds of kinship. The nobles developed a class consciousness. Royal favoritism toward a newcomer or a serf was resented and hindered. The greater nobles disliked the lesser for what seem to have been economic reasons. Willigis, archbishop of Mainz (975–1011), was born of noble parents who tilled their own land. A contemporary chronicler considered his rise unusual in view of his "low" birth, and other sources are even more outspoken on the unworthiness of such persons. The church continued to be an avenue of social mobility in the central Middle Ages, though for only one generation. Suger, counselor of Louis VI and Louis VII of France and abbot of St. Denis, was the son of a serf; Durand, who became bishop of Liège in 1039, was born a serf on the estates of the abbey of St. Lambert. Even in temporal positions the idea of social rise through service never died out, and persons of established families as well as those of low birth accepted honors granted by the king. But royal officials and nobles throughout western Europe in the early Middle Ages came from a small number of families.

Inheritance customs show changes in the nature of kinship. Inheritance of status in the Merovingian period was basically matrilineal, as in many primitive societies. Patrilineal inheritance of property and status became more common in the Carolingian period, particularly among the nobility. One inherited from the father the qualities that made him important—the ban power (the power of command over persons), the right to govern, titles, prestige, and lands. As social status became determined by paternal lines, the nobles thought of kinship increasingly in terms of lines of descent. Although extended family feuds did occur, they were less important from this time than quarrels between lord and vassal. Literary sources of the post-Carolingian period mentioning the sanctity of the kindred and the lost position of the man who had none come almost entirely from the Scandinavian and Anglo-Saxon worlds, where Roman ideas of the individual nucleated family had taken less firm hold than in France.

There remains the question of the fate of the primitive German aristocracy. Especially in areas that had been in contact with the West before the Carolingian conquest of Germany, the local aristocracy simply continued to function. There were exceptions, particularly in regions such as Saxony, where the Carolingians had to obliterate local resistance to their conquest. Although Carolingian forms were superimposed to a great degree on the German world, they took some time to have full effect. In particular, the idea of nobility as a separate class with rights transmitted by blood took hold later in Germany than in the West but remained in effect longer. Thus German society generally became more stratified than French society. This was less true of the nobility than of other classes, for the idea of ennoblement through service to a powerful prince was much stronger in Germany than in France, and mobility from below was correspondingly greater. In contrast to the West, Germany shows little evidence of the formation of a class of lesser nobles before the late tenth century, but drastic changes were to come in the central Middle Ages as the kings raised their own retainers and servile dependents to positions of high authority. These positions gave governmental authority, an important attribute of noble status, to such persons despite the contradiction implied in their servile origins.

Mobility among the nobles tended to decrease toward the end of the tenth century. Since strength and intelligence could create wealth and power, the aristocracy in the early medieval period took in a larger percentage of the total population than would be the case later. Biological replenishment from the middle and lower classes was less essential than it would become subsequently. Means of public control were unsophisticated, and the local governing class had to be rather large. But no one became a noble through usurping the ban power. The blood tie was essential for the legitimate exercise of governmental authority in one's own right. The nobility had been comparatively open at the time of its formation, but it was much less so by the tenth century and tended to perpetuate itself through cadet branches except in Germany, where the idea of ennoblement through service remained stronger than in the West. The population was growing tremendously by the year 1000, and the nobles, better fed and housed than the lower classes, produced proportionally more younger sons than did peasants and townsmen. The nobles in the central Middle Ages tried to close themselves off from outsiders in reaction to a serious problem of blueblood overpopulation, and this reaction was so severe that it brought on a crisis of the European nobility in the thirteenth century.

PEASANTS AND TOWNSMEN

The peasants and townsmen of the early Middle Ages are anonymous figures, leaving no literary remains of their own and inspiring no one to write of them. Social mobility for this group does not indicate economic or personal well-being in any sense, and much of the vertical mobility was downward.

The late empire was a troubled time for the Roman peasantry. The free farmers had been irretrievably weakened during the age of Rome's expansion. The free peasants never went out of existence even in Italy, where their position was weaker than in other regions of the empire. Most, however, either went to the cities or became tenant farmers on the estates of great lords. Slaves captured during the campaigns became the major work force on most estates. As the slaves died out, however, the lords had to obtain labor services from the free tenant farmers who rented land from them. Tenants also paid money rents in the late republic and early empire, but by the fourth century the rents were usually payments in kind (farm produce). This group of tenant farmers was the colonate.

The Roman state desperately needed money. Rather than enlarge the tax base by offering incentives to increase production, the government tried to guarantee certain revenues by freezing all people to their lands, occupations, and social status. This program obviously could not work, for enforcement, although crushing in individual cases, was spasmodic. Exceptions were allowed even among the upper classes, and various escape routes tended to drain persons away from the already weak Roman bourgeoisie in particular.

The colons, who lacked the wherewithal to buy their way into social groups whose members were exempt from taxation, were the most severely hit. They continued to lose their lands to lords in the fourth and fifth centuries. From 332, colons were frozen to their posts, unable to leave the land, but the law was not totally effective. They were personally free, if we may define the essential criteria of freedom as the right to use public courts, enjoy the protection of the state, and pay taxes to it. In contrast to many of the medieval servile classes, colons were not bound to their lords' persons. The lord could not sell them or otherwise alienate them from the land, even though the land was his.

It is doubtful that Roman colons continued as a class into the Merovingian and Carolingian periods. The total confusion of the fifth century seems to have permitted most to escape bondage. In 460 the emperor Majorian noted "those who do not wish to remain in the status into which they were born" and ordered the recall of such persons. The Theodosian Code forbade various classes to buy exemption from public duties and ordered annulment of such privileges previously granted, but such measures were repeated so often that the situation obviously was impossible. The code itself promised freedom by the early fifth century to slaves who would perform military service, a prior necessity of which was running away from their masters. We do find persons called colons in the Carolingian polyptyques (agricultural surveys listing land owned by the lord), the names of the peasants holding it, and their payments and services. Their juridical status was similar to that of the Roman colons, but their tie to the lord was stronger. They did not owe taxes to the state, for they were not totally free and were distinguished in the sources from free persons. The payments they made and the services they performed were assessed on their land, rather than on their persons as with the Roman colons, but they were not bound to the soil. Few colons mentioned in Carolingian sources have Romance names. The scribes who compiled the polyptyques probably had some slight acquaintance with Roman legal practices and social groups and simply took the class that most closely resembled the Roman colons and applied the name to them.

In southern Europe the picture is less clear. The colonate became less numerous even in Italy with the breakdown of the Roman state. Late Roman sources complain constantly of vacant territories whose tenants had died or abandoned them. It seems obvious that many tenant farmers, crushed by the burden of taxation and labor services on the lord's estate, fled into the forest and carved out farms of their own. Southern Europe in the Middle Ages was the land of the peasant allod, land held directly of the state and owing duties only to it. The state was weak, and the independent peasant proprietor was common. Some great estates did survive the Roman Empire, however, and part of their labor force was made up of persons who seem to have been descendants of the Roman colons.

There are few sources for the history of the Germanic peasants, who were to dominate settlement patterns in northern Europe, before the eighth century. The Roman historian Tacitus, writing at the end of the first century, shows the Germans practicing a sort of communal agriculture in forest clearings. They had private property, but agricultural implements and draught animals were so valuable that the local village regulated agricultural routine and communal plowing. The great German lords had slaves and semi-free peasants working their land for them, and this regime of village chieftaincies seems to have been continued after they entered Roman territory. But it seems beyond doubt that numerous Germans simply carved plots of land out of the forest, either singly or in groups, and kept their freedom. By the end of the fifth century, however, many of them had occupied land previously held by Romans in northern Europe. The Romans also had settled laets on land near the frontiers as social mixture with the Germans accompanied political fusion. These were free Germanic peasants who were to serve twenty years in the Roman legions, whereupon the land would devolve to them and their descendants to hold in perpetuity. As the Romans withdrew from their Rhine-Danube line, other Germans joined their fellows inside the empire. Indeed, only in the region from the German Rhineland through most of Belgium and into parts of northern France did the Germans make a sufficiently strong agrarian settlement to allow them to become the dominant linguistic group in the early Middle Ages.

Yet the free Germanic peasants were declining in number and moving toward serfdom by the Carolingian period. The spread of feudal relationships, with the increased military importance of mounted, armed warriors at the expense of the infantry service of the Germanic freeman, doubtless was related to this trend. Recent studies, however, show that the cavalry was neither unknown in the primitive period nor the normal rule under the Carolingians. It is true that the freeman lost his importance to the state as he lost his military value, but the state was too weak to give him much protection anyway, and the entire question seems more academic than real. More significant in the decline of the free peasant was the spread of the great estate, both secular and ecclesiastical, among the Germans. Roman lordship over the Germanic peasants of northern Gaul was weak, but the conquest of the area by Germanic chieftains resulted in the subjection of those holding the land, whether Roman or German. This need not have been permanent, for the kings were notoriously poor administrators. But they gave out their lands to temporal and ecclesiastical potentates, both of whom, but particularly the churches, were much more effective. This practice unquestionably hindered peasant mobility, for rude tests of determining servile status were applied, generally on the basis of the performance of certain types of labor service.

Most important of all, however, in the German peasant's loss of freedom and his mobility downward into serfdom was an agricultural change in the late

Merovingian and early Carolingian periods. Forms of exploitation were reverting toward neo-Roman models. The Germans reintroduced slavery into European agriculture. A serf is not a slave; he has some rights, such as that of holding property, and he cannot be sold away from his tenement. The slave, on the other hand, is the chattel of his lord. The supply of slaves had dwindled drastically as the Romans had ceased their conquests and their slaves either did not multiply or moved into the colonate. But the Germans, constantly fighting Romans and other Germans, found agricultural dependents an important form of booty. They normally used slaves to cultivate land taken from Roman peasants. The slaves were maintained directly on the lord's demesne (land cultivated by peasants for the lord), receiving food and clothing or occasionally a small wage and a cottage.

From the seventh century, however, we find new clearance of forest and expansion of arable land in the wake of a population expansion. The lords had to offer land to their slaves as an inducement for doing the extra work of clearance. Such a change also engulfed the free peasants who simply owed rents to the lord. This is not to say that most demesne slaves received lands from the lord; the reverse seems to have been the case. With the clearances, however, the manse (household unit of land) appears. The amount of land in a manse varied with fertility of the soil and the size of the household occupying it when the land was parceled out. The manses were designated either "free" or "servile" after the juridical status of their original occupants, and free manses generally were somewhat larger. Large manors, estates under great lords comprising demesne and hundreds or even thousands of peasant manses, were being created. The socially significant aspect of this development is that we now find persons of servile status occupying the lord's land in return for rentals or labor services, thus joining the peasant "aristocracy," for any peasant who lived on his personal tenement was considerably above the ordinary in wealth and social standing. An essential distinction between free and unfree thus was removed in the late Merovingian period. Both groups held land and performed labor services, for money was gradually going out of circulation. Distinctions between free and unfree did not disappear, but they came to have increasingly less meaning as classes and tenures merged. By the Carolingian period, freemen occupied servile manses and serfs occupied free manses. A mixture of classes was occurring in which slave was elevated to serfdom and free peasant sank into serfdom.

The change was in large part the result of ordinary social intercourse in the village. A recent study has shown that the sex ratio of men to women was extremely high on the estates of the abbey of Saint-Germain-des-Prés, near Paris. Marriage between persons of different juridical status was common, and in most cases the woman, who probably would be without a large dowry although with plenty of men from whom to choose a mate, married beneath herself. Since social status was passed through the maternal line on these estates, the result was the rise of many servile persons into the colonate within one generation. Whether this explanation can be generalized for other areas remains to be seen. Men apparently outnumbered women throughout Europe in the rough society of the early Middle Ages, but the ratio began to change in the ninth century and was totally reversed by the thirteenth. In this way the social milieu of the peasantry seems to parallel that of the nobility, where emphasis on patrilineal inheritance of status becomes pronounced only from the late ninth century.

There are other practical considerations. Within the village there was constant contact among the peasants. The performance of common duties in the fields contributed to social mixture and legal confusion. Mixed marriage, as we have seen, had important consequences. In areas where village custom was weak, lords often were able to claim that the children of such marriages followed the status of the lower parent, whether father or mother. Economic distinctions were not great. The marriage of an unfree man holding fifteen acres to the daughter of a colon with thirty acres who intended to divide his lands among his sons would be a rather good match for the girl. Such conditions, however, are not conducive to the maintenance of fast juridical distinctions.

We must also note population movement. This was an age of poor communications and little contact between distant regions, but there was considerable contact between one village and another. No estate was totally self-sufficient. Some peasants were required to do carrying services, involving the transport of produce either to market or to the lord's storage depot. This brought them into contact with other villas within the same lord's estate. Even leaving aside for the moment the question of a merchant class, peasants did exchange commodities with other villagers, and a certain amount of intermarriage and social mobility was the inevitable result.

Furthermore, a large labor force was on the move in the period of migration. The disruptions forced many peasants away from their homes in search of vacant land. There was enough horizontal mobility to cause the fundamental laws of tribes to concern themselves with it. Clause 45 of the Salic Law (law of the Salian Franks, the dominant branch of the tribe) orders that if even one resident of a village objects to the presence of a newcomer, the newcomer must leave. As the great church estates were built up, originally with slave labor, the comparatively advanced agricultural forms combined with the safety of numbers to attract many later settlers. The wanderers were not always desirable types. Some princes discouraged all horizontal mobility on the apparent assumption that even supposedly harmless migrants were actual or potential outlaws. Charlemagne even ordered the Irish missionaries wandering in his kingdom to settle and adopt a rule. Like the Roman emperors, Charlemagne was concerned with binding each person into a social status with precise obligations, and this royal desire may explain the sudden burst of record keeping on the great abbeys of central France. In one directive he informed an inspector that "there are no categories other than free and slave."

Peasants might rise within the manor and village as well as by moving away. Every estate had its overseer, generally from the lord's entourage, but it was normal also to have a steward. He was a peasant foreman who supervised his fellows and generally did the same services as they. He usually received a wage or a large tenement, perhaps two manses. Such persons might be free or servile. In the early Middle Ages the position was largely honorific, but later the local officers of the great lords were able to carve out petty lordships of their own at the expense of their careless masters.

Specialized duties on the estate made certain peasants quite valuable to the lord and contributed to economic and social mobility. Smiths, for example, were essential to a peasant population just entering the iron age, and they had a readier market for their wares than did simple agriculturalists. Some estates specialized in salt or mineral production in addition to growing the staple grains. The exploitation of the salt pans on the Lotharingian estates of the abbey of Prüm gives a good example. Salt was being processed by 892, when the abbey drew up a polyptyque, and those responsible for its production received extremely favorable conditions of tenure. In 967 the largest of the villages on these estates, Morville-sur-Seille, received a charter that shows a professional merchant class, the oldest such charter for a place in France. Persons performing military or messenger services for their lords had a great deal of physical mobility even if they were serfs. The value of their services to their lords made them a group apart from their fellows.

The pressure of population fostered horizontal mobility throughout the Middle Ages. The number of mouths needing sustenance was increasing from the seventh century, and the population continued to grow, save perhaps during the renewal of invasions in the ninth and early tenth centuries, until the late thirteenth century or in some regions the early fourteenth. By the early ninth century several households with no apparent blood tie might occupy the same manse. Manses were subdivided, with some peasants holding half or quarter manses. Technological improvements brought higher yields, and a family could be supported by a smaller piece of land than before. But yields always were low by modern standards, and progressive subdivision of holdings forced many off the land and forced others to expand their holdings by clearance. The serf was not always bound to his tenement, but there was a problem of where he might go. Accordingly, in the ninth and tenth centuries the rural population became progressively poorer in areas of high concentration, unless virgin land was available for clearance. Although merchant settlements did exist, they were large enough to relieve population pressure on the land to a significant degree only in the central and late Middle Ages.

The condition of the peasant on the manor was far from typical. There was too much diversity in agrarian life to allow us to speak of types. Furthermore, the manor was far from universal. Unfortunately, we know more of the economic aspect of nonmanorial farming than of social relationships. Peasants certainly were more likely to be free if they were outside the manorial structure. Many free peasants, however, did live on large estates, particularly in western Germany, southern France, and the Low Countries. They paid rents in kind or money to their lords. Although labor services tended to be regarded as a sign of servile status in the early Middle Ages, as they were later, some freemen worked on the lord's demesne. Liberty did not mean that a peasant was judged by his peers, for in most cases he was responsible to the court of the lord of his land.

The nonmanorial aspect of peasant social conditions was determined also by geography. In mountainous regions the open and elongated fields and dense settlement so necessary to the communal agricultural regime of the manor were impossible. Similarly, in marshy areas or those subject to flooding, as in the Netherlands and maritime Flanders, manors were unusual and most peasants were free. In rocky or wooded areas we find isolated peasant enclosures and small estates with peasant tenements that had services less burdensome than those of the manors. Peasants working in vineyard areas often were free and were paid daily wages. There was much horizontal mobility among peasants because of the environment. Knowing little of soil fertilization, they left poor land when it played out.

England, together with Germany east of the Rhine and north of Bavaria, the regions that had known Carolingian economic and social forms for only a short time, were only partially manorialized. They preserved their essentially Germanic social structures. In both England and Germany we find infinite social gradations, with each class having a different wergeld and owing different duties to the state. Both had a large serf population, and slaves remained important in both long after they disappeared in France. But the preservation of a comparatively large free peasantry before the year 1000 is striking in England and Germany alike. The fact that these areas were the strongest political units of their day may have contributed to this circumstance. Free peasants were important as sources of tax revenue (only in England do we find comprehensive taxation of the free population before the thirteenth century) and of soldiers. Most fighting continued to be done by infantry in both England and Germany until the eleventh century, and the free peasant thus could serve without buying a horse and heavy armament. Whether he could afford to be away from his farm for a campaigning season is another matter, and it seems clear that except for home guards, in which serfs often served, most of the infantry used by the English and German kings consisted not of simple farmers but of persons of means who had peasant dependents of their own to work their land for them.

In conclusion, therefore, we know little of the free peasantry of the early

Middle Ages beyond the fact that it existed. Free peasants were found chiefly outside the heavily manorialized Carolingian heartland of north-central France and western Germany, where they were a tiny minority in the ninth century and virtually disappeared in the tenth. Freemen preserved their liberty in Germany longer and were a sort of peasant aristocracy, but in the twelfth and thirteenth centuries they were united with those bound to the soil into a general class of *Leibeigenen*, those in a personal relationship of dependence to a lord. This development had occurred in fact but not in law two centuries earlier in France, for the serf's theoretical freedom of movement was no more than that; in law, the developments paralleled in time, as we shall see.

We know even less of the merchant and artisan classes than of the peasants in the early Middle Ages. The Roman middle class was neither numerous nor strong. There was little large-scale commerce. The wealth of most merchants was based upon rural estates. This class was driven increasingly out of the towns and toward the countryside as the Romans placed intolerable tax burdens on the municipal aristocrats and made their rank hereditary. Since money was easier to tax than land, merchants moreover paid a disproportionate share of the taxes. Most urban artisans were small operators who produced for a local market. They were frozen in their occupational guilds so that taxes could be collected more easily. As the producers and retailers of commodities fled the cities, only the proletarians on the grain dole were left.

We know little of the fate of the Roman artisans. The towns were overrun and depopulated by the Germans, but the artisans were returning by the early sixth century. Even so, most implements were made on rural estates rather than in the towns. The artisans of the early Middle Ages, particularly the makers of luxury items, were a very mobile group. The English historian Bede relates that in the eighth century the abbot of Jarrow sent to Gaul for masons and glass-workers. Furthermore, the abbot of Newcastle sent to Mainz in 764 for a glass-worker and a person who could make and play a zither.

The artisan of Germanic Europe operated as an individual. There is no evidence that Roman guilds, with their strict regulation of production and caliber, survived into the Middle Ages, though such occupational groups reappeared later. Since the level of technology was low, most types of artisanry took little training or talent. Both in rural workshops and in the pre-urban nuclei (tiny settlements growing up around episcopal palaces, princely redoubts, and Roman ruins), there probably was a substantial shift and migration of population. The market was essentially local, serving resident populations, nearby farmers, and the entourage of the local bishop or abbot.

Considerable controversy has raged about the merchants. The great Belgian medievalist Henri Pirenne propounded a thesis about them that once had considerable currency. According to Pirenne, numerous traders from the Near East frequented Merovingian Gaul. The economic unity imposed by the Romans upon the Mediterranean thus remained unbroken in the sixth and early seventh centuries. Local and interregional trade in northern Europe meanwhile stagnated. This thesis is simply erroneous. A recent study has documented a grand total of six references to Jewish and Syrian merchants in the written sources of the Merovingian period, some of them in contexts implying that trade with such persons was exceptional. There is considerable evidence of trade in luxury items and particularly slaves, but by European merchants. The sources show also a market for foodstuffs both in the agrarian villages and in the pre-urban nuclei. Transport facilities, however rudimentary, obviously were present, and this implies horizontal mobility of population.

We can even speak of a modest commercial revival along the great river valleys in the seventh century. There was a revival of continental trade with England, and this meant the expansion of agrarian centers along the trade routes into commercial settlements. We know little of the merchants who inhabited these centers. They were wanderers for much of the year, for goods could be sold only through personal contact. But they could not wander throughout the year, and they tended thus to settle in the off-season in the pre-urban nuclei along the great land routes and especially the waterways. This was essentially an interregional trade in goods produced locally. Much of the population of the Merovingian and Carolingian pre-urban nuclei farmed and trafficked in foodstuffs.

Wealth gave social advancement to the merchants. In eighth-century Lombard Italy the population was divided into three classes on the basis of wealth, not birth. An Anglo-Saxon merchant who made three trips abroad at his own expense was the legal equivalent of a thane, a noble who possessed at least five hides of land and owed military service. If his family maintained this position for three generations, the rank became hereditary.

It is obvious, therefore, that the physically mobile merchants were also able to move upward in the social hierarchy. By the time of Charlemagne some of the merchant settlements, although small, were thriving. Merchants were taken under royal protection. Some were sent into the newly conquered lands of the East as part of the royal program of opening these areas to trade and Christian influence. Many stayed and became important in local commerce. Certainly the embryonic towns had begun to draw some of the surplus population off the land and provide work for it.

The pre-urban nuclei, and with them mercantile activity in general, declined during the political confusion of the ninth century, but by the tenth century they had begun to expand definitively into true towns. Carolingian sources speak of guilds, but as charitable organizations. By the tenth century, however, we find traces of artisan and merchant occupational groupings. The merchants felt a community of interest with one another. By the end of the tenth century we find primitive sworn associations of all townsmen, rich and poor, against town lords who imposed restrictions upon them. The town still was very open socially, however, and would continue to be so until the late twelfth or early thirteenth century, when the urban sector of the economy became too large in proportion to the rural.

Where the early inhabitants originated can only be surmised in most cases. Some were serfs who sold the agricultural products of their lords on the town market and developed mercantile interests in their own right. A study of geographical forms in personal names—"von," "van," and "de" with place— suggests that most were from the immediate environs of the town. This can be documented statistically for the late Middle Ages, and it probably was even more true before the year 1000. Such persons were not always free. Arras, in northern France, developed on the estates of the abbey of St. Vaast, and most of the later town patriciate was descended from serfs who got their freedom after struggles with the abbot.

The lords have been seen as basically hostile to town development, but this view is not strictly correct. They were quite happy to have prosperous markets within or just outside their castle walls. They were hostile to settlements that began to have pretensions to political independence. It has been claimed that the towns were a refuge for local serf populations running away from their lords. Some charters of urban liberty from the eleventh century and later did provide that men of the town would be free. But no "town" of the period before the year 1000, consisting of a few hundred persons at most, was strong enough to resist a lord with an armed force seeking a runaway serf. By the turn of the eleventh century some were this strong, but for the early period we can only conclude that most inhabitants of the pre-urban nuclei were free peasants of the area, persons of uncertain extraction who had wandered far from home, or serfs who were not needed by their lords and whose absence from an over-populated estate would hardly be missed. It is no coincidence that most towns of Europe developed along the great rivers of France and Germany, the Low Countries, and Italy, areas of or near heavy rural overpopulation.

The pre-urban nuclei accordingly created a new source of mobility for the peasants. Technically, the free farmers in the Carolingian period may have been free to move about as they saw fit, but they had nowhere to go. Now, in addition to the obvious alternatives of seeking other lords or wandering far away to clear new homesteads, they could go to the towns. As commercial development brought more money into circulation, the economic power of the peasants was increased, although this trend became totally apparent only after the year 1000.

SOCIAL EUROPE IN THE YEAR 1000

Europe thus was in social ferment by the year 1000. The primitive Germanic aristocracy originally had distinguished itself by service to a chieftain. By the

Merovingian period the men of this aristocracy were landholders. They were joined then by a new group, which arose, just as the older aristocracy had, through personal prowess rather than through the blood tie and which in its turn also got lands. By the ninth and tenth centuries these two groups had virtually united and begun to close themselves off to outsiders. There developed class consciousness, made possible only by a population increase from the late Merovingian age, which allowed younger sons and cadet branches of noble houses to keep total numbers up without replenishing the old stock. As we shall see, high birth rates and particularly low death rates in the central Middle Ages led to a new crisis and a reassignment of roles between great and lesser nobility.

The peasantry was mobile despite juridical distinctions between classes. Economic criteria tend to be forerunners of changes in social status. France knew peasant movement upward from slavery and downward from freedom into a broader serfdom, a process hastened as the nobles increased their power and the kings lost theirs. In Germany and England a strong monarchy helped to preserve a substantial free peasantry. There was room for horizontal as well as for vertical mobility between manors and within manors. Marriage between persons of different manors held by the same lord was common. It was less ordinary between dependents of different lords, but it occurred if the lord gave his consent and (generally) if the peasants paid a fine.

The merchant classes were growing rapidly. By the year 1000 the suburbs around fortifications often were quite large and posed a potential threat to the lords of the fortifications. The merchant's profession allowed tremendous horizontal mobility, and his wealth could give him social advancement even into the nobility. The artisans were less mobile than the merchants, but the growth of a town class implied movement of population from the almost exclusively agrarian society of an earlier age.

The Central Middle Ages

The period between the eleventh and late thirteenth centuries was the age of the greatest economic prosperity that medieval Europe was to know. These centuries saw an expansion of Europe to the productive limits permitted by the agricultural and industrial technology of the day. The result could only be profound changes in social structure and patterns of social mobility.

THE NOBILITY

The European nobility underwent a crisis of major proportions. The nobles continued to reproduce themselves faster than necessary for the maintenance of a constant number within the group. Hence territorial principalities fractionalized in the eleventh and twelfth centuries as younger sons assumed governmental functions. We find emphasis on the ban power and the profession of knighthood as criteria of noble status. One could be qualified for knighthood and governmental authority, however, only if he were of pure noble blood.

The ban power was obtained easily enough. It simply involved the assumption of governmental powers and the recognition of this as legitimate by one's peers. The concept of knighthood was also united with nobility. In the early Middle Ages the Latin *miles* simply meant an armed, mounted soldier, with no connotation of nobility. But the profession of arms was normal for the son of a noble.

Lesser knights held the ban power over their dependents and often were of the blood line of the great noble families. The lesser nobility thus was not always distinguished from the greater by blood. All were knights or knights presumptive and hence might become noble if they were dubbed and acquired the other essential, the ban power. Thus in the twelfth and thirteenth centuries the older nobility of blood was joined by the knights to form an all-encompassing nobility in the lands of the old Carolingian Empire.

The nobles then closed ranks and tried to keep newcomers out. We find increased evidence of nobles' class consciousness in the late twelfth century. For the first time laws forbade non-nobles to bear arms. Punishment for crimes still varied according to social class. The concept of "estates" was formalized in the thirteenth century. This term was vague when applied to non-nobles, but it had precise connotations for the clergy and the high-born. From the late twelfth century we find stronger evidence than before that one could not inherit noble status from one parent if the other was not also noble. This ridiculous prohibition led to tremendous inbreeding and a biological crisis within a century. It certainly was not universally applied. Despite the legal merger of great and lesser nobility, the two were not considered social equals until the late fourteenth century. A person of the old titled nobility married beneath himself if he sought a bride from the lesser nobility. The division is shown most clearly in England, where the lesser nobles (or, in the case of England, aristocrats) found their natural allies in the upper bourgeoisie rather than among the titled nobles and joined the former to form the House of Commons in the fourteenth century.

There are peculiar cases. In the Namurois region of eastern Belgium, the studies of L. Genicot have shown that the terms "free" and "noble" were synonymous. But this can be deceptive. The nobles of the Namurois were not well off. The region is mountainous, a land of small farms. A large class of lesser nobles who were little more than prosperous peasants merged with the greater nobility around 1250. A similar situation occurs in the thirteenth century in the Forez of France, where numerous nobles were no better off economically than their peasants were. Such persons often did not bother to have themselves dubbed knights and thereby incur the obligation of expensive military service.

Hence at least before the late twelfth or the thirteenth century, when some nobles avoided being dubbed for financial reasons, all male nobles, except those in the clergy, were knights but not all knights were noble. Then the two groups merged and closed, but not at the same time in all parts of Europe. The closing occurred earliest in northern France and Belgium. A classic case is the Hauteville family of Normandy. Tancred of Hauteville, a minor baron, could not make provision for his twelve sons; the boys went to southern Italy and Sicily. Starting as mountain bandits, they succeeded in capturing Byzantine Italy and Saracen Sicily within two generations. There were too many lesser nobles and serfs, termed *ministeriales,* who were working their way into the lesser nobility. Few new ministerial houses were founded even in Germany after the early twelfth century. After the assassination of Charles the Good, count of Flanders, in 1127, ostensibly inspired by the count's threat to disgrace a powerful man by betraying his ministerial origins, there is no evidence that ministeriales entered the Flemish nobility. Too many people had too much to lose, so everyone kept quiet about the servile origins of his fellows in the hope of excluding others. Noble society in southern Europe remained mobile longer, and both in southern France and in southern Germany the ministeriales still had aspirations to noble status in the thirteenth century.

The term *ministeriales* takes in the serf knights of Germany and parts of Lotharingia and the Low Countries and, less precisely, their free counterparts in southern France. Military service by serfs was unusual in the early Middle Ages, but nothing in the nature of their status prevented it before the twelfth century. The German kings were in a singular position regarding their armies. They had extensive estates, and the heartlands of the royal domain in Saxony and Thuringia were areas where serfdom was rare. They had a large body of free peasant subjects upon whom they could call for military service. As in England, there was a carefully graded hierarchy of social classes, but with a more economic than genealogical basis of social advancement. The upper classes remained an aristocracy longer in Germany and England than in France. Social structures thus were somewhat "archaic." The lower levels of society in particular did not know the extent of mobility that had occurred in western Europe during the Carolingian period.

The ministeriales apparently originated as demesne serfs who were given various tasks, such as carrying and messenger service, that set them apart from their fellows. Many were manorial officials. They might perform military service as well, particularly as castle guards. We find little trace of the ministeriales as a separate social group before the eleventh century. The German kings had used ecclesiastical immunity to administer their empire. This avoided the ultimate disaster, enfeoffment to nobles, which would have diminished royal land

and power bases, and made the king the advocate or secular representative and defender of the most important ecclesiastical estates. But the church moved out from under royal domination, particularly from the eleventh century. As the kings lost power during the Investiture Controversy in the late eleventh century, the free populations of the empire fell under the direct control of dukes, counts, margraves, and other local potentates.

The German kings thus turned increasingly to their serfs, men devoted to themselves and dependent upon royal favor for personal and social advancement. They were placed in charge of castles and handled local business as viceroys. As soldiers, they could be knights, and knighthood was an essential aspect of noble status. Although they were serfs, they were free to move about as they chose. Ecclesiastical foundations also had ministeriales. In the middle of the eleventh century the ministeriales of the bishop of Bamberg were permitted to seek other employment if the bishop did not need their services and thus failed to give them fiefs. By 1100 the ministeriales had a class consciousness. However, as time went on, their military function became secondary. They also held the ban power by express royal authority, thereby fulfilling the other criterion of noble status. In a certain sense they never exercised it in their own right, but the kings of Germany were not able to control them in the thirteenth century. By an agreement of 1180 with the German nobility, the king in effect mediatized the ministeriales by placing them far down a list of descending "orders of escutcheons," as thirteenth-century legal texts termed it. The king could control them only through the temporal princes above them but under him in the hierarchy. The ministeriales became a nobility with local powers of government and the honors of knighthood by the process of social stratification taken to the political level.

Their unfree status was an embarrassment. By the thirteenth century, they were calling themselves knights rather than ministeriales. The merging of knighthood with the greater nobility into a single noble class was a merger of free and free in the West. In Germany it merged free and serf into a social grouping still quite distinct and only partially encompassing the order of imperial princes, a political grouping with social overtones. The case of the ministeriales is a classic illustration of how serfdom per se had become meaningless by the early thirteenth century, only to become significant again thereafter. Not all ministeriales became nobles. Some remained peasants, but they were generally well off and might even be petty lords of villages. Many entered the town patriciates and paid a nominal head tax to a lord as a sign of servile status; in fact they were totally free. This is particularly true of some of the episcopal towns. The ministeriales of Regensburg, for example, were basically a countryside class and lived outside the city, but they controlled the town magistracy until the fourteenth century. In many towns, especially those of middling size, they were among the richest inhabitants and occasionally designated themselves noble.

It has been claimed that western Europe knew no class similar to the ministeriales, but this seems incorrect. The technically servile status of the ministeriales has misled historians. Until the thirteenth century, when knighthood itself was becoming closed, class barriers or distinctions were by no means as significant as they might seem. The term ministerialis is sometimes used in southern France to indicate a free person moving toward the lesser nobility. But the normal French equivalent of the German ministerialis was *sergent,* who might be free or unfree (the word always meant a freeman in England). In France the sergent generally originated in the lord's household and was entrusted with various personal tasks, just as the ministeriales had been. The sergents eventually got land, and particularly positions as estate managers for their lords. Very early in the thirteenth century, just as the nobles were closing off to form a class, some managed to enter the nobility. Others, unable to buy their freedom (for knighthood and serfdom were impossible together in French law), remained well-off but servile. This cleavage occurred among the German ministeriales, but more in the fourteenth and fifteenth centuries than in the thirteenth.

Italy and the Anglo-Norman empire are peculiar cases. In common with much of the nobility of southern France, that of Italy was semi-urban. The great men of the countryside were also the great men of the city and developed commercial interests earlier than did their northern counterparts. But they often were also the bitter opponents of the townsmen as robber barons, particularly in Italy. The Italian nobility was not prosperous and tended to prey upon commerce. Their feuds also disturbed the citizens inside the towns. The towns thus conquered their surrounding countryside *(contado)* and forced the nobles to submit to city suzerainty.

There were different problems with the lesser Italian nobles, the vavasours, or rear vassals. These men held small plots of land in the countryside but were in an economic box because the consent of the lord had to be obtained for sale or other alienation of their land. Many wanted to sell all or part of their land and migrate to the towns. By the eleventh century, the Italian nobles were selling their fiefs, a privilege that their northern counterparts got only in the thirteenth. Vavasours went increasingly to the towns while maintaining some lands and family ties outside.

The growth of large towns in southern Europe made the local nobility more mobile. At Toulouse there were knights in both the Cité and the Bourg, the two nuclei around which the town grew. The primary difference between them and the burghers was in the wealth and military function of the knights. Such a situation could not produce great social stratification, and conditions similar to those in Toulouse are common in the South. The nobles formed the core of the early urban militia, but the distinction lessened in the eleventh century and later as merchants became rich enough to buy horses and serve. Merchants and knights united to form the first communal organization in the twelfth century.

The patriciates of Italy, like those of southern France, were not made up so exclusively of nobles as once was thought, but there was considerable mobility between noble and merchant classes. It was unusual for nobles to be in town patriciates of the North except in the case of the ministeriales. Nobles upon whose estates commercial settlements grew up often turned to trade themselves. But the social ethic of the Italian noble made him less reluctant than his northern counterpart to engage in commerce. Social distinction remained. The noble prerogatives of the feud and bloodletting, though by no means foreign to the townsmen, were a nuisance. They explain in large part the hostility that caused non-noble patricians to ally with the middle classes against the "magnates" in the thirteenth century and place them under civil disabilities. But by that time "magnate" had more the meaning of "outlaw" than of "noble," and by the fourteenth century persons were being exiled from towns as magnates who had no blood tie with the nobility. The nobility of southern Europe, and particularly Italy, was quite weak and must be thought of in an essentially urban or city-state context.

England and Normandy also vary from developments elsewhere in France. Normandy in the early eleventh century gives an example of two concurrent nobilities of blood and shows the paramount nature of the service aspect even as classes became more firmly defined. Like many territorial principalities, Normandy had too many nobles. The situation became totally chaotic with the accession of the bastard and minor Duke William I in 1035 and improved only when he reached his majority. William consciously drew upon a "new" service nobility to replace older men who defected. Obviously anyone can build up a wealthy class by taking property from one group and giving it to another, but William was favored by peculiarities in the Norman social structure. The distinction between feudal and nonfeudal tenure had practically disappeared in Normandy by this time. Persons not noble who did military service could hold fiefs hereditarily, a development coming much later in most of France. A barrier that tended to develop elsewhere between noble and commoner thus did not arise in Normandy, where society remained more mobile. The term *vavasour* also has a peculiar meaning in Normandy of small freeholders who had public military duties. The term was exported to England, and for a generation after the conquest the English vavasours were the equivalent of the Norman. The Norman vavasours were quite similar to the sokemen of the English Danelaw, sturdy yeomen of legend and probably of fact as well. But *vavasour* soon reverted to the vaguer meaning of rear vassal common to the continent in an age when the entire feudal relationship was being drained of its meaning.

The situation in England, just as in Normandy, was fluid after the conquest of 1066. The army William used to conquer England consisted largely of his nouveau riche nobility and mercenaries. The Norman nobles who replaced the

Anglo-Saxon aristocracy in the generation after the conquest were almost entirely men of recent accession to this "nobility of service," for most members of the older houses who remained loyal to William stayed in Normandy.

The Norman Conquest simplified the complex Anglo-Saxon social structure, but it introduced various levels of feudal landholding. The great tenants-in-chief, who held directly of the king, in their turn enfeoffed rear vassals, but often to such an extent that even the basic unit of the knight's fee (the amount of land considered necessary for the basic maintenance of a mounted soldier) became too small for its purpose. Both the great tenants-in-chief and their vassals were knights, but the two were often of completely different social levels. Only the tenants-in-chief formed a nobility in any sense. But not all descendants of these persons were noble, and they had no legal monopoly on the great offices of the realm. The ordinary soldier, the knight, was an individual of modest means. A recent study has shown that at the time of the Domesday survey (1086) the average holding of a knight was about one and a half hides of land, only slightly above the average for wealthy peasants. Many of course held less than the average. The position of the knight in England was thus similar to that of the northern French knight of the same period, a modest social status and economic position until knighthood began to become more prestigious around 1150. The turning point in the history of English knighthood apparently came under King Henry II (1154–1189). The smallest knightly tenements became ordinary free peasant tenancies and did not owe knights' service. By the end of the century legal standards held that five hides of land constituted a knight's fee. This meant that only the wealthiest knights remained knights and as such continued in the English aristocracy. Certainly the late twelfth century was a time of crisis for the lesser English knighthood. A recent study of the feudatories of Peterborough abbey in the twelfth and thirteenth centuries shows that most held on to a knight's fee until at least 1175, but this pattern broke in the last quarter of the century. Many lesser knights became poor because of the increased costs of their profession; others became wealthier by consolidation and purchase of estates. As an example, the house of Clapton held a substantial fief in the twelfth century of Roger of Lovetot, who in turn held it of Peterborough abbey. The fee remained whole until 1175. Then it was divided among five brothers, who in turn alienated it. It is true that this estate was partially reunited in the next century, but the example is instructive. Many other fees of Peterborough simply changed hands in the late twelfth century without being subdivided, as their holders fell into financial embarrassment.

The English upper classes were an aristocracy, not a nobility. They were conscious of blood ties but always were subject to penetration from below by other social groups if the latter obtained royal favor or could marry into a distinguished noble lineage. By the early thirteenth century there was even a large bourgeois element among the lesser aristocrats. This group, the gentry, was distinguished by local possession of the ban power by delegation from the king, although not in its own right. The status of the English "knights of the shire" was given by fiscal and social standing and local governmental function. It was not invariably hereditary, and it was military in name only by the late thirteenth century. The French social historian Marc Bloch argued that because the mass of the English peasantry was still servile in the thirteenth century, there was scarcely a difference between the peasant freeman and the local aristocrat. Studies are increasingly showing that in thirteenth-century England some peasants were free, but Bloch certainly was correct in arguing that the social hierarchy was less rigid in England, and perhaps in Germany, than in France. England had a nobility only at the upper reaches of society, and even there it is questionable, for only the eldest son inherited his father's title and noble status. The others inherited property but not a status except in the general feeling that a person of good birth was above the mass of mankind. Good birth was not a legal rank. Nevertheless, the English aristocracy was the most powerful in Europe by virtue of its performance of the local offices of royal government and its possession of great power over the peasants, most of whom were serfs. Patents of nobility purchased from the king developed later in England than in France for the simple reason that there was enough mobility in England to satisfy most aspirations.

By 1200, the European nobility was in a period of crisis. Fiefholding and fighting were no longer exclusive provinces of the nobles. We shall examine their reaction to the economic changes of the central Middle Ages in more detail when we discuss peasant mobility. Their incomes generally were tied to tenures held hereditarily for rentals by peasants. Nobles had other economic rights, such as judicial fines, peasant labor services, and forced peasant patronage of their mills. But until the late twelfth century most temporal lords were notoriously poor estate managers, a fact that led to substantial alienations of land. Sometimes it was given in charitable donation, but more often the lords granted leasehold tenements to peasants. Local officials of the nobles could in effect have many demesnes farmed for themselves rather than for their busy masters.

Thus the nobility suffered fiscal troubles around 1200. The crisis was furthered by inheritance customs. In England, land held by knights' service was transmitted by primogeniture unless it went to a woman (in which case it was divided) ; only the eldest son was able to inherit his father's title. Although feudal law in France varied by region, it often provided for the division of estates. All sons of a noble father were noble. The younger siblings might hold rear fiefs of the eldest or simply subdivide the estate with him. The fractionalizing of noble tenures was a serious problem in France. It is true that fiefs did not enter the land market to the same extent in France as in England, but the appearance is deceptive and reflects the stronger social class consciousness among the French nobility. Alienation of fiefs had reached the point in England that in 1290 a statute prohibited subinfeudation by providing that purchasers of fiefs would become vassals not of the seller but of the seller's lord. There is no equivalent of this provision in France. As early as 1209, the kings did try to prohibit subinfeudation to collateral heirs, but by the end of the century they were simply forbidding the alienation of fiefs to persons such as bourgeois, who could not do military service, exacting a fine, and letting the transaction stand.

Such changes in the fief obviously meant that many non-noble persons were entering feudal relationships. Even more, they meant that many nobles were becoming poor, particularly in France, though less in northern France, where some regions had primogeniture, than in the Midi, Provence, and Dauphiné, where extremely poor noble houses often had governing power only over the immediate household. But northern France still was overcrowded with nobles. In the thirteenth century lesser knights were recovering part of their lost position by entering royal bureaucracies. It is significant that most of the "new men" among the counselors of King Louis IX of France (Saint Louis) came from the northern petty nobility.

Some cadet lines of noble families saved themselves, and in the long run the fortunes of their families, by fortunate marriages. The marriage market was an important avenue of mobility within and into the nobility. The Wavrin family of Flanders and northern France is first encountered as vassals of the counts of Flanders. They made good marriages, beginning with the "countess" of Valenciennes around 1100. Roger III of Wavrin became seneschal of Flanders around 1140. Marriages brought new lands to the family: Oisy-Montmirail, Châtillon, and Béthune. But as the count strengthened his bureaucracy in the thirteenth century, as town power encroached upon the nobles, and as monetary inflation ate away the real value of their fixed revenues, the Wavrins had troubles. They sold the seneschalship in 1275. The house was eclipsed in the fourteenth century and maintained itself only through the lands of cadet branches, the lords of Comines and St. Venant. Cadet lines often did not fare so well. The Boneffe family was a younger branch of the house of Zétrud, related to the counts of Namur. Anselm Boneffe was called *nobilis* and *miles* in the twelfth century, as was his son. But of the son's three sons, one was called noble, one knight, and one neither. The Boneffes lost both titles in the next generation but became castellans of Bouvignes, thus dropping into the lesser aristocracy of professional administrators.

The troubles of main branches and cadet lines alike suggest the need for replenishment from other social groups, but in much of continental Europe in the late twelfth and thirteenth centuries the nobility was closing itself off. When two noble parents were needed to produce a noble offspring, noble houses tended either to have too many heirs and fractionalize estates or to die out entirely. The English gentry, an aristocracy rather than a nobility, maintained themselves in the face of economic pressures only by renouncing feudal obligations and going only as far as the rank of squire, in many cases never reaching knighthood. Although the pressures of the economy hurt the great nobles less than the lesser, the thirteenth century witnessed a birth rate crisis among the upper classes. Westphalia had 120 noble families in 1150, 98 in 1200, 64 in 1250, and 29 in 1300. Picardy saw a decline from around 100 noble *lignages* (extended families) in 1150 to 12 in 1300. Most families descended from the counts in Thuringia and Bavaria died out in the thirteenth century and were replaced by ministeriales, who were probably the most important element of most princely courts in Germany by the middle of the thirteenth century.

Biological necessity thus was dictating some relaxation of the strict hereditary criteria by the end of the thirteenth century. This could take various forms. The work of E. Perroy on the nobles of the Forez region of France, where noble *lignages* lasted only three or four generations on an average, has shown that replenishment came from ministeriales who grew prosperous managing church estates, collateral branches of the great noble houses, and lesser officials of the count. The peasantry, rather than the bourgeoisie as in most regions, was the ultimate point of origin for most. Absolute biological standards weakened. The first step usually was allowing a noble married to a commoner to designate his children as noble. Patents of nobility appeared, and in this way great families of town and countryside who lacked gentle birth made up for it with cold cash. The nobility did not cease to be a closed class in theory, but matters were rather different in practice in the late Middle Ages.

THE PEASANTRY

The economic growth of the central Middle Ages had tremendous effects on the social mobility of the peasantry. As the population expanded, new lands had to be cleared to feed the larger numbers. The initial impact of the change was felt in increased freedom of movement. Groups of peasant entrepreneurs wandered about until they found a territory needing clearance or reclamation from sea or marsh. Since the land was unproductive and brought in no revenue, its lord generally would be willing to give it to them on favorable terms. Thereafter he was assured of set rents, often payments in kind, and almost invariably judicial fines from cases arising in the new village. The peasants held their tenures as freemen. Such peasant specialists were a new feature of the agrarian labor situation of the central Middle Ages. The growth of groups with such skills greatly increased mobility.

The lords were less interested at first in founding new towns than were peasant entrepreneurs or even townsmen. But as they found revenues declining in an inflationary age, the lords eventually were forced to take an active interest. They founded "new towns," agrarian villages in the beginning which usually remained villages in the economic sense, and gave them charters of "elementary bourgeois liberties." In northern Europe this process usually involved freedom from serfdom, a minimizing or even abolition of forced labor services on the lord's demesne, heritability and alienability of tenure on the land, and freedom from arbitrary exactions. Declining revenues in an inflationary period thus forced change upon the lords, since "old custom" generally had fixed over a period of generations the amount of service or rent that peasant families owed for their land. The foundation of new villages worked to the advantage of both lord and peasant.

Indeed, if the medieval peasant had a golden age, it probably was the first half of the twelfth century. We have noted some of the ways in which enterprising peasant officials were able to take control of land from lords and elevate themselves into the squirearchy. By the central Middle Ages the exploits of some of these minor operators can be documented with more than statistics. Personalities begin to stand out. J. Boussard has noted the example of Constant le Roux, a serf of the abbey of Ronceray at the end of the eleventh century. Constant became extremely prosperous, although he was not a freeman, by being placed in charge of the abbey's wine cellar, then of some lands of the foundation. Free peasants had even greater opportunity to rise. P. Bonnassie has called attention to the striking case of the family of Llorenç, a prosperous free peasant in Aragon who died before 987. His son Vivas bought out his brother, then invested his money in the purchase of an enormous amount of land, most of it adjoining his own. This rise in fortune was continued by Vivas' three sons, the eldest of whom became a local squire with powers over peasant tenants and the local church. But perhaps typically, the family died out in the following generation. Even in the less mobile North such cases occur. In thirteenth-century England one Ketelbern of Canley, a free peasant of Stoneleigh, was the richest man in his village. He paid rents on behalf of his fellow peasants to the king, making a profit on the transaction. He finally married advantageously and became lord of Canley. His descendant, Robert of Canley, was to try unsuccessfully to have the other villagers declared villeins.

The bonds of serfdom were loosening, and with them the degrading tasks, ordinarily performed by serfs, that constituted tests of personal bondage. Rentals in kind still predominated but were being replaced in part by money payments, particularly in the vicinity of towns and other markets. The towns also gave the peasant convenient depots for sale of his surplus produce. Younger sons for whom there was no place on the farm might migrate to the towns, although by the early thirteenth century many town governments were reluctant to admit former bondsmen to bourgeois status. Unchallenged residence in the town for a year and a day was absolutely necessary, together in many cases with payment of a fee, and in Italy and parts of Germany and the Netherlands a much longer residence was required. Towns occasionally made reciprocal agreements with lords concerning the return of runaway serfs.

While social and juridical bondage became less severe, the old ties of kinship and lordship remained, but they were less potent forces than before. As families spread over greater distances, with some members holding a different juridical status from others, perhaps dividing into town and countryside branches, it could hardly have been otherwise. The old bonds were replaced to some extent with newly strengthened village organizations in which peasants were able to regulate their local affairs up to a point and negotiate with their lords. The peasants also founded secret societies, rural confraternities, and the like. In short, social cohesion was strengthened by village organizations, generally among the free peasants but occasionally in serf villages as well.

The great freedom of movement in the countryside was to continue and intensify. But the tendency that we associate with the late eleventh and early twelfth centuries for the peasant to move upward in the social scale could not continue in such a society as that of the Middle Ages, with political authority so stacked against the masses. It has often been assumed that England lagged behind the continent in the matter of peasant emancipation, for most of the population of Britain still was servile in the thirteenth century. But students of agrarian history are realizing increasingly that conditions were not so different as they seemed. In both England and much of the northern European continent, movements toward peasant freedom in the early twelfth century were weakened later and were virtually reversed in the thirteenth century.

Even in the twelfth century the bonds of serfdom were not totally relaxed. Younger sons, often living away from the family homestead, were more likely to buy their freedom than were the elder siblings, who tended to maintain the old ways. We must remember also that there were two types of unfreedom—those involving services tied to the holding of a piece of land and those that were personal, in which the peasant needed the lord's permission to move about freely. The two did not invariably coincide. Professor Fossier has wisely cautioned against euphoric generalizations about peasant "freedom," which meant nothing. Of importance were peasant "freedoms," liberating them from various duties and payments. One could have freedoms without being juridically free.

Peasants in the early twelfth century were being freed chiefly from labor services. With a surplus population in some areas as early as the tenth century, lords found it cheaper to hire labor than to maintain the administrative apparatus for compelling tenants to perform labor services. But freedom from labor services did not change one's status from serf to freeman. The peasant still was responsible to his lord's court and owed him an assortment of payments.

These payments were to be extremely important in the thirteenth century as a device by which lords reimposed or reaffirmed the servile status of many of their peasants. In the twelfth century we find less a movement toward enfranchisement of the peasants than a gradual merging of various peasant social groups. There is a new consciousness of class barriers in the thirteenth century.

Much of the problem in dealing with peasant classes is terminological. The English villein was a serf. The French villein was technically a free person who could move about at will. Particularly from the thirteenth century, however, the villeins became merged increasingly with the serfs. Thus serfdom went out of existence in some regions and was replaced with peasant villeinage, which on the continent implied a freer status. There was no statutory serfdom in the Mâconnais or Normandy after the early twelfth century, and it disappeared during the century in Burgundy. The Ile-de-France and Normandy were regions of a comparatively prosperous free peasantry in the late Middle Ages. But the reverse could occur: North and east of Paris and in central France, villeins tended to become serfs, as various peasant obligations came to be considered marks of servile status. Although peasants' economic prosperity tended to be greatest in areas ruled by great lords who were lax about administration, it is striking that serfdom persisted throughout the Middle Ages in the French Midi, Dauphiné, the Alpine regions, Provence, and central Italy, areas that had many small, impoverished nobles. The tendency for classes to amalgamate in the twelfth century is well shown by conditions on church estates. The rent-paying tenants of the great abbeys, although free, closely resembled the unfree peasants of the early Middle Ages who owed heavy inheritance taxes, marriage duties, high rents, and burdensome labor services.

For practical purposes, then, at the end of the twelfth century the distinction between servile and free peasants often was not great. There was a mystique about freedom then as now, and peasants were willing to make sacrifices to obtain it. But a good example of the state of affairs is given by the Capetian royal domain, where it was difficult for peasants to obtain liberty until the middle and late thirteenth century. King Louis X (1314–1316) finally forced his peasants to buy their freedom, but he did not free them from labor obligations. He lost no legal rights, for as lord of the land he was judge of free persons anyway.

In France the various peasant social classes tended to merge into serfdom after the Carolingian period. This merger was broken briefly in the eleventh and early twelfth centuries as many peasants became free. In many cases, however, the freedom was economically meaningless, particularly for those who did not use either their freedom or their position as serfs with personal mobility to leave the land. Thereafter freedom and serfdom again became virtually interchangeable in some areas, until a new legal consciousness in the thirteenth century perpetuated much more far-reaching class divisions.

Developments in Germany were somewhat different. The fusion of classes that characterized post-Carolingian France occurred in Germany only in the thirteenth century, and it tended to be a personal servitude, a tie of serf to lord, rather than the real bondage of serf to land characteristic of France. This is not to say that France knew little personal bondage or that Germany had no class of peasants bound to the soil, but rather that, taking the areas as a whole, other conditions predominated. Germany kept a larger class of landless demesne serfs in the central Middle Ages than did France, but from the twelfth century lords tended to give them lands on the principle that concession of a tenure implied the hereditary subjection to the lord of the tenant and his family. This development occurred only later in France. The German peasantry in a sense lost freedom by contamination with French ideas. Payment of the personal head tax was originally a sign of personal freedom in Germany, implying that the person paying it had free disposition over himself. In France it implied servitude on grounds of the lord's disposition over the peasant's person, as opposed merely to his property. The French meaning became current in Germany from the late twelfth century.

The German free peasant was thus sinking into serfdom in the central Middle Ages. As petty German lords increasingly made the royal judicial and administrative apparatus ineffective, they were able to mediatize the peasants under their own control. The earlier pattern had been reversed, and the French free peasant was a more common figure than his German counterpart by the end of the thirteenth century.

Various explanations can be offered for the social changes that began in the late twelfth century. Lords no longer were the barbarian huntsmen of old. They had been hurt by the early phases of the economic expansion and were forced to manage their estates more effectively. What was done was done, but the lords were able to impose new conditions in the wake of changed economic developments that turned the balance in their favor. It became unusual for bailiffs to carve out lordships of their own. There is evidence from the thirteenth century that when peasant families holding tenures at hereditary rent died out, they would be replaced by tenants holding the land for a term of years. The rental thus could be raised upon renegotiation. Of equal importance for the legal status of the peasantry, we find a new legalism and consciousness of law developing in the thirteenth century. As much of the peasantry became free, the new class of lawyers that was emerging out of the educational changes of the period began to apply the performance of certain labor services as tests of servile status. The most important of these were heriot or mortmain (payment of the best animal to the lord when the head of the peasant household died), a payment exacted when the peasant married someone from outside the estate, and the head tax. Liability to the personal tax, as opposed to the levy on property, continued to be regarded as a mark of servility in western Europe until the fourteenth century. The serfs paid as individuals, but free villages were taxed as communities by the lords and often had the right to apportion the levy among themselves. The amount of the head tax was generally fixed and annual even for serfs, but it was an important source of revenue for lords in an age of expanding population. Naturally there was an attempt to enforce payment from as many persons as possible.

Legal servitude thus began to revive significantly in the thirteenth century. There still was no effort to reimpose servile labor duties on free peasants who previously had escaped them, but the new concern with definition of free and unfree meant that the barrier between them became much more rigid and harder to breach in the thirteenth century than it had been in the twelfth. Lords also were trying to bind the unfree peasant to the soil, despite a surplus of labor. Roman Law, then in revival as a customary legal system in France, contributed to this trend, for Roman colons had been tied to their tenures. Certain territories also had been considered servile in the Merovingian period, and the thirteenth-century French jurist Beaumanoir declared that when a non-noble freeman inhabited such a territory for a year and a day, he became a serf of its lord.

Although personal servitude never died out and was becoming less extraordinary in the thirteenth century, it probably was a less severe burden than the economic bondage that lords were able to impose upon their peasants. They had economic monopolies that could be forced upon peasants as conditions of tenure. What had been the case earlier in fact became increasingly statutory. In particular, the lords built the imposition of judicial fines into a fine art. Since the amounts owed were not always specified in local custumals, they could abuse their privileges easily. Peasants in the twelfth century had generally obtained their freedom by organic, evolutionary processes of mutual advantage to lord and peasant, particularly land clearance. Often they acted as individuals or in small groups. By the thirteenth century the prosperity of many free communities led entire peasant villages to purchase collective manumission from the local lord. The lords exacted high prices for these charters and occasionally even forced freedom upon their peasants. In the middle of the thirteenth century serf villages were gaining manumission in the Paris region for rates as high as 20 lb. parisis. per person, an enormous sum for the time. Peasants impoverished themselves so severely by buying these charters that enfranchisement contributed to a growing problem of peasant indebtedness by the end of the thirteenth century. The lords always kept extensive rights even when granting freedom. For example, in 1248 the abbot of St. Denis freed the peasants of six villages from the marriage duty, the head tax, *mainmorte*, and "all other kinds of servitude." But other unspecified duties remained, and the men of these villages would again become serfs if they married one of the abbot's bondswomen. The abbot also kept all rights of justice. A similar charter given in 1249 to three villages by the abbot of Saint-Germain-des-Prés limited the peasants' right of alienation of their tenements and bound them to buy a certain amount of the lord's wine, grind their grain at his mill, bake in his ovens, use his winepress, and pay a share of the taxes that the king levied on the abbey.

The fundamental problem was ecological. Most of the great technological innovations that had made possible an increase of production were known by the early twelfth century and gradually spread over western Europe. But there were no new improvements until late in the Middle Ages. Even in the fourteenth century, seed yields were extremely low. As the population grew, Europe was expanding to its productive limits. All land that could be cultivated by the technology of the day was in use, and the constant use weakened the soil.

Population growth had generally worked in favor of all classes in the early twelfth century. Peasants had room for expansion of activity both on and off the farm. But the margin of subsistence was being reached as the population continued to expand. The hunger for land was such that some free peasants in thirteenth-century England declared themselves serfs simply to get a tenement. Some areas of Italy, the only part of Europe for which reliable statistics have survived from the thirteenth century, had as high a population at that time as in the nineteenth century, but with much lower seed yields and soil fertility. It is not surprising that the Italian peasants, though most were free, were economically depressed and subject to the fiscal exploitation of the large cities. David Herlihy's studies have shown overpopulation leading to a press on resources even as early as 900. Fragmentation of holdings led to renewed consolidation and to a rapid rise and fall of fortunes, particularly in allodial areas. But it also forced small-scale, inefficient agriculture. Flight to the towns, although possible, was made difficult by artificially long residence requirements—in many Italian cities it was thirty years before citizenship could be granted—for the towns also were becoming overpopulated.

Such conditions create a mobile labor force that will take work at any price. From peasant rents, fines, and the like, lords in the thirteenth century generally were able to get more money than they needed to hire labor to cultivate their demesnes, and indeed labor duties still were demanded as conditions of tenure. An agricultural proletarian class of free and serf was being created by the population expansion. Continued expansion of the economy was possible only in easternmost Germany.

Lords thus could impose the conditions that were most favorable for themselves. Some found the use of tenant laborers unprofitable and granted freedom to their peasants. Serfdom was generally imposed in Germany. In France the redevelopment of statutory serfdom was discouraged by the growth of royal justice and administration, for a free peasant was subject to the royal court, whereas a serf was judged by his lord. This distinction cannot be made absolutely, since lords held courts for free as well as for servile tenants, but only when the king's officers could do nothing about it. On the other hand, except in the royal domain, the kings made no great effort to eliminate serfdom in the large parts of France that still knew it in the early thirteenth century. In England the situation is ambiguous. The kings governed through local squires in part and tried to limit the courts of aristocrats to petty civil cases. They made no concerted effort to draw serfs into the overloaded royal courts in the thirteenth century, although many turned up there anyway in suit against their lords. But the nobles dominated royal administration in thirteenth-century England until 1272 and were very important in it thereafter. The French kings tended to rely on bourgeois, lesser squires, and even some peasants for their central administration. The distinction in attitude is not surprising. It may be only coincidence, but the English peasants were becoming free in the age of the strong kings of the twelfth century, yet tended to revert toward a continental form of serfdom during the baron-dominated thirteenth century.

THE BOURGEOISIE

Merchant and artisan groups were scarcely coherent social entities before the year 1000. As we have seen, migration studies suggest that during the early period most towns recruited most of their population from the immediately surrounding area. This pattern persisted in the central Middle Ages, but less strongly. Increased freedom of movement in the wake of population expansion brought persons from distant places to the towns. Merchants, of course, were wanderers by the very nature of their business. By the end of the thirteenth century more sophisticated business techniques would begin making it possible for some merchants to conduct business without leaving their home cities, but in the central Middle Ages most trade was conducted personally or in caravans. The typical merchant, however, resided permanently in a town to which he returned at the conclusion of the travel months; it is unlikely that the mobility imposed by the merchant's profession led to much permanent migration.

Criteria for social mobility within towns varied, but in general more avenues were open for the aspiring townsman than for the peasant, who might have to come to the town to take advantage of the institutional apparatus of mobility. First, the growth of princely bureaucracies created a need for a large trained personnel. The older habit of relying on the palace ecclesiastics and members of the feudal council no longer sufficed. Social advancement in the central Middle Ages, as before and after, depended in large part upon standing in the community, an intangible that had its base in economic prosperity. One attained economic prosperity by knowing how to run one's estate or counting house successfully. Accordingly, most towns of any appreciable size were centers of education. Churches had schools that taught the rudiments of reading and writing and occasionally arithmetic. In northern Europe, the churches often came into conflict with the townsmen by trying to keep a monopoly on education by papal charter, whereas the businessmen wanted local schools to teach the more mundane subjects. The tradition of municipal schools was quite strong in Italy. Both townsmen and peasants found that knowledge of the practical arts was of immense value in an age during which bourgeois mental attitudes began to take increasing hold of all elements in society—including the nobles, to a degree.

The development of the universities was important for social mobility. Bourgeois, peasants, and the sons of lesser nobles alike found their way into university studies. The study of law was particularly lucrative for aspiring parvenus. The kings needed persons trained in civil and canon law who could find theoretical justifications in ancient legal practice, as applied to present situations, for doing exactly what the kings wanted to do. No detailed university records have survived from this period, but studies of royal and princely lawyers show that many came from the upper bourgeoisie and the lesser nobility. These groups consisted of persons who wanted to rise socially, the one into the lesser nobility and the other into true social equality with the titled nobility. They saw royal service as the best avenue of advancement.

Although the bourgeois classes show tremendous variation in occupation and origin, they were in a sense less mobile than the peasants. The peasant had less to bind him to one place, at least before the land hunger of the twelfth century. But the urban upper classes in particular were tied to a single town. Migration of men of property from one city to another was unusual, although it did occur. Such men were more likely to aspire to estates in the surrounding countryside, while retaining their ties with the town. The development of mobility between town and countryside must be ascribed partly to the rural cast of social values of even the townsmen. The person to whom the poor townsman looked up socially was the rich townsman, but the rich townsman looked up to the wealthy man of the countryside, the landed aristocrat. Also bearing on this hierarchy of values may be the fact that some town patriciates were derived from the local nobility. Accordingly, as soon as a townsman had made money in trade, he tended to invest in land. Small groups of extended families held most of the land upon which the towns were built, then rented to tenants. Jean Boinebroke of Douai was a textile entrepreneur who dabbled in other commodities and in moneylending. He owned numerous houses and lots in Douai and rented most to textile artisans who worked for him. As was becoming increasingly common for town patricians, he also bought land in rural villages near Douai. Even in Italy, where the townsmen reinvested much of their money in their businesses, they put much into land, from which the return was quite slow. By the middle of the thirteenth century many older patrician families were moving to the countryside for at least part of the year, particularly in southern Europe but also in the North. This group of older landholding families took form in most regions during the crisis of the late twelfth century.

It is not surprising that townsmen occasionally rose into the lesser nobility even in the thirteenth century. In unusual circumstances a magistracy might try to hinder this linkage of nobility and town, especially if the local nobles were a political threat to the town. Lübeck, for example, forbade women who married nobles to inherit town property. But the contrary movement was more usual. It was quite common, especially in the late Middle Ages, for great bourgeois to buy rural estates or inherit them from members of collateral lines of their families. Nobles might also come to the towns. Not only yeomen but lesser aristocrats and knights were entering London in increasing numbers in the thirteenth century, forming a partly rural, partly urban aristocracy. The merchant dynasties of the late twelfth and early thirteenth centuries there as elsewhere were replenished more by the movement of substantial men of the countryside into the town than by the rise of poorer guildsmen who accumulated wealth, although this occurred as well.

Particularly in areas such as Flanders and Italy, where urban economic power was great, the position of the nobles weakened early and they were forced to marry bourgeois. As early as the 1230s the comital castellan of Ghent married into a town family, and such unions were common in Flanders by the 1290s, as nobles sought town money and townsmen sought social prestige. In England, class intermarriage owed as much to a less developed class consciousness as to noble penury. On the continent, the children of such unions generally were considered noble by the end of the thirteenth century, for the extremely narrow hereditary rules for noble status were breaking down in the face of economic and biological reality. Knighthood was the most convenient access route to the nobility for most townsmen, and some were dubbed in the thirteenth century. Bourgeois penetration of the nobility takes full force only in the fourteenth century, but it began earlier.

Mobility within the town is harder to pinpoint than is mobility between countryside and town. We know little of urban family structures in this period, let alone of their effect on social mobility. Studies from the more statistically reliable later period show a preponderance of women over men in towns. It is harder to say whether men outnumbered women in the countryside, but it seems likely. Then as now women had a longer life expectancy than men, despite high death rates from childbirth. Inheritance generally was patrilineal, however, and the nuclear conjugal family was the basic unit of accounting for the municipal administrations despite an exaggerated consciousness of the role of the extended family. The family often had the right to prevent alienation of property that would devolve by rigid inheritance laws upon certain family members. The family feud existed as an instrument of self-help, but it was a less important part of the social scene than it would become in the fourteenth and fifteenth centuries, for in the thirteenth century the state seemed capable of preserving order and defending the peace. Thus, although in a certain sense the central Middle Ages witnessed a relaxation of the bonds of the extended family, we must not think that elaborate kinship ties were disregarded or considered unimportant.

Most twelfth-century towns were comparatively open societies. The wealthy were the powerful and as such dominated town government, but there was little to preclude the accumulation of wealth. Death rates in towns were so high that replenishment even of the most wealthy and healthy houses was necessary. Most towns seem to have welcomed newcomers through most of the twelfth century, although this was not invariably true. Domination by "patricians" usually was narrow, but there was some broadening in the thirteenth century to include the richer guildsmen. The patriciate usually was founded on a group of extended families rather than on households; the city magistrates thus were chosen from a group of at least several hundred and in some cases several thousand males. Since, however, it is doubtful that any city in Europe even approached a population of 150,000 (including men, women, and children) at the height of the demographic crisis of the thirteenth century, and most were far below that, the patrician oligarchies were not as narrow as they may seem.

The late twelfth century saw a rapid rise and fall of fortunes within the towns as well as in the countryside. Social and economic dislocation and regroupment resulted. As late as the early twelfth century most town populations were relatively homogeneous economically and hence socially, since most towns still were chiefly centers of agrarian exchange and of a very crude manufacturing. But a sharp division between rich and poor occurs by the end of the century. This is connected with the development of artisan guilds.

We know little of early organizations of workers. England and Germany had them before France and perhaps Italy. They grew out of the charitable confraternities and included various occupational groupings. There were guilds of merchants at St. Omer by 1080, at Mainz by 1099, and at Oxford in 1100. By the early twelfth century there were guilds of cobblers at Rouen, butchers at Paris, and furriers at Saragossa.

There is no difference in kind between artisan and merchant guilds. The merchant corporations dominated town administrations in the thirteenth century simply because the merchants were richer, more powerful, and in many cases the employers of the artisans. Merchant domination grew out of an artisan organizational framework in some instances, particularly in Italy and England, as the wealthiest assumed control of the artisan guilds, for by the second half of the twelfth century the guilds, both merchant and artisan, began to downplay the charitable aspect (although it never was totally lost) and became more concerned with questions of production and quality. We begin to find entry fees, a requirement that excluded the poorest migrants into the city from the guilds. The guilds had their own inspectors and courts. A hierarchy developed: masters, journeymen (salaried laborers working for a daily wage), and apprentices. The master, who in most areas was the only one of the three who had full rights in the guild, dominated. Among the masters, the wealthiest assumed the direction of guild affairs.

Continued population expansion in the thirteenth century sharpened social antagonisms. Western Europe was absolutely overpopulated; it could not adequately nourish its entire population, and the towns were relatively overpopulated vis-à-vis the surrounding countryside. As migration continued, artisan organizations tried to seal themselves off, supposedly to protect the consumer from bad work done by untrained persons, but actually to protect the market for those already established in the town. Fragmentary statistics for salaries, particularly those paid for work on churches, show skilled workers receiving as much as twice the wage of the unskilled in the thirteenth century. This motif becomes painfully clear in the early fourteenth century. Skilled workers always had more freedom of movement than the unskilled and sometimes were called from different regions to work on projects. Horizons narrowed, furthermore, and each man became a specialist in a single aspect of an overall operation. It is true that as long as artisan guilds did not control town governments —and they rarely did in the thirteenth century—the rich entrepreneurs could give work to whomever they wished, a fact that undoubtedly allowed many outsiders to earn their daily bread. Moreover, the guilds in the thirteenth century were not so rigid as they might seem. Trades tended to be passed from father to son, but not always: We find many examples of persons named Baker who were weavers, and statistics from a later period show considerable mobility between guilds. But even in the thirteenth century the individual tended to think of himself in a political context only within the framework of his guild, and this tendency became stronger in the late Middle Ages.

For all its faults, the artisan guild was more open to mobility from below than was the merchant oligarchy. Accordingly, there was less tendency for the rich in England and Italy than in areas dominated by merchant guilds to seal themselves off by strict family ties or to monopolize supplies of raw materials. Accumulation of wealth was the chief criterion of social advancement in these towns, and Italy in particular was very wealthy indeed.

There were many ways of becoming rich in Italy in the central Middle Ages, most of them connected with various foreign luxury trades. In the great cities of northern Europe, wealth almost invariably came from textiles; cloth manufacturing was the only significant industrial operation aside from mining until very late in the Middle Ages. There was a limit to the market for textiles, in terms of population that might buy and in wealth of that population. But tastes were becoming more elevated and luxury items were expensive. The Italians capitalized on the luxury textile market and on importing luxury commodities such as spices from the East. Numerous studies have shown that new men were gradually displacing the rurally oriented magnates in the trade and industry of the Italian towns of the thirteenth century. The towns still provided opportunities for accumulating wealth. Although they tried to hinder migration from the countryside and had large industrial proletariats even in the central Middle Ages, the Italians had perhaps the most mobile social structures of Europe at the time among the towns that had developed extensive specialization within the labor force. Banking for the popes and as part of trading operations also made many new fortunes and created mobility.

Yet it is striking that while urban society in Italy in general remained more open than that in northern Europe, Venice, the richest commercial city of the peninsula, was a classic example of social immobility. Although the town patriciate was only formally closed in 1297, the Venetian merchant oligarchs were able to keep newcomers from displacing old families in wealth and in government. Defying all laws of genetic probability, the Venetian merchant oligarchy remained vigorous throughout the Middle Ages. The only significant industry at Venice was shipbuilding, a fact that undoubtedly meant a lower percentage of artisans there than at Florence or even Milan, which had more social unrest. This peculiar situation of a small, tightly knit, extremely wealthy urban society with little fear of trouble from the cashless multitudes continues to arouse an odd combination of admiration and bewilderment.

The Late Middle Ages

The crisis into which European society was plunged in the last quarter of the twelfth century intensified into an absolute disaster in the period after 1250. Many trends that we can only suspect from earlier evidence now become documented fact. The disorders of endemic warfare produced a tremendous movement of population, and the population losses from plagues and famines meant that social and economic relationships had to be readjusted. Despite the tendency of all groups to close themselves off and become juridical classes, practice was very different from theory. Hence our discussion of social mobility in the late Middle Ages involves a continuation of the essential features of the period from 1180 to 1250.

THE NOBILITY

Marc Bloch saw the period from 1250 to 1400 as the age of greatest social stratification in the Middle Ages, but he was misled by the letter of the law and by evidence of social attitudes. Statute forbade non-nobles in France to hold fiefs; in practice anyone could buy an exemption. The rule against marriage with a social inferior had practical effect only in Cyprus and in the upper reaches of the very stratified German nobility.

The nobles continued to feel threatened as a class, and with justification. There were repeated reactions against nouveaux, but these were not new. A conspicuous example comes with the death of King Philip IV of France in late 1314. Philip had used some bourgeois lawyers in his attempts to centralize authority and streamline the administration. Other lawyers were noble, and two, including the famous Guillaume de Nogaret, were bourgeois who had acquired patents of nobility. After Philip died, most of his low-born advisers were dismissed at the demand of the great nobles. Feelings of class had been aroused, and the bourgeois stood out beyond the proportion of their actual numbers.

Consciousness of social class as an essence transmitted primarily by blood was strongest among the lesser nobility, men who were too poor to become knights but who nonetheless had a little rural property. Such theoretical justifications seem to arise particularly among economically weak or declining groups. The greater nobles had become fanatically conscious of genealogy when they felt threatened in the twelfth century. Their class consciousness probably was diminishing except in outward form in the late Middle Ages. The political disasters of the fourteenth century made great princes out of many nobles, and they felt less need to justify their privileged existence. The lesser lords were trying to create an illusion of social superiority, which did not correspond to economic reality. Whatever we may say about barriers between classes, all evidence suggests that ties of family solidarity became stronger with all classes in the late Middle Ages, and this in turn furthered their social aims.

The fundamental fact, however, is that legal distinctions between classes by this time were simply tools to obtain what princes wanted. They could be used as needed, and exceptions could always be sold to enrich the princely coffers. Even servile status was no bar to advancement, although few serfs rose rapidly. Raoul des Presles, however, became the principal advocate of Philip IV at the Parlement of Paris at the age of thirty before the king bothered to emancipate him from serfdom!

In the twelfth and thirteenth centuries, the essential criterion of noble status had been the blood tie, but this had been a biological impossibility when strictly applied. Possession of the ban power had always been an essential aspect of noble status, although it is underemphasized in the sources. This power was essential for a noble as consciousness of blood ties increased and their real efficacy diminished in the fourteenth and fifteenth centuries. The children of a noble who married a commoner could inherit his seigniories. They accordingly could be noble. The same is true of persons who simply purchased seigniories. When all is said and done, in the late Middle Ages a noble simply was one who was recognized as such by others considered noble by the general community.

Knighthood continued to be a mark of nobility. But just as there had been two levels of both nobility and knighthood earlier, so now a third developed. This is the age of the "free companies" of mercenary soldiers. Latin sources of the period often call such persons *milites*, but they had no connection with the nobility. Knighthood was a separate social distinction that implied either nobility or status as an aristocrat, depending upon the region. Originally any knight could dub another. By the thirteenth century, however, kings claimed the power to dub as a regalian right, although they delegated this authority to their great feudatories. This deprived those who wanted to keep knighthood a distinction for a few—those who were already knights—of the right to recruit their own class, for the kings bestowed knighthood on those who served them well. Aspiring parvenus of diverse origins became knights, particularly bourgeois who served the king. Still, knighthood did not invariably mean noble status. From the time of Philip IV the kings openly sold patents of nobility to those with enough money. The *noblesse de la robe* originated before the close of the Middle Ages as a result of these practices. England continued as before to be more open than France. The De la Pole family, who began as merchants of Hull, became royal financiers and finally dukes of Suffolk, all within a few generations. Italian financiers who helped princes overcome financial troubles might enter the northern European nobility. Simon of Mirabello became bourgeois of Ghent, knight, lord of Perwez, brother-in-law of the count of Flanders, and finally regent of Flanders during the period of Jacques van Artevelde in the 1340s.

Noble status thus was much less rigid in the late Middle Ages than earlier, despite the theoretical closing of the class. There were avenues into the nobility for those who had enough money to purchase the rank. Desire to imitate the noble was an important motive of the bourgeois who bought rural land, especially after the depopulations of the fourteenth century forced land prices and rentals down. Possession of land brought social respectability. The nobles of town and of countryside owned land. The social aspirations implicit in the purchase of large estates outside the town usually were formalized by marriage into the nobility. The daughter of Jacob Willebaerd, a patrician of Ghent who owned land south of the town, married the lord of Oplinter. Jacques van Artevelde, so often portrayed as a popular reformer at Ghent, actually was a rich broker with estates outside the city. His position of political power brought him into contact with kings and princes, and his descendants married into several Flemish noble families.

Just as the townsmen were moving toward the nobility, so the nobles were moving toward the towns. Princes maintained residences in their major cities as always, but now it became customary for powerful local nobles to have town houses. Some held bourgeois status even while living outside the town on their seigniories for most of the year. The movement of noble to town in northern Europe is new with the late Middle Ages except for the ministeriales and the early core of nobles who had always been town dwellers. Most nobles who entered the cities became involved also in trade and finance in the late Middle Ages.

The noble always kept his essentially rural orientation, but he became increasingly involved in high politics, even to the point of becoming a courtier in the fifteenth century. He came into contact with other social groups, particularly the townsmen. As this occurred, it became easier for others to imitate every aspect of the noble life style. The formation of a closed juridical class hinders mobility in one sense but in another actually furthers it, for criteria are defined and cannot be denied. If knights are noble, the butcher whom Philip IV dubbed a knight in 1302 is the social peer of the count of Anjou. Hence there was increased movement into the nobility, particularly from the bourgeois knighthood, even as the titled nobles became more conscious of their own social pre-eminence.

THE PEASANTRY

With the peasantry the picture is much more kaleidoscopic. A large agricultural proletariat was working lords' lands for salary by the end of the thirteenth century. This class became larger in the late Middle Ages in the wake of land hunger, increasingly high rentals, and overpopulation before the plagues and famines. The problem was worse in England than on the continent, for by English law and custom only one son usually inherited his father's land; all tended to share in France. The plagues and famines reduced the population but did not lead to an immediate improvement in the condition of the survivors. A tendency to overproduce, then hoard for the next rainy day, drove grain prices down. By this time peasant tenants were producing largely for the market rather than for domestic consumption, and those who did not have enough capital to cover losses in the grain price became impoverished. Many fled to the towns, where they were cut down by the next plague in much greater relative numbers than in the countryside. In contrast to tenant farmers, the landless laborers who were left after the plagues did have a brief period in which wages rose astronomically despite attempted governmental control, for lords wanted their vacant lands cultivated at all costs. But this was only temporary, and many lords tried to reimpose demesne labor services as a condition of tenure to avoid paying the higher wages. One might expect that since so much good land fell vacant for lack of tenants there would be much consolidation of holdings by those who survived. There is some evidence that this occurred, but most documentation suggests that the ordinary peasant holding did not enlarge appreciably in the wake of the plagues. There simply was a limit to what one person or family could cultivate, and this limit precluded tremendous expansion.

At the same time, some agricultural consolidation did take place, with important consequences for peasant mobility. Those who were rich enough to employ laborers to cultivate were able to buy land rather cheaply and farm it. The land market became very fluid during these years. As we have seen, the economic expansion of the twelfth century brought an increase in tenancies held at hereditary rental. Higher death rates in the thirteenth century, which left some tenancies without heirs, enabled lords to change these to leaseholds at term. With the tremendous rural population decline of the fourteenth century, leaseholds became the rule and created opportunity for social advancement for those who could combine several leaseholds into a single property. The classic case of this is the English yeomanry. The Pastons, a family of social pretension whose men still did field labor in the fifteenth century, were wealthy peasants who accumulated enough leaseholds to force social acceptance as gentry, since in fact if not in law such leaseholds often amounted to ownership.

Other developments in the rural economy stimulated peasant mobility. Technological improvements in European agriculture in the fourteenth century meant that the West could be fed by fewer peasants, relatively as well as absolutely. Workers were thus freed for the diversification of grain crops, for pasturage of various sorts, and particularly for industrial operations. The extension of vineyards, as more luxurious tastes developed, created a sort of half-urban, half-rural salaried proletariat near some towns. The tendency to produce for a large town market, the lower grain prices, and the extension of grazing drove out many small farmers or forced them to take up a second occupation. The most important of these was weaving. Some rural weaving establishments were controlled by bourgeois, since labor was cheaper in the countryside than in the town and often nearer the source of supply. The village woolen establishments did not tend to produce for a luxury market, but they could export a good, ordinary cloth over a fairly wide area. The old village ties and the ethic of production for consumption had given way to production by all for the market even as early as the thirteenth century, but the trend was particularly marked in the late Middle Ages. As one would expect in such a time of economic change, many prospered while others were forced off the land.

Horizontal mobility among the peasants reached its medieval high point in the fourteenth and fifteenth centuries. We know less of vertical mobility. Such as occurred tended to be downward, save in the exceptional circumstances that we have noted. England is an exception, for mobility there tended to be upward. On the continent, many peasants still were serfs, but this dubious distinction had practical effects ranging from zero to virtual enslavement, depending upon circumstances and lords. Even in England, which had the largest servile peasantry of Europe after eastern Germany, peasants tended to come and go at will. Countless instances are recorded of peasants who left the parishes of their birth; if their lords pursued, they could defend themselves in a royal court on grounds that they were free. There were no records except the testimony of "good local men," who of course would not know whether the man was serf or free since records of his birth were elsewhere. In such cases the courts generally assumed that the person was free. The lords often did not bother to pursue. Villeins had to obtain their lord's permission to remain away from the manor in the thirteenth and early fourteenth centuries, but in this age of high population such leaves normally were granted in return for a nominal fee. After the Black Death lords tried to stop the drift away from the manor. They pursued fugitives more often and increased fines for permission to stay away. But where statistics survive, as for the estates of Ramsey abbey, there was no decline in the number of persons leaving the manor after 1350. The practice was simply too common by that time to be stopped. In 1395, for instance, the abbot of Ramsey allowed John Raven, a villein on the manor of Warboys, to stay on the abbot's land in St. Ives as a tanner in return for an annual head tax. Roving gangs of laborers worked first on one estate and then on another even in the thirteenth century. This condition was heightened by the plagues, as such workers searched for higher wages or vacant tenements that they might take over. Documents from Ramsey also show the state of migrant labor in late medieval England. John Smyth of Holywell, a serf of Ramsey, is shown by court rolls to be working at Colne in 1403 and 1405, at Sohamin in 1409 and 1413, at Ely in 1420 and 1423, at Ramsey in 1427, 1428, and 1432, and at Ely again in 1437. If there was no scarcity of needed labor as a result of the plagues and relative overproduction, there was a scarcity of desired labor, as lords wished to continue to increase production. A sign of this is the fact, confirmed by several recent studies, that the wage differential between skilled and unskilled labor decreased after the plagues in both town and countryside. Real wages unquestionably rose as grain prices declined, and there was some redistribution of wealth in favor of the lower orders of society.

Peasants also moved to the towns to an extent that the towns found disastrous. Such movement often was with the full knowledge of their lords, who would receive a small tax as recognition of servile status and occasionally the right of best chattel when the migrant died. Some lords tried to hinder this migration, but especially when a tenant had moved to a large and powerful town there was little that they could do. Simon Paris, a former sheriff of London who served as an alderman in 1308 after only ten years' residence in the city, was claimed by his former lord as a serf in that year. Although his brothers were still villeins on the manor of Necton, the lord's claim was denied, since bourgeois status at London had freed Simon from serfdom. Most peasants who went to the cities kept their ties with their old villages and especially with their fathers' holdings. This is reflected in nomenclature. The purse-maker Boudin van Straten of Bruges held land near Bruges at Straten. He almost certainly was a recent migrant. The ultimate origins of several wealthy families can be proven in this way. The Van Huysse and Van Leden of Ghent continued to hold land at Huise and Lede, both villages south of Ghent, throughout the Middle Ages, but they were never lords of the villages and probably came from the peasantry.

Servile status thus did not bar freedom of movement. But to what extent was the peasant population still servile in the late Middle Ages? Direct manumission of individuals or villages was unusual in this period. Except perhaps in England, the percentage of peasants who were serfs increased, as farmers ruined by the depression sought the security of an inalienable tenure, even if burdened by servile status and duties, in preference to the uncertainties and duties of freedom. In 1350 the English villager William atte Merrow was brought to court for refusing to serve in the local militia. He claimed that he and his ancestors were villeins and hence not bound to serve. The court was suspicious of this argument but allowed it on William's oath. It then expressly delivered him to his lord's bailiff, implying that he had not been acting as a villein or performing servile duties before he was called to military duty. The percentage of the peasant population that was servile varied among the English counties from 28 per cent to 48 per cent. Serfdom had never ceased to exist in parts of southern France. In other areas it began again in the late Middle Ages, particularly in the Laonnais, Champagne, and Burgundy.

Most peasants in central and eastern Germany also were serfs. Lords mass produced grain for export to western Europe and needed labor services from their tenants. This was one of the few areas of Europe that did not have a surplus of labor. By 1410 the peasants could leave their rented tenements only if they found others to replace them, and in 1526 peasants in East Prussia were forbidden to leave the land under any circumstances without the lord's consent. Although in some areas it had been possible immediately after the plagues for peasants owing servile duties to take over land without losing their freedom, this provision was unusual, and the German peasantry drifted into a miserable serfdom as the modern period approached.

In general, however, the most important social distinctions between peasants in the late Middle Ages were based on their economic situation rather than on juridical status. Extremes of poverty and prosperity are found within the free groups, and extremes of bondage and freedom of movement among the servile. The reimposition of servile obligations certainly hindered peasant mobility, but the process that began in the late twelfth century was irreversible, though it was to culminate only in the modern period.

MOBILITY IN THE TOWNS

The towns by their economic power exerted a tremendous influence on mobility among both nobles and peasants. The plagues of course had a profound effect on mobility among urban populations. There were higher death rates in the cities and towns than in the countryside, but immigration from the rural areas also increased tremendously in the late Middle Ages. Most great cities declined in absolute numbers while increasing in terms of the percentage of the total population. Some secondary centers actually grew during this period, probably as a result of the disappearance of smaller units nearby. Yet town markets contracted as relative population grew. More goods were being manufactured in the countryside for consumption there, and the rural depression would have subtracted customers from town merchants in any event. It is true that luxury markets were increasing as the overall standard of living became higher, but this development benefited chiefly the Italians. A reorientation of markets, often along national lines, brought difficulty for many larger centers. Governments tried to make their countries economically self-sufficient. The combination in the late Middle Ages of heavy migration, declining markets, national sentiments, and high death rates could only mean severe social difficulties for most towns, particularly the larger centers geared to export.

Studies of migration patterns show that in Italy the *contado* of the town always furnished most of its immigrants despite town restrictions on newcomers, perhaps because there were so many large towns in a comparatively small area. The North shows more variation. In the fourteenth century, from which the first reliable migration figures survive, the overwhelming majority of immigrants came from places less than a day's journey from the town. This was true of all urban centers, large and small. But as the towns shifted their economic emphasis in the late Middle Ages from local agrarian exchange to international or interregional trade, we find that the share of areas near the town in the total percentage of immigrants declined, while that of more distant places within the same general region increased drastically. Since population was becoming more concentrated in the late Middle Ages than before, and perhaps also because the northern towns began to follow the Italian example and exploit their hinterlands, we find a smaller percentage of migrants to towns coming from agrarian villages in the late Middle Ages, with a corresponding increase in migration from one town to another.

The towns thus became perhaps more open than in the early Middle Ages despite their persistent efforts to shut themselves off. There were distinct social effects. In the late Middle Ages most town administrations were controlled by wealthy artisans who rarely were still active in producing commodities. Rather, they were rich wholesalers and retailers who often controlled the productive facilities manned by others. In this sense they are quite similar to the merchant patricians of the thirteenth century, but they were of more recent origin and generally somewhat less wealthy. Indeed, even after guild regimes had come to power most of the richest townsmen continued to be merchants, particularly in the wine, textile, spice, and other luxury trades. In some towns these men enrolled in the guilds to obtain political influence. But in northern Europe, if not in Italy, many did not do this for the simple reason that they had no desire to participate in civic life. The same names reappear periodically in most town magistracies, whether the town had a guild or other form of government. Hence the result was the same, and only a tiny part of even the upper classes actually participated in town affairs in northern Europe.

Some towns, particularly those of Germany with little industry and thus a less explosive lower class, continued to have a separate merchant guild in the fourteenth century, although this guild normally did not form a patriciate that totally monopolized town offices. More often the merchant guildsmen shared government with the great men of the artisan guilds. Even where patriciates continued to exist, however, they were declining. Families often failed to reproduce themselves. High death rates in the late Middle Ages struck the comparatively narrow patriciates and forced replenishment, ordinarily not from recent migrants but from persons who had been in the city for a generation or two. One-fifth of the patriciate of Lübeck died out each generation and had to be replaced, and examples from other towns tend to confirm this picture. Migration to the countryside also diminished the numbers of the urban patricians. Many newly rich sought membership in a merchant guild or patriciate for the social prestige, even when it disfranchised them under a guild regime of artisans. A cycle of considerable importance for an understanding of continuing social mobility from below can be detected. Town governments were made up of persons who had become wealthy from merchandising. As they became rich, however, they invested in land inside and outside the town. As they became landlords, they tended also to leave active concern with town administration to others who were still active in trade. Even at their most narrow the merchant oligarchies were transitory and were replenished with new persons.

Town magistracies tended to close off during the late Middle Ages under both aristocratic and guild regimes. Although the ruling class rarely had a juridical base and often was made up of persons in power who simply perpetuated their domination, certain classes often got a set percentage of seats in the magistracy in the fourteenth century. This was particularly true of the group holding land upon which the town was located. At Toulouse the knights held 25 per cent of the seats, patrician *lignages* 22 per cent, the merchants 26 per cent, and the rest of the citizens 27 per cent. The Venetian "Golden Book" of 1297 made a division of "old houses," whose members had been in the town allegedly since the tenth century, and "new houses," persons with wealth of two centuries' standing. This aristocracy of from two thousand to three thousand members became a hereditary governing class from 1323. The landholders, weavers, and members of the "small guilds," which produced for an essentially local trade, controlled the magistracy of Ghent after 1360. The governing class thus took in some 10 to 15 per cent of the population except in the most tightly controlled oligarchies, and mobility between groups was sufficient to preclude an overly tight control. Nonetheless, town government was dominated by the rich, a fact that stimulated new (and generally unsuccessful) artisan uprisings in the late fourteenth century. Government at Florence, for example, was comparatively open. In the second half of the fourteenth century there were from five thousand to six thousand men in the twenty-one guilds that controlled the magistracy there. Using a household coefficient of 4.5, probably from twenty thousand to twenty-four thousand persons thus were represented. Since the population of the city after the Black Death was only around sixty thousand, including men and their dependents, the government was not particularly restrictive for the day, although it is true that only about a third of the five or six thousand ever held office. Nonetheless, a socially oriented revolt broke out among the unemployed Florentine artisans in 1378.

Guilds in their turn often became extremely restrictive as migrants poured into the cities, especially as town governments fell under guild domination. Even when participation in public life depended upon guild membership, fourteenth-century figures show that few towns registered more than two-thirds of their population in guilds, a figure perhaps unnaturally small in view of the large number of untrained artisans in the cities. Restrictions were made on entry into guilds, particularly by making mastership hereditary. Although the restrictions were not so absolute as the statutes indicate, there was constraint on mobility, ostensibly in the interest of preserving good quality but actually to keep a shrinking market for older families and not allow more competition. Such a system can never be absolute, for families die out. Rather, monopolies of great families developed within guilds. Talented newcomers could work, but only exceptionally could they become masters. The situation is demonstrated nicely by the butchers of Ghent. Mastership in this guild became hereditary in the early fourteenth century. There were 136 families of butchers in the guild in 1302, but the number declined to fourteen by 1463. By 1791 two families of master butchers held 70 per cent of the stalls in the great Vleeshuis. Thus the butchers evolved from a group of persons who cut meat into a class of rentiers who controlled the practice and monopolized a large part of the town's food supply. Further evidence that theory and practice did not correspond comes from salary figures. As in the countryside, salaries for unskilled laborers rose in relation to those of skilled in the late medieval towns. Labor thus was needed and used in the towns even as mastership was restricted. We are simply witnessing a period of concentration of commercial enterprises into fewer hands.

Historians have too often tended to view the urban upper class as one unit and the laborers as simply a second, all-encompassing social class. There is some reason for this in that the aristocratic lineages were more conscious of their political and social prerogatives than were those who had none. Intermarriage and movement into a better economic situation was easier for the less well off. But there are important distinctions in wealth among the artisans as well as the obvious distinctions between different guilds. Independent masters in most towns had a solid, though hardly fantastic, prosperity. At Schwäbisch-Hall in 1460 they comprised 35 per cent of the inhabitants and paid 34 per cent of a tax calibrated on the basis of ability to pay. This pattern seems to hold elsewhere. Under the masters were the poor, sometimes enrolled in a guild and sometimes not, generally including from 50 to 60 per cent of the population of the city but paying 10 per cent or less of the taxes. Comparative tax records surviving from the St. Jacob's section of Bruges for 1382–1383 and 1394–1396 show that only 17.4 per cent of the 1,395 persons who paid taxes in 1394–1396 also paid in 1382–1383, a figure indicating substantial mobility of fortune and high migration and death rates. Of those who paid in both years, roughly half paid more in the later record than in the earlier, 30 per cent remained stable, and 20 per cent declined. Some conspicuous examples are of interest. The wine merchant Jan Buerse paid 4.31 per cent of the taxes from this section in 1382, and in 1396 his share had risen to 10.06 per cent. The share of the broker Pieter van den Bussche rose from 4.31 to 6.89 per cent. Several men, particularly cloth merchants, rose from less than 1 per cent to 3.5 or 4 per cent. Declining figures tend to come from persons who operated for a local market, such as the wood dealer Willem Jans and the cheese merchant Jan Maertin, both of whom dropped from 3.7 per cent to less than 1 per cent.

The poorer artisans were quite hostile to the mass of the unemployed and propertyless, whose very presence tended to drive wages down and who may have constituted as much as 25 per cent of the population of some larger industrial centers. The poorer artisans helped to suppress the Ciompi revolt of the Florentine unemployed in 1378–1382. Double occupations also were quite common among this group and those slightly richer, and especially among persons whose wealth was increasing and who aspired to move into the urban upper classes. Common second occupations included moneylending on a small scale, innkeeping, and the wine trade, together with investment in urban and rural real estate. For example, the Londoner Philip le Tailor was a merchant of both grain and cloth but made most of his fortune in the wine trade in the late thirteenth century. His widow was the third highest taxpayer in London in 1292. William May, a leader in the revolt against the London patricians in 1263, was a prosperous skinner who also dabbled in the wool trade.

Mobility was comparatively strong within the guilds. In addition, as markets and needs underwent reorientation, new guilds displaced the old at the center of power. The victualing guilds often received monopolies during this period of uncertain food supply, but furriers and goldsmiths also prospered in an age of conspicuous consumption. The famous Jacques Coeur was the son of a furrier of Bourges who became a royal moneyer in 1374. Coeur took over his father's enterprises, made a fortune selling goods to the court of King Charles VII of France, and entered the nobility.

Migrants into the towns were not always of the poorer classes. R. Fedou has shown that many new citizens who had been rural notaries migrated to Lyon after the plagues and became jurists there. Persons with commercial contacts or family ties continued to move from one city to another. Hinrich Castorp, born in Dortmund around 1420, settled at Lübeck as an adult; he became burgomaster and one of the richest men of the city. The suspicion with which newcomers were regarded did not hinder some of them from becoming prosperous. "New citizen" was a separate status in some Italian towns and mobility out of it was not easy, especially as family ties were emphasized increasingly. But this point must not be overdrawn. The "new men" in Florence comprised two-fifths of the households in the upper 2 per cent of the tax assessment in 1352. All the great and aristocratic guilds show a strong influx of new men in the second half of the fourteenth century, despite the attempt of the older Florentine patrician families to impose civil disabilities on newcomers after 1343. The German cities also show opportunity for able migrants. Johannes Fugger emigrated from Graben in Swabia to Augsburg in 1367 and became a linen weaver. Augsburg did not have a strict guild or industrial regime and offered more opportunities for such a man than did many towns. His son became a linen merchant and had founded the family fortune by the time he died in 1409. In the next generation the Fugger bank was established. It was the richest house of Europe in the sixteenth century.

Periods of economic dislocation generally involve the rapid rise and fall of fortunes, and residents of long standing were no more immune to this than were newcomers. As we have seen, the survival of some tax records from the late Middle Ages gives a gauge of this form of mobility. The impositions show that wealth tended to be more evenly dispersed in small market towns than in large centers with substantial industry, but this was not invariably true. Towns strongly oriented toward long-distance commerce might have a tiny group of very rich taxpayers, while most of the inhabitants fell below the level of taxable incomes. Augsburg is the leading case of such development. Other cities, however, tended to have a more nearly even spread, such as Lübeck and the Hanse towns, and it is noteworthy that these places had less social conflict in the late Middle Ages than did the towns with more severe differentiations of wealth.

The town offered a wide range of potential employments, and generalizations about mobility within certain occupations or towns are suspect. A source of some urban social mobility in the central Middle Ages, but even more in the fourteenth and fifteenth centuries, was the plastic and decorative arts, which were becoming increasingly sophisticated. We have mentioned the role of education in social rise, particularly of the townsmen. The *noblesse de la robe,* actually an aristocracy with blood overtones but based on royal officeholding, was taking firm hold in France by the end of the Middle Ages. The increased opulence of princely courts and their frequent residence in large towns created work for townsmen and increased wealth. The court becomes the focus of parvenu social aspiration in the late Middle Ages, preparing the way in a sense for "modern" society. The late Middle Ages presented most of the opportunities for bourgeois if not peasant mobility that we associate with the more recent period. It also presented extremes of wealth, opulence, and grinding poverty, the less fortunate side of mobility, and an extent of economic and social differentiation not known in the more unitary and generally less mobile early and central Middle Ages.

The extreme dislocation of the late Middle Ages, and particularly the decreased power of the state in the wake of war, plague, and famine to provide security, brought about a resurgence of the power of the extended family and the blood feud. Although the hearth continued to be a tax unit and the household became smaller in the late Middle Ages, the moral and spiritual bonds of the family became stronger. Genealogies to glorify illustrious lineages were compiled by the bourgeois as part of their imitation of noble life style. The business, whether the simple shop or an extended mercantile-banking concern, was much more family-oriented in the town than in the countryside, where there was less necessary physical proximity. Sons tended to follow fathers in guilds, although not to the extent once believed. Kinship lines in some places were so extended that persons of the same name often were confused and innocent parties of no blood tie were assassinated during a feud. Magistrates deplored the violence and bloodshed of family feuds but were powerless to stop them. The kindred could supplement its ranks with armed retainers, just as ambitious princes were doing on a national scale. With high death rates, especially among the elderly, society was becoming younger in the late Middle Ages and, perhaps in part as a result of this, somewhat more reckless.

Barbarism and Mobility: A Brief Retrospect

With a young society dominated by males and imbued with exaggerated ideas of kindred, but with an equally overblown concept of the individual's right and duty personally to avenge wrongs, we seem to have come full circle. The characterization applies equally well to the society of the late Middle Ages, given its tone increasingly by the towns, and to the rural society of the Merovingian period. Society was mobile in both periods. How much had it changed in the intervening centuries?

We have noted the recurrence of similar patterns of mobility. Even as towns became powerful, their mores were taken from the rural world. Medieval society was conscious of the blood tie, but only in the twelfth century did that consciousness become so strong that an attempt was made to stop vertical mobility as a result of it. In the Merovingian age the major avenue of upward mobility was physical power; in the fourteenth century it was economic power. Indeed, since the one tended to involve the other, in both periods, in the power of command over other persons, whether peasant dependents or (on an unofficial level) employees, the distinction is perhaps fictive.

We must not overemphasize similarities between the ages of breakdown. During this thousand-year period the economy of western Europe underwent tremendous alterations that could not have been accomplished without social mobility. Classes arose, were penetrated by nouveaux, tried to close themselves off, and were forced by biological necessity to reopen. Class distinctions were real, but they could not be totally rigid. Then as now most people died in the status into which they were born, or perhaps even in a lower order of society. But a society consists of human groups interacting. This interaction produces mobility, a mobility that, however exceptional, provides the tone and the essential framework for less extraordinary social intercourse. Medieval society was mobile. The extent to which that mobility involved a progression is a question that we leave unanswered.

A Critical Bibliography

We are faced with two insuperable difficulties in attempting to write a bibliographical essay about medieval social history. Although there are numerous superannuated accounts of happy peasants dancing around maypoles, drawn largely from literary sources, the comparatively scientific study of social history for the medieval period is in its infancy. Most of the literature that does exist, and upon which this essay has been based, is in languages other than English and accordingly of difficult access for the general reader.

A convenient summary, although less helpful for the specific question of mobility than it might be, is Robert Fossier, *Histoire sociale de l'occident médiéval* (Paris, 1970). The companion volume in the same series also contains much information of value to the social historian: Guy Fourquin, *Histoire économique de l'occident médiéval* (Paris, 1969). Although now outdated in many of its interpretations, the standard brief treatment in English is Henri Pirenne, *Economic and Social History of Medieval Europe* (New York, 1937). A magisterially horrendous grab bag of misinformation, which generally should be avoided, is James Westfall Thompson, *Economic and Social History of Medieval Europe,* 2d ed., 2 vols. (New York, 1959). A convenient background to the early Middle Ages is the classic treatment of Mikhail Rostovtzeff, *Social and Economic History of the Roman Empire* (Oxford, 1926). A good brief summary of the literature of Rome's fall and its social causation is given in M. Chambers, ed., *The Fall of Rome* (New York, 1963).

Other general histories of value include the somewhat dated but still valuable work of P. Boissonnade, *Life and Work in Medieval Europe* (London, 1927). The *Cambridge Economic History of Europe,* vols. 1–3 (Cambridge, 1941–1966; vol. 1 revised, 1966), contains a mine of information for the social historian and excellent bibliographies. Georges Duby and R. Mandrou, *History of French Civilization* (New York, 1966), is the standard comprehensive treatment for France. Its much briefer counterpart for Italy is Gino Luzzatto, *An Economic History of Italy from the Fall of the Roman Empire to the Beginning of the Sixteenth Century* (London, 1961). An excellent account of early English society is given in Henry R. Loyn, *Anglo-Saxon England and the Norman Conquest* (New York, 1962); additional volumes are forthcoming in the same series, Social and Economic History of England, edited by Asa Briggs.

An excellent work on early medieval economy and society is Robert Latouche, *The Birth of Western Economy,* trans. E. M. Wilkinson (New York, 1961). The Nouvelle Clio series, which synthesizes recent research in broad areas of history, notes general directions that scholarship is taking, and provides excellent bibliographies, has published five works absolutely necessary for the study of medieval social history: R. Doehaerd, *Le haut moyen âge occidental. Economies et sociétés* (Paris, 1971); L. Musset, *Les invasions: les vagues germaniques* (Paris, 1965); Musset, *Les invasions: le second assaut contre l'Europe chrétienne (VIIe–XIe siècles)* (Paris, 1965); Léopold Genicot, *Le XIIIe siècle européen* (Paris, 1968); and J. Heers, *L'occident aux XIVe et XVe siècles: aspects économiques et sociaux* (Paris, 1963).

A convenient sketch of "daily life" in the early Middle Ages is given in Peter Munz, *Life in the Age of Charlemagne* (New York, 1969). Although its focus is chiefly political, most of what the student confined to English will find out about German society is in Geoffrey Barraclough, *The Origins of Modern Germany,* 2d ed. rev. (New York, 1963). A good collection of sources on the general subject is David Herlihy, ed., *Medieval Culture and Society* (New York, 1968). Richard W. Southern, *The Making of the Middle Ages* (London, 1953), is generally quite weak on social history but has interesting personal portrayals; of more use is Southern's *Western Society and the Church in the Middle Ages* (Harmondsworth, 1970). A classic of personal portrayal is Eileen Power, *Medieval People* (London, 1924); less good, but also useful, is Henry S. Bennett, *Six Medieval Men and Women* (New York, 1962).

An imaginatively written general history of considerable use to the social historian is Friedrich Heer, *The Medieval World: Europe 1100–1350* (New York, 1962). Three recent anthologies have translated important articles of leading European scholars and are of primary importance for the topics presented here: Sylvia L. Thrupp, ed., *Early Medieval Society* (New York, 1967), particularly the selections by Bertha Phillpotts, Lorraine Lancaster, Karl Bosl, Pierre Bonnassie, Jacques Boussard, Fernand Vercauteren, Marc Bloch, and Gino Luzzatto; Thrupp, ed., *Change in Medieval Society: Europe North of the Alps, 1050–1500* (New York, 1964), especially the articles of Marc Bloch, Léopold Genicot, Joseph R. Strayer, Edward Miller, and Edouard Perroy; and F. L. Cheyette, ed., *Lordship and Community in Medieval Europe* (New York, 1968), the articles by Walter Schlesinger, Jean François Lemarignier, Léopold Genicot, Georges Duby, Edouard Perroy, William Huse Dunham, and Karl Bosl. Jan Dhondt, "Medieval 'Solidarities': Flemish Society in Transition, 1127–1128," in *Lordship and Community in Medieval Europe,* contains interesting ideas of chronological progression. Several classic older accounts can also be used with profit, particularly Sidney Painter, *Mediaeval Society* (Ithaca, 1951); Austin L. Poole, *The Obligations of Society in the Twelfth and Thirteenth Centuries* (Oxford, 1946); G. G. Coulton, *Medieval Panorama: The English Scene from Conquest to Reformation* (Cambridge, 1938); and particularly the classic study of Achille Luchaire, *Social France at the Time of Philip Augustus* (New York, 1912). A recent collection of readings of value for the late Middle Ages is Anthony Molho, ed., *Social and Economic Foundations of the Italian Renaissance* (New York, 1969).

The standard work on the medieval peasantry and its relations with the landlord classes is and is likely to remain Georges Duby, *Rural Economy and Country Life in the Medieval West* (Columbia, 1968). Also good is B. H. Slicher van Bath, *The Agrarian History of Western Europe, 500–1850* (London, 1963). A classic older study, of less relevance for social than for economic conditions, is Marc Bloch, *French Rural History: An Essay on Its Basic Characteristics* (Berkeley, 1966). The reader should also see Marc Bloch, *Mélanges historiques,* 2 vols. (Paris, 1963). Several collections of Bloch's works have appeared in translation, notably *Life and Work in Medieval Europe* (Berkeley, 1967). Another good general study of the agrarian social scene is R. Boutruche, *Seigneurie et féodalité* (Paris, 1959), although it is concerned primarily with the aristocracy. More broad in scope is Guy Fourquin, *Seigneurie et féodalité au Moyen Age* (Paris, 1970). Specialized studies exist for Italy and Germany; see R. Caggese, *Classi e comuni rurale del Medioevo italiano,* 2 vols. (Florence, 1907–1909); and Gunther Franz, *Geschichte des Bauernstandes* (Stuttgart, 1963). The standard work on medieval slavery is C. Verlinden, *L'esclavage en Europe médiévale,* a one-volume series: *Peninsule iberique, France* (Bruges, 1955). The origins of the seigniory and its social relations have been treated often, most comprehensively of late by Robert Latouche, but a good recent study from the geographical-historical viewpoint is Adriaan Verhulst, "La genèse du regime domanial classique en France au haut Moyen Age," in *Agricoltura e mondo rurale in occidente nell' alto medioevo,* Settimani du studio del Centro ... Spoleto, 3 (1966) : 135–160. The social mixture of Roman and German has received an interesting treatment in André Joris, "On the Edge of Two Worlds: The Romance Regions of Northern Gaul in the Merovingian Empire," *Studies in Medieval and Renaissance History* 3 (1965) : 1–52. An extremely suggestive recent study of social relationships within the Carolingian manor is Emily R. Coleman, "Medieval Marriage Characteristics: A Neglected Factor in the History of Serfdom," *Journal of Interdisciplinary History* 2 (1971) : 205–219.

The peasantry in the period after Charlemagne has generally been seen as becoming increasingly servile through the tenth century, then freer. For classic statements of this view see the older general studies already mentioned and Lynn T. White, Jr., *Medieval Technology and Social Change* (Oxford, 1962), ch. 2. Other studies, particularly monographs dealing in depth with individual regions, are calling this picture into serious question. See in particular C. E. Perrin and G. Vernadsky, "Le servage en France, en Allemagne et en Russie au Moyen-Age," in *Xo Congresso internazionale di Scienze storiche, Relazioni* 3 (Rome, 1955) ; Gabriel Fournier, *Le Peuplement rural en Basse-Auvergne durant le haut Moyen Age* (Paris, 1962) ; M. Gonon, *Les Institutions et la société en Forez au XIVe siècle* (Macon, 1960) ; Guy Fourquin, *Les campagnes de la région parisienne à la fin du Moyen Age* (Paris, 1964) ; R. Boutruche, *La crise d'une société: seigneurs et paysans du Bordelais à la fin de la guerre de Cent Ans* (Strasbourg, 1947) ; Léopold Genicot, *L'économie rurale namuroise au bas Moyen Age,* 2 vols. (Louvain, 1943–1960) ; Georges Duby, *La société aux XIe et XIIe siècles dans la région mâconnaise* (Paris, 1953) ; Reginald V. Lennard, *Rural England, 1086–1135* (Oxford, 1959) ; Robert Fossier, *La terre et les hommes en Picardie jusqu'à la fin du XIIIe siècle,* 2 vols. (Louvain, 1968). Older accounts that can still be read with profit are Henri Pirenne, *Histoire de Belgique,* vols. 1 and 2 (various editions), and particularly Frederic W. Maitland, *Domesday Book and Beyond* (Cambridge, 1897). For an account of peasant emancipation in northern France and the Low Countries through the foundation of new towns, see Bryce D. Lyon, "Medieval Real Estate Developments and Freedom," *American Historical Review* 63 (1957) : 47–61. A superb treatment of social relations in the countryside is given by George C. Homans, *English Villagers of the Thirteenth Century* (Cambridge, Mass., 1942). Much less good, but with interesting selections from the sources, is G. G. Coulton, *The Medieval Village* (Cambridge, 1925), reprinted as *Medieval Village, Manor, and Monastery* (New York, 1960). A fanciful account that tends to view peasant conditions through rose-tinted glasses is Henry S. Bennett, *Life on the English*

Manor: A Study of Peasant Conditions, 1150-1400 (Cambridge, 1937). A different viewpoint is given in J. Z. Titow, *English Rural Society, 1200-1350* (London, 1969), and in R. B. Dobson, ed., *The Peasants' Revolt of 1381* (London, 1970). The village community in English society has been treated by various authors, recently by Warren O. Ault, *Open-Field Husbandry and the Village Community* (Philadelphia, 1965), a work that focuses on village laws and customs.

The issue of freedom and servitude in the late Middle Ages is treated in several of the general studies previously mentioned and in *Das Problem der Freiheit*, vol. 2 of the *Vorträge und Forschungen* of the Konstanzer Arbeitskreis (Constance, 1953). The reader should see also J. A. Raftis, *The Estates of Ramsey Abbey* (Toronto, 1957), and Raftis, *Tenure and Mobility: Studies in the Social History of the Mediaeval English Village* (Toronto, 1964); various books and articles by R. H. Hilton, the results of which are summarized in his recent pamphlet *The Decline of Serfdom in Medieval England* (London, 1969); and A. Bossuat, "Le servage en Nivernais au XVe siècle," *Bibliothèque de l'Ecole des Chartes* (1959).

On the noble classes there are numerous studies. Perhaps the best starting point is Joseph R. Strayer, *Feudalism* (Princeton, 1965). François L. Ganshof, *Feudalism*, trans. Philip Grierson, 3d Eng. ed. (New York, 1964), approaches feudalism from the standpoint of law and ceremony rather than as a set of social relationships, but his work is of great value for reference. An interesting collection of documents with commentary is given in David Herlihy, *The History of Feudalism* (New York, 1970). The standard work for the treatment of the aristocracy of the early Middle Ages and its ties with other social groups is Marc Bloch, *Feudal Society*, trans. L. A. Manyon (Chicago, 1961). I have disagreed with some of Bloch's interpretations in this essay, but my disagreement has been based on research conducted since he wrote. His accomplishment was fundamental.

The German aristocracy has received treatment recently by K. Leyser, "The German Aristocracy from the Ninth to the Early Twelfth Century," *Past and Present*, no. 41 (1968): 25-53. The student should consult also D. A. Bullough, "Early Medieval Social Groupings: The Terminology of Kinship," *Past and Present*, no. 45 (1969): 3-18. A work of fundamental importance in noting the early establishment of a nobility of blood is the three-part article of K. F. Werner, "Untersuchungen zur Frühzeit des französischen Fürstentums (9.-10. Jahrhundert)," *Die Welt als Geschichte* (1958-1960).

Some peculiarities of social development among the Norman upper classes are noted in David C. Douglas, *William the Conqueror: The Norman Impact upon England* (London, 1964). An extremely useful older work is Frank M. Stenton, *The First Century of English Feudalism, 1066-1166,* 2d ed. (Oxford, 1961). Stenton includes material on movement between classes and is useful for both England and Normandy. Still fundamental is Charles H. Haskins, *Norman Institutions* (Cambridge, Mass., 1918). Much material of value is contained in Frank Barlow, *The Feudal Kingdom of England, 1042–1066* (London, 1955).

The movement of knights into the nobility has been the subject of a substantial recent literature. A good review of German work, with accompanying bibliography, is Léopold Genicot, "La noblesse dans la société médiévale. A propos des dernières études relatives aux terres d'Empire," *Le Moyen Age* 71 (1965) : 539–60. Several critical articles have appeared recently for the Low Countries: Edouard Perroy, "La noblesse des Pays-Bas (à propos d'ouvrages récents)," *Revue du Nord* 43 (1961); Paul Bonenfant and Georges Despy, "La noblesse en Brabant aux XIIe et XIIIe siècles," *Le Moyen Age* 64 (1958) : 27–66; and Georges Despy, "Sur la noblesse dans les principautés belges au Moyen Age. A propos de travaux récents," *Revue Belge de philologie et d'histoire* 41 (1963) : 471–86. For France the reader should consult Georges Duby, "Une enquête à poursuivre: la noblesse dans la France médiévale," *Revue historique* 226 (1961). Good recent studies illustrating the plight of the lesser knights in England, from which examples have been drawn for this paper, are Sally Harvey, "The Knight and the Knight's Fee in England," *Past and Present,* no. 49 (1970) : 3–43; and Edmund King, "Large and Small Landowners in Thirteenth-Century England: The Case of Peterborough Abbey," *Past and Present,* no. 47 (1970) : 26–50. An escape route of the lesser nobles in France is shown in Quentin Griffiths, "New Men Among the Lay Counsellors of Saint Louis' Parlement," *Mediaeval Studies* 32 (1970) : 234–72. A particularly stimulating study of social conditions in southern France and Germany and their possible effect on intellectual developments is Herbert Moller, "The Social Causation of the Courtly Love Complex," *Comparative Studies in Society and History* 1 (1959) : 137–63. Sidney Painter, *French Chivalry,* is a good overview. For difficulties of the nobility in the late Middle Ages, see the general works already cited and Robert Boutruche, "Aux origines d'une crise nobiliare," *Annales d'histoire sociale* (1939) : 166–77, 257–73; and Edouard Perroy, "Social Mobility among the French Noblesse in the Later Middle Ages," *Past and Present,* no. 21 (1958) : 25–38.

Until quite recently there has been less work on towns and merchants than upon the rural classes, but as a whole it has been of higher caliber. The standard elementary treatments are Henri Pirenne, *Medieval Cities* (Princeton, 1925), and John H. Mundy and Peter Riesenberg, *The Medieval Town* (Princeton, 1958). A recent critique of Pirenne's ideas on Merovingian trade that summarizes the available source material on the question is Adriaan Verhulst, "Der Handel in Merowingerreich: Gesamtdarstellung nach schriftlichen Quellen," *Antikvariskt Arkiv* 39 (Stockholm, 1970) : 2–54. Nearly two decades ago A. B. Hibbert summarized research that contradicted Pirenne's hypothesis that wandering merchants constituted the core of the early town patriciates in his "The Origins of the Medieval Town Patriciate," *Past and Present,* no. 3 (1953) : 15–27, and recent studies of individual towns have confirmed Hibbert's reservations. The rural nature of the towns and the essentially local character of migrants coming to them until quite late has been shown among others by C. Higounet, "Mouvements de population dans le Midi de France du XIe au XVe siècle, d'après les noms de personne et de lieu," *Annales E.S.C.* 8 (1953) : 1–24. The reader is referred also to David Nicholas, "Medieval Urban Origins in Northern Continental Europe: State of Research and Some Tentative Conclusions," *Studies in Medieval and Renaissance History* 6 (1969) : 53–114; Nicholas, *Stad en Platteland in de Middeleeuwen* (Bussum, 1971), 31–37; and Nicholas, *Town and Countryside: Social, Economic, and Political Tensions in Fourteenth-Century Flanders* (Bruges, 1971), 222–249. Several excellent studies are contained in the volume of *Untersuchungen zur gesellschaftlichen Struktur der mittelalterlichen Städte in Europa,* vol. 11 of the *Vorträge und Forschungen* of the Konstanzer Arbeitskreis (Constance, 1966).

The educational aspect of social mobility is shown nicely in Franklin J. Pegues, *The Lawyers of the Last Capetians* (Princeton, 1962). An older standard account is Helen Waddell, *The Wandering Scholars* (New York, 1927). Well-written and stimulating is the short work of Jacques Le Goff, *Les intellectuels au moyen âge* (Paris, 1960) ; a good short account of related questions is John W. Baldwin, *The Scholastic Culture of the Middle Ages, 1000–1300* (Lexington, Mass., 1971).

The history of the Italian towns in the Middle Ages and of their social problems is facilitated by the fact that surviving documentation is much richer for the cities of the peninsula than for the towns of the rest of Europe put together. Hence there are numerous good accounts. A solid work for a wider audience by a specialist is Daniel Waley, *The Italian City-Republics* (New York, 1969). Waley's *Mediaeval Orvieto* (Cambridge, 1952) also merits close attention. Other works of interest include, Yves Renouard, *Les hommes d'affaires italiens au Moyen Age,* 2d ed. (Paris, 1968) ; the source collection of Robert S. Lopez and Irving W. Raymond, *Medieval Trade in the Mediterranean World* (New York, 1955) ; Iris Origo, *The Merchant of Prato* (London, 1957) ; Gene A. Brucker, *Florentine Politics and Society, 1343–1378* (Princeton, 1962), and Brucker, *Renaissance Florence* (New York, 1969) ; the comparative study of Jean Lestocquoy, *Les villes de Flandre et d'Italie sous le gouvernement des patriciens (XIe–XVe siècles)* (Paris, 1952) ; Jacques Heers, *Gênes au XVe siècle* (Paris, 1961) ; J. K. Hyde, *Padua in the Age of Dante* (New York, 1966) ; David Herlihy, *Pisa in the Early Renaissance* (New Haven, 1958), and *Medieval and Renaissance Pistoia: The Social History of an Italian Town* (New Haven, 1967). The older study of Ferdinand Schevill, *Siena* (London, 1909), has been replaced by several articles by William Bowsky and Bowsky's *The Finances of the Commune of Siena* (London, 1970).

The towns of northern Europe are less well represented in easily available treatments. A fascinating view of two major centers is given in Urban T. Holmes, *Daily Living in the Twelfth Century: Based on the Observations of Alexander Neckam in London and Paris* (Madison, 1952). Also recommended are Jacques Le Goff, *Marchands et banquiers du Moyen Age* (Paris, 1964), and Philippe Wolff and Frédéric Mauro, *L'âge de l'artisanat, Ve–XVIIIe siècles,* vol. 2 of Louis H. Parias, ed., *Historie générale du travail* (Paris, 1960).

Despite the impulse given to urban studies by Henri Pirenne, no medieval town in the Low Countries has received a definitive treatment except the minor centers of Huy and St. Trond. Pirenne's *Belgian Democracy, Its Early History* (London, 1915) is a good beginning. H. van Werveke, *Gand: Esquisse d'histoire sociale* (Brussels, 1946), is a pleasant popularization. See also the works of André Joris, *La ville de Huy au Moyen Age. Des origines à la fin du XIVe siècle* (Paris, 1959), and J. L. Charles, *La ville de Saint-Trond au Moyen Age. Des origines à la fin du XIVe siècle* (Paris, 1965). The best recent studies of English towns are Gwyn A. Williams, *Medieval London: From the Commune to Capital* (London, 1963); Sylvia L. Thrupp, *The Merchant Class of Medieval London* (Ann Arbor, 1948); and J. W. F. Hill, *Medieval Lincoln* (London, 1948). Excellent for social mobility is Eleanora Carus-Wilson, *Medieval Merchant Venturers* (London, 1955). Several good studies on French towns and merchants have appeared, notably Philippe Wolff, *Commerce et marchands à Toulouse, vers 1350 vers 1450* (Paris, 1954); John H. Mundy, *Liberty and Political Power at Toulouse, 1050–1230* (New York, 1954); J. Schneider, *La ville de Metz au XIIIe et XIVe siècles* (Nancy, 1950); Charles Higounet, ed., *Bordeaux pendant le haut Moyen Age* (Bordeaux, 1963); Yves Renouard, ed., *Bordeaux sous les rois d'Angleterre* (Bordeaux, 1965); René Fedou, *Les hommes de lois lyonnais à la fin du Moyen Age. Etude sur les origines de la classe de robe* (Paris, 1964). An excellent recent collection on urban social structures in the Low Countries is W. Blockmans, I. De Meyer, J. Mertens, C. Pauwelyn, and W. Vanderpijpen, *Studien betreffende de sociale strukturen te Brugge, Kortrijk en Gent in de 14e en 15e eeuw* (Heule, 1971).

A useful survey of social development in the German towns of the late Middle Ages is Philippe Dollinger, "Les villes allemandes au moyen âge. Les groupements sociaux," *Recueils de la Société Jean Bodin, 7. La Ville* (1956), pp. 371–401. Philippe Dollinger, *The German Hansa* (Stanford, 1970), gives colorful accounts of several merchant careers. A suggestive recent study of a small Portuguese center is R. C. Hoffman and H. B. Johnson, "Une ville portugais en mutation. Póvoa d'El Rey à la fin du quatorzième siècle," *Annales E.S.C.* 26 (1971): 917–40.

Most standard works on late medieval economic history give an account of aspects of social crisis. A convenient introduction in English with an excellent bibliography is Philip Ziegler, *The Black Death* (London, 1969). Other works of particular interest to the social historian are J. Calmette, *The Golden Age of Burgundy* (New York, 1963); and particularly the classic by Johan Huizinga, *The Waning of the Middle Ages* (New York, 1924).

Several works of general interest for medieval English society should be noted. Timothy Baker, *The Normans* (London, 1966), and O. G. Tomkeieff, *Life in Norman England* (London, 1966), are good studies designed for a wide audience. Much benefit still can be obtained from Paul Vinogradoff, *Villeinage in England* (Oxford, 1892). The chapters by O. Corbett and Eileen Power in the *Cambridge Medieval History* on social conditions are still good. Beginners can read with enjoyment and profit the works of George M. Trevelyan: *Illustrated English Social History*, 4 vols. (London, 1949–1952), and the classic *England in the Age of Wycliffe, 1368–1520* (London, 1899). Some material of use is found in George G. Coulton, ed., *Social Life in Britain* (London, 1918). For a statistical approach the reader should consult J. C. Russell, *British Medieval Population* (Albuquerque, 1948), and Russell, *Late Ancient and Medieval Population* (Philadelphia, 1958). Recent studies of value, with decent bibliographies, are F. R. H. DuBoulay, *An Age of Ambition: English Society in the Late Middle Ages* (London, 1970), and J. R. Lander, *Conflict and Stability in Fifteenth-Century England* (London, 1969). Of a more literary orientation is Paul M. Kendall, *The Yorkist Age* (New York, 1962).

We have noted some literature concerning the family and kinship bonds. It is striking that scholars have neglected this topic. The studies of Professor David Herlihy have pioneered a new approach through quantitative analysis. Of his many publications, see particularly "Land, Family and Women in Continental Europe, 701–1200," *Traditio* 18 (1962): 89–120; "Women in Medieval Society," The Smith History Lecture, 1971 (Houston, University of St. Thomas); "The Agrarian Revolution in Southern France and Italy, 801–1150," *Speculum* 33 (1958): 23–41; "Church Property on the European Continent, 701–1200," *Speculum* 36 (1961): 81–105, and "Family Solidarity in Medieval Italian History," in *Economy, Society, and Government in Medieval Italy: Essays in Memory of Robert L. Reynolds* (Kent, 1969). Much of our material on demographic trends in southern Europe has come from these articles. A different aspect of the family has been examined in Sidney Painter, "The Family and the Feudal System in Twelfth-Century England," *Speculum* 35 (1960): 1–16. The effect of the revival of the blood feud in a fourteenth-century city is described in David Nicholas, "Crime and Punishment in Fourteenth-Century Ghent," *Revue belge de philologie et d'histoire* 48 (1970–1971): 289–334, 1141–76.

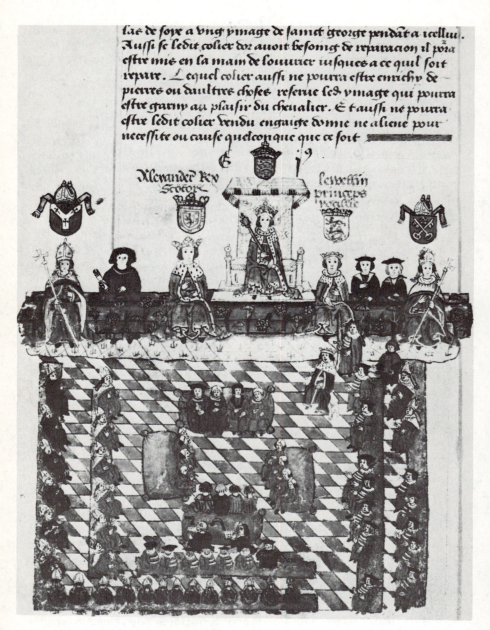

The Parliament called by Edward I of England, probably in 1279. On the outer benches sit secular and ecclesiastical peers. Judges sit in the middle on woolsacks. On the bench behind the two clerks with scrolls are representatives of the commons.

3.
Political Institutions

DONALD E. QUELLER

SOCIETIES CONSIST of "patterns of culture," as Ruth Benedict insisted in her well-known anthropological study bearing that title. The technology, ideas, and institutions of a society form a configuration or (to borrow a term from psychology) a *Gestalt* of coherent elements—economic, social, religious, educational, political, and many others. Each reinforces the whole. The congruity of the various elements, indeed, defines the society. In *Centuries of Childhood* Philippe Ariès, in a modest but significant example of cultural congruence and cohesion, points out how household architecture affects the structure of the family. When the long central hallway, serving only as a passage to the rooms branching from it, supplanted the old multi-functional hall where the family ate on a removable table, where the master received his guests and perhaps conducted his business, and where several curtained beds occupied the corners of the room, then the traditional extended family began to give way to the nuclear one. Occasionally some element of a culture fails to adapt to the overall configuration and we find cultural lag. The religion of classical antiquity with its many gods and goddesses, more than human in their power but human and even petty in character, is an outstanding example. It had suited well the pattern of the Homeric age, but it was a primitive anachronism by the time of Plato and Aristotle, Sophocles and Euripides, so that Plato wished to ban from his Republic immoral tales of the seducer Zeus. Insofar as a religion or other element of a culture lags behind the whole it is nonfunctional. Conversely, in a period of rapid change, such as the High Middle Ages, roughly the twelfth and thirteenth centuries, first one element of a culture and then another leaps forward, upsetting the balance and hampering smooth interaction; but in a healthy society most of the elements adapt to the new conditions created by the advanced elements.

It is no longer particularly radical to believe, as Karl Marx did, that the economic element in society is basic, the substructure of the entire cultural edifice. Men must have food, drink, clothing, and shelter, as Engels said (and as Aristotle knew long before him), before they can interest themselves in politics, art, religion, science. It does not follow, however, that we must be persuaded by the Marxist assertion that the entire superstructure of a culture is determined by the economic substructure. Yet the concept of an economic substructure is useful, for the fundamental modes of production do more than merely influence or condition the superstructure. They limit it in a rather more basic way than do, for example, political structures or religious ideas. A society of nomadic sheepherders like the ancient Hebrews, to take an extreme example, could hardly evolve a parliamentary democracy and it required a considerable time for them to achieve the primitive kingship of Saul and David. On the other hand, the elements of the superstructure also react upon the economic substructure. Whether one accepts Max Weber's still controversial views or rejects them, it is undoubtedly true that Protestantism, and especially Puritan religious views, provided more favorable soil for the growth of capitalism than did Catholic teachings.

The Middle Ages offer splendid, though certainly not unique, advantages for the study of patterns of culture and historical change. The time span is long, about a thousand years, and within this period radical changes in the configuration of western European culture occurred. European society from the fall of the Roman Empire until about the eleventh century presented a recognizable and distinct pattern; it developed another out of the rapid changes and adjustments of the twelfth and thirteenth centuries, and a third, somewhat less distinct, in the fourteenth and fifteenth centuries. Some medievalists believe that the traditional division of ancient, medieval, and modern history does not adequately stress the pattern of culture that began to emerge toward the end of the eleventh century—a turning point in European history more significant than the Renaissance, the Reformation, or the French Revolution, and, in fact, the real historical watershed between the age of localism following the fall of ancient civilization and the Industrial Revolution.

This essay will relate the slow working out of the medieval foundations of the modern state to parallel changes in other aspects of the society and especially to those in the economic substructure. The early portions will deal with the efforts of western Europeans after the failure of the Roman imperial system to devise local substitutes for an effective state. Their primitive culture and especially the enfeebled economy could not sustain a centralized government. To provide themselves with a minimum of law and order, they developed feudalism. The remainder of the essay will concentrate upon the rise of the monarchical state, though some attention will be paid to the parliamentary assembly—the servant of medieval monarchy that later became its conqueror or master. Underlying the growth of effective monarchical governments was an increase in the numbers, importance, and specialization of bureaucrats. The sweeping changes in the configuration of the culture rested upon the economic revival of the High Middle Ages. This essay will not summarize the political histories of the emerging medieval states but rather will depict the common factors in the development of political institutions in medieval Europe.

Germanic Peoples and Germanic Kingdoms

In about the middle of the first century B.C., while Roman civilization was still flourishing, Julius Caesar provided our first description of the barbarians who, half a millennium later, were to inherit the ruins of the Roman Empire in the West. German society was based upon a predominantly pastoral economy. Climate and vegetation did not require the Germanic peoples to be nomadic; they were settled and supplemented their cattle raising with agriculture. At first there was no marked inequality of wealth or social status among them. They were illiterate; they had no need for writing, for their patterns of life were fixed by custom and their transactions were neither widespread nor complex. Urban life, commerce, writing, and the political state are mutually supportive elements of a civilized culture and usually develop together.

The clan was the basic economic, social, and political unit of the German barbarians. More extensive, but less closely knit than the clan, was the tribe, and at a yet more remote level the people, such as the Alemanni, the Burgundians, and the Franks. The Germans had no state. The instruments of public power were not highly developed. The armed host of a whole people occasionally assembled to decide issues of war and peace; there were informal councils of leading men in times of crisis; war leaders were chosen for specific campaigns. These represent a rudimentary political system. In addition to the clan, tribe, and people were war parties recruited by leading men to steal cattle and plunder. War parties later became important in the evolution of medieval government, but initially they were not institutionalized and disbanded after each foray.

The traditional legal recourse of the Germans was the blood feud. This was a system of private justice granting the injured party or his clan the right and responsibility to take revenge upon an offender or his kindred. In the absence of public justice rendering enforceable judgments, the blood feud provided a needed sanction against wrongdoing and an incentive to the clans to keep in check their most aggressive members. Because of the lack of public officials to judge right and wrong and a public force to uphold justice, the blood feud was preferable to anarchy and was suited to a society dominated by clans.

During the century and a half after Julius Caesar, German society was transformed by Roman influence, particularly by the impact of the Roman trader. The desirability and availability of the goods of the advanced culture undermined the egalitarianism and the clan structure. Enterprising Germans, tempted by the merchant's wares, strove successfully to break the communal bonds of the clan and to become more wealthy than their kinsmen and neighbors. By A.D. 98, when Tacitus wrote his famed *Germania*, the economic and social underpinnings of German society had changed drastically. Tacitus has been criticized for romantically contrasting the purity and virility of the German barbarians to the decadence of his Roman compatriots. He is probably guilty as charged, yet much of his description rings true. His well-known account of the German mania for gambling, which led men to stake their very freedom, reflects the breakdown of the egalitarian society and the rise of slavery and aristocratic slave holders brought about by commercial dealings with the Romans. Such sweeping economic and social changes could not fail to be reflected by developments in the Germans' early political institutions.

The traditional clan structure decayed while at a higher level the institutions of the peoples were undergoing a modest development. The assemblies of free warriors under arms gained in importance. They began to meet periodically, rather than occasionally, and they decided all important questions affecting the whole people, most of which continued to be questions of war. That the assembly remained primitive was reflected in the warriors' expression of approval by clashing their weapons upon their shields and in their raising up on their shields a newly elected king. Nevertheless, the assemblies were gaining a limited judicial capacity over crimes closely connected with war and threatening the whole people, such as treachery, desertion, cowardice, and homosexuality (an unnatural crime for which the people could anticipate punishment by defeat in battle). Generally kings still possessed little power, remaining mere war-kings, elected to lead a specific campaign. Some of the advanced peoples, such as the Chatti, the Cherusci, and especially the Marcomanni, however, elected kings for life from recognized royal clans. Although warfare remained primitive, lacking, for example, any system of supply or skill in besieging fortified places, the most advanced peoples under their kings did display a new discipline. The old agglomerations of armed clans fighting more or less independently gave way to the beginning of unified armies sufficiently effective so that the less progressive peoples in time had either to imitate them or submit to their superior force.

As the military organization of the Germans between the times of Caesar and Tacitus underwent a modest centralizing tendency, the administration of justice also improved. Alongside the blood feud, ameliorating its harshness and socially disruptive qualities, the Germans placed the wergeld. Under this system of justice an offending party or his kin could pay the aggrieved party or his kin a sum fixed according to the seriousness of the crime, thus canceling the right to take revenge. The wergeld was a primitive system of justice, but it did provide a formal means sanctioned by society for obviating the violence of the blood feud. Judges elected by the assembly of warriors, and thus representing the public, moreover, were beginning to gain jurisdiction over some private wrongs. The wergeld and more significantly the expanding authority of judges show that justice was becoming more than a private or family matter; it was a public concern of the people as a whole.

Another advance was called by Tacitus the *comitatus*. Similar to the raiding party recruited by a leader in earlier days, the comitatus became institutionalized and enduring, a permanent war party for plundering. Possessed of wealth unknown among the Germans in Caesar's time, the leader of the comitatus maintained his following about him on a permanent basis, providing them with supplies, military equipment, and booty. They owed him loyalty in battle and were considered shamed if they survived a defeat in which their leader perished. The comitatus consisted of recruits from various clans and peoples, and it stood outside the ordinary political structure as an independent military force. On the one hand it hastened the decay of the old Germanic society by weakening the tie of kinship and by widening the gap between the wealthy and powerful and the poor and weak. On the other hand scholars see in the comitatus the roots of the personal bond between medieval lord and vassal and of the private feudal army.

From the end of the first century to the end of the fourth century the history of the Germans is obscure. Through a generally peaceful infiltration of the Roman frontier by Germans as slaves, hostages, workers bound to the soil, and soldiers in the Roman armies, the process of the mingling of German and Roman cultures was underway. In the late fourth and fifth centuries numerous Germanic peoples—Visigoths, Ostrogoths, Vandals, Angles, Saxons, Jutes, Franks—overran the Roman Empire and established successor states upon its ruins (see map). The political system of the Franks, the most important of the successor states, may serve as an example of them all.

Under their great and bloody king Clovis (481–511) of the Merovingian line the Salian Franks expanded in the fifth century from their base on the west bank of the lower Rhine over most of what is today France and some of

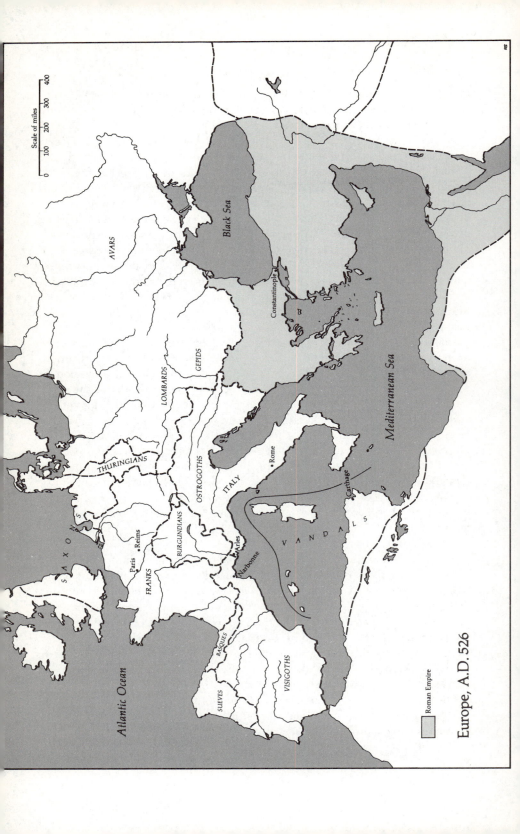

Europe, A.D. 526

Roman Empire

the lands to the east of the Rhine. The Franks, like the other Germans, had wanted not to destroy the Roman Empire but to enjoy its fruits. Clovis, in fact, had gained the loyalty of the Roman inhabitants of his realm by converting to a barbarous version of orthodox Christianity, in contrast to the heretical Arianism of the other Germans.

The Franks took over, as best they could, the decaying framework of the Roman state. J. M. Wallace-Hadrill has written: "the administrative shape of Frankish Gaul is for the most part sub-Roman and the men who run it use old Latin terms [*civitas, pagus, villa, fiscus, rescriptum*], sometimes inaccurately, but never with any sense of constraint." The imposition of degenerate Roman forms upon a barbarian cultural base is illustrated by the sixth-century codification known as the Salic Law—the law of the Salian Franks. The economic basis of the king's power consisted in his succession to the Roman imperial fisc, which included not only movable treasure but the vast imperial estates. The Frankish king's judicial and legislative powers also presuppose a sub-Roman form of government rather than a purely Germanic one.

Though it possessed a few Roman elements, however, the Salic Law was basically barbarian. Roman Law would not have been meaningful for Frankish society, which remained agricultural and rural. The ancient blood feud, modified by the wergeld, remained the basis of what law and order existed among the barbarians. The law of the Franks, moreover, did not apply to the Romans, the Visigoths, and other peoples within the Frankish empire. Each man retained the law of his own people in traditional fashion as a personal possession. The concept of a single legal jurisdiction extending over a territorial kingdom was still alien to the Germans. The Franks also retained the Germanic concept of the kingdom as the property of the king, and this proved tragic, for their custom was to divide the inheritance among the heirs. In efforts to reunite the kingdom brothers repeatedly betrayed brothers and the land was frequently tormented by bloodshed and civil war.

Much as they wished to be the successors of the Roman Caesars, therefore, the Germanic kings were powerless to halt the long-term decay of government in the West. The economic substructure of commerce and towns, money and taxes, essential to strong, centralized public authority, did not exist. Europe was entering upon half a millennium of profound economic depression. The successors of Dagobert (628–638), the last effective monarch of the dynasty of Clovis, are known as "do-nothing" kings. Anarchical conditions prevailed and only the powerful could thrive. Ordinary freemen had to commend themselves to wealthy lords for protection, becoming serfs. The royal governments, unable to rule, granted land to be governed by the increasingly powerful lords. The grants were originally conceived as delegations of authority, but weak royal governments proved unable to prevent the wrongful detention of the lands and the efforts of the recipients to make both lands and jurisdictions hereditary.

Many even gained from the kings grants of immunity, the renunciation of all royal power within their domains. Public power passed into the hands of private landholders; the state was dissolving into estates.

In the soil of the ensuing chaos, enriched by the detritus of Roman government, feudalism and feudal monarchy would in time grow. From feudal monarchy, in turn, medieval national monarchy would develop. Before turning to the growth of feudalism, however, let us consider the survival of the Roman ideal of imperial and universal government.

The Medieval Empire

The disintegration of the Frankish kingdom was temporarily interrupted and the ideal of universal and imperial authority was given new life by the Frankish ruler Charlemagne (king of the Franks, 768–814; emperor, 800–814). In 752 his father, Pepin III the Short (752–768), had displaced the last of the "do-nothing" Merovingian kings and assumed the royal title for his own house. Charlemagne (Carolus Magnus), after whom the dynasty is called Carolingian, extended the rule of the Franks over most of western Europe, from the Elbe to the Ebro and from the North Sea to central Italy. On Christmas Day in the year 800, the Frankish king was crowned Roman emperor by Pope Leo III, marking the birth of the medieval Roman Empire in the West.

From its beginning, however, the medieval Roman Empire was an anachronism. The venerated political structure of antiquity could not be imposed upon a society that had radically changed and could not sustain it. For all its outward greatness, Charlemagne's government rested upon a feeble economic foundation, which was rural and local. His achievement in gaining a brief respite from the political disintegration afflicting the West depended upon his dynamic personality and military prowess, and it had not, nor could it possibly have had, an adequate institutional base. Even a Charlemagne, lacking the sums of money necessary to maintain a corps of educated bureaucrats and a standing professional army, could not reestablish the state. In spite of his imperial pretensions, he remained, like his predecessors, a Germanic king striving to govern his far-flung lands with attenuated political authority. Institutionally the results of his efforts were ephemeral. Ideologically, however, Charlemagne and his empire remained extremely influential throughout the Middle Ages. In the centuries after Charlemagne until the new urban revolution and the beginning of the rise of the modern state, while political institutions disintegrated to the local and personal level, the illusory ideal of universal empire ruled the realm of political thought.

Not only history's achievements, however, but its illusions can be instructive.

The crux of the failure of the medieval empire was financial. Charlemagne's resources, though enormous for his day, were quite insufficient to support a genuine state. Direct taxation was virtually nonexistent, although some revenues, not very significant and difficult to collect, bore some resemblance to it. The king did possess indirect taxes, such as tolls, and coinage and justice yielded profits, but the returns were not great. The weakness of Carolingian political institutions and the shape of those of succeeding generations are revealed in the lack of a clear distinction between public finance and the private resources of the emperor. The crown lands were his main source of income, as they would be for rulers throughout the age of localism. Tribute and booty from Charlemagne's wars provided a welcome supplement, revealing again the still primitive nature of the Carolingian Empire. Its basic weakness, like that of all medieval government prior to the twelfth century, was lack of money. Wanting cash, some substitute, often a grant of land from the royal domain, was given to reward those who served the ruler. From the point of view of the king, as we shall see, payment in land had serious defects.

The Carolingian army reflects the basic weaknesses of the Carolingian state. At its nucleus were royal vassals, men bound to the emperor by ties of personal loyalty. Because of their armor and horses, their services were extremely expensive. The king either supported them at court or, increasingly, rewarded them with rural estates for their maintenance. The vassals were supplemented by the militia of freemen, who were required to fall out upon summons at their own expense, equipped with arms and food for three months. To diminish the burden upon poorer men, Charlemagne reformed the militia by providing that they could combine to send one of their number to fight. An unforeseen result of this relief from military duty was the further degradation of arms-bearing freemen into defenseless serfs.

Carolingian justice was burdened with similar defects. It was administered not by salaried and educated judges, for both money and education were wanting, but by unsalaried laymen. As earlier among the Germanic peoples, the law remained personal rather than territorial. Every man was judged according to the law of his own people. The king-emperor did cause the unwritten laws of the various peoples to be codified according to the Roman pattern, although their contents remained un-Roman. The emperor made law, as had his Roman imperial predecessors. His capitularies, which were administrative commands in appearance, often were a kind of statutory law resembling the imperial edicts of Roman times. Although a few of the trappings of Roman law and government remained, however, the antique legal system had long since broken down.

Carolingian central government, which focused upon the palace, revealed a confusion, typical of the Middle Ages, of the private servants of the ruler with political officials. Public responsibilities were performed by the chief members of the king's personal household—the seneschal or steward, who was head of the household staff and responsible for provisioning the court; the butler, who had charge of the drink; the constable, who saw to the mounts; the chamberlain, who looked after the royal bedchamber and, since the king's valuables were kept there, was treasurer as well as valet. The count of the palace appears more like a public official, for he presided over the royal tribunal in the king's absence. The king's chapel, under his chaplain, was the center for ecclesiastical affairs. Its clerics (clerks) wrote some royal documents, but it was more like a small secretariat than a full-scale chancellery. The household was ambulatory, for the king had to move about a great deal to exercise his authority in person, although Aachen became a favorite residence and a quasi-capital in the late years of the reign. Personal government through household officials was characteristic of the Middle Ages and continued into modern times alongside more institutionalized structures; witness the powers of "kitchen cabinets" and special advisers to heads of state on particular problems or activities.

The king was assisted by an advisory council summoned at his will and composed of household officials and any others whom he wished to consult. There was also a larger annual assembly in the spring. This was not the traditional assembly of arms-bearing freemen, which had disappeared. The new body was decidedly aristocratic, being composed of counts, bishops, and other people of significance. Its function too was merely consultative; the king did not require its consent. Sometimes he summoned smaller assemblies, of churchmen, for example, to advise him on special problems. Under the king the household officials, councils, and assemblies were the organs of the central government.

In a vast empire, plagued by poor communications and weak institutions, making royal authority consistently effective at the local level was a problem. Charlemagne and his successors never solved it. The key institution of territorial government was the county, of which there were two hundred or more, governed by counts. The count represented the emperor and was supposed to be responsible to him. He was to safeguard royal rights, maintain public order, serve as local judge, collect fines and tolls, and muster the local militia for service under his command. Each count had a small staff, perhaps a viscount and a notary, and subordinates whose role was similar to his, though performed in the subdivisions of the counties, called hundreds. The count's position was attractive, for he possessed much landed wealth and power. Counts were usually selected from the old Frankish nobility and often, for especially sensitive appointments, from the royal dynasty itself. Remote or frontier provinces or marches required especially strong military forces, and their governors gained the title of duke or margrave. Charlemagne was particularly careful to place loyal men in these positions. Nevertheless, the counts, dukes, and margraves acquired local power that in time could be turned against the royal authority they were supposed to represent. Not easily removable, they later succeeded in making their positions and their lands hereditary. The localization of power in the hands of the counts in the ninth and tenth centuries played an important part in the rise of feudalism.

Charlemagne recognized the danger of regional particularism and sought to combat it by institutionalizing the *missi dominici* ("messengers of the lord"). F. L. Ganshof, the distinguished Belgian authority on Carolingian history, has written that the *missi dominici* were "commissioners of the king used in order to make his personal action felt in a specified region . . . to say it was the king who acted in the person of the *missi* would not be an exaggeration." They were to represent the king's interests, to check the local authorities, and to receive complaints against them in yearly courts or assizes. For his missi Charlemagne relied upon powerful and wealthy men, high nobility, counts, bishops, and abbots, believing them less subject to bribery or intimidation than lesser men. Unfortunately, these men were burdened with other responsibilities, so their effect upon local government was limited. For two or three generations the missi functioned reasonably effectively, but in time their visits became less regular and they were more often and unwisely appointed to serve in areas where they already held local power. Although ultimately unsuccessful, the use of the missi represents an intelligent effort to reinforce at the local level a fundamentally weak political structure.

Governing of the Carolingian Empire was a task made impossible by its size, the difficulty and slowness of communication, and the lack of an economic base able to support more than rudimentary and makeshift political and administrative institutions. That it had any success was due to the vitality and personal interventions of Charlemagne. In fact, the prolonged residence of the aging king-emperor at Aachen in the last decade or so of his reign marked the beginning of decline, which accelerated after his death in 814. After the brief respite under Charlemagne, the disintegration of government resumed.

Under Charlemagne's son, Louis the Pious (814–840), it became common for lands, jurisdictions, and immunities held of the king-emperor to pass on to the sons of their holders. Noble families thus became rooted in landed properties and local powers; the authority of the central government dwindled. The counts, above all, began the slow process by which their lands and positions would eventually become hereditary. Local magnates were on the way to becoming the virtually autonomous lords of the feudal age. As the sons of Louis fragmented the empire in fratricidal wars, they accelerated the acquisition or usurpation of imperial lands and rights by local lords. Even the title of emperor disappeared for a time after 924, though the memory of the empire and the renown of Charlemagne lived on.

In the anarchic tenth century the successors of the Carolingians in East Frankland had certain advantages over those in the West. Most of the estates of Charlemagne had been located in Germany, and these offered a basis of wealth, lacking in the West, to the kings of the East Franks. Feudalism spread more slowly in the East than in the West, and the old Germanic militia of freemen persisted until the eleventh century, providing a measure of local defense and a counterbalance against the aristocracy.

Thus when the imperial title once again appeared in 962 it was in Germany under Otto I (king of the East Franks, 936–973; emperor, 962–973) of the strong Saxon dynasty, and with the Saxons and their successors it remained. The empire of the Saxons was much smaller than Charlemagne's, including only Germany, Burgundy, and north and central Italy. Like his great predecessor, Otto I recognized the political weakness of the empire before the predatory magnates. Lacking an institutional means of control, he thus entered into an informal alliance with the bishops, whose offices were clearly not heritable, raising them as rivals of the lay lords. They received extensive grants of lands and political jurisdictions, in return for which they served the king-emperor in council, diplomacy, and war. Insofar as the Ottonian empire possessed an officialdom, it was composed of ecclesiastics. In the long run, however, Otto's enhancement of the political power of the bishops exacerbated the tensions between the two authorities claiming universal jurisdiction, the empire and the church. This conflict dominated medieval political thought (even after it was made obsolete by the rise of national states), and it was largely responsible for the ruination of the empire in the great Investiture Struggle of the eleventh century. Even more than Charlemagne's *missi dominici,* Ottonian dependence upon the bishops was a patchwork response to the forces of political decentralization. To a somewhat lesser extent the same may be said of the Salian dynasty's use at a later date of ministeriales, lowborn men, often of servile origin, raised to high military and government offices.

No solid institutional solution to the splintering of political authority could be attempted until the twelfth century, when Europe once more became prosperous enough to begin to construct states. Then the solution would be found in new entities, not in the archaic claimant to universal rule, the empire of Charlemagne. Meanwhile, although the imperial ideal remained a force, western Europeans sought to gain some measure of defense and domestic tranquillity on the local level under the feudal pattern of government.

Feudalism

Feudalism too was a makeshift, a substitute for a state. At a minimal and local level it was successful in halting and eventually reversing the decline of political authority. When western European society would once again possess the resources to construct states, it would do so by building upon the antecedent feudal structure.

From inception to moribund old age feudalism can be traced through several rather clearly distinguishable phases. Its ancestry goes back to the German war band and Roman land tenure. In the Merovingian age feudal institutions were embryonic. The limited success of the early Carolingians in preserving royal government interrupted feudal development, but the anarchy of the ninth century brought about the birth of feudalism in northern Gaul between the Loire and the Rhine. In the same area it received its characteristic form and greatest strength in the tenth and eleventh centuries. It remained vital in the twelfth and thirteenth centuries, although its raison d'être was being undermined by the revival of the economy and the rise of feudal monarchies. After 1300, while the class ethos of feudalism flourished as never before, its political and military importance was reduced by the growth of the nation state.

At its birth, amid the crises of the ninth century, feudalism was not a coherent theory of government but a conglomeration of improvised devices to preserve some semblance of peace and order in a society threatened with chaos. Powerful Charlemagne himself had not been able to reverse the deterioration of government institutions since the Pax Romana. The contraction of the economy, which once had been stimulated by a flourishing Mediterranean commerce, was characterized by a near-subsistence agriculture on the local level, not allowing the resources for an effective central government. Even before Charlemagne's death his empire was beginning to suffer the raids of piratical Vikings. As the menace increased, the central government proved incapable of providing defense, which was its fundamental duty, and so the responsibility passed by default to the greater local landlords, who could offer some protection by building wooden forts and gathering about them a few fighting men to resist the invaders. Civil war among Charlemagne's grandsons further weakened the central government. Not only was the empire dismembered as they concentrated their warlike efforts upon one another, but they permanently damaged royal power by purchasing the loyalty of their followers with grants of land and jurisdiction. Their monarchies ceased to be able to govern. Feudalism filled the need of a poor society, plagued by foreign attack and domestic discord, for a political system suited to its capabilities. In spite of its own almost anarchic character, it offered some protection against the Viking marauders and provided a rough-handed justice.

The elements interwoven in the ninth century to form feudalism were vassalage, the fief, and the delegation of public authority into private hands. Vassalage was a form of military retainership originating in the Germanic comitatus, although the Roman practice whereby lesser men commended themselves to greater ones also played a part. Unlike the aristocratic fighting men of the comitatus, commended men were ordinarily of the lower classes and they performed all sorts of services for their lords, including servile ones. Some of them, however, served as military retainers and eventually fused with those of more exalted origin. The term "vassal" comes from *vassus*, which at one time signified a slave. After the fusion of the Germanic and Roman elements and with the increasing importance of expensively equipped and highly skilled heavy cavalry in the eighth century, however, it took on an honorable connotation by its association with men who fought for a lord in the new manner. The fief, also called a benefice, was usually a grant of land; it appears to go back to a Roman land tenure called *precarium,* which was originally at the will of the landlord. The political character of feudalism, necessitated by the breakdown of central government, originated in the grants of immunities to the holders of great estates from late Roman times. The origin of the elements of feudalism is of more than antiquarian interest; the subject illustrates the way in which a society under the stress of change grasps, modifies, and combines the institutions available to it in order to adapt itself to new conditions.

Personal contract between lord and vassal, the proprietary fief, and the decentralization of political and legal authority in private hands combined to create feudalism in the ninth century. The vassal had originally been maintained at the court of his lord, but the Carolingians first widely employed the granting of benefices or fiefs as a reward for service, since even the strongest of the Carolingian monarchs had relatively little money with which to maintain their followers. A few vassals continued to reside at the court, but the combination of vassalage and fief became customary. When the vassals left the court to reside on their own fiefs, the old quasi-familial loyalty that was the fruit of daily contact weakened. While the bond between lord and vassal remained strong, the original personal character gave way in some measure to a more institutional one. The addition of the third element, governmental authority, truly characterized feudalism. The collapse of central government in the age of civil wars and Viking invasions made government a private possession of vassals holding fiefs. The wealthier and more powerful vassals possessed fortified towers made of wood, which became centers of local protection and jurisdiction. The fate of the late Carolingian monarchy hinged upon its ability to halt the diffusion of government power. It could not. In fact, the agents of royal authority, especially the counts, joined the great vassals in assuming and usurping the functions of government.

Theoretically the granting of fiefs and governmental powers had been conditional and the king could take them back for himself or regrant them to others. Certainly in the early stages the arrangement was considered to lapse with the death of either party. In the course of the troubled ninth century, however, the holders of great estates and offices had considerable success against weakened monarchs in making them hereditary, although the process was then by no means complete. This was one more major step in the localization of political authority.

The conditions that gave rise to feudalism were not limited to northwestern France. It spread throughout West Frankland by the end of the tenth century and then, in one form or another, throughout most of western Europe. Feudalism, due to the different traditions and institutions of the various areas, the earliness or lateness of its introduction, and the fact that it was local in character, existed in many varieties. Also, there always remained, especially in Germany, lands outside the feudal nexus. Despite exceptions and variations, fully developed feudalism of the tenth through the thirteenth centuries possessed certain common characteristics.

Basic was the concept of the feudal contract with its reciprocal rights and duties. The lord owed the vassal military protection, justice in the lord's court, advice, and material support, customarily in the form of a fief. The vassal owed the lord aid and counsel. The aid was customarily military, the provision of fully equipped and mounted knights. Counsel signified the vassal's duty to advise and assist his lord in the latter's governmental responsibilities. When vassals had been household retainers, before the granting of fiefs, the amount of service required of them was unlimited. Once settled on their own estates, however, with government responsibilities of their own, their services to the lord necessarily became fixed. They customarily owed, for example, only forty days of military service a year. When the lord summoned them to assist in governing, they owed suit to court. The lord also had the right to certain payments from his vassals, but these were not a regular source of income. The lord's right of wardship over minor heirs, the right to control the marriage of heiresses and widows, the right to a payment when an heir took over the fief, all were vestiges of the days before the fief became hereditary. If the lord required aid beyond the customary terms of the feudal contract, as kings increasingly did for the defense of the realm, he could only summon his vassals and demand their consent.

This feudal contract was sanctioned by the Germanic ceremony of homage and the oath of fealty. In performing homage, the vassal became the man (*homme*) of the lord. The bond thus created was taken seriously, probably more seriously, for example, than marriage. This is not to say that it was never violated, any more than one could say it of the marriage bond, but the ceremonial and psychological sanctions were powerful, even if the military and legal ones were not. For a vassal to raise his sword against his lord was an unspeakable crime. In the chanson *Raoul de Cambrai* the hero recounts the evils of his lord Raoul, who is worse than Judas, yet he can only conclude, "He is my lord." Henry II (1154–1189) of England, who showed little respect for his marriage vows, gave up his attack on Toulouse when he discovered that Louis VII (1137–1180) of France, his lord for his continental fiefs, was in the city. Henry was too clever a king, moreover, not to be concerned with the example for good or evil that he set for his own vassals. The church lent its support to the chief institution standing between society and anarchy through fealty, an oath of loyalty to the lord taken upon the Scriptures or sacred relics. Theoretically, the carefully sanctioned bond between lord and vassal could be broken only by a formal act of defiance, although it required a rash vassal to break a handful of straw and throw it in the face of his lord, so the requirement was rarely honored. When vassals had performed homage to more than one lord, as they eagerly did in return for fiefs, confusion resulted. In theory the vassal should provide each of his lords with the required number of knights, leading one band or the other himself, and possibly fighting against his own men. Sometimes this actually occurred, although self-interest and common sense, those two great arbiters of human affairs, usually prevailed. An attempt to regulate the confusion was made through the institution of liege homage, by which a vassal vowed to be loyal to a particular lord above all others, but the avidity for fiefs was so compelling that vassals also offered liege homage to more than one lord. The holding of multiple fiefs from different lords was both manifestation and cause of the collapse of central authority, for such a vassal possessed a diversified base of power and was effectively governed by no one.

In return for homage and fealty the vassal was invested with the fief, the material means for bearing his obligations. A vassal who owed only his own service as a knight received a small fief. A manor was considered a fief sufficient to support a single knight. More powerful vassals received great fiefs for which they owed perhaps twenty or fifty knights, who could be household retainers of the old-fashioned sort or hired, though in the fully developed feudal pattern they customarily received smaller fiefs of their own carved out of the greater ones. This was called subinfeudation. Those who received fiefs in this way might in turn subinfeudate, and the process could be repeated as long as there was enough land to attract a vassal. Thus there were, as the eminent American medievalist Joseph R. Strayer has emphasized, levels of feudalism. At each stage in the process the lord retained some lands, called his demesne, for his own support and that of his establishment. When money revenues would become increasingly important, the wealth of a lord's demesne would be more significant than the number of vassals who owed him allegiance.

In the fully developed feudal system each vassal and subvassal obtained jurisdiction along with his fief. At the highest level delegated feudal jurisdictions extended over duchies and counties, occasionally even over kingdoms. The feudal castle symbolized governmental authority at the higher and middle levels. At the lowest level each lord of a manor, or more often his bailiff, presided over the manorial court attended by both free and servile tenants.

While this localization of government forestalled anarchy, feudalism was a poor substitute for a state, and members of the feudal class continued to rely heavily upon the ties of kinship for their protection. Even in the feudal courts kinship was important. A man's relatives would serve as oath helpers, swearing as character witnesses that his own oath was a dependable one, thereby clearing him. Though far from ideal, the system was somewhat effective in a strongly religious society that took oaths seriously. When a noble faced trial by battle, kinsmen also often assumed the burden and risk of upholding the honor of the family, as in the famous trial of the traitor Ganélon in the *Chanson de Roland,* where one relative died in the trial by arms and, as a result of this proof by defeat, thirty more were hanged. Probably more important than the judicial resolution of disputes was the feud or vendetta of one kinship group against another. Though the feud more often prolonged disputes than it resolved them, it remained an essential device for protection in a society where justice was rude and unreliable and private warfare was a right.

Even so, in an age when central government had failed, the kinship was not entirely thrown upon its own resources, for local feudal government did provide some measure of order and justice. Crude as it was, from it we have received the concepts of limited government under fundamental law, the social and political contract, the consent of the governed, and even representative government. In its own age and even at its crudest, it offered a rough-hewn order and protection to a society that could sustain nothing better.

Feudal Monarchy in the Tenth and Eleventh Centuries

The tenth and eleventh centuries continued to be an age of agricultural localism, of an economy barely above the subsistence level. The political superstructure could be no stronger than the economic substructure would sustain. There was simply not enough wealth for rulers to hire administrators and pay soldiers. So, by delegation or usurpation, local power passed into the hands of local landlords. Perched precariously atop the shaky feudal structure, however, monarchy survived as the repository of the remaining authority of central government.

The theory of tenth- and eleventh-century feudal monarchy, based on the memory of Charlemagne, was in marked contrast with its insubstantial reality, grounded in the localized society. According to theory the feudal king had an exalted status. As successor to Charlemagne he was the font of law and justice. He possessed a sacredness as a result of his anointment with chrism (consecrated oil), a rite that for a time possessed the solemnity of a sacrament. Although later Carolingian monarchy had assumed a feudal character, the king remained at the head of the feudal hierarchy, and his vassals owed him military service and suit to court. The feudal king of the tenth and eleventh centuries, however, lacked the means to enforce the rights and perform the obligations that were in theory his. His treasure was so small that it could be carried about with him in a chest shared with important documents. The king was often weaker than his vassals, to whom he had yielded lands, rights, and authority. After they had departed from the royal court to live on their fiefs, the old personal bond between the king and his vassals had been impaired. Counts, dukes, and margraves assumed complete responsibility for defense and justice in the lands under their jurisdiction. As the price of their support in his own struggles, the king granted to many magnates immunities within their territories from royal justices, tax collectors, and other representatives of the central government. Strayer asserts that about the year 1000 there was no state in western Europe.

More or less similar conditions existed throughout Europe north of the Pyrenees and Alps at this time, and political institutions naturally adapted themselves in more or less similar ways. Historians and anthropologists perhaps too often discover cultural borrowing where there may be only a common-sense adaptation along the same lines. Cultural choices (of political institutions, for example) are rather narrowly restricted, if the view expressed here concerning the way a society is put together and functions is correct. Since the conditions were only "more or less" similar, however, the adaptations were not identical nor quite contemporary.

Of the three major feudal monarchies, France may be considered typical. It was the homeland and heartland of feudalism, and it became feudalized earliest and most thoroughly. In the tenth and eleventh centuries, indeed, it was the only unequivocally feudal monarchy. Germany and Anglo-Saxon England had not assumed a truly feudal character but remained basically Germanic kingdoms (see map).

Since East Frankland (or Germany) did not become a feudal monarchy in the period under consideration, we may confine ourselves to indicating the most significant factors distinguishing its political structure. In an age in which political power was based upon landed wealth it was important that the greater part of the estates of Charlemagne had been situated in the newly conquered lands in the East. After the breakup of the Carolingian Empire, therefore, the German successors to that mighty emperor possessed greater resources and less diminished powers that did those in the West. The ancient Germanic kingship also was buttressed by a semi-theocratic character gained through anointment and the loyal support of the bishops. During the turmoil of the Magyar invasions of the ninth century the dukes of Saxony, Franconia, Swabia, and Bavaria made serious inroads upon the central government, but the Saxon dynasty's successful defense against the Magyars and its revival of the imperial tradition in the tenth century cut short this development. Feudalism thus did not become firmly established in Germany until the twelfth century, and even then feudalization was far from complete. In the tenth and eleventh centuries, East Frankish monarchy remained stronger than that of

Europe, ca. A.D. 1000

	Holy Roman Empire
	Non-Christian territories
······	Religious frontier of the Great Schism

Scale of miles
0   100   200   300   400

NORWAY

SWEDEN

DENMARK
Lund
Roskilde

HEATHEN BALTS
Riga

POMERANIA
Gniezno

BILLINGS
Hamburg
Magdeburg
Paderborn
Cologne
Mainz   Trier

KINGDOM OF THE GERMANS
Regensburg
Prague
Salzburg

POLAND
Cracow

PRINCIPALITY OF KIEV
Kiev

PETCHENEGS

ORTHODOX CHURCH
CATHOLIC CHURCH

MAGYARS
Gran
Kalocsa

CROATS
Aquileia
Venice
Spalato
Zara
Ragusa

SERBS

BULGARS
Preslaw

Black Sea

Constantinople

BYZANTINE EMPIRE

Athens

Mediterranean Sea

SCOTLAND
Edinburgh

IRELAND
Dublin

WALES

ENGLAND
York
London
Canterbury

To Norway

Atlantic Ocean

KINGDOM OF FRANCE
Rouen
Paris   Orléans
Reims
Tours

DUCHY OF BURGUNDY
Besançon
Lyons
Cluny   Vienne
Arles

KINGDOM OF ITALY
Milan
Pisa
Ravenna
EXARCHATE
LANDS OF ST. PETER
Spoleto
Rome
Naples

Palermo

MUSLIM EMPIRE

Toulouse
Narbonne

COUNTY OF BARCELONA
Barcelona

KINGDOM OF NAVARRE
Pampeluna
Burgos

KINGDOM OF CASTILLE
Santiago de Compostela
León
KINGDOM OF LEÓN

CALIPHATE OF CÓRDOBA
Toledo
Córdoba
Seville

MUSLIM

the West Franks. When later, however, western monarchies began to build upon new feudal foundations, Germany would be left behind as a political backwater.

Anglo-Saxon England existed on the periphery of European civilization until the Norman Conquest, although it shared many of the characteristics prevalent on the continent. Although England was comparatively prosperous, it too suffered from the general economic backwardness of the early Middle Ages. Anglo-Saxon monarchy, even more clearly than the East Frankish, was based on old Germanic foundations, in spite of the presence of elements of feudalism. English thanes performing military service in return for land grants look very much like continental fiefholding vassals, but among the Anglo-Saxons political and legal jurisdiction never fully merged with thaneship and landholding. The central government of the monarchy, in fact, was relatively strong. In the lengthy warfare against the Danes, Alfred (871–899) and his successors developed an army, a fleet, an administrative and financial system, which enabled royal government to perform its basic duties, to protect its subjects and render them justice. The king was not entirely dependent upon the nobility for the defense and government of his realm. Local government in the shires and their subdivisions was well integrated with central government through effective royal officials, especially the sheriffs. This sound Anglo-Saxon substratum of government would continue to be important after the Norman conquest and later even upon the continent.

West Frankland, the homeland of feudalism, alone was sufficiently feudalized before the late eleventh century to come under the rubric of feudal monarchy, and therefore most of our attention will be directed to it. The West Frankish kings were poor, and the majority of the demesne lands that the later Carolingians had possessed there had been expended in return for military support in the chaotic ninth century. Whatever their theoretical position, the kings had no power to enforce their rights. In the tenth century the magnates had managed to weaken the throne still more by emphasizing its elective character at the expense of the idea that the ruler must be chosen from a royal clan. They passed the crown back and forth between the Carolingians and the Robertians, the descendants of Robert the Strong. The rivalry of the two great houses naturally played into the hands of counts, dukes, and others who continued to gain lands, jurisdictions, and immunities for themselves. The election of Hugh Capet (987–996) of the Robertian line in 987 put an end to this profitable game, although the nobles did not intend or anticipate that it should. By that time, however, West Frankland had ceased to have an effective central government and had become a collection of almost independent principalities.

Yet the kingship survived, albeit feebly. The West Frankish feudal monarch of the tenth and eleventh centuries occupied a threefold position: He was the king, the successor of Charlemagne; he was the feudal suzerain, the lord at the pinnacle of the feudal structure; he was the direct ruler of his own duchy, his demesne, the Ile-de-France.

As king he had the duty to defend the realm, to maintain public order, and to protect and foster the church. To carry out these responsibilities he ought to have been able to summon the militia of freemen, to rely upon the counts as agents of the monarchy, and to issue capitularies as Charlemagne had done. In fact he could do none of these. The theory of monarchy was for the most part incompatible with actuality. The militia no longer existed. The counts pursued their own ends and made their offices hereditary. They and other powerful nobles ignored the king's commands, if he was foolish enough to issue them. Lesser men sought a measure of security under the protection of the greater, to whom they owed a loyalty stronger than that they felt to the king. What remained of royal administration was traceable to the Carolingian household officials. The chief of them continued to be the steward, responsible for provisioning the court. He stood over the provosts, who supervised the royal manors, from whose fruits the king and his court were sustained. This sort of government descends almost to the level of household management, but the crown did retain a few advantages. Anointment with chrism gave the king a certain sanctity, which was of no small importance in a religious, not to say superstitious age. The king also possessed social prestige, which could be politically useful, for example, in contracting advantageous marriage alliances. Of course the king could not fulfill his royal duties. Only after a slow process of building upward from the local level would he be able to do so.

As feudal suzerain at the head of the hierarchy the king should have been able to command the military and governmental services the vassals owed their lord, but he could not. Until the twelfth century the dukes of Aquitaine and the counts of Toulouse refused to perform homage, and although the dukes of Normandy recognized that they owed homage and service to court, they would perform these obligations only if the king met them on the border of Normandy. The counties and duchies were virtually autonomous. The king's great vassals had acquired by subinfeudation many more vassals of their own than they owed in knights' service to the king. The counts of Champagne, for example, owed ten knights' service but commanded about two hundred knights. Such powerful nobles regarded the king as one of themselves, at the most as "the first among peers." The feudal authority of the king as suzerain had to be established before France in the thirteenth century would possess an effective government.

Whatever real power the kings of the West Franks possessed in the tenth and eleventh centuries came from their third role as direct rulers of the royal demesne. Here were the manors that provided their rather pitiful economic base. Here were the petty vassals who owed them loyalty, not as kings but as dukes of the Ile-de-France. In their capacity as dukes of France they were numbered among the other great lords of West Frankland. Even their control over the demesne was shaken, however, as feudalism progressed within the duchy, as it did within the kingdom and also within other principalities. Petty vassals threw off their obligations and defied their lord. The provosts strove to make their office hereditary, and they became part of the feudal structure. The first step in the building of royal authority would have to be the regaining of firm control over the royal demesne.

The one success enjoyed by Hugh Capet and his successors during this period was the gradual establishment of a hereditary right to the throne. Hereditary monarchy was far from the minds of the magnates when they elected Hugh, but he contrived to associate his son with him on the throne, and his successors managed to do the same for over two centuries, by which time the hereditary principle had become fairly well established. Fortune smiled upon the Capetians in this endeavor, for they continued to produce male heirs and the family was sufficiently long-lived that these heirs were usually mature men before they received the reins of government.

That the early Capetian monarchy was able merely to survive the centrifugal effects of feudalism may be counted as an accomplishment. Rivalries among the great feudal lords prevented them from uniting against the weak king, whom they feared no more than others of their own group. In a sense, the very impotence of the monarchy may have aided its survival.

Pitiful as the kings of the West Franks were in the eleventh century, a rudimentary institutional basis for an effective feudal monarchy was present. The king possessed some prestige, and his crown was surrounded by an aura of sanctity. He was the head of the feudal hierarchy, however incapable he was of enforcing his feudal rights. Vigorous kings of the future, like Louis the Fat, Philip II Augustus, and Saint Louis, aided by a reviving economy, could build on these foundations. They would start at the bottom, at the local level, reestablishing their authority within the narrow demesne. They would then begin to assert their rights as feudal suzerains, and in time would attain the splendor of thirteenth-century French kingship. Powerful Norman and Angevin kings of England, William the Conqueror, Henry I, and Henry II, would also create a strong feudal monarchy, preceding their Capetian rivals, moreover, by a century. Before about the twelfth century, however, western European society lacked the necessary economic basis for effective kingship.

Feudal Monarchy in the Twelfth and Thirteenth Centuries

About the eleventh century appeared the first signs of an economic revival, culminating in the twelfth and thirteenth centuries. It changed the face of Europe and established the foundations of the ascendancy Europeans enjoyed for so long and for which they are still vigorous contenders. Population boomed.

Forests separating scattered manors and villages were cleared, swamps were drained, the sea was pushed back with dikes, and a great deal of new land was put under the plow. The clearing, draining, and diking required economic resources, so leadership was assumed by prosperous feudal lords. Many of them profited from the resultant increase of wealth, but none more than the kings, who played a large role in the expansion of the arable land. The growth of agricultural production made possible and in turn was stimulated by a revival of interregional trade. A money economy began to supplant the subsistence economy of the manor. The agricultural surplus also permitted a revival of towns as thriving centers for commerce and industry. Feudal monarchs, notably the Capetians, took the lead in chartering towns and founding prosperous fairs. In return for the privileges granted to townsmen, the kings received rents, infantrymen (called *sergents*), and the support of walled strongholds friendly to the royal cause. With new money revenues they were able to employ mercenary soldiers and professional administrators, thus lessening their dependence upon their vassals. The expanded trade, moreover, created a need for a more extensive and centralized government than local landlords could provide. Indeed, the basis of feudal particularism was undercut, for feudalism was a makeshift pattern of government created for the poverty-stricken and localized society of the ninth and tenth centuries.

In the centuries of political disintegration the centrifugal feudal element had nearly overwhelmed the monarchical. In the twelfth and thirteenth centuries, however, feudal monarchs who could generally enforce their rights brought the monarchical element into balance with the feudal. This development occurred in France and England; it aborted in Germany. Whereas only West Frankland could be used as a suitable model of tenth- and eleventh-century feudal monarchy, England and even Germany can illustrate the characteristics and problems of the feudal monarchy of the High Middle Ages.

For didactic purposes France, though not the earliest to achieve a strong feudal monarchy, provides the best example, for there is almost a straight evolutionary line from the feudal anarchy of the eleventh century to the strong but still feudal monarchy of Saint Louis IX (1226–1270). French development may be followed step by step, logically and progressively, in a way not possible elsewhere. Louis VI the Fat (1108–1137), and Louis VII (1137–1180) gained control over the royal demesne, and Philip II Augustus (1180–1223) greatly expanded it. The kings slowly gained the strength to assert their rights as suzerain. To cap the structure Philip Augustus and Saint Louis presided over the development of new monarchical institutions of government.

England developed an effective feudal monarchy extremely early, more than a century before France did, but its pattern of development was irregular, and it is therefore not so useful a model. It began abruptly with the Norman Conquest; the anarchy of 1135–1154 interrupted its development; and, after it reached a pinnacle of systematic organization under the Angevin Henry II (1154–1189), it had to suffer the weak reigns of Richard Lion-Heart (1189–1199), John (1199–1216), and Henry III (1216–1272). Nonetheless, the framework of government constructed by William the Conqueror (1066–1087), Henry I (1100–1135), and Henry II was so strong that it survived and thrived through almost a century of royal misrule, an institutional accomplishment of no mean proportions.

The German monarchy was handicapped by archaism and universalism and never succeeded in entering upon the path followed by England after the conquest and more gradually by France a century or so later. The Salian kings, such as Henry IV (1056–1106), the contemporary of William the Conqueror, looked back, as had the Saxons before them, to try to emulate the empire of Charlemagne. They repeatedly wasted their energies and resources in attempting to play the role of emperors of Rome. The bitter struggle over investitures between Henry IV and that other representative of universalism, the Roman pontiff Gregory VIII, wrecked the monarchy and opened Germany to destructive, though never fully developed, feudalism. The great magnates emerged with the gains, as had the magnates of West Frankland in the strife-torn ninth century. Frederick Barbarossa (1152–1190) strove valiantly to establish an effective feudal monarchy, but he did not succeed in restraining the particularism from which Germany continued to suffer until the age of Bismarck.

In order to stress the common themes dominant in a pre-national age, we will approach the growth of strong feudal monarchy analytically, instead of treating France, England, and Germany separately. This technique results in a sacrifice of chronological development in each country but has the advantage of emphasizing a model of monarchical development against which the various monarchies can be measured. Each of the feudal monarchs first strove to establish control over a large and prosperous demesne. When they had gained this minimal basis of strength, they began to enforce their feudal rights against the great vassals. Finally they developed monarchical institutions. The three steps are not sharply divided chronologically, but, despite overlapping, there is an ordered and logical progression. As the monarchical element grew stronger, specialized bodies slowly evolved out of the undifferentiated feudal court, the curia regis. More effective means of exercising the authority of the central government at the local level were devised. Professional officials of modest origins and greater loyalty to the king were employed to man the new institutions. Greater armies, less dependent upon the vassals of the king, were put into the field. All this was supported by a growth in the financial resources of the monarchs. In England, precocious as it was in the growth of kingship, the feudality reacted vigorously in the thirteenth century to keep the balance of feudal and monarchical elements from swinging decisively against them, resulting in the constitutionalism of the Magna Carta and, less directly, the beginnings of the rise of Parliament.

The demesne consisted of the lands under the direct rule of the king, free from the intervention of magnates who were the tenants-in-chief of the crown. It was a feudal king's secure base and the source of most of his income. If monarchical power were to grow, a king required firm control over a sizable, strategically located, and wealthy royal demesne. This was obtained at an early date in England when after 1066 William the Conqueror simply retained for himself 15 per cent of the land while seeing to it that his followers gained no comparable bases of power. This gave the English king a tremendous advantage over his own vassals and over his Capetian rival. The French kings did not at so early a date enjoy the privileges of conquest. Throughout most of the twelfth century, in fact, Louis VI and his son Louis VII had to struggle to regain firm control over the petty vassals of the Ile-de-France, the Capetian royal demesne, thus beginning modestly two hundred years of virtually uninterrupted growth of royal power. At the beginning of the thirteenth century Philip II Augustus seized the most important of the French possessions of the English king, including the prosperous and well-governed duchy of Normandy, incorporating them in a demesne that was at once quadrupled. From this time, in place of feeble and insecure feudal incomes, the Capetians would dispose of superior financial resources. Normandy, in particular, as a result of its relationship since 1066 with the advanced English monarchy, provided a model of strong feudal institutions, which the Capetians could adopt for their own purposes. In Germany when Frederick Barbarossa came to the throne in 1152 the royal demesne of his predecessors was depleted. His only real base of authority was his own familial duchy of Swabia. Unlike the Ile-de-France, however, and the later accretions to the French royal demesne, Swabia was not the possession of a monarchy becoming fairly clearly hereditary but merely of the house of Hohenstaufen, where it would remain when the kingship passed to another dynasty. Modern scholarship holds that Frederick's invasions of Italy, once thought to represent the vain pursuit of the old Carolingian imperial dream, were a rational effort to gain alternative financial resources. Although his well-known campaigns in Lombardy failed before the combined strength of the Lombard towns and the papacy, he did gain sources of great wealth in central Italy. In Germany, however, when in 1180 Frederick defeated and humiliated Henry the Lion, possessor of the two great duchies Saxony and Bavaria, and confiscated his fiefs, he was unable to achieve what Philip Augustus accomplished a quarter-century later, the assimilation of the forfeited fiefs into the demesne. The German magnates, whose support against Henry the Lion was essential, granted it only on condition that Frederick accept the principle that all forfeited lands would be granted in fief within a year and a day. Several eminent scholars believe that a German legal principle required this redistribution of the confiscated fiefs, but the better view, summarized in the recent biography of Barbarossa by Peter Munz, is that the emperor was driven by political necessity. Whatever its reason, the precedent constituted a permanent obstacle to the growth of a German royal demesne. The English kings had gained a sizable and wealthy demesne in the late eleventh century, and the French Capetians had expanded theirs in the early thirteenth, but the German kings never gained this essential basis for the growth of an effective feudal monarchy.

The second stage in the development of strong feudal monarchy was the successful assertion of the rights of the king as suzerain. In England William the Conqueror, after retaining vast demesnes for himself, granted the remainder of the land of his foes to his followers in return for the service of four or five thousand knights. His vassals were not permitted to erect unauthorized castles, which might be used to defy the king. During the anarchy of 1139–1154 this prohibition was widely violated, and an early and important work of Henry II was to reassert and enforce it. In 1086 William the Conqueror also exacted the Oath of Salisbury Plain from all landholders of substance, requiring that they swear allegiance to him before all others. Replacing the old Anglo-Saxon council, he introduced into England the continental curia regis as the highest feudal court of appeal. The conquest enabled William to establish at once a rational and well-ordered feudal pattern. In France a half-century later Louis VI was able to enjoy only a few minor successes beyond the Ile-de-France. A limited number of appeals began to come to the French king's court from subvassals who claimed not to have received justice in the courts of their immediate lords. Philip Augustus had great success in enforcing his rights as head of the feudal hierarchy. He increased the feudal levy, squeezing out many intermediate lords, making more knights immediate vassals of the king. He had some success in restraining private warfare, and he made great use of feudal warranties and hostages whereby subvassals guaranteed the lawful behavior of intermediate lords. Under the saintly Louis IX the right of the subvassals to appeal unjust decisions to the king's court was more widely recognized. All this still falls short, however, of English institutional development a century earlier. In Germany, on that same occasion in 1180 when Barbarossa took his revenge on Henry the Lion for refusing to aid the king in Lombardy, he did succeed in asserting his feudal rights. Henry, at least according to Frederick's interpretation, had been disloyal, so his fiefs were confiscated and new and loyal men were raised to high estate. This did not crush Henry's power, however, for Germany had never become thoroughly feudalized and he possessed many lands of his own (allods) in addition to his lost fiefs. Thus, although the English kings had been able to enforce their feudal rights after the Norman Conquest and the French rulers followed gradually in the twelfth and thirteenth centuries, the German king's suzerainty, like his ability to construct a royal demesne, was extremely limited.

The feudal element and the monarchical element were not distinct. Feudalism assumed kingship, just as monarchy in those centuries based itself upon feudalism. As the imbalance of the tenth and eleventh centuries was redressed, the feudal elements shaded into the monarchical. Nowhere is the transition more clearly shown than in the evolution of the curia regis. In origin it was a characteristic feudal body, the assembly of the king's vassals, along with his few officials, gathered to perform their duty of aiding him in governing. It was undifferentiated and unspecialized, not clearly distinguishing judical, adminis-trative, and legislative functions, or possessing much in the way of special skills. As the economy revived and the work of royal government increased, the whole curia, including the vassals who had interests and responsibilities else-where, could not be in continuous session, so there appeared a smaller curia, dominated by the ministers of the king. This functioned on behalf of the larger body in the intervals between assemblies to conduct the routine tasks of government. The smaller curia was much more amenable to the will of the king, and its increasing importance marked a major advance for monarchy.

Royal government also became more effective as specialized bodies grew out of the originally undifferentiated curia. This happened gradually as increas-ingly technical tasks fell into the hands of those competent to handle them. Chancery emerged as a specialized body of clerks under the chancellor respon-sible for the increasingly burdensome task of writing the king's letters and doc-uments. With the increase of wealth royal finance became more and more complex, so that smaller bodies of financial specialists emerged from the royal courts. In England the Exchequer began to appear in the twelfth century un-der Henry I and was quite clearly defined under Henry II. Its routine records, the first we have from the Middle Ages, are known as the pipe rolls, incom-plete for the reign of the former king but continuous under the latter. As in other developments, France trailed behind English government in the twelfth century, for the Chambre des Comptes did not begin to emerge until the reign of Philip Augustus, and it received its developed form only in the fourteenth century. Another increasingly specialized task was the administration of justice, necessitating the appearance of professional courts. The English Exchequer had a judicial aspect with regard to debts owed the crown, the origin of the jurisdiction of this first of the three common law courts. Early in the thirteenth century the other two appeared, as the Court of Common Pleas was fixed at Westminster for the convenience of litigants, while King's Bench continued to follow the peregrinations of the king. Not until the reign of Saint Louis did the Parlement of Paris begin to specialize out of the undifferentiated French curia. Other activities of government that were not so technical were not specialized so early.

One test of the success of a monarchy was its ability to integrate central authority and local government. Since local government was the stronghold and the very heart of the power of the feudality, the devices used to increase royal power on the local level had to be nonfeudal in origin. A great advantage to William the Conqueror and his successors was the Anglo-Saxon heritage of sheriffs and shire and hundred courts. William also initiated the Domesday Inquest, a survey of the entire land in 1086, to learn what rights he had inherited from the Anglo-Saxon monarchs. Much earlier than elsewhere in northern Europe the English rulers had established the king's peace over the entire realm, making an act of violence an offense against the king and subject to royal justice. Through the use of the new possessory assizes Henry II's judges would even restore a plaintiff in possession of lands from which he had been disseized pending the determination of right. The king's law was justice common to all England, or the common law. It was made more effective when Henry I intermittently and Henry II on a regular basis sent out itinerant justices from the royal court to bring the king's law to the people. The itinerant justices or sheriffs summoned juries of presentment (precursors of grand juries) to charge those suspected of serious crimes. Juries also came to be employed as expert witnesses for determining the facts in civil cases and, after the outlawing of the ordeal in 1215, in criminal cases as well. These royal devices nearly overwhelmed the feudal system in England. No other medieval government, save that of Norman Sicily, approached the English in the effectiveness of royal authority throughout the realm. France lagged far behind. Not until the early thirteenth century did Philip Augustus institute new paid officials called *baillis* and *sénéschaux,* whose salaries and tenure were at his will, to form a link between royal and local governments. He modeled them upon the officials used by the English kings for their continental possessions. Saint Louis, who desired no more than his rights as a feudal monarch, found it necessary to appoint *enquêteurs* to restrain the zeal of other royal officials.

These ministers of the king and many lesser officials were often of modest origins, not possessed of independent wealth and power, like the great vassals, but dependent upon royal favor. One of the best known was Suger, who rose from poverty to become abbot of the royal monastery of St. Denis and served as regent while Louis VII was on crusade, from 1147 to 1149. Even more famous, because of his subsequent martyrdom, was the English chancellor Thomas Becket. Among the royal servants were petty nobles and middle-class clerics, more and more of them trained in law or in the new notarial discipline. For years of distinguished service a clerk might hope to be rewarded with ecclesiastical preferment, perhaps ultimately, like Becket, with a great bishopric. Laymen of comparable importance received money fiefs. On the lower levels of service the payment of royal wages was increasingly common. Even businessmen, once regarded with scorn, were employed in high positions, as when Philip Augustus, departing on crusade, left the Great Seal and the royal treasure in the custody of six merchants. The new officials did not think in feudal terms, and they saw their own advancement in the expansion of royal power.

In military force the English kings also had a great advantage. William the Conqueror retained the militia of freemen, a pre-feudal Germanic inheritance that had survived in Anglo-Saxon England, while it disappeared in France. Under William's successors it was allowed to lapse, but the vigorous Henry II restored it by the Assize of Arms of 1181, for it made the king less dependent upon his vassals. In 1166 Henry had also seen to it that all those who held fiefs and owed military service to his vassals offered allegiance to him, thus negating the possibility that a vassal would command a feudal levy larger than his own military obligation to the king.

Fundamental to most of these changes, of course, were the financial resources of the king. The demesne as the feudal king's basic source of wealth has been mentioned, as have various supplementary feudal incomes. A distinctly feudal device, adapted, like the curia regis, to changed conditions, was scutage, a cash payment in lieu of knights' service. Scutage is a splendid example of the adaptability of the feudal monarchy of the twelfth and thirteenth centuries to the new economic substructure and of its transitional character between the poor feudal monarchies of the earlier period and the later national monarchies. King's preferred scutage, since it offered much greater flexibility, a peculiar virtue of money, than did feudal military service. Under the Assize of Arms Henry II succeeded in claiming scutage not for the service of the four or five thousand knights directly owed to the king but for all those knights enfeoffed by his vassals, one more manifestation of the strength of twelfth-century English monarchy. Royal incomes were added to feudal ones. Kings customarily had a right to export and import duties, which naturally increased with the expansion of trade. William the Conqueror and his successors continued to collect for special purposes the Anglo-Saxon gelds (general land taxes), the only national direct taxes in northern Europe at this time. Much later, the Capetians gained a new source of income through the obligation of communes and abbeys on the royal demesne to supply sergents (soldiers below the rank of knights) to the king as set forth in the *Prisée des Sergents* (*Levy of Sergeants*) of 1194. These obligations were promptly commuted to payments in cash to the great advantage of the king. So feudal incomes were adapted and royal revenues added to swell the coffers of twelfth- and thirteenth-century monarchs. The needs of the improved governments, however, exceeded even the expanded resources.

This was particularly true in England, where Henry II, building on the foundations of William the Conqueror and Henry I, had constructed a monarchical government strong enough to function, and especially to provide revenues, during the prolonged absence of the king on the continent. In face of the royal initiatives, the feudal forces had to struggle to preserve the contractual concept of government. The magnates had exacted from Henry I in 1101 a Coronation Charter promising to respect their feudal rights and renouncing the abuses of his two predecessors. Henry II also issued a charter of liberties. The culmination of this baronial effort was the Magna Carta forced from King John in 1215. It was a conservative document representing an attempt to redress the balance of power, which had been shifting strongly against the feudality in favor of the king. Fundamentally feudal (and clerical), the Magna Carta did contain some provisions favoring the towns and some protecting all freemen. Designed chiefly for the protection of the feudal magnates, it restricted the king's power to extort money for reliefs, wardships, and marriages of widows and heiresses. The necessity of gaining the consent of his vassals for extraordinary aids was affirmed. To posterity, it has stood for constitutionalism, the primacy of law; posterity has generally been ignorant that it was based upon the conservative principle of the feudal contract. An interesting aspect of the Magna Carta and other efforts by the feudal magnates in England and elsewhere to redress the balance of power in their own favor was that they showed no inclination to destroy the structure of twelfth- and thirteenth-century feudal monarchy. The order that it had bestowed had benefited them, as well as the common people, so they fought only to restrict and control it.

A makeshift pattern of government offering only crude protection against external enemies and internal violence to a localized society no longer had appeal for a booming urban society stimulated by an active interregional commerce. It no longer appealed to the local feudal lords themselves. Stronger central governments were needed, and the enhanced economic prosperity provided the necessary resources to strengthen the monarchical element in feudal monarchy.

Bureaucracy

Every institution had to adapt to the economic revolution of the High Middle Ages, and the success of its adaptation determined whether the institution flourished or withered. In the ninth century feudalism was an adaptation to a localized and agricultural society; its raison d'être disappeared with the revival of a money economy. The strong feudal monarchies of the twelfth and thirteenth centuries and the emerging national states at the end of the thirteenth century successfully exploited the opportunities offered by the economic revival to overcome feudal localism and to become more centralized and more efficient. Government assumed a larger role than previously. There were many more and more significant contacts between government and governed. Numerous and capable officials were required to preside over the courts and collect revenues. Loyal to the ruler upon whom their careers depended, these officials were the sinews of government, and they contributed greatly to the development of public authority. They formed a new institution, universal in a different way, the bureaucracy. Not only the kings of England and France, but the emperor, the church, the city-state, and the surviving feudal magnates employed the new professional civil servants. In the history of political institutions the growth of bureaucracy is at least as important as the closely interdependent rise of monarchy, and it is certainly more significant than the achievements of this or that monarch, even a Henry II or a Philip Augustus. The administrators were usually of similar background and education. They functioned in much the same manner everywhere. They may even be considered interchangeable parts in similar governmental machines, and, in fact, during a long transitional period, foreigners, especially Italians, were often engaged.

The current model of bureaucracy, based on nineteenth- and twentieth-century experience, includes factors such as payment of regular salaries, specialization of function, qualification for office, and a hierarchical structure of authority. Medieval bureaucracy does not precisely match this modern model. The standard is useful, however, in giving us a means for measuring the extent of bureaucratization in the Middle Ages.

A key characteristic of the new officials was that they were salaried. The feudal custom, because of the lack of money, had been to grant a fief to the vassal, who exercised jurisdiction over it. This was fraught with problems because the recipient established hereditary rights over his land and his authority. Salaried officials were much more subject to the ruler's control than were vassals. The change came gradually. For a transitional period certain intermediate forms of remuneration, such as income-producing church benefices or even money fiefs, were common.

Another important characteristic of bureaucracy was differentiation and specialization of function. Each official was increasingly responsible for a certain kind of government business, although especially trusted servants continued to receive special assignments outside their customary field of activity, as they still do. The technical areas of drafting documents, law, and finance split off earliest from the generalized service.

Closely related to differentiation and specialization was qualification for office. Inherited status, social position, and personal considerations became less important than specialized training as the tasks of officials became technical and complex.

The keeping and systematizing of records also were important in the development of bureaucracy. Records represent an accumulation of knowledge and experience available for future reference. By their use the exercise of authority can be reduced to a defined and sophisticated routine. The officials who control the store of knowledge possess an instrument of great power.

A bureaucratic structure possesses distinct levels of authority through which the successful bureaucrat ascends as his career progresses. In a fully developed bureaucratic system there is a chain of command, although it was typical of the emergent bureaucracy of the Middle Ages that the highest authority (for example, the king) often intervened directly at the lower levels, by-passing and undercutting the intermediate officials. Whether directly from the top or through a chain of command the various activities were allocated and coordinated.

The older feudal administration, such as it was, was based upon the household of the ruler. The household officials—the steward, the chamberlain, and others—were in the domestic service of the lord. Those of a great lord, such as a king, were of very high status, the more personal service being the most exalted. Some of them early acquired public functions. The chancellor, who was usually the best educated of the household officials, acquired a staff of clerks constituting the writing office. It followed naturally that the chancellor also gained custody of the lord's seal. Since the chamberlain was in charge of the lord's valuables, he became the first financial officer, and he too soon required a staff of clerks. As professionalization of government progressed, other household offices, such as those of the steward and the marshal, became primarily honorific.

At about the beginning of the twelfth century (the date varies from place to place), bureaucratic administration was barely embryonic. The chancellor and the chamberlain, the most important members of the household, were usually neither great vassals nor true bureaucrats. They were almost always clerics of modest background who may have been educated at a cathedral school, entered the service of their lords as clerks, and risen to high position as they gained his favor. They were not yet paid a fixed salary but were rewarded with benefices. Their specialization and functional differentiation were not great; they often performed various tasks the ruler assigned them. They also still owed the domestic duties with which their offices had first been associated.

The twelfth century saw the beginning of the transformation of this pre-bureaucratic administration into the true medieval bureaucracy. Kings, in their efforts to establish their authority over the territories they nominally ruled, required new sources of revenue and legal justifications. These in turn demanded the creation of administrative organizations, extensive records, and a loyal, full-time, salaried staff with a greater degree of specialization. In short, a bureaucracy had to be created.

Bureaucratization did not occur simultaneously in all areas of government. Perhaps the most laggard has always been diplomacy, where, even today, ambassadors are often drawn from outside the professional service. In medieval diplomacy prestige and display were even more important than they are now, so wealthy and powerful nobles and bishops always headed important missions. Even in the diplomatic field, though, in the thirteenth century lawyers and notaries served as secretaries of missions to carry out the routine work and to provide professional expertise to the dignified ambassadors. No specialized foreign service developed, however, although G. P. Cuttino has revealed the barest hint of one in fourteenth-century England. In general, lawyers, notaries, and clerks were drawn from their regular duties and assigned to diplomatic tasks.

Financial administration, on the other hand, involves a lot of detailed technical work and therefore lent itself to early specialization and bureaucratization. Bryce Lyon and A. E. Verhulst have written a comparative study of medieval financial institutions in England, Normandy, Flanders, and France. In each area, the bureaucratic financial administration grew out of the household administration under the chamberlain. By 1200 England, Flanders, and Normandy possessed continuous financial records kept in similar fashion. They had separated the treasury and the keeping of accounts. The enlarged treasury no longer followed the court but split off under a treasurer. Regular sessions of the court reviewed accounts and considered the legal questions involved in finance. Most important, each of these specialized and functionally differentiated bodies was staffed by professional bureaucrats. France at first lagged behind the others, but with the conquests of Philip Augustus and the absorption of well-governed Normandy into the royal demesne, Capetian government swiftly narrowed the gap.

A class of men possessing the professional skills and imbued with the values necessary to staff the burgeoning bureaucracies was produced by the universities. The older cathedral school had offered a broad and liberal education with considerable emphasis on the classics, but it had not provided its students with specialized vocations, such as law. The early university, on the other hand, was not a center of liberal learning but was extremely professional in its orientation. It was the training ground and the licensing agency for the young men who wished to enter the administration of church and state. By the middle of the twelfth century it was clear that the futures of the professional bureaucracy and the university were intimately linked.

The backbone of every administration was made up of clerks and notaries trained in the *ars dictaminis* or the *ars notaria,* the writing of business letters and legal documents. To provide himself with well-trained notaries, Frederick II founded the University of Naples in 1224. According to the tradition of the older *ars dictaminis,* the student learned grammar and rhetoric and, as the requirements of commerce increased, the forms of business letters. The *ars notaria* was more specifically oriented to the drafting of legal and governmental documents. The top levels of administration were commonly occupied by more highly educated lawyers. Legal education at the universities was much lengthier and more demanding than notarial training, which was of the "how to do it" variety.

It is not without reason that the thirteenth century has been called the century of the lawyers. Judges, lawyers, and notaries with some legal training formed the age in their own mold. The government of Frederick II (1220–

1250) provides a clear testimony to the importance of the law and the professionals who administered it. The emperor's most important official was Piero della Vigna, who had been trained as a notary and lawyer at Bologna. Della Vigna himself was probably the author of the Constitutions of Melfi, in which the outlines of the centralized state were set forth. He also exerted his influence over the University of Naples and its education of students for the bureaucracy. The lawyer-counselors of Philip IV, such as Pierre Flotte and Guillaume Nogaret, are also famous. From the thirteenth century, even in the ecclesiastical hierarchy, lawyers were more likely than theologians to rise through the ranks to the papacy—and for good reason, for they were better trained to govern a vast and complex institution.

In the Roman Law and the canon law derived from it lawyers and statesmen found at hand a structure of constitutional, juridical, and political concepts consonant with the emerging outlines of the new society. They employed it to fill in the outlines. In the early Middle Ages political issues and institutions had been clothed in religious garb. Monarchy was surrounded with sacred ceremonies and symbolism. Theorists wrote of the delegation of authority by God and sought sanction in sometimes strained citations of the Scriptures and Church Fathers. This fashion did not suddenly disappear, of course, and vestiges of it survive today, but it did not really suit the new secular society. Legal concepts did, and with the rise of Roman Law politics began to adopt the legal dress in fashion for centuries. Lawyers found increasing employment in government, beginning the domination they seized from churchmen and have continued to enjoy.

Polemicists searched the Roman and canon law for concepts to support their positions. They discovered a mélange of principles, for the constitutional concepts of earlier republican jurists had found their way into the Justinian codification along with the absolutistic ideas of the late empire. The French monarchy fastened upon the absolutistic threads exalting the power of the ruler. England made more use of those that were constitutional, emphasizing the obligation of the monarch to govern according to law. Among the provisions exploited for establishing the principles of representation and consent was the well-known *Quod omnes tangit ab omnibus approbetur (What touches all must be approved by all)*. In general the maxims of Roman Law tended to strengthen the power of the state. In contrast to feudal society, where private relationships predominated, Roman Law reintroduced the concept of the *res publica,* not the "republic" but the commonwealth. The impersonal tie of public law between king and subject began to supplant the personal feudal relationship of lord and vassal. Kings learned that they had a duty to promote the common welfare and to preserve the *status regni* ("state of the kingdom"), another new abstraction. They found it easier to gain financial aid through the Roman practice of corporate representation and full powers, by which representatives could bind their constituents to payment. Lawyers discussed the maxim that "necessity knows no law," and the extremely influential *Glossa Ordinaria,* the standard commentary on the Roman Law, even adopted it. The new servants of the rising state thus were armed with a formidable array of ideological weapons.

In the fourteenth and fifteenth centuries, the bureaucrats became increasingly professional. They served longer apprenticeships, were more specialized, and followed more detailed and routine procedures. Nevertheless, one must not exaggerate the degree of bureaucratization in the High and late Middle Ages. Medieval practice did not conform to the nineteenth- and twentieth-century model. Personal relationships (which even now cannot be ignored) were much more important than modern theory would allow. The able man was often called upon to perform a variety of tasks, a practice counter to the principle of differentiation and specialization. Sometimes a single office was split between two incumbents, so that each might serve as a check on the other, thus violating the concept of a unified hierarchy of control. The payment of salaries only gradually prevailed over the use of benefices, money fiefs, and other semi-feudal devices. Even in the late Middle Ages rulers had to take precautions against the tendency of offices to become hereditary. The bureaucratization of medieval governments was far from complete.

Still, the development of bureaucratic government and a tradition of professionalism is one of the most important and enduring contributions of the Middle Ages to the history of government. The bureaucracy of the thirteenth century continued to develop through the turmoil of the fourteenth and fifteenth centuries. It served well the absolute monarchs of early modern times. Its importance in our own day is clear enough, and its vices are commonly cursed. Our brief glance at its medieval origins, revealing its superiority over feudal government, may remind us of its virtues.

Beginnings of National Monarchies

Under the rubric of "feudal monarchy" we have considered medieval governments where the feudal element outweighed the monarchical, like early Capetian France, as well as those in which the elements were almost evenly balanced, like twelfth-century England and thirteenth-century France. The equilibrium of the strong feudal monarchies, however, was precarious. The raison d'être of feudalism—to provide minimal governance for a localized society capable of sustaining nothing more—had passed away with the coming of the economic revolution, and the feudal element became a long surviving anachronism. By the end of the thirteenth century England and France became emergent nation states. Categories such as "feudal monarchy" and "national monarchy" possess a certain arbitrariness, for there is no sharp line between them. The fluid, complex institutions themselves are the stuff of history; the historian merely attempts to emphasize trends by using categories such as "feudal" and "national," which are only mental constructs. In reality there was much overlapping. National characteristics such as common law appeared very early in English history, but they existed in the twelfth century side by side with substantial feudal elements, including a king whose interests centered upon his continental fiefs.

The first of the western European polities where national characteristics prevailed over feudal was Norman Sicily, contemporary with Norman and Angevin England. Textbooks commonly pay far too little attention to it, probably because the early seeds of nationalism failed to bear modern fruit there. France and England did not achieve national monarchies of a similar sort until the late thirteenth and early fourteenth centuries under Philip IV (1285–1314) and Edward I (1272–1307). Germany and Italy did not become nation states until the nineteenth century.

The most precocious of the national states was twelfth-century Norman Sicily. The conquest of the island by Roger de Hauteville from 1061 to 1091 is much less well known than the contemporary feat of William the Conqueror, but until the collapse of the Norman state after 1250 it was certainly no less significant. Like William, Roger (1085–1101) established a highly centralized feudalism. His followers also received scattered fiefs as their reward, and he too ordered a survey of his rights in 1088. Roger took over, as did William, a nonfeudal military force, a tax on property, and strong local institutions. He too combined and integrated the institutions of his predecessors, in this case Greeks and Muslims, with Norman feudalism. Roger, however, succeeded to a land much wealthier and more advanced than England, already possessing a real bureaucracy, educated, specialized, salaried, and subject to the will of the ruler. Roger inherited a central financial and judicial institution, the Islamic *diwan,* which was far advanced in record keeping.

On these foundations his son and successor, Roger II (count, 1105–1130; king, 1130–1154), one of the great state builders of the Middle Ages, constructed the first national monarchy far in advance of the most successful of the northern kingdoms. In 1127 he seized Apulia and subsequently had himself crowned king of the combined Norman lands in Sicily and South Italy, henceforth called the Regno, or Kingdom. Roger II combined the assimilative and organizational ability of the Normans with the government experience and institutions of the Greeks and Muslims to form the strongest government in western Europe, free of dependence upon the feudal class. The government was run by professional bureaucrats, mostly businessmen, many of them foreigners, including Muslims. These officials were economically enlightened and efficient. They managed the royal demesne, collected taxes, and fostered the economy. In the Regno, in fact, we can discern a proto-mercantile system, a conscious strengthening of the economy for the sake of the power of the state.

The government possessed monopolies on lumber, salt, and other important products. The judicial system was highly centralized with appeals culminating in the *strategoi* and the viscounts. (Notice the mixture of Byzantine and feudal titles.) Roger II even controlled a national church in the Regno as papal legate, an unprecedented role for a secular ruler. In addition to his feudal vassals and infantry from his demesne the king employed many mercenary troops, and he did not hesitate to use Muslims, even against Christians. He also constructed a powerful fleet, the lack of which had been the Normans' greatest weakness. By the end of Roger's reign in 1154, the naval power of the Regno was greater than that of Venice, Genoa, or Pisa.

The Regno achieved the peak of its political development under Emperor Frederick II (king, 1197–1250; emperor, 1212–1250) in the first half of the thirteenth century. In 1194 it had come into possession of the German emperor Henry VI (1190–1197), son and heir of Frederick Barbarossa. Three years later Henry died, leaving the kingdom by inheritance to his half-Norman infant son Frederick. Upon reaching majority and gaining the imperial crown, Frederick undertook to build up the strength of the Regno, which had deteriorated during his childhood and the struggle for the empire. He planned to use the southern kingdom, according to his biographer Ernst Kantorowicz, as a base for gaining control over the empire. He never achieved this, but in the Regno he established a centralized bureaucratic absolutism. He promulgated an authoritarian code of law, the Constitutions of Melfi, which enhanced the king's authority and restricted that of all others. The large bureaucracy not only controlled the law, public works, taxes, and the like, but even business and agriculture. Regular direct taxes had not been a part of the early medieval pattern of government, but it gradually was recognized that a ruler might demand financial aid in case of necessity. The rise of mercenary armies and salaried bureaucracies made the necessity permanent, so Frederick claimed almost regular annual taxes, though he continued to preserve the fiction of singular emergency. The power of the feudality was crushed. The development of a national monarchy had a strong impact upon education and the orientation of learning, for Frederick founded a university at Naples to educate servants of the state. Upon the Constitutions of Melfi, the curriculum of the University of Naples, and the whole of the Regno, the influence of the Roman Law, codified under the autocrat Justinian, was great. Frederick's lifework, impressive as it was, however, was not enduring. During most of his reign he was in bitter conflict with the papacy, which, after his death in 1250, enlisted Charles of Anjou to conquer the Regno. Before the end of the thirteenth century it was divided and the elaborate government structure fell to pieces. It had been a precocious but not enduring experiment in national monarchy.

France continued to display a remarkably gradual development of monarchy until the fourteenth century. Philip Augustus and Saint Louis created a strong feudal kingship. Anticipatory signs of nationalism were also present during this period. Philip's triumphal procession to Paris after his great victory at Bouvines in 1214 hints at the growth of national patriotism. Although Saint Louis tried meticulously not to infringe upon the feudal rights of his vassals, his pious and just character endowed the French crown with an extraordinary aura of sanctity, which strengthened national feeling. At the end of the thirteenth century Philip IV created a national monarchy, subordinating all more limited jurisdictions to the crown. Ironically, the gradual growth of royal power and the slow decline of the feudal class in France gave the Capetians some advantages over their more advanced rivals across the Channel. The survival of provincialism in France proved an advantage to the monarchy, which did not have to face united opposition. On the other hand, not so much authority passed into the hands of local bodies because a national bureaucracy had time to develop gradually to take over as feudal government receded. The royal officials vigorously extended the powers and revenues of the king, for thus they enhanced their own importance.

Under Philip IV, as government became increasingly complex, specialized institutions continued to split off from the curia regis. The Chambre des Comptes, the financial office, was gradually emerging, although it traditionally counts its institution only from 1320. In the other field of early expertise and specialization, the judicial, the Parlement of Paris, the high court of France, had begun to emerge from the undifferentiated curia in the reign of Saint Louis, and it gained official status between 1278 and 1320. The Parlement itself developed three separate chambers for specialized tasks, with a fourth for cases coming from southern France where Roman Law prevailed. The right of appeal from lower jurisdictions to the Parlement of Paris was a significant step toward French nationhood and a source of conflict with the English king, who held southwestern France as a fief from the French crown. On several occasions Philip IV convened his vassals along with representatives of the communes to hear and support the monarchy on some specific issue. These national assemblies of the early fourteenth century were to enhance royal power, not to oppose the monarchy or to share power with it.

The need for money for war dominated Philip's reign. Warfare had become vastly more expensive than in the feudal age, and as kings became aware of what they could accomplish with increased financial resources their needs outdistanced the expansion of their incomes. Philip resorted to oppressive taxation, including the then questionable taxation of the clergy, which led to the first great conflict between the universal church and the new nationalism. Like Frederick II, Philip IV preserved the fiction of extraordinary necessity, but in the following century the fiction was dropped. The enquêteurs that the saintly Louis had instituted to redress wrongs were used by Philip to scour the land for money. He negotiated for extraordinary aids with local assemblies, not like the English kings with a national parliament. Although much less convenient than the English system, in the long run this was to be an advantage to the French monarchy, for the local assemblies had less power to resist and the national assembly did not become like its English counterpart a partner in government.

The English monarchy, enjoying the advantages of the Norman Conquest and the creative efforts of William the Conqueror, Henry I, and Henry II, had a considerable headstart on France in the development of a national state. It had early developed a common law, shire and hundred courts, sheriffs and itinerant justices. The early appearance of a strong, centralized, feudal monarchy in the twelfth century, however, had left much of local administration, which was reasonably well integrated with the central government, in the hands of landholders of the area. A royal bureaucracy, more amenable to the will of the king, did not develop as fully at the local level as in France, which had not achieved an effective feudal monarchy so quickly.

Under Edward I at the end of the thirteenth century, however, the English bureaucracy was gaining in size and authority, though it was less numerous and powerful than the bureaucracy in France. One of Edward's main tasks, in fact, was to by-pass earlier bureaucratic innovations such as the Exchequer and the Chancery, which had gone out of court, achieved institutional forms of their own, and could no longer be controlled easily by the king. Edward fell back upon his private household. To get around the Exchequer he made the Wardrobe, the financial branch of the king's household, which formerly had relatively minor responsibilities, the principal royal treasury. Similarly the Privy Seal, kept in the Wardrobe, replaced the Great Seal controlled by the chancellor. These measures to gain greater efficiency moved away from institutionalized procedures toward more personal ones. Since our theme has been the triumph of feudalism over anarchy and of the state over feudalism, we have tended to consider institutionalization progressive. Its very advantage of dealing with a large quantity of business according to a fixed routine, however, carries with it a certain rigidity, so that the king found it necessary to restore a balance between the institutional and the personal characteristics.

Like Philip IV, Edward strove to increase royal powers at the expense of others. His great codifying statutes did much to strengthen the position of royal justice. Various statutes limited the powers of ecclesiastical courts and attempted to force the magnates to submit documentary proof of their grants of jurisdiction. The most sweeping example yet of the legislative power of the king, the statutes contributed to the growth of positive law in opposition to the ancient customary law interpreted by judges. The limitation of the judges by the codifying statutes, moreover, limited the influence of Roman and canon law, in which the great thirteenth-century jurists had been well steeped. Gradually the improved royal courts won jurisdiction from feudal courts employing obsolete procedures.

The development of the English Parliament in the late thirteenth and early fourteenth centuries was no more intended as a limitation upon royal power than were Philip IV's assemblies in France. The strength and national character of the English institution was for a time a source of strength for the king.

Germany and Italy failed to follow the French and English pattern of growth of national monarchy. The second half of the thirteenth century witnessed the definitive failure of German kingship. The efforts of Barbarossa to build an effective feudal monarchy had not succeeded. Frederick II had concentrated his efforts upon the Regno, allowing the powers of the king-emperor to decline in Germany. After the fall of Frederick's house, though the form remained, the German kingship had little significance. The nobles were dominant, especially the newer secular princes of the East. From 1254 to 1273 Germany suffered an interregnum and a farcical double election. By 1273 the fragmented character of Germany was established. After the interregnum was ended, the great princes, such as the Habsburgs and the house of Luxembourg-Bohemia, exploited the royal office, when they could obtain it, as a means of building their own strength. The famous Golden Bull of 1356, which firmly fixed the electoral procedure, in effect guaranteed the right of the princely houses to dominate a weak monarchy. Like France and England, Germany had shared in the economic revival of the twelfth and thirteenth centuries, but circumstances such as the Investiture Struggle and the late introduction of feudalism handicapped the development of a national monarchy. The development of political institutions in the western countries was reflected in Germany, but within the various principalities rather than at the national level.

Although Italy led the economic revolution and the revival of Roman Law, it also failed to give birth to a national monarchy. Italy lacked an indigenous king, unless we accept the half German and half Norman Sicilian, Frederick II. Italy developed a polity of thriving and jealously autonomous city-states, feuding with one another and rent by internal factions. The large ones tended to swallow the smaller ones, but none seriously threatened to gain national hegemony over Italy. By the end of the thirteenth century, despite the pious hopes of patriots like Dante, the fate of monarchy in medieval Italy was sealed.

Supported by the prosperity of the twelfth and thirteenth centuries and making use of legal and political concepts from Roman antiquity, the kings of Sicily, France, and England, however, had enhanced their powers and formed national monarchies. They enjoyed new incomes, were served by specialized and efficient institutions, and employed mercenary troops. One of the most important factors in the rise of the national monarchies was the growth of a skilled and salaried bureaucracy, bound by its own interest to the enhancement of royal power.

Parliamentary Institutions

The economic revival of the High Middle Ages brought in its wake the rise of a middle class of prosperous townsmen and rural landholders. The wealth of the bourgeoisie, and in England the rural gentry, gained them a political significance that none below the feudal class had enjoyed in earlier centuries. Their new political strength and consciousness was brought to bear, especially in England, through parliamentary institutions.

The word *parliament* is derived from the French word *parler* ("to speak"), and it was used broadly in the Middle Ages to signify a conference, for example, of leaders on the battlefield or of vassals performing their duty to assist the king, duke, or other feudal lord in his governmental duties by constituting his court. The feudal court gave rise to parliamentary institutions, but it is important to remember that in the beginning a parliament was not an institution but an occasion, a meeting of the court. In these assemblies no clear distinction was made between judicial, legislative, and administrative functions of government, but most of the duties of the court were judicial. Another important role was to grant consent to an extraordinary levy (or aid) required by the lord, usually for the defense of the realm. The early assemblies were not rivals of the rising monarchies but instrumentalities of royal authority. In the early days of national assemblies, the king proposed the business and the role of the parliament was to assent.

The feudal court was the basis of later medieval parliaments, but certain concepts from Roman Law—corporate personality, procuratorial representation, public utility, and common welfare—were required before the institutions could take shape. The town, the shire or province, the nation itself, had to have a sense of corporate entity and a legal recognition of that status. They also required an instrument by which one or a few could represent the many composing the corporate body. They needed a sense of their common goals. Corporate representation through a procurator probably rose first out of the necessity for monasteries and cathedral chapters to be represented by an advocate before ecclesiastical courts. Procuration with full powers was a Roman device by which a representative could perform a conclusive legal act for another person. Such representation of the middle class along with the personal attendance of the great lay and ecclesiastical lords in augmented feudal courts provided a forum in which some consensus could be attained among the most important groups concerning the new goals of the public utility or the common welfare. In this way the newly important middle class began to have a small voice in government.

Usually the public utility or the common welfare required money. The key to the rise of parliamentary institutions is taxation. The kings of the more advanced realms in England, France, and Spain were no longer able to "live of their own"—that is, off the fruits of their demesne lands and irregular and insufficient feudal revenues. The new wealth had given rise to more advanced and much more expensive forms of government. Salaried bureaucrats and mercenary soldiers were costly. Therefore the new sources of wealth, the lesser landholders and the bourgeoisie, had to be tapped. When the king felt that the consent of these new men to the levies that they would have to pay was necessary or desirable, he summoned their representatives to parliament. In the beginning they did not regard it as their right to be represented, for they would usually have preferred to try to avoid the burdens, but to respond to the summons of their lord was their duty.

The growth of parliamentary institutions was widespread in western Europe, but the developments were far from identical. Different patterns of parliamentary development emerged in England, Spain, and France.

In England parliaments in the late twelfth century consisted of the temporal and spiritual magnates with the small council of ministers of the king meeting primarily as a court of justice but also to counsel the monarch. By the thirteenth century the king maintained an expensive bureaucracy, and his ordinary revenues could not keep up with his expenditures, especially in time of war, inflation, or other crisis. He had to resort to extraordinary aids, but article 12 of the Magna Carta had confirmed the feudal custom that the king could levy no extraordinary aids without the common counsel of the realm. Since the prosperous landed gentry and the townsmen would have a considerable share in the burden, it gradually became the custom to seek the consent of their representatives. The king could summon whomever he wished to his court, although political reality required that he obtain a consensus of the most powerful and wealthy, euphemistically called in the Middle Ages the "greater and wiser part." In 1254 for the first time knights of the shire representing the landed gentry met with the magnates in parliament, and in 1265 Simon de Montfort, during his brief rule over England in rebellion against the king, summoned two knights from every shire and two burgesses from every town to parliament. For those who seek the first English Parliament (the capital letter is used purposefully), the assembly of 1265 will not do, however, for it was not summoned by the king. Edward I's parliament of 1295 is called the Model Parliament, for the king summoned not only the traditional lay and ecclesiastical magnates but two knights representing every shire and two burgesses for every town. In several ways it did not closely resemble a modern English Parliament. Notably, it also included procurators representing the lower clergy of each diocese, who later formed their own assembly. What is important, however, was that the newly wealthy classes had gained a small voice in government.

The augmented feudal parliaments in England gradually began to conceive of themselves as representing the community of the realm, the beginnings of a concept of the modern state. Their basic function remained judicial, and, as royal power grew and the prestige of the king's court made it more and more clearly the highest tribunal in the land, it was much in demand. Even today the distinction between judicial and legislative authority is not clear, and it was much less so in the Middle Ages. When questions concerning the law arose out of judicial proceedings, they were settled by statutes enacted by the king, often with the consent and perhaps the advice of Parliament. That body first began to gain initiative through petitions introduced by members for approval by the king. In time the Commons, the knights of the shire and the burgesses, learned to unite in support of petitions for the redress of grievances. These were then passed on to the magnates. If they also approved, the petitions would be submitted to the king for enactment into law. The king retained, however, the alternative of issuing statutes in his small council. In the fourteenth century Parliament discovered a coercive power that made it a partner in government rather than a humble petitioner. The king customarily summoned Parliament to gain its consent when he needed money. Soon Parliament learned to use its power to consent to or refuse financial aid to bargain with the king for his approval of its petitions.

The medieval Parliament attempted to gain control of the king's ministers, which would have introduced something very like modern parliamentary government with a cabinet, but this attempt failed. Parliament had more success in deposing kings. As a result of a baronial uprising, Edward II was tried and deposed by Parliament in 1327. Parliament went a step further in 1399, not only asserting its right to depose Richard II but assenting to the succession of Henry of Lancaster instead of the apparent heir. No medieval parliament achieved or even conceived of parliamentary supremacy, but the English Parliament did gain real and significant powers.

With hindsight it appears surprising that the English mother of parliaments was preceded by parliamentary bodies in the several Spanish kingdoms, for Spain has been known since the Middle Ages for autocratic government. Perhaps nowhere other than in Italy, however, did towns and townsmen flourish so vigorously so early. The role played by the towns in the reconquest of the peninsula from the Muslims shaped the rise of the cortes (parliaments). The kings assumed leadership in the struggle against the Muslims, feudalism was relatively retarded, and towns owing direct allegiance to the crown were chartered in the newly conquered areas as centers of security. The military and administrative importance of these centers led to the early summons of townsmen to the king's court. As early as 1163 in Aragon and 1187 and 1188 in Castile and Leon townsmen were summoned to join the lay and ecclesiastical magnates in approving important decisions. These townsmen do not appear to have been procuratorial representatives of their town corporations. Not representatives of a "third estate," they were the ordinary magistrates of the towns in their capacity as heads of administrative subdivisions of the realm.

Unlike the English assemblies, the early cortes were summoned not for financial reasons but for purposes that might be called feudal, such as to assent to decisions concerning succession to the throne. Like the English Parliament, on the other hand, the Spanish cortes emerged from the feudal court and were primarily judicial. Before the middle of the thirteenth century, however, the financing of the wars against the Muslims had become a problem, and procurators with full powers were being asked to consent to aids in the names of their town corporations. Here, too, the right of petition gave rise to a legislative capacity, though the king remained the ultimate lawgiver. The cortes also sought guarantees of the rights of nobles and townsmen in the Acts of Leon of 1188, which have been extravagantly compared with the Magna Carta, the General Privilege of Aragon of 1283, and the Privilege of the Union, also of Aragon, in 1287.

The cortes continued to flourish from the end of the thirteenth to late in the fifteenth century, then declined before the rising autocracy of Ferdinand and Isabella. Once the Catholic kings had made use of the cortes to carry out desired reforms, they ceased to employ them. The origin of parliamentary assemblies in the feudal court meant that they were summoned at the pleasure of the lord. The cortes of Castile met only nine times between 1475 and 1503 and not at all between 1482 and 1498, perhaps the most vital period in Spanish history—that of the conquest of Granada, the discovery of America, the institution of the Spanish Inquisition, and the expulsion of the Jews. In Aragon also Ferdinand rarely summoned the assembly; he preferred to raise funds by arbitrary methods. Since he succeeded in doing so, the history of the cortes, so promising in earlier centuries, was abruptly cut off.

The development of parliamentary assemblies in medieval France differed from both the English model and the Spanish ones. The key to the difference was the tardy development of French unity. In the course of the thirteenth century, when Philip Augustus and Saint Louis constructed a strong French monarchy, the king's court became the recognized court of last resort, but the judicial function remained predominant. In sharp contrast to England, in France the word *parlement* referred to the judicial specialists of the royal court.

A national representative assembly did not develop out of the feudal court of the French kings. Provincial loyalties were so strong that no general assembly could speak for all France. Philip IV did summon assemblies augmented with representatives of the bourgeoisie on various occasions, but the role of the assemblies was passive and his purpose appears primarily propagandistic. The famous assembly of 1302 heard the king's charges against Pope Boniface VIII. That of 1308 listened to his complaints against the Templars, the trumped-up charges that were the basis for the confiscation of the order's property. In 1314 the delegates of the towns joined the magnates in Paris to hear the reasons for a new tax. No importance was attached, however, to their consent, for the tax had already been approved and the collectors had been appointed to negotiate with local assemblies. When in the middle of the fourteenth century seeking consent did become customary, it was gained in local assemblies, for no national assembly could grant it effectively. Some scholars have regarded the assembly of 1302 and its successors as the earliest Estates-General, but recent opinion would deny it. Indeed, discussions about the first this or that are semantic and antiquarian, rather than historical, for they attempt to impose a more recent model upon the functioning reality of an earlier society. Certainly, though, the early-fourteenth-century assemblies in France did not closely resemble the fully developed Estates-General.

In brief, parliamentary assemblies developed more or less fully in England, Spain, and France under the aegis of the king. New classes had gained wealth and prominence, and the feudal courts were expanded to give them recognition. Because of the late development of national unity in France, a national parliament did not evolve in the Middle Ages. The various Spanish kingdoms saw a very early blossoming of parliamentary bodies, but these were blighted as Spain began to become unified at the end of the Middle Ages. Only in England did the parliamentary plant take root in fertile soil and grow to maturity.

Late Medieval Absolutism

The economic boom that had been the stimulus and the foundation for the development of political institutions in the High Middle Ages leveled off in the late thirteenth century to be succeeded by a long and severe depression in the fourteenth and fifteenth centuries. The fourteenth century was characterized by chaos—collapse of the economy, plague, depopulation, war, civil disorder. However, the monarchical gains of the twelfth and thirteenth centuries, though threatened, were not wiped away and in time most states sought refuge from disorder under the rule of a despot. The late medieval despotic governments foreshadowed the pattern of rule which was to prevail until the French Revolution.

Although the rise of feudal and national monarchy in the High Middle Ages had spawned many political institutions, the further centralization of power in the hands of despots, at least in the early stages, was not fruitful for institutional development. The elaboration of institutions designed originally to facilitate the exercise of royal authority reached a point where they threatened the decision-making power of the despot. The problem is not peculiar to the Middle Ages. Sometimes a level of institutional complexity is reached where the decision-making power becomes attenuated and the man at the head of the institution can no longer dominate the process, various parts of which fall into the hands of specialists. As the bureaucrats became more specialized, moreover, they became less competent to deal with broad policy issues than their thirteenth-century predecessors had been. Rather than suffer blunting and fragmentation of their power, those striving to enhance centralized authority were willing to sacrifice the benefits of institutional development. Some institutional proliferation, such as the rise of the Wardrobe and the Privy Seal in England, actually represents an effort to escape the ossification of the old bureaucracy in favor of a return to personal household governments. Paul Kendall, the recent biographer of Louis XI (1461–1483) of France, puts it succinctly when he states that the king had no ministers but only devoted agents of his will.

The internal dissension, factionalism, class riots, and dynastic strife of the late Middle Ages provided the occasion for despots to grasp power. Men submitted to despotism, as they have repeatedly, to gain the cessation of turmoil and the opportunity to lead their private lives in relative peace. First of all, the Italian city-republics, torn by the strife of class and party, succumbed to rule by one man. In France the aftermath of the Hundred Years' War and the bitter struggles between the princely factions of Armagnac and Burgundy gave way to the despotism of Louis XI. Similarly in Spain the dynastic struggles and the breakdown of law and order of the reigns of John II of Aragon and Henry IV of Castile were followed by the tyranny of Ferdinand and Isabella. Even England, with its Magna Carta and its Parliament, flirted with despotism under the house of York and emerged from the dynastic wars of York and Lancaster under the strong rule of the Tudors.

The rise of the despots hastened the decline of the once powerful feudal nobility. The importance of the landed wealth of the aristocracy had dwindled before the rise of commercial riches, and its military importance had eroded in the face of new tactics and technology. For a time in the era of disorders the greatest and wealthiest of the feudal dynasties, combining old feudal ideals with new money and means of warfare, had made a last bid for power. They built great stone castles and enlisted private armies composed of recipients of money fiefs and hired mercenaries. In some ways this movement resembled the earlier feudal disintegration, so it is called bastard feudalism. But the conditions of the fourteenth and fifteenth centuries were far from those of the ninth and tenth, so the resemblance is quite superficial. The Wars of the Roses in England and the struggles between Burgundians and Armagnacs in France mark the last cruel efforts of a kind of feudalism to dominate a world in which feudalism was an anachronism. Where the foundations of strong monarchies had been laid in England, France and Spain, bastard feudalism failed before the rise of despotic monarchies. The use of the cannon in warfare, which rendered the castle, the symbol and stronghold of feudal aristocracy, vulnerable, sealed the fate of the feudality. In Germany, it is true, the great nobles had already succeeded in throwing off the royal yoke. There the rise of despotism occurred at the level of territorial dynasties rather than at that of the monarchy. Remnants of the old social order lingered on, of course, and the feudal class survived for centuries as a costly vestige of a bygone age, those in the highest ranks as courtiers, others as powerless members of an honorary elite. Although the tyrants surrounded themselves with the splendor of a court nobility, they relied for the most part upon men of humbler origins. Despotism, indeed, tended to break down the hierarchical structure of medieval society, leveling all classes under the tyrant. Some people were much wealthier than others, and some had more influence, but political power belonged to the despot alone.

Although our attention has been focused upon the rise of national monarchies, late medieval despotism appeared first in the Italian city-states, so we must at least glance at despotism south of the Alps before we turn to the two greatest despotisms of the age, the France of Louis XI and the Spain of Ferdinand (1479–1516) and Isabella (1474–1504). The northern and central portions of Italy were distinguished in the Middle Ages by the survival and early flourishing of urbanism, the weakness of feudalism, and an early revival of commerce. The prevailing polity of the High Middle Ages was the autonomous city-republic dominated by local oligarchies. These were increasingly afflicted by strife between the rich and the poor and between the old rich and the new rich. By the middle of the fourteenth century many Italian city-republics had delivered themselves into the hands of *signori* to gain respite from endemic civil strife. The great Lombard metropolis of Milan was one of the first to accept a tyrant, submitting to a brief despotism under the Della Torre as early as the thirteenth century, supplanted in the early fourteenth century by the Visconti, who assumed a ducal title in 1395. When this dynasty failed, the Milanese quixotically sought to restore the republic, only to fall swiftly under the signory of the famed mercenary Francesco Sforza (1450–1466), who established a new dynasty. In somewhat similar fashion the Estensi gained power in Ferrara, the Gonzaga in Mantua, the Montefeltro in Urbino, the Pallavicini in Cremona. The papacy itself became another Italian despotism. Florence and Venice, which retained republican forms of government, though they too adapted to the new pattern of statecraft, were atypical. After 1434 Florence fell under the boss rule of the Medici, who possessed the power of despots, though they retained republican institutions. Venice, on the other hand, developed after 1297 a sort of collective despotism of the patrician oligarchy.

The way the tyrant rose to power made his rule difficult and dangerous, for he himself had set the pernicious example of overthrowing the constituted authorities. Political life was marked by bad faith, intrigue, assassination, and poisoning. Atrocities were commonly committed in the name of "reason of state." This is hardly the setting in which stable political institutions develop. The tyrants commanded no standing armies. Mercenary troops, the *condottieri,* here today and hired by someone else tomorrow, were the mainstay of Italian despotism. One institution common to the age was the secret tribunal designed to act swiftly and arbitrarily to protect the vital interests of the government. Despite the arbitrariness of despotism toward possible rivals, however, most of the Italian despots, like the tyrants of ancient Greece, were supported by the good will of the masses, to whom they offered security and relative relief from exploitation. Sforza enjoyed great popularity. Federigo of Montefeltro was beloved by the people of Urbino.

Italian despotism lacked two closely related elements crucial to the rise of the absolute state in France and Spain—dynasties with an aura of legitimacy and popular feelings of nationalism. Like Germany, Italy failed to achieve nationhood in the Middle Ages. The petty Italian despots could not match the power of the national autocracies, so Italy became a prize contested between its powerful neighbors, France and Spain.

The incipient national monarchies in France and Spain tardily followed the example of the Italian city-states. Through most of the tumultuous fourteenth century France suffered under kings who were weak and even insane. They were faced, moreover, by a feudal reaction against the abuses and oppressions of Philip IV, who had pushed France more aggressively in the direction of national monarchy than the society could then tolerate. For the first time since Louis the Fat had begun to build the power of the French monarchy two centuries before, the growth of monarchical authority received a major and long-lasting setback. France was thus handicapped in the Hundred Years' War against England by a comparatively regressive organization and old-fashioned feudal military tactics.

Under the pressure of invasions and defeats at the hands of the English a new national spirit arose, manifested in Joan of Arc's mission to drive the hated enemy from France. After the triumphal conclusion of the war France emerged with grievous material losses. The fighting had taken place on French soil, and in the intervals of the conflict unemployed mercenaries had plundered France unmercifully. The monarchy, however, enjoyed the prestige of the victory and the benefits of a sense of nationhood forged in the fires of bitterness against the foreign invader. The king became a symbol of the recently embattled nation.

Taking advantage of the new nationalism and the prestige of the monarchy, Charles VII (1422–1461) and his ministers, such as the financier Jacques Coeur, reformed the government, providing a firmer institutional basis for national monarchy than France had enjoyed even in the days of Philip IV. The bureaucracy of lawyers and financial agents flourished and began to take on the characteristics of a distinct social class, between the aristocracy and the bourgeoisie, the class that was to become the *noblesse de la robe*. The king gained permanent taxes on the basis of precedents at least theoretically temporary, and he no longer had to seek consent to their renewal. With the proceeds he was able to maintain a standing army. Despite all his powers, he was not yet master of the kingdom, however, nor were the feudal elements crushed. The greatest nobles, in fact, especially the duke of Burgundy, possessed within their own lands princely powers and institutions comparable to those of the king. Their destruction was to be the work of Charles' son, Louis XI.

To this end Louis XI devoted his life. He sent his bureaucrats into some seigniories to collect taxes and to administer justice in violation of ancient feudal immunities. He sought to prevent the nobles from exercising their traditional privileges, above all the right of possessing private armies. However necessary these had been during a period of disintegrating royal power, they were intolerable to the rising national monarchy, which sought to concentrate all military force in its own hands. The hard-pressed lower nobility, which had been weakened by inflation and by the Hundred Years' War, sided with the king, as did the middle class. With the death of Duke Charles the Rash in battle in 1476 the fate of Burgundy, the greatest of the principalities, was sealed and the royal authority assured.

Louis XI cleared the ground for the French absolute monarchy of early modern times. Almost all France was absorbed into the royal demesne. An efficient bureaucracy executed the king's will. Louis maintained a standing army supported by regular taxation, for which he did not seek the consent of the estates. When the third estate, the nobles, and the clergy were summoned, they could only hear the business presented by the king; they had no initiative. When in 1468 they sought to remonstrate against abuses of law and financial extravagances, they were rebuked by the king and submitted meekly. Set beside the ideals of medieval kingship, as embodied in Saint Louis, Louis XI was ignoble, crafty, deceitful, untrustworthy, a generally base character, but politics was then gaining its divorce from morality. With the support of the middle class and the lower nobility Louis destroyed the last great obstacle before the religious wars to the monarchy of Henry IV (1589–1610). With regard to political institutions, however, this was more a period of ground clearing and restoration and extension of precedents than of rich innovation.

Through the fourteenth and the greater part of the fifteenth centuries the Spanish kingdoms also were wracked by class struggles, civil wars, and political instability. These were ended in the late fifteenth century by Ferdinand of Aragon, perhaps the greatest of the late medieval despots, whose marriage to Isabella, heiress of Castile, brought about the unification of Spain. Like his contemporary Louis XI, Ferdinand was a ruler of renowned duplicity, one of the models for Machiavelli's *Prince*. He exploited the desire for law and order (at least in Castile) to curtail all privileges and to subject all classes to the crown. Repression of civil disorder was achieved through the adaptation of an old institution, the Hermandad (Brotherhood), an alliance of towns to repress banditry and private warfare. It had been employed earlier at the local level and was revived under the patronage and control of the crown. A tax, which was considered oppressive, was levied upon all, including the clergy and the nobility, to support a militia-police and judges to put down robbery, arson, rape, housebreaking, and acts of rebellion.

Other actions were taken to repress the nobility, whose turbulence contributed to lawlessness. Baronial castles were destroyed, and laws were made removing the protection from punishment that rank had provided. Lands and revenues usurped during the preceding times of turmoil were reclaimed. The nobles retained no real political power. Administration was placed in the hands of low-ranking legists. The aristocrats were converted into courtiers, possessing great honor and prestige but under close surveillance by the monarch. They were not allowed to adopt titles and heraldic devices appropriate for royalty. The number of nobles was even increased in order to diminish the importance of possessing a title.

Spain possessed one peculiar problem. The *Reconquista,* completed only in 1492 with the fall of Granada, had left Spain with a large population of Muslims. There were also many Jews. The spirit of long-lasting warfare against the infidel and the use of Jews as tax collectors had fanned the fires of religious bigotry. Isabella first established the Spanish Inquisition, the greatest institutional innovation of the period, against converted Jews and Muslims who had not clearly abandoned their old beliefs. It finally resulted in the expulsion of both Muslims and Jews, an economic disaster for Spain. It is the character of the institution and its relationship to despotism, however, that concern us here. This was far from the ecclesiastical inquisition of the thirteenth century, however distasteful to modern sensibilities even the earlier institution might be. The methods of the Spanish Inquisition were those we associate with tyranny —the presumption of guilt, the anonymous accusation, torture, the grisly spectacle. The Spanish Inquisition, moreover, combined the authority of the church with the new power of the crown in such a way that royal power was served as much as religious orthodoxy was. The sovereign insisted upon appointing the officials of the Inquisition; papal influence was kept to a minimum; confiscated property (as in the past) fell to the crown. Both the spiritual and secular swords were wielded by the crown. Spain had gone a long way toward the great modern idolatry that makes religion a servant of the national state.

Even England toyed with absolutism of a peculiar sort at the end of the Middle Ages. First, however, the English monarchy, like the French, passed through a period of weakness. Edward I, like his rival Philip IV, had grasped power unscrupulously and had created a reaction against the monarchy. His successors too were inferior in ability. During the fourteenth century the English monarchy was effectively checked by the nobility acting through Parliament. Twice, in fact, in 1327 and 1399, Parliament deposed kings. The latter case, the deposition of Richard II, followed upon his attempt to free the monarchy from parliamentary control and to govern by authoritarian means. His successors, the Lancastrians, who owed their throne to parliamentary support, sought to rule with the cooperation of the nobility and Parliament. Especially under the weak and mad Henry VI (1422–1461) the balance shifted radically in favor of Parliament, which, however, proved its incompetence to govern.

The turmoil of the middle of the fifteenth century permitted the dynasty of York, which won the crown from the unfortunate Lancastrians, to introduce absolutism. In this they had the support of the middle class, which, as in France, viewed absolutism as the preferable alternative to feudal anarchy. Edward IV (1461–1483), the first of the Yorkist kings, did not need to call upon Parliament often for money, and so it was seldom summoned. Yet the position of Parliament was by this time so well established that laws were always made in that body, although the king proposed them. In this combination of royal absolutism and the constitutional role of Parliament Tudor absolutism is prefigured. This is in marked contrast, of course, to French government, where no representative body checked the king. Other contrasts were the relatively small size of the paid bureaucracy in England and the lack of a standing army.

The beginnings of the despotism of early modern times dominate the institutional development of the last centuries of the Middle Ages. It was not a great age for the growth of subordinate institutions, not as great as the fecund twelfth and thirteenth centuries, for the despot feared to share his power. On occasion there was even a retreat from institutionalization in favor of more personal government. Some subordinate institutions, such as the Hermandad and the Spanish Inquisition, however, were adapted from earlier bodies. The France of Louis XI and the Spain of Ferdinand gave birth to the absolute government that was to dominate western Europe until the French Revolution. England, too, experimented with a unique kind of despotism. Italy and Germany joined in the prevailing trend (Italy even taking the lead), but on the local rather than on the national level. In the area of political institutions the rise of despotism marks the transition from medieval to modern history (see map).

Conclusion

Other authors, most notably Joseph R. Strayer in his presidential address to the American Historical Association in 1971, have noted the similarities and dissimilarities of European society in late antiquity and in the late Middle Ages. Above all, both were periods of economic collapse. From this there followed social turmoil, a weakening of established political institutions, and a striving toward new means of achieving law and order. The intensity and the duration of the economic failure of late antiquity, however, far exceeded those of the depression of the late Middle Ages. As should be expected, therefore, the political adaptations of the fourteenth and fifteenth centuries were not so radical as those of the fifth to ninth centuries. The basic institutional developments of the intervening period absorbed the shock of depression, were altered, and, for the most part, survived.

The Germanic kingdoms that rose on the ruins of the Roman Empire provided only a pitiful, primitive substitute for an orderly political existence.

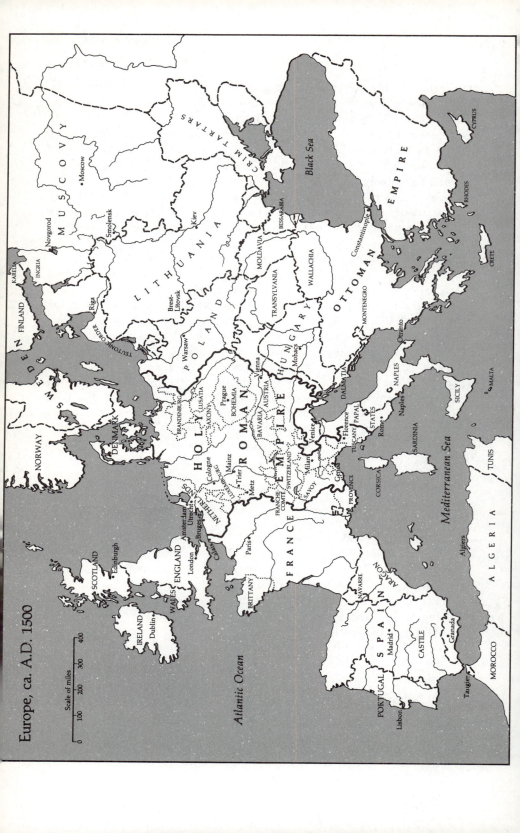

Europe, ca. A.D. 1500

Without the economic means to sustain the state, public authority passed largely into the hands of private landholders. The memory of the ancient empire survived and was revived in a Germanic form by Charlemagne and the Ottonians, but, although its prestige was strong, the imperial ideal was fundamentally anachronistic. The realistic response that saved Europe from utter anarchy was feudalism, founded upon the rural and local economy. It gave some form to political chaos and offered a measure of protection and order. Monarchy barely survived in the early feudal centuries, for kings were merely titular heads of a system over which they had almost no control. When the economy revived, however, and Europe entered upon the boom of the twelfth and thirteenth centuries, a few fortunate monarchs seized upon newly available resources to enforce their rights as feudal suzerains. Several even achieved a monarchical predominance over the feudal element that may be regarded as a simple and early form of national monarchy. A great aid in achieving strong feudal and national monarchies was the use of trained, specialized, and salaried bureaucrats of modest origins who served their royal masters capably and faithfully. Many of them came from the revived middle class. Throughout western Europe this newly influential class also found expression in parliamentary assemblies, although only in England did Parliament survive the Middle Ages as an effective institution. With the depression, famines, plague, and social unrest of the fourteenth century came a regression to quasi-feudal political forms, but the depression was not so deep or the political institutions so weak that the latter were destroyed. In response to disorder, in fact, men submitted to despotic rulers, who established the political model for future centuries.

Through all these changes political institutions of necessity maintained a rough coherence with other elements of the culture—economic, social, intellectual, educational, and religious. They were always limited by what was economically possible, but political institutions, in turn, affected the economy and other elements of the culture. Occasionally they were out of step with the cultural configuration: The medieval empire, for example, was an anachronism; Philip IV, for another, pushed for monarchical powers somewhat more vigorously than was consistent with the cultural pattern of his day. The apparent exceptions, however, prove the rule that political institutions are part of a total cultural configuration and that the better they are adapted to it the more vigorously they will thrive.

A Critical Bibliography

For the only written evidence we possess on the Germans before Tacitus, see Julius Caesar, *The Conquest of Gaul;* the Penguin translation (Harmondsworth, 1951) by S. A. Handford is good and inexpensive. The most important written source is Tacitus, *Germania,* published in A.D. 98; the Penguin translation (Baltimore, 1967) by H. Mattingly, can be recommended. Whether Tacitus knew Germany at first hand and the degree to which he romanticized the "noble savage" to shame his Roman compatriots are matters of debate. Gregory of Tours, *History of the Franks,* is a barbarous but vivid history of a barbaric nation; the translation by O. M. Dalton (Oxford, 1927) is recommended. The distinguished British scholar E. A. Thompson, who has a number of works on the Germanic peoples to his credit, has published a small and excellent scholarly survey, *The Early Germans* (Oxford, 1965). Another of the very best recent scholars is J. M. Wallace-Hadrill. See his survey of *The Barbarian West, 400–1000,* 3d ed. rev. (London, 1967). Other good recent works include Richard E. Sullivan, *Heirs of the Roman Empire* (Ithaca, 1960), and William Carroll Bark, *Origins of the Medieval World* (New York, 1960). Eleanor Shipley Duckett, *The Gateway to the Middle Ages* (New York, 1938), focuses on the sixth century; it is a standard work, well regarded, based upon much learning, but too anecdotal. Another older and excellent work is by the outstanding French medievalist Ferdinand Lot, *The End of the Ancient World and the Beginnings of the Middle Ages,* trans. Philip and Mariette Leon (New York, 1966).

A member of Charlemagne's palace school and secretary to Louis the Pious, Einhard the Frank provides our best source for the Frankish emperor in *The Life of Charlemagne,* trans. Samuel Epes Turner (Ann Arbor, 1967). The best survey of Carolingian history is Heinrich Fichtenau, *The Carolingian Empire,* trans. Peter Munz (Oxford, 1957). Geoffrey Barraclough, *The Origins of Modern Germany* 2nd ed. rev. (New York, 1963), is the best survey in English of German medieval history, though it is marred by the author's understandable concern, at the time when he wrote it, about the Germany of Adolf Hitler. Richard E. Sullivan presents edited selections from various historians in *The Coronation of Charlemagne* (Boston, 1959). Jacques Boussard, *The Civilization of Charlemagne,* trans. Frances Partridge (New York, 1968), is also worth attention. A small sample of the abundant scholarship of François L. Ganshof, the distinguished Belgian historian of the Carolingian age, has recently been made available in English in *Frankish Institutions Under Charlemagne,* trans. Byrce and Mary Lyon (Providence, 1968). Ganshof's learning is immense. Those who can read French or German should seek out his works in the original languages. James Westfall Thompson, *The Dissolution of the Carolingian Fisc in the Ninth Century* (Berkeley, 1935), is a more specialized work than would normally appear in a select bibliography, but it is important for understanding the differences between East and West Frankland.

The fundamental work on feudalism is that by the great French historian Marc Bloch, *Feudal Society,* trans. L. A. Manyon (Chicago, 1961). As his title indicates, Bloch deals with feudalism in broad terms, including the manorial component. François L. Ganshof, *Feudalism,* trans. Philip Grierson, 3d Eng. ed. (New York, 1964), on the contrary, treats feudalism strictly as a political and military institution and has a strong legalistic emphasis. Both are very scholarly. Bloch is highly readable, Ganshof more technical and difficult. Carl Stephenson, *Medieval Feudalism* (1942; reprinted Ithaca, 1967), is a highly simplified handbook for beginners. For what it purports to be, it is excellent. Joseph R. Strayer, *Feudalism* (Princeton, 1965), like Ganshof and Stephenson, defines feudalism strictly in political and military terms. See Strayer's "The Two Levels of Feudalism," in *Life and Thought in the Early Middle Ages,* ed. Robert S. Hoyt (Minneapolis, 1967), and his "Feudalism in Western Europe," in *Feudalism in History,* ed. Rushton Coulborn (Princeton, 1956). The Coulborn volume is an attempt at a comparative study of feudalism in various societies. Another recent work of great value is R. Boutruche, *Seigneurie et féodalité,* 2 vols. (Paris, 1959, 1970; vol. 1 revised, 1968). Charles Seignobos, *The Feudal Regime,* trans. Earle W. Dow (New York, 1904), is still worth reading. So is Paul Vinogradoff, "Feudalism," in *Cambridge Medieval History,* vol. 3 (New York, 1922). On a more specialized topic, see Frank M. Stenton, the great authority on Anglo-Saxon England, moving beyond his earlier interests to *The First Century of English Feudalism, 1066–1166,* 2d ed. (Oxford, 1961). The first chapter of Lynn T. White, Jr., *Medieval Technology and Social Change* (Oxford, 1962), presents the fascinating thesis that feudalism resulted from the use of the stirrup; it has been recently criticized. Sidney Painter, *French Chivalry* (Ithaca, 1957), deals with the changed chivalry of the High Middle Ages. On the economic background, see Robert Latouche, *The Birth of Western Economy,* trans. E. M. Wilkinson (New York, 1966). For the spirit and "flavor" of feudalism, read *The Song of Roland,* trans. Dorothy Sayers (Baltimore, 1966).

A brief, simple outline of the feudal monarchies of Germany, France, and England is offered by Sidney Painter, *The Rise of Feudal Monarchies* (Ithaca, 1963). To Barraclough's work on Germany already mentioned may be added the older James Westfall Thompson, *Feudal Germany* (Chicago, 1928), and the more recent Friedrich Heer, *The Holy Roman Empire,* trans. Janet Sondheimer (New York, 1968). The best and only up-to-date survey of the feudal monarchy in France available in English is Robert Fawtier, *The Capetian Kings of France,* trans. Lionel Butler and R. J. Adam (London, 1968). The magisterial Frank M. Setton, *Anglo-Saxon England,* 3d ed. (Oxford, 1971), towers over the numerous other works on the subject. Peter Hunter Blair, *Anglo-Saxon England* (Cambridge, 1966), is modern, briefer than Stenton, and also useful. An old favorite of mine is Charles Petit-Dutaillis, *The Feudal Monarchy in France and England from the Tenth to the Thirteenth Centuries,* trans. E. D. Hunt (New York, 1964). The author insists, contrary to narrowly nationalistic historians, that after the Norman Conquest, England

and France cannot be intelligently studied in isolation from each other.

Joseph R. Strayer, *The Medieval Origins of the Modern State* (Princeton, 1970), is a brief but masterful essay. See also the collection of Strayer's articles, *Medieval Statecraft and the Perspectives of History* (Princeton, 1971). Gaines Post, whose articles have been collected as *Studies in Medieval Legal Thought* (Princeton, 1964), has contributed more than any scholar to revealing the influence of Roman and canon law upon the rise of the state. See also *Post Scripta: Essays on Medieval Law and the Emergence of the European State in Honor of Gaines Post,* ed. Joseph R. Strayer and Donald E. Queller (Rome, 1972.) On Sicily we have the recent work by Denis Mack Smith, *Medieval Sicily, 800–1713* (New York, 1968). Charles Homer Haskins, *Norman Institutions* (1918; reprinted New York, 1960), remains important. On France, in addition to Fawtier, see Margaret Wade Labarge, *Saint Louis* (Boston, 1968), for a recent treatment of the ideal medieval king. Franklin J. Pegues, *The Lawyers of the Last Capetians* (Princeton, 1962), is also valuable. David Douglas, *William the Conqueror* (Berkeley, 1964), is not only a thorough study, but it challenges the conclusions of Haskins on the government of Normandy. See John E. A. Jolliffe, *Angevin Kingship,* 2d ed. (London, 1963). J. C. Holt, *Magna Carta* (Cambridge, 1965), is the most recent work on the Great Charter. There are many fine constitutional and legal histories of England. A good recent one is Bryce D. Lyon, *Constitutional and Legal History of Medieval England* (New York, 1960). We needed a study of Frederick Barbarossa, and now we have two: Peter Munz, *Frederick Barbarossa* (Ithaca, 1969), and Marcel Pacaut, *Frederick Barbarossa,* trans. A. J. Pomerans (New York, 1970). Ernst H. Kantorowicz, *Frederick II,* trans. E. O. Lorimer (London, 1931), is the standard work on its subject. With all respect to the author, whose later works inspire awe, I find this book excessively romantic and ripe for supplanting. For a study of the transition from the feudal to the national monarchy, see Bryce D. Lyon, *From Fief to Indenture: The Transition from Feudal to Non-Feudal Contract in Western Europe* (Cambridge, Mass., 1957).

The greatest work on medieval administration remains Thomas F. Tout, *Chapters in the Administrative History of Medieval England,* 6 vols. (Manchester, 1920–1923). On the same subject see S. B. Chrimes, *An Introduction to the Administrative History of Medieval England* (Oxford, 1952). A comparative study of financial institutions has recently been done by Bryce D. Lyon and Adriaan Verhulst, *Medieval Finance: A Comparison of Financial Institutions in Northwestern Europe* (Providence, 1967). See also Joseph R. Strayer, *Administration of Normandy Under St. Louis* (Cambridge, Mass., 1932). For a specialized study of incipient bureaucratization in a field subjected late and only partially to that process, consult George P. Cuttino, *English Diplomatic Administration, 1259–1339,* 2d ed. rev. and enl. (Oxford, 1971).

On the origins of representative government see Maude V. Clarke, *Medieval Representation and Consent* (London, 1936). For its origins in the two laws consult Post, *Medieval Legal Thought,* already mentioned. The best brief survey of medieval political thought remains Charles Howard McIlwain, *Growth of Political Thought in the West* (New York, 1932). For the origins of the English Parliament consult George L. Haskins, *The Growth of English Representative Government* (Philadelphia, 1948). Any of the many good English constitutional histories may also be used. A general discussion of the French Estates and Parlement is found in Achille Luchaire, *Manuel des institutions françaises* (Paris, 1892). Thomas N. Bisson, *Assemblies and Representation in Languedoc in the Thirteenth Century* (Princeton, 1964), is an excellent regional study. See also Joseph R. Strayer and Charles H. Taylor, *Studies in Early French Taxation* (Cambridge, Mass., 1939). Spanish medieval history, and especially the history of Spanish representative institutions, has been sadly neglected by historians from beyond the Pyrenees, but see Joseph O'Callaghan, "The Beginnings of the Cortes of Léon-Castile," *American Historical Review* 74 (1969): 1503–37. For Italy see Antonio Marongiu, *Medieval Parliaments,* trans. S. J. Woolf, 1st ed. in Italian 1949 (London, 1968). Brian Tierney, *Foundations of the Conciliar Theory* (Cambridge, 1955), treats the conciliar movement in the church.

On the rise of the Italian despots one must start with Jacob Burckhardt, *The Civilization of the Renaissance in Italy,* 1st publ. 1860, trans. S. G. C. Middlemore, rev. and ed. Irene Gordon (New York, 1960). See also Ephraim Emerton, *Humanism and Tyranny: Studies in the Italian Trecento* (Cambridge, Mass., 1925), and Maude V. Clarke, *The Medieval City-State: An Essay on Tyranny and Federation in the Later Middle Ages* (London, 1926). The latter is not up to the quality of the author's later work, *Medieval Representation and Consent,* already mentioned. Hans Baron, *The Crisis of the Early Italian Renaissance,* rev. ed. (Princeton, 1966), illuminates the relationship between tyranny and civic-mindedness and offers a starting point for much subsequent scholarly discussion. On Spanish absolutism the standard work in English remains Roger Bigelow Merriman, *Rise of the Spanish Empire,* 4 vols. (New York, 1918–1934). Merriman makes some comparisons and contrasts with France and England. J. H. Mariéjol, *The Spain of Ferdinand and Isabella,* trans. Benjamin Keene, 1st ed. in French 1892 (New Brunswick, 1961), was used by Merriman and may still be consulted. For a more modern treatment, see J. H. Elliott, *Imperial Spain, 1469–1716* (New York, 1964). There is a new biography of the Spider King of France by Paul Murray Kendall, *Louis XI* (New York, 1971). One of the great late medieval sources is Philippe de Comines, *The Memoirs,* ed. Samuel Kinzer, trans. Isabelle Cazeaux (Columbia, 1969–); there are various editions and translations.

DOMINVS FRANCISCHVS PETRARCHA

Petrarch, with book in hand, in the robes of an academician, by Andrea del Castagno.

4.

Literacy and Learning

ROBERT E. LERNER

EARLY CHRISTIANITY had a strong anti-intellectual strain. In the first chapter of his First Epistle to the Corinthians the Apostle Paul warned that God "will destroy the wisdom of the wise, and will bring to nothing the understanding of the prudent." He asked of the Christians of Corinth, an ancient Greek intellectual center, "Hath God made foolish the wisdom of this world?" and answered his rhetorical question in the affirmative by saying: "The Greeks seek after wisdom, but we preach Christ crucified . . . unto the Greeks foolishness; but unto them which are called, both Jews and Greeks, Christ the power of God, and the wisdom of God."

For centuries since Paul, indeed up to the present time, some Christians have wished to turn their backs on learning as the foolishness of the world and devote themselves to the "wisdom of piety," or the unencumbered worship of God. Had this sentiment prevailed, the West would never have emerged as a leader of the modern world, for widespread knowledge of reading, writing, and computation, and habits of logical thought are foundations of Western civilization and material accomplishments. These skills and habits were won for the West without possibility of recall in the Middle Ages, even though at the beginning of that period they were in danger of being lost or at least limited to a mandarin elite. Not only was there a strong anti-intellectual strain in early Christianity, but as the Roman world decayed, the usefulness of Roman education decreased, and by the seventh century it almost entirely disappeared. Afterward, there were some dark periods in the history of education. At the end of the ninth century, for example, King Alfred the Great of England lamented that when he came to the throne there was so little learning that he could not remember a single man south of the Thames who could understand the Latin offices or translate a letter from Latin into English.

During the early medieval period in western Europe, from the fifth century to the mid-eleventh century, there was only a tenuous hold on an intellectual tradition. But in the High Middle Ages, notably the twelfth and thirteenth centuries, learning triumphed, and though there was some reaction in the later Middle Ages, western Europe had by then become too committed to learning to shut its books. Indeed, by 1500, even before the greatest impact of printing, literacy was far broader than it had been in 1300. Not long after 1500, Erasmus, a Pauline thinker in many respects, could maintain that without education man becomes a wild beast but with it he is a divinity, and hundreds of thousands of men in western Europe in their own ways, great or small, were proving the truth of his adage.

The reasons for this momentous change were manifold, but simply stated the triumph of learning in the West was the result of the interaction of changing material circumstances and changing attitudes. Since the former have been treated in the previous essays in this volume, they will not be dwelled upon here, though they will always be called into view, for the history of knowledge is inseparable from the sociology of knowledge or the story of the interaction of political, economic, and social structures with ideas. In particular, however, we will stress ideas and attitudes along with the practical achievements they helped call forth. In other words, the following essay will be a brief account of what men in the Middle Ages thought about learning, and how and to what extent they became learned.

Augustinian Foundations

The writings of Saint Augustine (354–430), after Scripture, were the fount and origin of the thought of the medieval West. As a boy Augustine received a typical Roman education and wept over Virgil's story of Dido and Aeneas. Later, though his parents had wished for him to become a lawyer, his taste for the academic life was so strong that he became a professor of rhetoric, rising to teach in Carthage, Rome, and Milan—the leading cities of the western Roman Empire. When he was converted to Christianity, he abandoned his professorial career, but thereafter he was eminently qualified to deal with the problem of how a Christian should come to terms with classical culture and education. Augustine did not single-handedly save Christianity from obscurantism. Other Church Fathers stated views similar to his, and the Greek Church reached an accommodation between classical culture and Christianity without any significant aid from him. Nonetheless, in western Europe the influence of Saint Augustine more than that of any other revered authority influenced the course of medieval education.

Two of Augustine's relatively unfamiliar letters tell us much about his attitudes toward learning. The first he wrote to an old and beloved student named Licentius, a talented, enthusiastic, and sensitive young man, but from Augustine's view one who was too flighty. Licentius was a Christian; indeed, he had once shocked Augustine's prudish mother by loudly singing the Seventy-ninth Psalm in the privy and answered her complaints by asking, "Do you think that if some enemy had locked me in, God even there would have refused to hear my voice?" But he had the soul of a poet. He could notice how falling leaves alter the flow of rivulets, and when a magician entertained him with tricks, he could tell Augustine that such was a good example of wisdom. In his letter Augustine rebuked Licentius for writing Virgilian poetry, becoming overly concerned with the rules of grammar and versification, and in general being too preoccupied with temporal values. Even though Licentius had once been his star pupil, Augustine excoriated him in the harshest language: "If you found a golden vase you would present it to the Church of God; you have received from God a fine intelligence, pure spiritual gold, and yet in your lust you offer yourself as a drink to Satan."

Years later Augustine wrote to another young man, this time a stranger. A young Greek student named Dioscoros was departing from the schools of Carthage and, having learned that Augustine, who was then bishop of neighboring Hippo, had once been a famous teacher of rhetoric at Carthage, sent him a list of philosophical and literary questions in the hope that he might obtain one more neatly wrapped bundle of knowledge before he left for home. Dioscoros wrote in a manner bordering on effrontery, lightheartedly assuming that Augustine had nothing better to do with his time than respond to his letter. In his answer Augustine quickly put the young man in his place by saying that a good bishop, pressed by the claims of his church, should not turn aside to expound on some fine points of Cicero to a single scholar. But that was just rhetoric. After some persiflage about Dioscoros' obvious wish to gain knowledge for the purpose of showing off at home, Augustine went on to do his bidding by writing what amounted to a short treatise on the relationship of classical philosophy to Christianity. He refrained from answering Dioscoros' questions about literary style because he thought they were entirely out of accord with his religion and office, but despite his initial protestations, he conceded that philosophical questions could be answered by a bishop. In so doing, he showed limited approval for Platonism and followed the classical pattern of discussing in turn ethics, natural science, and logic.

At first sight there seem to be some inconsistencies in Augustine's two letters. In the first he harshly scolds a beloved pupil for turning to literature, classical learning, and worldly things, accusing him of serving the Devil. In the second he grants the request of a presumptuous stranger, who has also become enamored of literature, classical learning, and worldly things, to comment on classical thought, and he does so at length in a way that follows classical methodology and expresses limited approval for some pagan philosophy. Nonetheless, the differences are only of tone or mood rather than of substance or doctrine. In both letters Augustine entirely rules out classical studies for their own sake: The ultimate truth is Christ and the Christian must devote himself entirely to him, for in the end the only knowledge of importance is that which leads to blessedness. In his letter to Dioscoros, however, Augustine also makes clear that certain parts of the classical tradition can be appropriated in providing for a truly Christian culture.

It would be tempting to interpret Augustine's position as a subconscious compromise born from a lingering love for the pursuits of his youth. Such indeed seems to have been the case with the almost equally influential Saint Jerome (347–420), who was called contemptuously by a contemporary Christian "our rhetorician" and who has the best title of all the Latin Fathers to being called a humanist. Jerome, like Augustine, had had the best available Roman education and retained a special fondness for the works of Cicero. He continued to read the latter and quoted him in his Christian writings until he had a terrible nightmare in which he was called before the judgment seat of God, where, despite his protestations, he was told that he was not a Christian but a Ciceronian. Jerome then vowed never to own or even to read a secular book again; but though he kept his promise for about fifteen years, he thereafter slipped back to his practice of quoting the classics. When reminded by an antagonist of his oath, he denied that he should be bound by anything that had happened in a dream because according to the Prophets dreams were not to be trusted. Elsewhere he justified his use of the classics with a text from Deuteronomy that allowed Israelites to take to wife captured Gentile women on the condition that they shaved their hair and pared their nails. According to Jerome, a Christian could use pagan writings if he purified them in the same way, but his very choice of image suggests that he thought his desire for them was not unlike illicit sexual lust. Deep down he still thought that one must be either a Ciceronian or a Christian, and because in the end he kept on trying to be both he was never able fully to resolve the conflict in his soul.

This was by no means the case with Augustine. Unlike Jerome, he never suffered from pangs of conscience because sometime after his conversion he became certain that he was no longer a Ciceronian but a Christian. Wisdom for him was solely the contemplation of the truth that is God, and the surest avenue on earth toward that truth was knowledge of Holy Scripture, which he believed contained all that was necessary for a Christian to know. In his maturity Augustine once wrote to a young pagan who loved the classics that "such is the depth of the Christian Scriptures that, even if I were attempting to study them and nothing else, from boyhood to decrepit old age, with the utmost leisure, the most unwearied zeal, and with talents greater than I possess, I would still be making progress in discovering their treasures." Yet the view that the Bible was a far greater classic than Homer or Virgil led him to the conclusion that one needed a preparatory education in order to study it.

Augustine set forth his position on this subject most fully in a treatise called *On Christian Doctrine*. He argued there that divine revelation is found in a book, the Bible, and that a certain amount of intellectual training is necessary to apprehend it. First he stoutly defended this position against the Christians who believed that Scripture could be learned by miraculous inspiration without the intermediary of human instruction. He cast doubt on the story that after three days of prayer an illiterate Christian slave once miraculously learned the entire Bible. Though he conceded that the Holy Spirit had spoken directly to the apostles, he intimated that that was not likely to occur often and insisted that Christians should not stop teaching their children in the expectation of such miracles. Then he explained that words, even those in Scripture, are only signs, not things to be loved for themselves. But signs signify things—in the case of Scripture things of paramount importance. To understand the biblical system of signification one must understand the meaning of words agreed upon by human conventions and for that it is necessary to have a liberal education.

What was the meaning of this now much abused term? The phrase "liberal education" originally had nothing to do with liberal as opposed to conservative. On the contrary, a liberal education was designed for a free man (*liber* is Latin for free) or a man of leisure, which in effect meant that it was an aristocratic education and, by Augustine's time, in fact a conservative one. It aimed at making a man a perfect aristocrat in the ability to think clearly, argue persuasively, and serve the state. For that reason it was largely verbal, resting primarily on the study of grammar, which meant reading, writing, and the rigorous analysis of literary texts, and then on rhetoric and dialectic, the arts of speaking and reasoning well. It proceeded, for those who cared to advance so far, to arithmetic, geometry, astronomy, musical theory, and ideally philosophy. For those who needed specialized professional training it could culminate in law or medicine, but these studies were professional and so no longer counted among the liberal arts.

Augustine had been nurtured in the system of liberal arts, and in *On Christian Doctrine* he prescribed this system as the preparatory stage for studying the Bible. Most of all he stressed the need for grammatical studies, clearly the most important of the liberal arts for the purposes of reading. Repudiating to a degree his own past, he denigrated rhetoric. But somewhat surprisingly he included in his program all the other liberal arts, even astronomy, geometry, and music, which had hardly any discernible use for the study of Scripture. This was the basic program followed in the Middle Ages. After studying some of the liberal arts, the student ideally went on to study the Bible (in other words, theology, known in the Middle Ages as the "queen of the sciences") or else pursued medicine or law. Similarly, even in our own day, medicine and law are not part of the American undergraduate (liberal arts) curriculum. *On Christian Doctrine* preserved the fundamentals of the old learning by making it preparatory for the new and therefore has been called by Henri Marrou with full justice "the fundamental charter of Christian culture."

That being said, it must be added that Augustine's program was not the fundamental charter of the modern academic ideal. Augustine believed that the liberal arts had been so perfected that the Christian had only to learn their rules rather than, as the modern slogan would have it, "push past the frontiers of knowledge." Originality was to be shunned. Augustine respected "experts" and believed in dragons because they had been described in books. In Marrou's words, Augustine's cultural program amounted to "less an active formation of intelligence than the acquisition of a mass of useable knowledge." For that purpose the best books to read were handbooks (we would say textbooks). Augustine had once planned to write such books treating the useful contents of each of the liberal arts, but he managed to complete only one, on music. A contemporary of his, however, named Martianus Capella, did cover all the arts in a work called *The Marriage of Mercury and Philology,* which became one of the most popular schoolbooks of the Middle Ages. In the following two centuries other important compilations were put together by Boethius, Cassiodorus, and Isidore of Seville, and these performed the inestimable service of preserving chunks of classical knowledge for the Middle Ages. Still, they were handbooks, encouraging their readers merely to absorb their often arid or misguided contents rather than to think critically about them.

Augustine approved of handbooks not only because he thought that the liberal arts had been perfected but because he did not want them to be studied too much. (It is ironic that in making this point he used an adage—"nothing in excess"—taken from Terence.) Learning for him had above all to be subordinated to its end, the knowledge of Christian truth. Thus he entirely ruled out scientific curiosity. Virgil had once written, "Happy is the man who is able to know the causes of things." To this Augustine answered that knowing the causes of physical phenomena is not essential for man's salvation, and he maintained that "knowledge is good, but for men, who misuse everything, it is not good to know everything." He agreed with Saint Paul that "knowledge puffeth up, but charity edifieth" and was certain that belief came before understanding. Reason alone could not reach wisdom unless aided by divine guidance, and therefore one always had to subordinate one's studies to the love of God and remember to be humble. As he told the complacent student Dioscoros: "I wish you to submit to Him with complete devotion and think of no way of gaining the Truth other than the way constructed by God who saw how faltering were our steps. That way is first humility, second humility, third humility, and however often you should ask me I would say the same."

Was Augustine's program of Christian culture designed for an elite—equivalent to the elite that in his day would have received a liberal education—or for all Christians? Most likely Augustine did not conceive of an educated elite in the sense of the clergy as opposed to the laity. He himself had published a commentary on Genesis before he was ordained, and there had been a number of lay commentators on sacred doctrine of whom he approved. But he undoubtedly conceived of Christian culture as something esoteric because he delighted in the belief that much of the Bible was wrapped in allegory so difficult that even with training it could be understood by only a select few. For the others Augustine did not forbid purely technical or vocational studies. These he hardly ever mentioned, but he did say that "all human instruction helpful to the necessary conduct of life" should not be shunned, and he approved of the "useful mechanical arts." But he never said that all Christians should know how to read and write. In fact he wrote a little treatise, *On Catechizing the Unlearned,* which assumed that many would remain illiterate. They were to be taught the rudiments of Christian doctrine orally, and they had to accept them on faith. For teaching such people Augustine advocated simplicity: The teacher was to avoid excessively lengthy presentations and speak in a simple, thoroughly comprehensible manner.

Such were the Augustinian foundations of medieval education—liberal education for an elite leading to biblical studies, technical education for others, and the catechizing of the unlearned. The modern secular reader will probably regret Augustine's purely theocentric orientation, and modern liberals will deplore his closed-mindedness and elitism, but we may all be thankful that he put his stamp of approval on classical education and proclaimed exultantly to God in his *Confessions:* "May whatever useful things I learned as a boy be of service to Thee. May it be of service to Thee that I can speak and write and read and count." Most fittingly the earliest surviving representation of Saint Augustine shows him in the dress of a scholar, with a scroll in one hand and fingering a book with the other (fig. 1).

Education in the Barbarian West

Augustine never called for parochial schools. He and his contemporaries believed that Christians were to be catechized in the faith by the church but that otherwise Roman schools already in existence were perfectly utilizable vehicles for transmitting the liberal arts. In Augustine's day a number of orthodox

1. *Fresco of Saint Augustine, probably from the sixth century, in the Church of the Lateran, Rome.*

Christians even taught in these schools without altering Roman curriculum or pedagogy. Only during the barbarian invasions of the fifth century did the Roman schools begin to disappear and Christian ones take their place, but the transition was slow and lasted several centuries. Most barbarian rulers had no implacable hostility toward Roman education, and in some areas remnants of the Roman system survived for a century or two. Christian alternatives, on the other hand, were initially limited both in quantity and quality. Thus in certain areas for long periods of time there was hardly any education at all, and from the fifth to the eighth centuries literacy in western Europe ebbed. But at the same time characteristically medieval modes of education were slowly emerging.

The reasons for the slow death of the Roman schools are easy enough to understand: No one closed them down; there just was less and less need for them. Education in the liberal arts was meant for the children of the Roman upper classes who were to have careers in law or government, but after the Germans took power in the West in the fifth century, Roman urban life and government began to disappear and the Roman aristocracy began to die out. With a diminishing clientele Roman schools too began to disappear. The first to go were the public schools. In the heyday of the Roman Empire municipalities had maintained public schools primarily for the recruitment and training of officials, but in the fifth century, when the Roman state in the West was replaced by barbarian kingdoms, these schools ceased to function. Thereafter there was still some private education on the Roman model for those who desired and could afford it. Our sources are too sparse to allow for precision on this subject, but it seems that such private education for aristocrats continued in Italy until the Gothic and Lombard wars of the middle and later part of the sixth century and in the most Romanized part of France—the south— until the second half of the seventh century, when it disappeared not as the result of any calamity but as part of a process of attrition. By this time Roman education was becoming mummified because it had less and less relation to public life: Certain leisured men entertained themselves by collecting precious books or writing precious prose and had their sons trained to do the same, but eventually they died or went financially or culturally bankrupt.

The fate of the Roman educational system hinged on the attitude of the barbarian conquerors. Had the Germans who occupied the western Roman Empire wholeheartedly adopted Roman education, it doubtless would have survived. But they did not. Most barbarian rulers and aristocrats had no animus against Roman education and culture, but neither did many of them consider it appropriate for themselves and they certainly did not embrace the Augustinian ideal of learning the liberal arts for the sake of biblical studies. As one fifth-century Roman complained, the conquerors "laid claim to ignorance as if it were their property." The Germans preferred to train their sons in the arts of war, almost a full-time occupation, and beyond that they encouraged only the recital of the exploits of tribal heroes and verbal inculcation of the rudiments of the Christian faith. Toward Roman education their attitude was not one of hostility but of indifference.

There are exceptions to every rule and one that must be mentioned here is the case of the Ostrogothic king Theodoric the Great, who ruled Italy from 493 to 526. Theodoric wished to preserve Roman civilization and therefore insisted on a solid education for his family, patronized scholarship, and maintained public professorships in the schools of Rome. His reign proved to be merely an interlude in the progressive decay of education, but he did have a long-term influence in his patronage of two outstanding scholars, Boethius and Cassiodorus, both of whom came from illustrious old Roman families and held high office in his government.

Boethius (480?–525), almost as if he sensed that Theodoric's program of supporting classical culture would not outlive its patron, aimed to rescue the best of classical thought for future generations by writing translations, commentaries, and handbooks. In this he was far too ambitious. He intended not only to translate the complete works of Plato and Aristotle from Greek into Latin but also to show in a series of commentaries that the two philosophers were in basic harmony. Even though he began this stupendous project in his twenties, he had completed only the smallest part of it by the time of his death in his forties. He managed to translate some of Aristotle's logical treatises, as well as an introductory work on logic by the Neoplatonic philosopher Porphyry, and to write his own commentaries on these works as well as handbooks on music and arithmetic and treatises on theology. In music his work was ill-advisedly dogmatic and in logic his own position was often indecisive because of his aim to harmonize, but nonetheless his contribution to the subsequent development of learning was enormous because he did provide a repository, small though it may have been, of ancient thought in certain areas. In logic his translations were all that the West possessed of the Greek heritage until the twelfth century, and, more importantly, he created in his translations and his own commentaries a vocabulary of logical terms that were necessary for any discussion of logic and allowed later logicians to speak with precision.

Boethius upheld the dignity of the human intellect. Though a committed Christian, he believed that one should try to "join faith to reason," and he discussed theological matters, such as the doctrine of the Trinity, solely on the basis of rational analysis without any quotations from the Bible. In his most widely read book, *The Consolation of Philosophy*, written while he was awaiting execution for alleged treason (it is still not known whether the charge was justified), he argued that God alone is the supreme good and the only ultimate source of happiness, but he wrote as a philosopher, not as a theologian, making no explicit reference to Christian revelation. Few of Boethius' contemporaries thought philosophy much of a consolation, but men who thought so in later times would be greatly in his debt.

Boethius is often called the last of the Romans because although he was a Christian he was a layman dedicated to philosophy and he lived and died in government service. His contemporary Cassiodorus (477?–570?) never showed much interest or aptitude for philosophy. He lived twice as long as Boethius did and in the later part of his long life retired from public service into a monastery, thereby typifying the onset of the Middle Ages. As Theodoric's first secretary Cassiodorus had been a perfect anachronism, playing the role of Roman statesman, trying to shore up a Roman system of bureaucratic government, and writing pompous and turgid letters for his German ruler while Roman government and culture were on the verge of collapse. But after Theodoric died and Italy succumbed to protracted wars, Cassiodorus founded the monastery of Vivarium in southern Italy and lived there in retirement for the last decades of his life.

In so doing, he by no means turned his back on classical culture. Rather, his aim was to place the best of classical culture in the service of Christianity. He had read Augustine's *On Christian Doctrine* and was a fervent adherent of the Augustinian principle that study of the liberal arts was a necessary preparation for study of the Bible. While at Vivarium he wrote his most important and influential work, *An Introduction to Divine and Human Readings,* which is a digest of theological and secular studies, including the liberal arts, meant for the edification of his monks. (Cassiodorus, unlike Augustine, intended liberal education only for monks.) Since the *Introduction* was comparatively short and included knowledgeable recommendations for further readings, it proved to be a useful handbook and bibliographical guide for later generations. In addition to encouraging his monks to read, Cassiodorus had them copy manuscripts, secular as well as sacred, thereby making Vivarium the first important monastic copying center in the West. His timing in this was fortunate. Elsewhere copying had almost stopped and many precious works were being destroyed by disasters of war. By the time of Cassiodorus' death his monks had copied fewer than one hundred large volumes, but within them were many important works of classical antiquity that otherwise would not have been preserved. These, along with the contents of Cassiodorus' rich private library, helped to spread learning in later centuries.

Unfortunately, Vivarium was an anomaly. Even during Cassiodorus' lifetime it was more of a copying house than a center of education and after he died even copying activities at Vivarium ceased. Much unlike Cassiodorus, the typical monastic leaders of his time were anti-intellectual ascetics. Monasteries for such men were places for fasting, vigils, and the singing of Psalms, and they were happy to compare this regimen to military life. For them classical studies were to be avoided. Saint Caesarius of Arles, a sixth-century French author of rules for monks and nuns, compared the liberal arts to the plagues of Egypt and his contemporary Saint Benedict, the founder of the monastic order that was subsequently to do much for the preservation of classical culture, made no provision in his Rule for the cultivation of the liberal arts.

Thus the continental monasteries of the fifth, sixth, and seventh centuries eschewed study of the classics and even intensive study of the Bible and the Fathers of the church, but this did not mean that they abandoned learning altogether. The active monk at least had to know the Psalms, and therefore he was supposed to know how to read. Indeed, a sixth-century rule said simply that "all who wish to claim the name of monk cannot be ignorant of their letters." The same Caesarius who compared the liberal arts to plagues insisted that all nuns learn how to read, and Saint Benedict went farther by providing in his Rule for regular times for divine reading and by referring as a matter of course to the monastic use of tablets, styluses, and books. Recruits normally entered monasteries as children, often as young as six or seven years old, and in the monasteries of the West they were taught first to read.

Priests also were supposed to know how to read so that they could celebrate mass, and in the course of the sixth century, with the disappearance of the old Roman schools, it became necessary to provide some education for them as well as for monks. Occasionally this service was performed by monasteries, but it could not be depended on. Instead, some bishops began to supervise primary education in their dioceses in order to ensure the training of recruits, thereby founding the episcopal schools that were to be the central institutions of medieval education for centuries to come. In addition, some of the bishops who were concerned about the evangelization of the countryside encouraged similar clerical education in rural parishes. A milestone in this development was a decree issued by a southern French council in 529 to the effect that all parish priests were to take on students for the priesthood and teach them how to read the Psalms and other ecclesiastical texts. The disorganized state of the church made it impossible to put such orders widely into effect, but at least in a few places after the sixth century a young priest or aspirant to the clergy could obtain the rudiments of primary education.

Since the schools in monasteries, episcopal centers, and parishes were the ancestors or models for all medieval schools and subsequent schools in the West, it is worthwhile to describe their pedagogy. To begin with, they were truly parochial. Though they occasionally took in laymen, they aimed at training monks or priests; therefore they taught letters and Christian virtues together and they thoroughly subordinated the secular to the spiritual. Whereas Roman education had aimed at preparation for participation in public life, the new ecclesiastical education was much more like that of a choir school and characteristically the first book read by all was the Psalter.

Furthermore, since books and writing materials were prohibitively expensive, a great stress was placed on oral instruction, and writing was often not taught at all. Students learned first to recognize the letters of the alphabet, but then, instead of reading the Psalms from pages, they were made to repeat verses out loud after their teachers until they learned them by heart. Thus reading was actually secondary: It helped monks and priests to "recognize" Psalms they already knew, but those whose education went no farther probably were not able to read any texts other than those they had learned by heart. A few students might, after learning the Psalter this way, have gone on to study Latin grammar more carefully, but during the following centuries these were at most a handful. Later, when books became more plentiful, reading was taught more thoroughly, but until modern times the amount of oral repetition was still overwhelming.

Clerics were supposed to know all 150 Psalms by heart—a most arduous process, which could take anywhere from six months' to three years' time. During this period the teacher customarily enforced the most rigorous—many would say barbarous—discipline (fig. 2). The beating of children was recommended by several biblical texts including the "wisdom of Solomon" in Proverbs, which proclaimed that "foolishness is bound in the heart of a child; but the rod of correction shall drive it far from him." Throughout the Middle Ages, just as in ancient times, the rod was the symbol of the schoolmaster. Around the year 700, one noted teacher was rewarded by the king of the Lombards with a staff decorated with silver and gold, and we can be sure that if he saved that one for display he put others to frequent use.

Only in certain monasteries was there a tendency toward lessened severity in the treatment of children. The Benedictine Rule in particular urged moderation and discretion in the discipline of children under the age of fifteen, and even argued that the opinions of youths should be taken into consideration since "Samuel and Daniel judged their elders" and "often the Lord reveals to the youngest that which is best to do." Some early medieval monastic writers stressed the innocence of boys and enumerated their four winning qualities as "not persevering in hot anger, not nursing grudges, not taking delight in the beauty of women, and always saying what they think." Nonetheless, even in Benedictine monasteries children were beaten as part of the educational process. In the tenth century children in one monastery were beaten every year five days before Christmas, not because of any specific misbehavior but merely because it was customary.

A final salient feature of early medieval education was its esotericism. The clergy was coming to consider itself more and more as a caste apart from the laity and regarded its rudimentary education as one of its most distinctive traits. Monks in particular thought of themselves so much as members of a secret society that one of the earliest western monastic rules maintained that monks in the presence of laymen should read the most difficult texts so that the secrets of God and the monastic life would not be divulged. Other monks developed sign language or intricate written codes to keep "the lowly and the foolish" away from the mysteries, which should be known only by the initiated. On occasion certain laymen were admitted into ecclesiastical schools to learn how to read, but their number was limited, they were regarded as foreign bodies, and they were usually dismissed after they had learned a few Psalms.

2. Corporal punishment in a medieval school, from a German manuscript of the fifteenth century illustrating the life of Saint Augustine. The three "bad boys" at the left are sticking out their tongues instead of reading; the punished child is trying to shield his rear to ward off blows. At the left Saint Augustine is praying to an apparition of Christ that he not be beaten.

This is not to say, however, that there were large numbers of people knocking on church doors to demand an education. With the decline of town life, most people in early medieval Europe were peasants who did not even imagine that they might learn to read. Literacy, given the economic state of the time, could only be a luxury for a few, since the peasantry was engaged in a desperate struggle with the soil and peasant children were set about this struggle as soon as they were physically able. The barbarian aristocracy was interested primarily in the arts of war. Thus by the second half of the seventh century most rulers and their lay functionaries could not even sign their names on official documents. At that time even church schools seem to have been decaying or dying out, and writing became so rare that it took on for some a supernatural significance: The entrance to one French burial place has a meaningless inscription ("grama, grumo"), as if the mere presence of magical letters would keep away violators. Western Europe clearly was threatened by the triumph of abracadabra.

The Carolingian Renaissance

From this fate western Europe was saved first by the activities of a few Englishmen and then by the Carolingian Renaissance, a movement for the revival of learning that took place between the middle of the eighth and middle of the ninth centuries. The Englishmen may be compared, not at all flippantly, to the Royal Air Force pilots of whom Winston Churchill said that never "was so much owed by so many to so few." While scholarship and literacy were disappearing on the European continent, a few Englishmen from the mid-seventh to the mid-eighth centuries were cultivating it on their remote island until some of them were able to bring their learning across the Channel and help initiate the Carolingian Renaissance, which then secured a tradition of learning for western Europe. Few Englishmen have had such a decisive effect on European history as they did.

Their story is all the more remarkable because until their time England was one of the most backward and illiterate parts of Europe. The reason Englishmen turned to studies in such a dark century as the seventh was that England was then being evangelized for Christianity and some of the clergy had to learn Latin. This need was more pressing in England than on the continent because in England Roman civilization had been obliterated and no one knew Latin until the coming of Christianity. In the old Roman areas on the continent the Latin language was evolving into the vernaculars spoken today. Although scholars are not sure how far this process had progressed in the seventh century, it does seem that young priests felt no need to learn Latin as if it were a foreign language. But in England Latin had to be learned from the start and a concerted and rationalized attempt to teach it was necessary.

England was converted to Christianity and Latin from two opposite directions, Ireland and Italy. The Irish influence came first but was less lasting. After the time of Saint Patrick (ca. 450), Ireland had became a leading Christian outpost, and because it was a haven for literate refugees fleeing from English and continental turbulence it also became a center of learning. In the sixth century Irish monks as a group were the best educated men of Europe and probably the most zealous Christians. Many were ardent missionaries, and by the early seventh century they were making considerable inroads into England. Some English centers of learning continued to owe much to Irish scholarship in succeeding decades, but the Irish had their own ecclesiastical traditions, which were very independent of Rome, and Pope Gregory the Great (590–604) regarded their success as a threat. In 597 he sent a Benedictine monk named Augustine to missionize England for Rome, and the struggle of the Roman party against both paganism and the Irish continued for much of the seventh century. Ultimately Rome was triumphant owing to the persistence of a number of heroic missionaries, to the claim of Rome to apostolic succession, and to the fact that the Germanic Anglo-Saxons often regarded the Celtic Irish as traditional enemies.

The Roman effort to win England brought the island learning as well as religion. In 669 the papacy sent two men, Theodore of Tarsus and his assistant Hadrian, to reorganize the English Church and tighten its bonds with Rome. Theodore was a Greek well versed in secular as well as ecclesiastical learning, and his companion, who came from North Africa, had similar attainments. One of their greatest accomplishments was the establishment of episcopal and monastic schools at Canterbury, which succeeded in planting offshoots and educating members of the clergy in southern England for several generations. Their counterpart in the north was a remarkable native nobleman turned monk named Benedict Biscop, who had escorted Theodore and Hadrian on their trip from Rome to England. Benedict first directed the monastic school at Canterbury and later founded the twin monasteries of Wearmouth (674) and Jarrow (685) in his home of Northumbria. So dedicated was he to the Roman obedience that he made six trips to Rome—a frightfully arduous journey in that age—and every time he returned to England he brought back with him a number of precious books, which he deposited in the libraries at Wearmouth and Jarrow. They probably did not total more than three hundred, but they contained a good selection of the Latin Fathers and also some secular Latin works, some of which appear to have been copied originally at Cassiodorus' monastery of Vivarium a century earlier.

The man who put Benedict Biscop's collection to its fullest use was the Venerable Bede, a monk at Jarrow from 685 to 735 who had been educated by

Benedict himself and who afterward was so occupied in Benedict's library that he used it to write thirty-six books of his own. Indeed, he hardly ever left it for the outside world. He once described a Roman wall entirely on the basis of literary sources, although it was less than ten miles away from his monastery. Still, it would be false to think of Bede as an "ivory-tower intellectual," for much of his scholarly work was purposely meant to be practical. Aside from his famous *History of the English Church and People*—one of the greatest narrative histories written in the Middle Ages—he wrote treatises on grammar and spelling to help the English clergy master the fundamentals of the Latin language. He also wrote treatises on computation and cosmography that aimed at helping the clergy to draw up ecclesiastical calendars and to reckon the date of Easter. Bede's precision in such matters, particularly his observations concerning the periodicity of tides, earned him the title of "the first scientific intellect produced by the Germanic peoples of Europe," but it is important to bear in mind that he was motivated by no vain curiosity but by the pressing need felt by the English Church to celebrate ecclesiastical holidays uniformly on the approved days. He was hostile toward any study of the liberal arts beyond the simple learning necessary for managing churches, and having done his best to provide instruction in this, he spent most of his time writing commentaries on the Bible. Thus it can be said of Bede's learning, as V. H. Galbraith has justly said of the entire Anglo-Saxon educational movement, that it was "marked by an insistence on correct Latinity and a total subordination of learning to the Church."

Bede's erudition was furthermore not typical of the England in which he lived. Even his own monastery housed illiterate monks, and although he had trained a few disciples to help him in his scholarly work, he complained about not having had enough. In most other monasteries the educational standard was the semi-literacy necessary only for reading the daily offices, and outside the monasteries the situation was far worse. Some priests were illiterate and knew no Latin at all, a condition that applied to all the laity except for a tiny minority of princes and aristocrats trained to read in monasteries. Bede lamented the lack of education among the clergy, but the ignorance of the laity did not much bother him. Like most of his monastic contemporaries, he was an elitist who believed that the lay condition was only a concession to human weakness. In the best of worlds all men would be monks, but since this could not be, monks would have to remain as a class apart, distinguished, among other traits, by their special education. Like many of his continental brethren, Bede prescribed the use of a secret sign language, not to keep monastic silence but to be employed by monks in the presence of strangers to their community.

Educated English monks thus felt no calling to spread education to large numbers, but they did wish to spread the faith and they propagated some clerical education as they did so. One of Bede's contemporaries, Saint Boniface, the Anglo-Saxon "Apostle of the Germans," was the first to help bring back learning to the European continent. Boniface had obtained a thorough grammatical education in the south of England and might have become the Bede of Wessex had he not early felt the missionary calling and devoted his life to evangelizing central Germany for Christianity and the Roman obedience. In so doing, he stressed the importance of instruction in Latin and stocked his monastic foundations, especially Fulda—a future center of the Carolingian Renaissance—with books from Rome and England, including some works of Bede. Boniface left for his last mission with a small library and was martyred by the pagans, it was reported, with a book in his hand.

Meanwhile in England, a direct line of intellectual descent was passing down from Bede himself. One of Bede's students became archbishop of York, where he opened an episcopal school and taught, among others, a young Anglo-Saxon named Alcuin (730–804), who then rose to become the school's director. By the late eighth century Alcuin had become so famous a schoolmaster that he was invited by the Frankish ruler Charlemagne to help direct studies on the European continent. He accepted and in his last years presided over the Carolingian Rennaissance. Whatever England had owed in the way of learning to the continent was paid back with generous interest.

It is impossible to appreciate the nature of the Carolingian Renaissance unless one recognizes, in the words of the British scholar J. M. Wallace-Hadrill, that "learning and good letters were no mere hobbies of the Carolingians and their friends; they were conditions of survival." Charlemagne was impelled to patronize learning for several pressing reasons. He ruled over a vast realm, roughly comprising modern France, the Low Countries, western Germany, northern Italy, and parts of northern Spain, and he knew that he could have no efficient administration without written records. But when he came to his throne in 768 hardly any men could read such records, let alone write them. Worse, among the few who were literate, there was a bewildering lack of uniformity in language in Charlemagne's far-flung kingdom. The ruler not only needed many more men who could read and write, but he needed a language that could be taught and comprehended so that all literate men would be certain to understand each other and help unify his realm. The language that Charlemagne patronized was not his native German but Latin, the language of the church, for Charlemagne was thoroughly religious. Indeed, another reason for encouraging education, and probably the one uppermost in his own mind, was to promulgate the Christian faith. Charlemagne wanted desperately—some might say fanatically—to extirpate paganism beyond his own lands and to inculcate Christianity more deeply within them. For these purposes he needed a clergy that understood the faith well enough to preach it, as well as scholars who could standardize scriptural and liturgical texts and scribes to make such texts available to priests and missionaries.

Charlemagne, though strong-minded, was a nearly ignorant man and relied for the implementation of his educational program on the efforts of scholars lured from abroad. Among these Alcuin stood out as something like the ruler's minister of education. His interests and abilities meshed perfectly with Charlemagne's needs. Alcuin would today be dismissed as a drudge because he was not an original thinker but was fascinated by schoolmasterish subjects such as grammar, spelling, and handwriting and rose to his greatest heights not as a creator of new works but as an editor of old ones. Nonetheless, if there was ever a scholar whose work was relevant in the sense of being practical it was he. He wished to establish uniform principles of Latin grammar and spelling in order to facilitate teaching, writing, and the promulgation of a linguistic standard throughout the Carolingian realm. This desire led him inevitably to the study of the pagan Latin classics, but like Saint Augustine he insisted that they were not to be read for their own sake. He was convinced that real wisdom was to be found not in the "lies of Virgil" but only in the "truth of the Gospels." Alcuin's own grammatical work was not inspired textual analysis but rather the presentation of prosaic injunctions such as the warning to distinguish the word *ara* ("altar") from *hara* ("pigsty"), but uneducated Carolingians needed such knowledge most of all.

Just as there were pressing practical needs in Alcuin's day for reforms in grammar and spelling, so were there needs for reforms in handwriting. After the fall of Rome, regional diversity in handwriting had become extreme, and writing became difficult to read because scribes in some areas preferred to write very esoterically, using difficult signs and swirls, and because in others they became careless and sloppy (fig. 3). Communication and education could not spread until this tendency was reversed, and in his last years as abbot of the monastery of St. Martin of Tours Alcuin helped to do that. Though the then current cursive scripts increased speed in writing by the use of ligatures between letters, they were all but illegible and gradually in the late eighth century were replaced by a script known as Carolingian minuscule, characterized by small, separate, and highly legible letters. Alcuin did not invent this script. It had been evolving before he became aware of it, and it was not perfected until after his death. But under his direction the monastic scribes of Tours helped develop it and, most important, were responsible for its widespread diffusion in their copies of religious texts spread by Charlemagne's authority. Soon all western Europe was using the same script, and manuscripts became easier to read not only because the new script was so legible but because words were carefully separated by spaces and

3. Nearly illegible pre-Carolingian handwriting of the Historia Francorum *of Gregory of Tours. The eighth-century script was executed at the Burgundian monastery of Luxeuil.*

phrases were initiated by capitals in contrast to the older Roman practice of omitting spaces and punctuation (fig. 4). Carolingian minuscule evolved into Gothic script in the twelfth and thirteenth centuries, but in the fifteenth century the Italian humanists returned to it and it is the basis of modern typography. Just as Molière's *bourgeois gentilhomme* did not know he was talking

4. *Nonpunctuated sixth-century writing (uncial) from* Breviarum Alarici, *written in southern France. The sixth line reads, "in eclesia vel martyrium vel clericum."*

prose, the modern reader may not know that he is at this moment reading Carolingian minuscule (fig. 5).

Alcuin's influence in the editing of ecclesiastical texts was as pronounced as it was in grammar and handwriting. In this area too the previous centuries had seen the growth of regional diversities and carelessness, making

BEATISSIMO PAPAE DAMASO
HIERONIMUS

Nouum opus me facere cogis ex uetere · ut post exemplaria scrip
turarum toto orbe dispersa · quasi quidam arbiter sedeam.
& quia inter se uariant quae sint illa quae cum greca consenti
ant ueritate decernam · Pius labor · sed periculosa praesump
tio · iudicare deceteris ipsum ab omnibus iudicandum · senis muta
relinquam · & canescentem mundum ad initia retrahere paruu
lorum · Quis enim doctus pariter uel indoctus cum in manus uo
lumen adsumpserit · & a saliua quam semel inbibit uiderit discre
pare quod lectitat Non statim erumpat in uoce me falsarium
me clamans esse sacrilegum · qui audeam aliquid in ueteribus
libris addere mutare corrigere · Aduersus quam inuidiam du
plex causa me consolatur · Quod & tu qui summus sacerdos es
fieri iubes · & uerum non esse quod uariat etiam maledicorum
testimonia conprobatur · si enim latinis exemplaribus fides est
adhibenda respondeant · quibus tot sunt exemplaria pene quod
codices · si autem ueritas est quaerenda de pluribus · Cur non
ad grecam originem reuertentes eaquae uel auctiosis inter
pretibus male edita uel á presumptoribus imperitis emendata
peruersius uel á librarius dormitantibus aut addita sunt aut
mutata corrigimus · Neque uero ego deuetere disputo testamento
quod á lxx senioribus in grecam linguam uersum tertio gradu
ad nos usque peruenit · Non quaero quid aquila quid srmmachus
sapiant · Quare theodotion inter nouos & ueteres medius incedat.
sit illa uera inter praelatio quam apostoli probauerunt · De nouo

5. Carolingian minuscule, from Loisel Evangeliary. *The first three and a half
lines after the title read:* "Novum opus me sacere cogis ex vetere ut post examplaria
scripturarum toto orbe dispersa quasi quidam arbiter sedeam et quia inter
se variant quae sint illa quae cum greca consentiant veritate decernam."

the establishment of fresh editions a pressing concern for good Christians. Alcuin addressed himself to this Herculean task almost single-handedly. First he edited and established a uniform Christian liturgy; then he turned his attentions to the greatest book he knew, the Bible. Before his efforts, most copies of Scripture were in one way or another incomplete; where complete texts existed there was little agreement on the correct order of books; and worst, the contents of the books often varied. Remedying this by careful study, Alcuin established a complete, ordered, and comparatively uncorrupt text of the Bible, which became widely accepted and remained the basis of the Roman Catholic Bible until recent times.

The clarification of grammar, the design of a simple, legible handwriting, and the editing of Christian texts all facilitated the spread of Christian education, but this could proceed only with the establishment or reinvigoration of schools. Charlemagne himself could hardly write, but he regretted this inability and supported three types of educational institutions— the so-called palace school and schools located in the bishoprics and monasteries of his realm.

Palace schools had existed intermittently at the courts of earlier rulers for the purpose of teaching noble young men the rudiments of reading and primarily how to fight and deport themselves. Before Charlemagne's time instruction in reading was almost forgotten in favor of athletics and comportment, but Charlemagne countered this trend. He insisted on thorough attention to reading at his palace school, and there is some evidence that he himself warned noble boys not to be lazy in their grammatical studies, even beating a young student for making mistakes in Latin. In addition to formal elementary education at the palace, when Alcuin resided at Charlemagne's court he presided over an informal palace literary society. In an atmosphere of camaraderie and tippling Alcuin would conduct discussions of learned subjects with Charlemagne, the king's noble friends, and other scholars or promising students who were at court. No doubt the quality of these sessions was below that of a Platonic symposium, but they helped to give a certain prestige to intellectual matters in a society that was still very crude. Education of both sorts at the palace did not last long because Charlemagne's empire quickly fell apart. Nevertheless, the ruler's patronage of instruction at court was responsible for the training of a new generation of intellectuals who managed to continue working and to pass down their learning to others even while the empire was expiring.

Much more lasting in the institutional sense were the Carolingian schools located in the bishoprics and monasteries. There too Charlemagne's initiative was decisive. In particular, he ordered the establishment of schools for reading, singing, and computation in every bishopric and every monastery in his realm. Of course it was one thing to issue orders in the sprawling and lightly governed Carolingian Empire and another to have them carried out. We do not know how effectively this particular order was implemented, but we do know that a number of bishops and abbots took it seriously. Some episcopal and monastic schools had been formed out of necessity after the fall of Rome, and in the course of time began to decay or disappear. Charlemagne's legislation, as well as the existence of a new supply of scholars trained at the palace school, gave new impetus to teaching throughout most of Europe at a time when it might otherwise have stopped. Another period of chaos in the late ninth and early tenth centuries once more threatened the existence of schools, but by then enough abbots and bishops regarded the support of education as part of their duties that the Carolingian tradition, though sometimes interrupted, ultimately endured. The Carolingian episcopal school in Paderborn, for example, remained to become an important center of studies in the eleventh and twelfth centuries and still exists as a high school, which is more than eleven hundred years old.

It is important to bear in mind, however, that the Carolingian schools had limited aims and clientele. Charlemagne's order that schools teach singing shows that their purpose was still largely ecclesiastical. Unquestionably the highest aim of Carolingian education was knowledge of the Bible. In this period Saint Augustine's *On Christian Doctrine* first became a popular text, and Charlemagne himself ordered, in the spirit of Saint Augustine, that monks should diligently pursue the study of letters in order to penetrate the mysteries of Scripture. Supposedly any children who wished to learn were to be admitted to church schools, but in fact most who were instructed were meant for the clergy. In 817 the abbots of the Benedictine Order—as a result of Carolingian reorganization, the only monastic order in the West—even agreed that they would educate only the inmates of their own monasteries. Although this rule was violated in certain monasteries, it was typical of the monastic lack of inclination to assume a burden for educating outsiders. Even after Charlemagne's reforms most of his lay functionaries could not read administrative orders. There were a few educated laymen in the Carolingian Empire, but they were exceptions and they too were educated first in the Psalms. Furthermore, some of the so-called educated men could do no more than barely read. Louis the Pious, Charlemagne's son, was a layman whose education was far better than average because of his royal position, but even he, though accounted learned for being able to read and speak Latin, was unable to sign his name.

The monks seldom rose to scholarly heights because they avoided speculation, and the few who wrote scriptural commentaries—the greatest Carolingian intellectual endeavor—were seldom original. But many monks did at least participate in the great Carolingian undertaking of copying manuscripts. In the edict that ordered the establishment of schools, Charlemagne insisted that the "Catholic books" used in churches should be scrupulously corrected and that "if there is need of writing the Gospel, Psalter, and Missal, let men of mature age do the writing with all diligence." Fearing that Christianity would be corrupted by the use of corrupt books, Charlemagne encouraged an unprecedented wave of copying of "corrected" texts, many of them freshly edited by Alcuin. But Carolingian copying did not stop there. Since Alcuin recognized the value of studying the pagan classics for the purpose of learning good grammar, he and his disciples in the next two generations busied themselves with finding the best surviving texts of the classics and having them recopied by monastic scribes. Owing to the decline of literary interests in the preceding centuries, such texts had become exceedingly scarce and some of Alcuin's disciples exhausted great energy finding them. In some cases the search must have become an end in itself, especially when it resulted in the recopying of such an egregiously non-Christian work as Lucretius' *De rerum natura,* which would have been lost forever if it had not been preserved by Carolingian treasure hunters. The writings of Tacitus too, and what we have of Livy, owe their survival to the energy of Carolingians. In fact, most of the best manuscripts of all the Latin classics we have today were copied by Carolingian scribes, who thus took a place next to Cassiodorus' scribes of Vivarium as preservers of the Latin literary heritage.

It is hard to imagine the tremendous exertion demanded by copying. Today, when handwriting is regarded as an expression of personality, we write as freely and often as eccentrically as we please, but in the Middle Ages the scribe was supposed to write so regularly that one man's handwriting could not be distinguished from another's. The method of holding pen in hand was more arduous than our own, and the necessity to shape letters artistically yet in a thoroughly uniform way was extremely taxing. In fact, copying was imposed on monks as an ascetic discipline—the only one, as an early medieval writer commented, that simultaneously engaged mind, eye, and hand. In addition, physical circumstances were not the best. Light was usually poor (Americans still complain about poor light in most European libraries—one reputedly entering the manuscript room of the Bibliothèque Nationale in Paris with a miner's helmet), and cold was often so intense that scribes were obliged to interrupt their work when their hands became numb. To heighten the ascetic atmosphere of the copying room, silence was enforced, a practice that prompted some scribes to express themselves silently in manuscript margins with remarks like "The light is too dim," "I don't feel well today," or, to explain lacunae, "Here mice ate away the original." Considering all these trials, it is easy to understand why it was said that "sweeter than the view of his harbor to the sailor is the view of the end of his manuscript to the tired scribe."

The tremendous expense of labor in copying manuscripts was but one of the many expenses that limited the Carolingian Renaissance. Added to the labor that went into the production of manuscripts was the cost of parchment, made from the skins of domestic animals at a time when such animals were in short supply, and the cost of bindings made from the skins of wild animals. Charlemagne once had to grant a monastery an entire forest in order to provide it with enough game to supply skins for manuscript bindings. Such expenses could not be widely maintained in a Europe that was poverty-stricken, eking out its existence on a pitifully backward agricultural base. Rather than growing out of any real change in economics or society, the Carolingian Renaissance was imposed from above primarily for religious and political reasons. Because bread and labor were scarce even at its peak, it extended only to the narrowest, primarily clerical, elite. Nor did the quality of those educated make up for the lack in quantity. A late ninth-century biographer of Charlemagne—"the stammering monk of St. Gall"—claimed that Alcuin's teachings "bore such fruit among his pupils that the modern Gauls or Franks came to equal the Romans and Athenians," but that was inflated nonsense.

Nonetheless, the very occurrence of the Carolingian Renaissance was as good as a violation of the laws of economic determinism, and Carolingian accomplishments in the face of such great odds were remarkable. Alcuin and his disciples succeeded in resuscitating the writing and teaching of Latin, thus making it the language of learning for centuries to come as well as a constant influence even on non-Romance European vernaculars. They promulgated a clear method of writing, which is still in use, and they preserved the basic texts not only of the Christian but also of the Roman literary tradition. Charlemagne's schools too were the foundations of many schools to come. In all this the Carolingians provided Europe with cultural unity at a time when it was threatened with thorough fragmentation. Indeed, the preservation and welding together of the Roman and Christian inheritance was the greatest achievement of the Carolingian age. Charlemagne's empire expired a century after Charlemagne, but its methods of expression and schools lasted a thousand years and in some cases are with us still.

Bridges Between the Carolingian Renaissance and the High Middle Ages

Europe experienced a second wave of invasions—of Vikings, Hungarians, and Arabs—which reached its peak in the late ninth century and the first half of the tenth century. Scholars have recently disagreed about the severity of these invasions, but the fact remains that they were severe enough to help bring about the termination of Carolingian rule throughout western Europe and to bring to the fore local leaders who were best able to offer security to their localities. These leaders, however, were brute warriors who, when they had no foreign enemies to worry about, lost no time in fighting each other. Europe around the year 900 was in political chaos, and one hundred years later the situation was hardly better. The tapering off of the invasions brought respite from external dangers, but only in Germany did a strong dynasty emerge in the course of the tenth century to bring a modicum of internal peace. Yet remarkably, despite all this turbulence, schools survived, a testimony to the impressive staying power of Carolingian institutions and attitudes.

The area in which education was most endangered was England, where, after the departure of Alcuin for the continent, the decay of intellectual life was greatly accelerated by Viking invasions. As early as 793 Alcuin was horrified by reports of a Viking sack of a monastery and declared that "never before has such a terror appeared in Britain as we now suffer from a pagan race." This incursion was just one of the first. A year later the Vikings destroyed Bede's monastery of Jarrow. There was comparative peace in the first half of the ninth century, but Vikings began to winter in England after 850 and came close to conquering the entire country in the last decades of the century. It was then that King Alfred the Great began to turn them back and concurrently to provide for a revival of learning. Unable to find scholars in his own kingdom of Wessex, he imported them and with their aid set up a court school where upper-class youths were taught to read and write. Unlike Charlemagne, Alfred was persuaded that the vernacular should be taught before Latin so that all upper-class Englishmen would learn to read English. To further this program he translated with the help of one of his scholar friends several basic Latin works. But this concern for disseminating learning in the language of the laity was unprecedented for Alfred's time and doomed to failure. Alfred's court school vanished after his death, and learning again became such a near-monopoly of the clergy that even most of Alfred's successors on the throne were illiterate. Yet teaching did go on in the monasteries, especially after a great monastic reformation of the middle of the tenth century when monks reestablished broken links with the continent and again started to copy manuscripts in a rush to make up for lost time.

No contemporary ruler on the continent cared as much for patronizing learning as Alfred did. During the worst period of renewed invasions, from the last decades of the ninth century to the first decades of the tenth century, the outposts of literacy were not rulers' courts but, as later in England, monasteries. A surviving ninth-century plan of one of these, the monastery of St. Gall at the foot of the Alps, shows that it was big enough to house farm buildings, artisans' quarters, baths, and hospitals, as well as a school and library.

Tucked away relatively safe from invasion, St. Gall and a few other monasteries like it such as Corbie in France, Corvey, Reichenau, and Fulda (Saint Boniface's foundation) in Germany survived as self-sufficient nuclei during the times of trouble. Fortunately these monasteries were direct beneficiaries of the Carolingian Renaissance, for a number of Alcuin's leading students had retired into them when the empire began to decay and there they educated monks and abbots who passed their literate traditions to succeeding generations of monks. Many of these heirs of Alcuin were, like him, bibliophiles who were zealous about collecting, copying, and preserving books. Therefore all the monasteries mentioned had good libraries housing not only biblical and patristic but classical texts; in the middle of the tenth century a monk of Corvey could thus describe the deeds of Saxon rulers in language modeled on the prose of the Roman historian Sallust. Later in the Middle Ages a monk wrote that "a monastery (*claustrum*) without a library (*armarium*) is like a castle (*castrum*) without an armory (*armamentarium*); our library is our armory." This sentiment was most keenly felt by Alcuin's heirs in an age of iron.

Along with libraries, the monasteries had schools for the education of inhabitants. These no doubt varied in quality, but a leading institution like St. Gall was a nest of literacy and Latinity. This was learned painfully by a visiting Italian grammarian who in 965 was humiliated in St. Gall by the laughter of the monks for unwittingly using in conversation the accusative instead of the ablative case. In addition to its interior school, St. Gall also had a separate school, kept physically apart, for the instruction of outsiders, but in this it seems to have been atypical. Even though our lack of sources for the history of the tenth century makes it unclear how many other monasteries had such outer schools, clearly few monasteries were extensively concerned with educating the laity, and in all probability monastic education of nonmonks was less widespread in the tenth century than in Carolingian times. Monasteries, of course, were also hardly conducive to the free play of ideas. In the early eleventh century, Lanfranc, one of the most learned men of his day, was "corrected" in the pronunciation of a certain Latin word by an illiterate monastic superior and according to his admiring contemporary biographer gladly then said the word in the wrong way as a sign of obedience.

Teaching also continued in schools attached to cathedrals. During the invasions the activities of these schools seem to have been sharply curtailed or even interrupted, but by the second half of the tenth century several sprang back to life. In Cologne, for example, a cathedral school had been founded in the time of Charlemagne and in the middle of the ninth century was still turning out students. Thereafter, a century of inactivity intervened until the school was reinvigorated by Archbishop Bruno, the brother of Emperor Otto I of Germany. Bruno had received a good monastic education and loved his books so much that according to his biographer he took his library with him wherever he went "as if it were the ark of the Lord." The same biographer credits him with restoring the liberal arts and educating a number of students who then spread knowledge in many places. Similarly, at Liège the cathedral school was reinvigorated in the late tenth century by the learned Bishop Notker, who had been educated at St. Gall. When Notker traveled, he supposedly took his students with him and kept on drilling them in their scholastic exercises.

Most important of all the tenth-century cathedral schools was that of Reims. The original establishment was Carolingian, but the late ninth century saw an interruption of educational activities. At the very end of the century, however, an energetic archbishop had the dilapidated school building rebuilt and invited a scholar who had a monastic education and who could trace his line of teachers directly back to Alcuin to reinaugurate the teaching of reading and the liberal arts. Thereafter, teaching at Reims appears to have been uninterrupted, and the school reached its zenith in the late tenth century under the direction of Gerbert, the greatest intellect of his time. Gerbert, who rose at Reims from the rank of schoolmaster to archbishop and died as Pope Sylvester II (999–1003), was most unusual for his day in being interested in the advanced liberal arts—arithmetic, geometry, astronomy, and music. He taught all these as well as advanced grammar, rhetoric, and logic (he left the most elementary teaching to someone else) to a large number of students, many of whom traveled great distances to sit at his feet. Among these were a future king of France, Robert the Pious, and several young men who later directed schools of their own in the late tenth and early eleventh centuries, foremost among whom was Fulbert, subsequently bishop of Chartres.

In considering the accomplishments of schools like Reims under Gerbert, however, two limitations must be taken into account. First, the nature of their clientele had not changed since Carolingian days. Education at Reims and other cathedrals was meant expressly for the future cathedral canons and rural clergy; laymen by and large were accepted only when they were as privileged as the heir to the throne of France. As for the clerical students, occasionally a lowborn youth could gain an education if he was going to enter orders or was already in them, but most seem to have been young men of relative means, for most peasant families needed their children to help in the fields.

Second, Reims under Gerbert was as atypical in late tenth-century Europe as Jarrow was atypical in England at the time of Bede. Indeed, the attainments of teachers like Bruno, Notker, and Gerbert were recorded (and perhaps exaggerated) by admiring chroniclers precisely because they seemed so unusual. Others were even hostile to such learned men. A certain German supposedly once had a vision in which he saw Bruno being judged by Christ for vain pursuit of philosophy, and after Gerbert's death a legend cropped up that he had been a magician in league with the Devil. The knowledge possessed by Bruno and Gerbert would have been considered elementary in following centuries, but in their age they were intellectual giants regarded by some with suspicion for knowing or wishing to know too much. In short, almost all men in late tenth-century Europe, even including an appreciable proportion of the clergy, were illiterate, and most who were literate were just barely so.

It was long the fashion to revile the tenth century as an age of utter darkness, and in reaction to that some recent scholars have tried to introduce the notion of a "Tenth-Century Renaissance." But neither characterization will do. Learning was preserved in the tenth century, but in a most limited way. Because historians know that after 1050 there was a true intellectual awakening, some fall into the habit of reading history backward and making the tenth century a "period of incubation" or an age of "darkness of the womb." Of course students of one generation were taught by masters from an earlier one, but as we will see, there was a thorough quantitative and also qualitative difference between the learning of the High Middle Ages and that which came before. Looking at events from the other direction, it seems best to regard education from around 850 to around 1050 as an extension of the Carolingian tradition of having schools in monasteries and cathedrals for the primary purpose of educating the clergy to propagate the faith. If contemporaries of Bruno of Cologne thought that he was in danger of damnation because of his pursuit of philosophy, one wonders what they would have thought about Peter Abelard.

The Renaissance of the Twelfth Century

An oft-repeated joke of the twelfth century told in one version of events that purportedly took place two hundred years before. In the middle of the tenth century the king of France supposedly was not only illiterate but had no desire to learn. Once when he visited the city of Tours he undiplomatically mocked the literate count of Anjou for his knowledge of Latin and "for singing like a priest," but the count had the last word. After the king returned to Paris, the count sent him the following terse missive: "To the king of the Franks, the count of Anjou: greetings. Know, my lord, that an unlettered king is a crowned ass" (*rex illiteratus, asinus coronatus*). It is most unlikely that these events ever transpired in the tenth century, for then no one much cared whether kings were crowned asses or not; the story is told here because it represents new attitudes of the twelfth century, when there was a true renaissance or rebirth of learning.

Unlike the Carolingian Renaissance, which was imposed artificially from above, the Renaissance of the Twelfth Century—to be understood as beginning about 1050—grew spontaneously along with and appreciably as a result of greatly changed material conditions. Starting about 1050 and continuing through the twelfth century, the medieval economy made a quantum leap toward prosperity. Improved farming techniques and cultivation of new lands boosted agricultural productivity. With a broader agricultural base, population increased and the western European economy became more diversified, causing the growth of existing towns and the foundation of many new ones. Western Europe, previously a "Wild West," was becoming wealthier than it had ever been before. In addition, concurrent with economic growth was the growth of secular governments better able to reduce private warfare and the vast increase of the administrative and judicial operations of papal government.

These changes allowed momentous changes in the history of education. With greater wealth and population, education became much less a luxury. Europe had far more of the wherewithal than it did in Carolingian times to support study, and its greater population meant that more men could be spared for studious occupations. The growth of cities also spurred the progress of education, for cities provided legal liberties as well as domiciles for teachers and clusters of students. At the same time, stronger governments not only helped economic development by increasing peace but also allowed scholars to travel with less fear of being assailed on the roads by brigands or robber barons. Furthermore, the growth of bureaucratic governments called for trained officials, and lowborn men could thus rise through the ranks at court if they were well educated. This was a considerable incentive to go to school. Finally, even religious changes worked in the same direction, for the growth of papal government called for trained officials and the newly strengthened papacy encouraged the thorough training of priests in order to upgrade the promulgation of the faith.

Nevertheless, not every religious change helped to encourage education. The twelfth century did see a sharp decline in educational activities in monasteries. The monastic ideal of the twelfth century, embodied by the new and widely influential Cistercian Order, was one of total withdrawal from the world. As cities grew, Cistercians moved away from them into woods, hills, and swamps. There, divorced from secular society, they taught no outsiders. More important, they had no schools for their own inhabitants because they eschewed the practice of recruiting children and stipulated that entrants, who had to be at least fifteen years old, had to have had some education before being admitted to the novitiate. The insistence of the greatest Cistercian of the twelfth century, Saint Bernard, that "the duty of the monk is not to teach but to weep" was in the twelfth century a frequently repeated slogan. Caught up in such sentiments, older monasteries abandoned their teaching of outsiders and curtailed internal instruction. Teaching had usually been regarded by monks as either peripheral to the monastic vocation or even as a serious distraction. In the eleventh century the monastic reformer Saint Peter Damian was delighted to see a monastery in which there were "no schools for boys to enervate the rigor of sanctity," and he would have been gratified to know that in the following centuries there would be many more of these monasteries.

Perhaps one reason the monasteries felt they could do without schools was the fact that education in towns and cities was burgeoning. In the late eleventh and twelfth centuries such education was carried out in two different ways—either by the private instruction of clerics, often wanderers, hired by the rich to be tutors for their children, or, more frequently, in schools attached to cathedrals and collegiate churches. The great majority of students were, as earlier, destined for the priesthood or monastic life, except in Italy, which, though the home of the papacy, had a more secular tradition than the North because an urban economy had first developed there.

In Italy the clergy had a near-monopoly of instruction until the thirteenth century, but there more well-to-do laymen were students than they were in the North. As early as 1041 a German poet contrasted Italy as a country where "all the youths are obliged to sweat in schools" with Germany, where education was scorned as vain and worthless for all but the clergy. Even a generation before then, the young Lanfranc—later to become archbishop of Canterbury—was educated while still a layman in Pavia in "the liberal arts and secular law." The study of law in particular became an Italian specialty. In the eleventh century it was taught in Rome and Ravenna in addition to Pavia, and in the twelfth century it became concentrated in Bologna. There, around 1100 a great layman and jurist named Irnerius firmly established the teaching of Roman law on the basis of the complete text of Justinian's *Corpus Juris,* and around 1140 a monk named Gratian just as firmly established the teaching of canon law (that is, church law) on the basis of his own compilation and analysis of canon law texts, known as the *Decretum*. Both Irnerius and Gratian began dynasties of teachers who made Bologna the center of European legal studies throughout the rest of the Middle Ages. Of course not all Italian students went on to law, but in the twelfth century not only most priests and papal functionaries but also lay urban administrators learned at least how to read.

North of the Alps, Germany had a plentiful number of schools in the twelfth century but was the one major country that did not see steady educational progress. In the tenth and most of the eleventh centuries it had been the best governed area of northern Europe, but from the 1070s to the 1150s it was seriously weakened by the Investiture Controversy and civil wars. Political turmoil by no means interrupted educational activities, but it did hamper them. Thus, while Germany had several unrivaled cathedral schools in the eleventh century, outstanding German students in the twelfth century—Otto of Freising and Rainald of Dassel, for example—gravitated for their studies to France.

One of the few vivid accounts we have of the education of a twelfth-century German is exemplary. A certain Vizelin, who came, as a contemporary biographer reported, from a family "more distinguished for honest ways than for noble blood," was sent as a boy around 1100 to a church school in his home town of Hameln but did not attend to his studies. Asked by a hostile priest what he had learned there, he replied the *Achilleis* of the Roman poet Statius —a striking indication that pagan classics were being read even in small church schools—but could say nothing about what he was supposed to have read. Intent on reforming himself, he then went to the cathedral school of Paderborn, "where studies were flourishing," there worked so hard that even his teacher urged him to relax, and soon rose to become a teaching assistant. Afterward, in the early 1120s, he became director of studies at the cathedral school of Bremen, but then he felt that his own education was unfinished and went to France to study theology for three years at the leading school of Laon. Finally, he became a bishop and died as a missionary to the Slavs. From the evidence of this story alone we can safely say that there were a good number of church schools for beginners in Germany, even if the best products of these schools promptly moved on to France.

In the twelfth century the best English students like Thomas Becket, John of Salisbury, and Stephen Langton also left for France, despite the fact that in England, unlike Germany, political stability was growing. Local schools were proliferating and expanding, but the trouble was that they had a lot of catching up to do. Until the Norman Conquest in 1066 the only educational centers in England were monasteries, which were disinclined to teach outsiders. After the conquest, therefore, when the number of youths seeking education was growing, many schools were founded in cathedrals and churches, but they had to be staffed by Frenchmen. Most, with the exception of Oxford, never reached French standards and even Oxford at its medieval prime was staffed mainly by teachers who had gained some of their own education in France. In addition, England had come into such a French orbit as a result of the Norman Conquest—in the twelfth century the kings still spoke French —that aspiring Englishmen felt they would be considered provincial if they did not visit France. Thus, bright or ambitious students generally left for France (or Bologna if they wished to study law) after receiving preliminary education at home, and most English institutions contented themselves with offering introductory studies.

Of course France would not have attracted so many students from Germany and England, as well as from many other countries, if it had not had distinguished teaching to offer. Education in France underwent a great transformation both in quantity and quality about the year 1100. Good evidence of this comes from the writings of a French monk, Guibert of Nogent, who, in his autobiography written in 1115, reported that when he was a boy (around 1075) there was "such a scarcity of teachers that there were almost none in the villages and hardly any in the cities, and those who by chance could be found had such slight knowledge that they could not even be compared to the wandering scholars of today." Guibert was educated (if that is the word) by a schoolmaster who, because he had learned grammar late in life, was "utterly unskilled in prose and verse composition" and who out of insecurity subjected Guibert to "a hail of blows and harsh words" in trying to make his student "learn what he could not teach." Just a generation later, however, Guibert wrote that there was "a great number of schools" and that grammar was "flourishing far and wide."

These assertions were not exaggerated. The cathedral of Poitiers had "a master of schools" in 1077 and thereafter an unbroken series of such masters, including from 1105 to 1135 an influential teacher named Hilary. From 1087 to 1092 the cathedral school of Tournai so thrived under its schoolmaster Odo that a chronicler called it a "second Athens." In the first three decades of the twelfth century the cathedral school of Laon was pre-eminent in theology under the direction of Anselm of Laon, "the light of all France," and his brother Ralph. In the 1120s the cathedral school of Reims regained the luster of the days of Gerbert under the theologian Alberic, who brought it a new "diadem"; and the cathedral school of Chartres was directed from 1119 to 1126 by Bernard of Chartres, "the most abounding spring of letters in Gaul." Most northern French cathedrals had respectable grammar schools attached to them in the early twelfth century, but Paris not only boasted a cathedral school that was already flourishing around 1100 but also had leading schools attached to the collegiate churches of St. Geneviève and St. Victor. These schools pulled ahead of the others by the mid-twelfth century. Around 1140 the logician and theologian Gilbert of Poitiers lectured to four students at Chartres but to three hundred at Paris, and between 1137 and 1147 the Englishman John of Salisbury was able to hear at Paris the lectures of at least ten different masters, including some of the greatest intellects of medieval times.

This sudden French intellectual explosion is as difficult to account for fully as the later outburst of poetry in Elizabethan England. Exclusively economic answers will not suffice because the most developed urban economies of the twelfth century were to be found in Lombardy and Flanders, neither of which had schools to rival those of northern France. Not that northern France was poor: It was an expanse of rich farm land made richer by new agricultural techniques; commerce was aided by a good system of rivers; and though except for Paris there were no cities as large as those of Lombardy and Flanders, there were many middle-sized towns to provide markets. What the area around Paris had in addition that Lombardy and Flanders did not have was a growingly assertive monarchy. In particular, Louis VI, who for practical purposes took over from his father around 1100 and died in 1137, subdued the turbulent local nobility and brought more peace to the area than it had had for hundreds of years. He made travel on the roads safe and in the words of his contemporary biographer, "looked after the needs of churches, and guarded the security of priests, working men, and the poor, duties which for a long time no one had discharged." Without the stability brought by his reign, scholars would have feared for their lives and no doubt have gone elsewhere. Louis— no Charlemagne—did not designedly patronize schools, but he was sufficiently aware that the cathedral school of Paris was becoming a leading educational institution to send his own son there even though he himself had been educated in a monastery (a fitting token of the twelfth-century shift from monastic to urban cathedral schools).

Sufficient wealth and political stability made the growth of learning possible in northern France, but only the presence of great teachers and new attitudes toward learning ensured French, and particularly Parisian, dominance in matters intellectual. The greatest of these teachers, whose reputation brought throngs of students to northern France and helped to establish a lasting intellectual pre-eminence for Paris, was Peter Abelard. Fortunately we know more about this singular man, born around 1079, than we do about most of his contemporaries because he left an autobiography. One of the first items he reports in this work shows how knowledge was spreading in France in the late eleventh century. Abelard's father, though a simple knight from Brittany (one of the more backward parts of France), had gained a smattering of letters and wanted his children to gain even more learning before they turned to feats of arms. Abelard was the eldest son and customarily would have inherited his father's title, lands, and occupation, but once launched on studies, he "gladly" left to his brothers "the pomp of glory in arms" and, preferring "the battle of minds in disputation," fled, as he said, from the "court of Mars" to the "bosom of Minerva." Had he lived earlier, his father would likely have stood in his way or he would have had few places to flee to other than a monastery, but times had changed.

After leaving Brittany, Abelard studied at Loches, Paris, and Laon, taught near Paris at Melun and Corbeil, and then taught at Paris both in the schools of St. Geneviève and the cathedral. Everywhere he went he attracted droves of students from all parts of Europe. In 1118, for example, a contemporary noted that Abelard's students included Romans, Englishmen, Germans, Swedes, and natives from all over France. His arrogance and new ideas and methods made him many enemies, but even after one of his books was condemned by the church he continued to attract students. Though his enemies compared his errors to a plague spreading over France, he was silenced only by a second ecclesiastical condemnation. A story told a century later shows that his drawing powers and persistence as a teacher had not been forgotten.

Supposedly the king of France suddenly forbade Abelard to teach in his lands. Upon hearing this news, Abelard climbed a tree and his students flocked to hear him from below. The king then prohibited him from teaching in the air, but when Abelard started lecturing from a boat, the king conceded defeat and allowed the indomitable teacher to continue his course of lectures in Paris.

Aside from Abelard's great popularity as a teacher, what must be stressed here is the fact that he pursued knowledge as a career. Before his time even Alcuin, though dedicated to disseminating education, was first of all a churchman and minister of Charlemagne, and others who taught did so still more peripherally, most often as monks. But Abelard represented a new class of men who were pre-eminently scholars and teachers and who therefore have been called with justice by J. Le Goff the first professional intellectuals of the West. For Abelard the profession of teaching and scholarship was one fully equivalent to that of knighthood and at odds with monasticism, which he believed was a profession not at all conducive to the study of secular books. He expressed this new attitude most fully in a famous passage of his autobiography when he said that he ran a school "since to dig I was not able, and to beg I was ashamed, so having recourse to the profession I knew, I was driven to work with my voice instead of with my hands." A generation after Abelard men started speaking forthrightly about the "business of scholarship," and this attitude led later to the foundation of universities.

What led men to enter this new "business"? Questions of motivation are among the hardest for historians to answer, but in this case a good start can be made from Abelard's own opposition of study for "money and praise," which he admitted were his original motives, to study for "the love of God." The latter was, of course, still the dominant apologia. In the twelfth century it was universally acknowledged that theology was the summit of learning and many still argued, along the lines of Saint Augustine's *On Christian Doctrine,* that the liberal arts should be pursued solely for the sake of preparation for biblical studies. The popularity of *On Christian Doctrine* in the twelfth century was enormous; J. B. Reeves even maintains that "no book on education has ever been studied more attentively or profitably than this was in the twelfth century." Thus, in the spirit of Augustine men said that the liberal arts were "the footmen of theology" and compared the appropriation of the arts for the purposes of theology to the biblical beating of swords into plowshares. No doubt other motives for becoming educated were overpowering, but it will not do to say that twelfth-century men merely paid lip service to the Augustinian argument. Even Abelard, the personification of the new professionalism who in some careless scholarship now ranks as an atheist, regarded theology (a word that he coined) as the highest of studies and devoted himself to studying and teaching it with the greatest absorption.

Those earlier, however, who sought wisdom for the love of God were not in the "business of scholarship." Only in the twelfth century, when teaching left the monasteries for the cities, could a man make a regular living at it and think of it as a profession. Sometimes he might have been supported by the church. A twelfth-century ideal, stated in a decree of the Third Lateran Council in 1179, was that education should be free for all, and this was to be achieved by having every cathedral church in Christendom provide a benefice (a steady income usually from the profits of a certain piece of land) to support one master who would then be able to teach all the students who came to him —rich and poor alike—without fee. This was not an entirely impossible goal because most cathedral chapters were prospering from landowning, market taxes, and donations and could afford one benefice to support teaching. Nonetheless, it is certain that not all cathedrals did as they were supposed to, even after the order of 1179. Furthermore, this decree made no provision for ubiquitous private tutoring, the teaching of public law (a secular subject that could not be financed by church benefices), or the problems of Paris, which by then had dozens of masters. The provision of benefices for teaching remained a practice that did support an impressive number of teachers, but the church became forced to tolerate the fact that many teachers had to support themselves by taking fees. Abelard regularly lived off the fees of his students in the beginning of the twelfth century, and as time went on the practice became more and more frequent. By the end of the century it became a commonplace to concede that teachers of the liberal arts could charge for their instruction because their skills were equivalent to the mechanical arts. Teachers of theology, on the other hand, were casuistically forbidden to stipulate charges in advance because theology was a "spiritual gift," but if they had no benefice, they were allowed to accept "donations" after their lessons were over.

In addition to "money," the young Abelard's other motive for becoming a teacher was "praise." This must have been an appreciable consideration for him and others, for even with the taking of fees the likelihood of becoming rich in the twelfth century in the teaching profession was small. In fact, one of the most impressive aspects of the Twelfth-Century Renaissance was the new prestige it gave to the pursuit of knowledge and the profession of teaching. It was said that "learning makes one noble," that "the liberal arts are powerful swords" (a forerunner of the modern cliché that "knowledge is power"), and that "as much as men are removed from the beasts, so are educated men removed from the illiterate." Great teachers became celebrated figures, and Paris, the home of most of them, was praised for its "philosophers" and admiringly called a "city of letters." Teaching came to be recognized as one of the most honorable of the professions, and by the thirteenth century one writer even said that "the status of the philosopher is more perfect than the

6. *A detail of the liberal arts on the west portal of
the cathedral of Chartres. On the left, over Pythagorus,
is a personification of music; on the right, over
Donatus the grammarian, a personification of grammar
as a schoolmistress threatening boys.*

status of the prince." The most famous visual evidence of the exalted place
accorded to the liberal arts is the west portal of the cathedral of Chartres,
decorated in the 1140s, on which sculptured personifications of the seven liberal arts, accompanied by their prototypic exponents (Aristotle, Euclid, and
others), surround the infant Jesus enthroned in the lap of the Virgin (Fig. 6).
At Paris too in the first decade of the thirteenth century the liberal arts were
represented at the front of the cathedral in direct relationship to Christ.

With the arts so exalted, their earthly teachers must have felt proud, but
finally it must be assumed that many of them pursued scholarship as well for
its own joys as from any other motives. In 1158 the German emperor Frederick
Barbarossa issued privileges for scholars who left their homes "for love of
knowledge," and though this motive was otherwise not often stressed, that no
doubt was because it went without saying.

Pure love of learning, of course, was a less compelling motive for those who became educated for careers other than teaching. Students of law in particular had a reputation for being materialistic careerists in an age when law was becoming known as "the lucrative science" and its successful practice the best means for rapid advancement in the government of both church and state. Medicine too had its profit-making attractions. Those who did not go on to law or medicine could, if they had been well trained in the arts, gain positions at royal courts or rise in the clergy. Eloquent testimony to the profit motive behind much of twelfth-century education was the lament of a student of Abelard around 1150 that "Christians educate their sons . . . for gain, in order that the one brother, if he be a clerk, may help his father and mother and his other brothers, saying that a clerk will have no heir and whatever he has will be ours and the other brothers'." With the opening of positions in law, government, and the church, education became a means for advancement not only in income but also in status. Most who were educated were wealthy, but in the twelfth century, more often than before, many were not and were able to rise through the ranks by means of their education. The most familiar examples are Thomas Becket, who rose from a humble background to become chancellor of England and then archbishop of Canterbury, and John of Salisbury, who was born a "plebeian" but because of his reputation for learning died as bishop of Chartres.

The instances of Becket and John of Salisbury bring us to the most difficult question concerning twelfth-century education: To what degree was it still a clerical preserve? Despite the fact that throughout the twelfth century—aside from the teaching of law, medicine, notarial skills, and mechanical crafts— the clergy had a monopoly of instruction, one of the outstanding medievalists of our day, R. W. Southern, refers with good reason to the institutions staffed by the clergy as "secular schools." How can we make sense out of the paradox that twelfth-century schools were clerical and yet "secular"?

Let us look at the clerical side first. Not only were all twelfth-century teachers except professionals and craftsmen in church orders, but in northern Europe students in schools had clerical status and looked like priests. Not that all really were priests, but by virtue of being students all were awarded the legal privileges accorded to the clergy, and all wore the clerical tonsure to make sure that these privileges would be honored. Furthermore, the large majority of twelfth-century students, outside of the possible exception of Italy, if not already priests became so after their studies were finished. For these reasons, the term "cleric" was often used to denote a man who was literate and the term "layman" one who was illiterate. As late as the thirteenth century an Italian imaginatively argued that "layman" (*laicus*) originated from the word for stone (*lapis*) because the layman is "rough and ignorant of letters." Similarly, the English word for cleric, "clerk," continued for a long time to be a synonym for student (as in Chaucer) or for a man who could write—which is why it now means an office worker who keeps records—while the French word *clerc* even today has the connotation of intellectual.

Despite all this, twelfth-century education was taking on many secular qualities in its environment, goals, and curriculum. Student life obviously became more secular when it moved out from the monasteries into the bustling towns. Most students wandered from town to town in search not only of good masters but also of worldly excitement, and as the twelfth century progressed they found the best of each in Paris—excellent teachers and also the throbbing life of a rapidly growing capital. An early thirteenth-century preacher told of how masters and whores in Paris sometimes shared houses, one lecturing above while the other plied her trade below, hardly an arrangement that provided the atmosphere of a monastery. More important than environment was the fact that most students, even though they entered the clergy, had secular goals. Theology was recognized as the "queen of the sciences," but very few went on to it. Instead they used their study of the liberal arts as a preparation for law, medicine, government service, or advancement in the ecclesiastical hierarchy.

This being so, the curriculum of the liberal arts became more sophisticated and more divorced from religion. Teaching was still almost exclusively in Latin, and the first book most often read was the Psalter, but further education was no longer similar to that of a choir school. In particular, the discipline of rhetoric was transformed from a linguistic study into instruction in how to compose letters and documents; there was a new stress on logic; and in all the liberal arts and philosophy texts more advanced than those known in the early Middle Ages were introduced. Sometimes the preoccupation with logic could be laughable, as when logicians supposedly debated whether since "mouse" is a syllable and a mouse eats cheese then a syllable eats cheese. But training in logic was necessary to help men think rationally, and in the words of Joseph R. Strayer, "it was only when the rules of logic had become an unconscious habit of all European thinkers that the teaching of formal logic could be abandoned."

Along with the rise of logic came the translation of Greek and Arabic philosophical and scientific works. Most important was the translation of almost all the writings of Aristotle, as well as his sophisticated Arabic commentators, which helped to bring about an intellectual revolution based on Greek rationalism. On a more prosaic level, contact with Arabs resulted in the introduction in the twelfth century of the Arabic numeral system and the concept of zero. Though most Westerners first resisted this and made crude jokes about the zero as an ambitious number "that counts for nothing and yet wants to be counted," the system steadily made its inroads first in Italy and then throughout Europe, thereby vastly simplifying the arts of computation and record keeping. (The reader who wonders about this is invited to try doing his income tax returns with Roman numerals.)

The intellectual accomplishments of the twelfth century are the subject for another essay; what should be pointed out here is that they were carried out in an unprecedented atmosphere of receptivity, open-mindedness, and independence. A distinction does have to be made between studies in the liberal arts and studies in theology, which naturally were subject to more constraints. Abelard, for example, was free to argue as he pleased in logic but was twice condemned when he sought to push logical methods too far in theology. The independence of the liberal arts, on the other hand, was most forcefully stated by a great twelfth-century thinker, William of Conches, who maintained that a philosopher is by no means bound to accept the authority of the church in matters unconnected with faith and morals. Open-mindedness was pushed even farther by the Englishman Adelard of Bath, who insisted that science should be based on reason and boldly said that he regarded authority as "matter for contempt." In contrast to Saint Augustine, who attacked intellectual curiosity if it was not clearly subordinated to the search for divine wisdom, the twelfth-century scholar Hugh of St. Victor—who otherwise was a very Augustinian thinker—urged his readers to "learn everything" and "hold no learning in contempt, for all learning is good." Of course many still attacked untrammeled question raising, in the spirit of Augustine, as idle and even dangerous, forcing William of Conches to complain that every question raiser in his day was decried as a heretic. But in the twelfth century such men were fighting a rearguard action; conceivably they were in the majority, but they were not having their way in the leading schools.

In theology, few immediately followed Abelard's attempt to inject logical arguments into theological discourse and the impact of Aristotle was not fully felt until the thirteenth century, but theological studies did become more systematic and professional, especially as a result of the widespread use of Peter Lombard's *Book of Sentences,* written in the mid-twelfth century, as a basic textbook. This was a collection of texts from the Bible and Fathers on both sides of basic theological questions followed by Peter's judgment. Though it lacked originality or brilliance, it had in the words of J. Pieper, "the somewhat boring solidity which is after all one of the prime qualities of a good textbook," and it must rank as one of the world's epoch-making books because it became the basis for almost all further theological inquiry during the Middle Ages.

Growing professionalism and accomplishments in twelfth-century Western intellectual life led to growing self-confidence. Actually, Europeans were doing little more than absorbing the knowledge previously set forth by Greeks and Arabs, but they were beginning to feel that they were on the same level with them or even higher. In the twelfth century the theory that learning was passed like a baton from the Egyptians to the Greeks to the Romans to the West was often repeated. Thinkers now forgotten like Berengar of Tours, Manegold of

Lautenbach, and Anselm of Laon were compared to the philosophers of Athens. A manuscript illumination dating from about 1150 shows a certain Adam of Petit Pont, then a famous logician but now unknown to all but specialists, in equal company with Plato and Aristotle and debating with Socrates (fig. 7). Though Europe still had no intellects to compare with Aristotle, the fact that it thought it did helped it to push on to the point where with Saint Thomas Aquinas in the thirteenth century it would. More than that, in receptivity to new ideas and spread of learning Europe was advancing to the point where it would outstrip every other part of the world.

7. Dialectic portrayed as a Christian queen surrounded by Plato, Aristotle, Socrates, and Adam of Petit Pont, in a pen drawing of a twelfth-century Boethius manuscript now in Darmstadt.

8. *A student emptying his chamberpot on the head of King Louis IX of France, from a fifteenth-century manuscript.*

The Thirteenth Century: The Emergence of Universities and Lay Primary Schools

Twelfth-century kings were not supposed to be crowned asses, yet many of them were. By the thirteenth century, however, the spread of learning no longer passed them by and most were at least literate. Some were outstandingly so: Emperor Frederick II (1215–1250) knew several languages, took a lively interest in science and theology, and wrote a treatise on falconry that historians of science count among the best of medieval zoological works. Alfonso X of Castile (1252–1284), known as "the Wise" or "the Learned," studied astronomy, helped compile his country's laws, and has rightly been called by J. B. Trend "a bad king but a good editor." Saint Louis IX of France (1226–1270) studied throughout his life and translated on sight passages from Latin into French for the benefit of less learned members of his court. Of Saint Louis it was said that once when he was going to church in Paris at dawn a university student unwittingly emptied his chamberpot on the royal head, but the king, instead of punishing the student, rewarded him because he had risen so early to study (fig. 8). This is just a story, but it indicates how much men of the thirteenth century prized studiousness. The story's locale is also significant: By the thirteenth century Paris was the home of a university, a new institution that there and elsewhere was one of the most salient features of the new map of learning.

The material underpinning of thirteenth-century culture was the same as that of the twelfth century. The European economy continued to expand until roughly the last quarter of the thirteenth century, and wealth continued to be amassed to support teaching and scholarship. Moreover, there was greater peace for most of western Europe, providing an ideal climate for the pursuit of learning. The growth of secular governments and the papacy continued to provide jobs for the learned, and increasingly some education was considered to be a prerequisite for advancement to the upper echelons of the clergy. Thus incentives for learning were numerous, and teachers and students became assertive enough to form their own self-interested corporations.

These corporations were known as universities. In the early twelfth century scholars like Abelard often quarreled with each other, but by the end of the century they had become wise enough to band together against common enemies. There were two different original corporative patterns: Those of Bologna and of Paris. The former city had a "university" or guild of students, a fact often pointed out by modern advocates of student power. Of course the situation then was very different. The great majority of students who came to Bologna came there to study law and were thus not beginners. Often they were in their thirties or even forties and had attained high governmental positions. They needed a guild because they were not native to Bologna, though their teachers were permanent residents, and they needed to secure exemptions from local dues and restrictive jurisdictions. By the thirteenth century they had fully achieved this goal because of their potent threats of withdrawing to rival cities. They also managed to reduce their teachers to subservience because teachers of law were laymen who were not supported by the church and therefore depended for their livelihood on student fees. The Bolognese pattern, once established, became the model for most other subsequent medieval universities in Italy.

The North followed the model of Paris, which had a university of masters and students and was dominated by the former. In the second half of the twelfth century Paris became recognized as an unrivaled center of studies. Ironically, while the rate of education increased, the number of leading French schools decreased because cathedral schools like Laon and Chartres, dwarfed by the fame and resources of Paris, limited themselves more and more to preparatory curricula. A reflection of the concentration of studies in late twelfth-century Paris was the growth of a bookselling industry, which took the copying monopoly away from monasteries and produced books less elegantly but more rapidly and cheaply than they were provided in the earlier Middle

9. *A manuscript of the Psalms written in 1105 in the monastery of Saint Martin of Tournai showing few ligatures or abbreviations. The first two lines read: "Anno ab incarnacione domini millesimo centesimo quinto et a restauracione huius cenobii quartodecimo scriptus est liber iste," the only abbreviated words being "domini" and "liber."*

Ages. With a new emphasis on cheapness and speed came a new readiness to abbreviate words to save not only time but also precious parchment space, and a new script, the Gothic, first developed in Paris in the late twelfth century, which allowed scribes to work more quickly because it had more ligatures than did Carolingian minuscule (figs. 9, 10). The book industry was only centered in Paris because so many students were there and Parisian teachers who had control over this growing network of higher education began asserting their strength.

Their enemies were two—local ecclesiastical authorities and local secular authorities. Since teaching at Paris grew out of church schools, it was still controlled in the twelfth century by church officials, primarily the chancellor of the cathedral of Notre Dame. This officer had the legal right to grant the license to teach on the island of Notre Dame (at that time still the central city), and for this he often took money. The masters, of course, wanted independence from the chancellor, and in the first half of the thirteenth century they gained it by threats of strike and an actual two-year strike from 1229 to 1231, when they left for other cities. The rights of the masters to promote their own students were stated in a papal bull of 1231 that called Paris "the parent of sciences" and obliged the chancellor to give the license to students already

10. *A manuscript of Peter Lombard's commentary on the Pauline Epistles,
written in Paris—almost certainly as a commercial product—in 1239 showing the
new greatly abbreviated and cramped Gothic style. The first line of the left column
reads, "-ra providendo. Quasi pro animabus vestris rationem reddituri, ideo,"
every full word being abbreviated.*

judged worthy by their masters. In the meantime the masters had asserted
themselves against town officials who tried to maintain jurisdiction over un-
ruly students. As early as 1200 the king of France agreed that his provost and
judges would in cases of criminal students defer to the judgment of ecclesiastical courts. This date could be considered the foundation date of the "university," which in fact evolved over a long period of time.

Once the academic personnel of Bologna and Paris established themselves
as universities and their rights became recognized by popes, kings, and local
church and lay authorities, it was not long before other universities were recognized or founded in their wake. Generalizing roughly, the earlier ones developed out of pre-existent centers of learning or were spontaneous growths,
and the later ones were founded from above. Thus Oxford, which had been a
center of learning throughout the twelfth century, was awarded a papal charter in 1214, and Cambridge—always an insignificant university in the Middle
Ages—grew out of a migration from Oxford in 1209. In France an old medical
school at Montpellier was recognized by the papacy as a university in 1220,
and the old cathedral school of Orléans benefited from the great exodus
of Parisian masters in 1229 to become a papally recognized university

in 1235, while in Italy universities at Vicenza (1204) and Padua (1222) grew out of migrations from Bologna. But in Spain a different pattern was begun by the foundation of a university at Palencia in 1212 by the king of Castile, who invited leading scholars to teach there. Thereafter, Emperor Frederick II founded a university at Naples in 1224, and Pope Gregory IX did likewise at Toulouse in 1229 for the purpose of combating heresy. Subsequently most universities were founded by edict or bull, although those established in such a fashion often foundered. (Palencia, for example, disappeared about 1250 and Naples and Toulouse constantly had to be revived by official patronage.) Nonetheless, by one means or another the university form of academic organization became firmly established, and by the end of the Middle Ages at least eighty universities had been organized in Europe.

Along with the proliferation of universities in the thirteenth century came ever mounting prestige for intellectual endeavors. Until the thirteenth century it was customary to say that the world was ruled by two powers, the spiritual and the secular. Supposedly Scripture referred to these powers when Peter said to Christ, "Lo, here are two swords," and Christ answered, "It is enough." But in the course of the thirteenth century men no longer thought that it was enough, and several began independently to maintain that the world was ruled by three powers: church, state, and scholarship. A German, for example, argued that as Italy had the papacy and Germany the empire, so France equally shared in the direction of Christendom with its University of Paris, and a Frenchman wrote that the three parts of the French fleur-de-lis symbolized knighthood, faith, and wisdom.

Within the universities themselves, particularly the University of Paris, greater stress was being placed on the powers of the human intellect. As early as the middle of the eleventh century a French schoolmaster, Berengar of Tours, was arguing that "reason is incontestably the best guide in the search for truth," for whoever does not have recourse to reason "denies that which honors him the most, since his reason is the image of God in him." But Berengar was condemned for hersey when he used rational methods to expound on the mystery of the Eucharist. Though logic gained much ground in the twelfth century, most men still shrank from applying its methods to theology. Saint Thomas Aquinas (1225–1274), however, in the thirteenth century achieved in the Aristotelian milieu of the University of Paris the greatest synthesis of faith and reason. While circumscribing certain "mysteries of the faith" as impenetrable to unaided human understanding and insisting, as any Christian must, that ultimate wisdom and happiness consist only in the vision of God, which cannot be attained fully on earth, Thomas stressed the power of man's natural reason. Reason, he argued, could be used first to demonstrate "preambles of the faith," such as the existence of God, second to illustrate by analogy the content of the faith, and third to refute any objections against the faith. He insisted that human science and sacred wisdom fully complemented each other and singled out man for being "a rational creature." For him, as for Aristotle before him, man was distinguished from the animals by his ability to "contemplate the truth," or as Dante, who is said to have "set St. Thomas to music," phrased it, "man's basic capacity is to have a potentiality or power for being intellectual." With such an attitude, Dante challenged the Augustinian idea that Christians need learn only the knowledge contained in old handbooks by maintaining that he wanted to "publish truths that have not been attempted by others," and in several areas western Europeans were first beginning to do just that.

Unquestionably there was great improvement in the quality of learning in the thirteenth century. What of the quantity? We cannot answer this question with precision, but there is no doubt that the number of schools continued to grow. First of all, when talking of the spread of universities, we are not merely talking about the spread and discovery of rarefied knowledge among a thin caste of intellectuals. Rather, although the majority of universities had advanced faculties of law, medicine, or theology (rarely did early universities have all three), they were dominated numerically by arts faculties for relative beginners. Entrants to the arts faculties of medieval universities were by modern standards astonishingly young. Insofar as it is possible to generalize from our scant records, most students seem to have entered between the ages of twelve and fifteen. Students younger than that were by no means rare. There are documentary references to students at the medieval University of Paris who were seven years old and many references to students of less than ten.

These young students were trained at an elementary level. There were no formal requirements or examinations for admission to the arts faculties. In practice only a knowledge of how to read some Latin, obtained at home from parent or tutor or at an elementary school, was necessary. Once the student arrived at the university he was trained in grammar—a more extensive course in the reading and speaking of Latin—and was taught to write. Having attained this level of education, the majority of students—roughly 70 per cent —left the universities without having been awarded the lowest degree. In other words, medieval universities served the functions, roughly, of American third to seventh grades for the majority of their students. According to the best modern estimates, in the thirteenth century Paris had some seven thousand students and Oxford about three thousand per year. In both cases these are appreciable figures. Those for Oxford, for example, indicate that about one out of every thousand Englishmen gained some education at that university alone.

Moreover, the universities were not the only sources of elementary education. Not only did church primary schools continue to grow, but the thirteenth century witnessed the emergence of lay primary schools. These were designed primarily to educate future businessmen, but, so far as we know, the curriculum of the earliest lay schools hardly differed from that of clerical ones. Far too little research has been done on the emergence of such schools—which ultimately did much to transform medieval civilization and lay the foundations of modern society—but undoubtedly in the thirteenth century the church was irrevocably losing its monopoly of instruction.

As usual in the history of secularization, Italy seems to have been in the vanguard. Law schools, such as the one at Bologna, which flourished throughout the twelfth century, were from the start secular. The University of Naples, founded by imperial fiat in 1224, was fully a state institution whose faculty stood under royal jurisdiction and aimed to provide royal administrators. Exactly when the first secular primary school was founded is impossible to say, but unquestionably a number of them were directed by local governments in the cities of northern Italy by the second half of the thirteenth century. Arezzo in Tuscany, for example, paid a Sienese grammar teacher around the middle of the century a *maximum salarium* to stay in Arezzo permanently, but after 1262 Siena succeeded in outbidding for this teacher's services. Even a smaller city like San Gimignano decided to employ a teacher of grammar in 1270. By 1340 lay education in Florence had made enormous strides. According to a contemporary estimate, from eight thousand to ten thousand students, or roughly 40 per cent of the Florentine children, were enrolled in the city's elementary schools. Even if these figures are inflated, as they might be, Florence almost certainly had a higher literacy rate than that for the total population of Italy or Spain as late as 1850.

The extent of education in Florence and in other Italian cities was highly exceptional in comparison to that in the rest of Europe, but by 1300 a good number of lay primary schools could be found in the North, particularly in commercial cities. At first these met the opposition of the church. The earliest northern lay school we know of was founded by burghers in Ghent after the middle of the twelfth century when a fire destroyed the local church school, but the burghers had to fight against the clergy, which complained about their "insolence" in challenging the church monopoly of education. Even though in 1191 the countess of Flanders ruled that anyone capable should be free to open a school, the local clergy managed to win back educational prerogatives and hold on to them during the thirteenth and apparently also during the fourteenth century. In neighboring Ypres, on the other hand, the church tried to maintain an educational monopoly, but by 1253, though the collegiate church controlled the "major" schools, anyone was free to open a "little school," where sons of merchants and even artisans learned the rudiments of literacy.

Elsewhere, northern European church officials seem to have stopped opposing the foundation of city schools, allowing them instead to function as complementary or parallel institutions to their own. Thus, in 1262 the town council of Lübeck founded its own school and maintained control over its teachers and curriculum even though it conceded certain formal rights to an ecclesiastical official and fully cooperated with him. In 1267 the city of Breslau founded its own school for students who had to journey too far to the cathedral school. In England towns like Lancaster and Nottingham founded their own schools in the later thirteenth century because there were no collegiate churches to provide schools in those localities.

The proliferation of schools led to a great thirteenth-century surge in lay literacy, which can be seen most visibly in the history of documents. From Carolingian times until the twelfth century there was a great paucity of official documents and records throughout western Europe. At a time when few outside of the clergy knew how to write and even many clergymen were functionally illiterate, it was impossible to have large chanceries issuing documents and there was little point in doing so since few people knew how to read. The documents that do survive from this period are beautiful specimens displaying a leisured and florid calligraphy; they were not mass-produced and might often have been calculated to impress illiterates with their magnificence. A monastery, for example, might display a royal charter granting it rights over local peasants and count on the elegant appearance of the document alone to cow the illiterate peasants into submission.

In the thirteenth century, however, all this changed. First of all, the number of written documents began rapidly to multiply. The published edition of the documents issued by the archbishop of Mainz for the period from 742 to 1288, for example, is divided into two volumes, of which the second, allotted to the period from 1160 to 1288 is considerably larger than the first. Similarly, equal-sized volumes containing the documents issued by the duchy of Styria are divided in this way: 798–1192, 1192–1246, and 1246–1260. Unquestionably this proliferation of documents came about because more laymen could write them and read them.

Second, the rapid increase in the number of documents to be written and the fact that they were most often drawn up by professional laymen paid by the piece meant that they were written less beautifully and much more hurriedly. Around the year 1200, documents began to be written in a cursive script, with letters connected to speed writing instead of being separately spaced as previously. Certain ceremonial documents were still written in the beautiful old minuscule, but most were written in cursive. The two scripts were written concurrently in 1226 when the imperial chancery of Frederick II issued a magnificent ceremonial document in old-fashioned minuscule at the same time that it produced its first document fully in the cursive that was to be the wave of the documentary future. Since more people could read, the less impressive appearance of documents did not matter; content took precedence over elegance. Marc Bloch tells, for example, of how some French peasants were so little impressed with a royal diploma issued around 1179 that enserfed them to a local monastery that they persistently fought the order in royal and papal courts for the next half-century. Certainly, not all these peasants could read— probably almost all could not—but because they had one or more representatives who were literate they became far too sophisticated to be overwhelmed merely by elegant calligraphy and there was no point in wasting scribal energies on them.

Another visible example of increased lay literacy comes from the history of coins. In Germany in the twelfth and early thirteenth centuries, die-cutters often were so illiterate that they could not put legible inscriptions on the coins they issued. But some believed their products would not look right unless they were adorned by letters. Therefore, counting on the fact that most users of their coins were as illiterate as they were, they put letters in random order on them and few ever knew the difference (fig. 11). (Beginning students of numismatics sometimes waste much time seeking to make sense out of such inscriptions in gibberish known to experts as *Trugschrift*—German for "illusory writing.") This practice, however, was abandoned in the thirteenth century when die-cutters either became better educated or felt they could no longer pass such coins without complaints from their users.

Similar evidence could be multiplied, but we may best end this discussion of the growth of a literate laity in the thirteenth century with brief reference to Dante, who reached the middle of his life when the century ended. Dante, of course, was not at all typical, but his example does show to what heights lay education could rise. As a boy he seems to have learned Latin grammar in a Florentine lay school of the sort that then was proliferating, and later he attended "the schools of the religious," probably some of the advanced church

11. Trugschrift *(illusory writing), a* German one-sided penny (bracteate), *ca. 1180–1190. The coin shows an unidentified lay ruler with lily-scepter and bears the nonsensical inscription (reading clockwise)* "VDAICI— ENPOF." *The first word may be a halting attempt at the Latin for* "Ulrich"; *the second is completely meaningless.*

schools of Florence. He almost certainly never went to a university, but this did not prevent him, though he remained until his death a layman, from becoming one of the most learned men of his day. His Latin treatise *On Monarchy,* for example, draws from the Bible, Aristotle, Cicero, Virgil, Boethius, Saint Thomas, and many other Roman and Christian writers. He loved to write and had no false humility but trumpeted forth the assertion that he wished "not to be charged with burying [his] talent." When a layman could know so much and write so self-confidently as Dante, the clerical pre-emption of learning in Europe was certainly coming to an end.

The Later Middle Ages

A great crisis for western European civilization began in the last decades of the thirteenth century when the European economy slowly began to stagnate and wars challenged the strength and stability of the western monarchies. In the fourteenth century matters became far worse. Until 1348 the economy was burdened by acute food shortages and afterward followed a time of agricultural glut as the result of the Black Death, which ultimately drove down prices and caused severe deflation. Concurrently, throughout the fourteenth century Europe was wracked by fearful wars, and the prestige of the papacy, first self-exiled to Avignon, then rent in the Great Schism of 1378 to 1416, reached a low ebb. In the fifteenth century there was some slow recovery on economic, political, and religious fronts, but until the last decades of that century recovery in most areas outside of Italy was halting and sometimes hardly noticeable. Thus for the better part of the period from the 1270s until the 1470s most of western Europe was tested by economic, political, and religious trials that sometimes threatened to nullify previous accomplishments and bring European civilization down again to ruins. Yet that threat never materialized, and before 1500, even before the full conquest of the New World, economic and political stability was returning to Europe. In the same way, in the later Middle Ages there were severe challenges to the spread of education, but ultimately high medieval institutions withstood the troubles of the time and by the end of the fifteenth century they emerged stronger than ever.

Roughly speaking, the era characterized by buoyant confidence in human intellectual powers began in Paris around the time of the arrival of Peter Abelard in about 1100 and ended in 1277 when the bishop of Paris condemned 219 articles attributed to philosophers from the Parisian arts faculty. Most of these "errors" arose from untrammeled philosophizing and reliance on an Arabic interpretation of Aristotle. Some explicitly placed reason above revealed theology by saying that "there is no more excellent state than the practice of philosophy" (40), "true wisdom is only the wisdom of the philosophers" (154), "all the good which is possible for man consists in the intellectual virtues" (144), "Christian law impedes education" (175), and "what the theologians say is based upon fable" (152). It is not likely that even the boldest of the Parisian philosophers said all these things in earnest, but many of the propositions might have been aired for theoretical debate in the prevalent climate of intellectual freedom. Above all, what certainly horrified the bishop, and no doubt many theologians, was the fact that philosophers not yet fully trained in theology were treating theological problems from a strictly philosophical point of view.

The Parisian condemnation of 1277 opened a sad chapter in the history of official attempts at thought control. Although it was not aimed directly at Saint Thomas Aquinas, dead in 1274, who had taught in the theological, not the arts, faculty and who had occupied a middle position between the extremes of reliance on reason and revelation, insofar as it was aimed against Aristotelianism and rationalism it succeeded in inhibiting further utilization of Thomistic methods. Thereafter, on the one hand the spirit of collaboration between philosophy and theology that had dominated most of the thirteenth century was replaced by an atmosphere of mutual suspicion, and on the other hand church officials became emboldened to launch a series of trials against prominent thinkers. Ironically, one of the greatest late medieval thinkers, William of Ockham, was tried by the papacy from 1324 to 1328 for arguing, among other things, the anti-Thomistic extreme that man's intellect unaided could know practically nothing about God. But this is just an example of how in the fourteenth century official displeasure extended in all directions and resulted in the trial for heresy of most of the best minds of the age. Men had to be careful about expressing what they thought, unless they were willing to risk ecclesiastical censure.

The year 1277 is convenient for marking the end of an era, but it would be artificial to argue that ecclesiastical condemnations alone caused the growing reaction against confidence in the human intellect. After all, Saint Thomas, in trying to harmonize reason and revelation in one grand guide to theology, was undertaking an enormous task, which he did not even finish before he died. Scholastic theology and the building of cathedrals are often compared. By the 1270s both were soaring perhaps too high and were unable to go much farther. The enormous cathedral of Cologne was left unfinished, like Thomas' *Summa,* and the cathedral of Beauvais began to fall apart in 1284. Furthermore, whether or not one agrees with the view that Thomas was attempting too much, there is little doubt that by the fourteenth century events were militating against intellectual self-confidence and optimism. In an age of growing economic and political turmoil, as well as of terrible natural disasters, orderly laws did not seem to be in effect. This situation probably encouraged the most influential theologians to follow Ockham in stressing God's omnipotent unpredictability. There continued to be Thomistic theologians in the fourteenth century, particularly within Thomas' Dominican Order, but there were no great ones and it is likely that this would have been so as the result of internal intellectual pressures and external events even without official ecclesiastical condemnations.

Outside of the schools of higher learning anti-intellectualism that had nothing directly to do with complex intellectual currents or doctrinal proscriptions was growing. Of course even in the twelfth and thirteenth centuries there had always been men like Saint Bernard and Saint Francis who were impatient with rationalism and learning, but in those centuries they were fighting a losing battle. Saint Francis was reported by contemporaries to have said that he was sent by the Lord to be "a new-born simpleton in the world," that the Lord would "confound" men through their "learning and wisdom," and that learning would be the ruin of his order. But despite the force of Francis' sayings, learning did infect his order. Soon after his death Franciscans became professors at the University of Paris, where one of them, Saint Bonaventura, became the greatest scholastic theologian of the thirteenth century after Saint Thomas. The intellectual climate of the age warmed most Franciscans so much to learning that one of those who remained faithful to the founder's anti-intellectual ideal lamented that "Paris has triumphed over Assisi."

By the fourteenth century, however, anti-intellectualism became a popular ground swell, expressed, as one might expect, particularly by those who did not go to universities. The English mystic Richard Rolle said, "In all our actions and thoughts let us give greater weight to divine love than to learning and argument." The Dutch religious reformer Gert Groote made his motto "the greatest knowledge is to know that man knows nothing." A German heretic named Hermann Kuchener maintained that once when he was illuminated by God he could have offered instruction to all the theological masters of Paris, and the Czech reformer Milič of Kroměříž went so far as to argue that study of the liberal arts was a deadly sin. Most powerfully, in the middle of the fifteenth century Thomas à Kempis, one of the most popular writers of his age, wrote that "rightly we find in the Gospels that 'blessed are the poor in spirit, for theirs is the kingdom of heaven,' but nowhere do we read 'blessed are the masters of arts.' "

Saint Augustine, whose influence had been somewhat eclipsed in the thirteenth century, enjoyed a new vogue in the later Middle Ages and his impatience with rationalism and "vain curiosity" was stressed. Milič, citing Augustine, maintained that "the intellect gets nothing from its own exercise unless it is given by God" and misquoted Augustine as saying, "Who is Aristotle? He trembles in Hell." Characteristically, in the fourteenth century the legend circulated that when Saint Augustine was meditating on the Trinity by the seashore, he noticed a small boy using a shell to spill water from the sea onto the sand. After he realized that the child was hoping to empty the ocean in this way, he concluded that the human mind trying to fathom the mystery of the Trinity was engaged in a task no less futile.

Augustine's impatience with excessive learning was shared in the four-teenth century even by the great Italian poet Petrarch, who ridiculed "the crazy and clamorous" scholastic philosophers of "contentious Paris." Petrarch claimed that Aristotle knew no more about happiness than "any pi-ous old woman, any faithful fisherman, shepherd, or peasant." Against the "vanities of philosophers," he opposed—in language often taken directly from Saint Augustine—the truth of Scripture. Against knowledge he opposed virtue, as in his apothegm that "it is better to will the good than to know the truth." For him the only necessary knowledge was that which is necessary for salvation. That, he believed, could be achieved "without much learning, even without any, as is clearly shown by the long line of illiterate saints," thereby upholding miraculous illumination against study of the liberal arts even more than Augustine himself had done.

Nevertheless, Petrarch was always a scholar. In an early dialogue entitled *The Secret,* purporting to be a conversation between Saint Augustine and himself, he made Augustine cite Horace, Virgil, and Cicero. Even though Augustine in this dialogue urged Petrarch "to try to put into practice what you know, instead of plunging into deeper and deeper inquiries," Petrarch, acknowledging the truth of such remarks, ended by admitting that he did not have the "strength to resist that old bent for study altogether." This was true enough. Later, in *On His Own Ignorance,* he criticized too much learning but at the same time ostentatiously paraded his own and said more boldly than before that he would "never regret [his] studious efforts."

Petrarch's ambivalence toward learning may be taken as typical of the attitudes of the later Middle Ages. Most good Augustinians agreed—in consonance with Saint Augustine himself—that knowledge of the liberal arts was a necessary preparation for theology, and few in the later Middle Ages went so far as Milič to condemn their study entirely. On the contrary, priests were still supposed to know at least the basics of Latin grammar. Though human reason may have been denigrated, the growing threat of heresy and frightful bewilderment about disasters and plagues made the need for an instructed clergy more urgent than ever. A remarkable testimony to the conviction that learning was needed to fight heresy is found in a set of frescoes on the wall of a Dominican church in Florence, executed some twenty years after the first onslaught of the Black Death. On one wall Peter Martyr and Thomas Aquinas oppose heretics and Jews by argument and reference to Scripture. In the group around Thomas one Jew is reduced to ripping up a book and another is stopping his ears, but others are taking notice and two have already been converted (fig. 12). Another fresco depicts Christian learning by personifications of the seven liberal arts and seven theological sciences, each matched with a specific human representative; above them is Saint Thomas, open book in lap and enthroned impassively over three heretics (fig. 13). Learning, then, in this view was still regarded as an underpinning of Christianity.

Nor was justification of learning limited to the rationale of defending the faith. Italian humanists of the fifteenth century continued to harbor Petrarch's distrust of untrammeled rationalism but returned to the classical ideal of propagating education—particularly in grammar and rhetoric—to achieve eloquence as well as to gain "moral worth and fame." They believed that education was a necessity for finding the way to a virtuous and good life and, in the words of a typical humanist, Pier Paolo Vergerio, that education "calls forth, trains, and develops those highest gifts of body and of mind which ennoble men."

Aside from such humanistic views, which were limited in place and time, all over Europe it was widely believed that kings and officers of state should be educated in order to perform their government functions. The greatest French king of the fourteenth century, Charles V (1364–1380), was not only learned enough to be called "the Wise," but he was also a patron of learning who

12. Detail from a fresco in the Spanish Chapel of the church of Santa Maria Novella, Florence, done by Andrea da Firenze, ca. 1365. The black and white hounds attacking the wolves of heresy in the foreground at the feet of Peter Martyr and Saint Thomas are visual puns for the Dominicans, who dressed in black and white and called themselves "hounds of the Lord" (Domini canes).

gathered around him some of the greatest intellects of his day. Charles' concern for education is shown in a contemporary manuscript illumination that portrays him sending his boys to school and sitting in a classroom himself (fig. 14). Education was also still a matter for local and national pride. Bologna's late medieval coins, for example, bear the proud legend *Bononia docet* ("Bologna teaches"). Similarly, in 1348 the German emperor and king of Bohemia, Charles IV, founded a university at Prague so that, as his charter said, "the faithful subjects of our realm who hunger unceasingly for the fruits of knowledge should not be forced to beg of others but should find a table prepared for them in their own country."

The reference to men hungry for knowledge was not entirely rhetorical, for even in a period of anti-intellectualism there were always those who loved study for its own rewards. Such was a German named Peter Turnau, who said in the early fifteenth century that he became a teacher "to inform boys and in

13. *"Christian Learning," another fresco from the cycle by Andrea da Firenze in the Spanish Chapel of Santa Maria Novella, Florence, ca. 1365.*

14. *Charles V of France as patron of learning, from a manuscript of Aristotle's Ethics, ca. 1376. At the top left the king smilingly receives a manuscript (the figure behind him is inexplicable). At the top right he orders his boys to school, perhaps to the disquiet of their mother. At the bottom left the king himself sits in school. At the bottom right is another schoolroom scene.*

so doing to learn himself." Chaucer's Clerk of Oxenford would rather have had "twenty bookes, clad in blak or reed, of Aristotle and his philosophie than robes riche"; the poet said of him, "gladly wolde he lerne and gladly teche."

It is not surprising, then, that men continued to seek education. Indeed, far from declining, literacy and learning increased in the later Middle Ages. Old incentives were still present. Per capita income by the late fourteenth century was beginning to rise, and education was becoming cheaper. Despite the Black Death, economic depression, and wars, governmental and ecclesiastical bureaucracies continued to expand. Even the papacy in the period of its residence in Avignon expanded its bureaucratic apparatus inordinately, and in Germany as central government collapsed, every petty principality and free city vastly increased the issuance of its own documents. Augsburg, for example, issued as many documents from 1347 to 1399 as it had from 1104 to 1346 and Frankfurt as many from 1314 to 1340 as from 794 to 1314. New jobs called for more men who could at least read and write, and the numbers of the educated continued to swell, especially since education was not quite the luxury it once had been.

Ironically, though the European economy was contracting instead of expanding in the fourteenth century, the sharp decline in population caused by the plague, natural disasters, and wars resulted by the end of the century in a rise in per capita wealth. Poor people especially were not as a rule (with inevitable exceptions) so poor as before because their labor was in greater demand and the price of most staples had fallen. Cities too were less badly hurt by the depression than the countryside, for city industries were better able to adjust to the new economic facts of life. Some cities, particularly in Italy and Germany, even became richer and stimulated the continued growth of education. Finally, learning became decidedly less expensive when in the fourteenth century cheap paper replaced precious parchment as the standard writing material, and after the middle of the fifteenth century the invention of movable type greatly reduced the cost of making books. In earlier times books had to be chained down to prevent theft and bore imprecations damning anyone who stole, mutilated, or even approached them without washing his hands; now they were coming more and more within reach of the many.

Instead of chronicling the progress of learning country by country, we may conclude by touching upon three interrelated trends of late medieval education—the emergence of education in European vernaculars instead of Latin, the education of lower classes, and the continued progress of secular as opposed to clerical education. These topics have been slighted by scholarship in favor of the easier and more glamorous institutional history of universities, and therefore much work will have to be done before fully authoritative results can be presented. The following remarks are based on sparse returns but sketch the rough outlines of late medieval patterns.

The most dramatic innovation was education in the vernacular. With the exception of a brief English interlude under King Alfred, formal education in medieval Europe was conducted in Latin until about the thirteenth century. In the twelfth century original literature in the western European vernaculars began to emerge, but we have no hard evidence that men were trained to read these languages before they knew Latin. Vernacular literature, until deep into the Middle Ages, was meant primarily for illiterate aristocrats and therefore was meant to be read aloud. Such literature was no doubt often created by men—such as Wolfram von Eschenbach (1170?–1220?), a knight who was the greatest of all German epic poets—who were illiterate and dictated to scribes. We have seen that in the thirteenth century many cities founded independent lay schools, primarily for businessmen, but Europeans so regarded Latin as the language of learning that teaching at these schools too was initially conducted in Latin.

Scholarly research has not yet seriously broached the question of exactly when the teaching of literacy was first conducted in the European vernaculars. Very roughly, the answer seems to be in the course of the thirteenth century. Interestingly enough, the first to have been educated in this way seem to have been women. In European aristocratic circles until the sixteenth century most men had no patience for book learning and were often proud to be ignorant of letters; women far more often were taught to read by tutors. Up to the thirteenth century they were first taught Latin. Apparently sometime in that century it became common to teach them in their vernaculars instead, and by the end of the century more educated women knew how to read their vernaculars than knew how to read Latin. For them in particular vernacular works were written and Latin works translated. In 1298, for example, a writer presented a treatise to Philip IV of France in Latin and gave the same work in French to Philip's wife, the same woman who commissioned a French translation of another Latin treatise and for whom the lord of Joinville wrote his *History of Saint Louis*, the greatest vernacular history up until that time. In the thirteenth century women also began to write in the vernaculars. Among the earliest writings in Dutch are the religious poems of a woman named Hadewich, which date from the first half of the thirteenth century. The first large work of German religious prose was written around 1250 by Mechthild of Magdeburg, a woman who stated outright that she knew no Latin.

Most of these female writers were probably taught privately, but by the early fourteenth century there were schools that taught reading in the vernacular instead of in Latin. Once more the leader of Europe was Italy. We do not know when the earliest vernacular schools were founded there, but by 1340 of the eight thousand to ten thousand students reported to have been enrolled in elementary schools in Florence, approximately six hundred were said to have learned Latin; the majority were educated only in the vernacular. In northern Europe widespread vernacular education came much later. Indeed, we do not know whether before 1500 any schools taught in the vernacular at all in England—an anomaly in King Alfred's time—and France. We do know that the vernacular was taught in Germany occasionally in the late fourteenth century, but only in the course of the fifteenth century was a number of vernacular schools founded there.

In the areas that had no vernacular schools and even in those that had them, some teaching of reading in the vernaculars must have been done in non-noble homes in the later Middle Ages, for a growing number of businessmen, town officials, and sometimes even artisans could read and write in their vernaculars but not in Latin. Many laymen were able to write subtle religious works but were still scorned by the clergy as "illiterate" for not knowing Latin. For example, we have late medieval references to "German books written by men ignorant of letters" and to "an unlearned layman" who read and wrote books in German. Even Ruysbroeck, the greatest of late medieval Flemish mystical writers, was referred to by the chancellor of the University of Paris as "an illiterate unlearned man" (*idiota unus sine litteris*). These are indications that the educated clergy was still trying to preserve a privileged position by signaling out its knowledge of Latin and disparaging vernacular learning—one fourteenth-century cleric going so far as to lament that "schooled laymen and unlearned clergymen ... are confounding the Church." But mass education could obviously only make headway if conducted in the vernaculars and the trend in that direction, though it long had to run counter to clerical opposition and naive reverence for Latin, was becoming strong enough in the later Middle Ages to triumph in modern times.

We have even less information about a second late medieval educational phenomenon—the education of an appreciable number of students who came from families that were not wealthy. To say with accuracy how the later Middle Ages compared to the High Middle Ages in this respect is impossible, but apparently as time went on education became less expensive and more attainable by greater numbers. The education of poor students was supported sometimes by their parents but more often by the church, secular governments, or private benefactors. A rich London grocer, for example, provided in a will of 1432 for the regular income of a schoolmaster who would "instruct all boys whatsoever," without having to take fees from them, their parents, or their friends. At the university level church benefices were often used to support students who could not pay their way, and in the later Middle Ages residential colleges founded to help the indigent proliferated. The results can be seen in early university matriculation figures. At the University of Cologne from 1400 to 1470 from 16 to 20 per cent of all students were classified as paupers; at Leipzig in 1409 the percentage of paupers was as high as 28; and at Freiburg from 1508 to 1514 about 17 per cent of the university membership was classified as poor. In terms of absolute numbers such figures mean little; no doubt the vast majority of poor people in late medieval Europe remained totally illiterate. Nonetheless, education was clearly not barred to the poor, and there seems to have been a modicum of truth in the claim of Pope Pius II (1458–1464) in a bull permitting the foundation of the University of Basel in 1459 that "the pursuit of knowledge has the power to raise up the lowly born."

Scholars have paid most attention to our third trend, the secularization of learning and in doing so have too frequently exaggerated it. Reading in the later Middle Ages, as throughout the medieval period, customarily began with the Psalter, and there was still much emphasis on learning creeds and prayers by heart. A fifteenth-century mnemonic device for learning the alphabet reminded small children that A stood for the Trinity—three in one—because it was shaped by the intersection of three lines but was still one letter, that D stood for the Devil, and that P stood for sin (*peccatum*) brought upon man by Eve. Nonetheless, conceding that in the late Middle Ages a very large amount of education was still controlled by the church and that primary education customarily began with religious texts (even in nineteenth-century America children were taught that A stood for Adam, through whose fall "we sinned all"), it still must be said that the high medieval trend toward challenging the clerical monopoly of learning was continued on all levels.

To begin with the lowest, there can be no question that lay literacy continued to spread. In England "benefit of clergy" was accorded to criminals who passed a literacy test on the old assumption that only the clergy could read, but fifteenth-century records show that men who were classified as "clerics" because of their literacy were often laymen, sometimes of such lowly status as butchers, tailors, fishmongers, and laborers. By 1488 the government complained that "upon trust of privilige of the Churche divers persones lettred hath ben the more bold to committe murder, rape, robbery, thefte, and all othre myschevous dedys." Although children who learned to read started with the Psalter, purely secular subjects were rapidly developed throughout western Europe and it was quite easy to study business methods as well as notarial arts, law, and medicine. An archaeological discovery in Lübeck shows that students in the lay city school there were in 1370 practicing how to write letters about politics and also about the herring trade.

European universities too were becoming increasingly secular. Lay students could not only go into law, medicine, government, or business but could also get jobs as teachers. For example, the London grocer who wished to have a free school in 1432 stipulated in his will that the teacher there be "a master, an honest man, sufficiently advanced and expert in the science of grammar and a Bachelor of Arts, but by no means in holy orders." With the growth of lay professions, the percentages of lay students at universities sharply increased. Whereas earlier the majority of students at northern European universities were in priestly orders, in Heidelberg from 1409 to 1419 48 per cent of the matriculants were in orders and in Cologne from 1389 to 1465 only 35 per cent were so. Thereafter, even those percentages sank so sharply that in Cologne in the next hundred years a mere 10 per cent average of matriculants were in orders and in Heidelberg the percentages fell from 26 per cent from 1449 to 1463 to 15 per cent from 1471 to 1485 to 8 per cent from 1505 to 1515. Some of those classified as lay at the time of their matriculation probably became priests later, but even so a pronounced trend from clerical to lay student populations at universities is apparent.

A remarkable document of 1460 also shows that the raison d'être of universities was becoming almost as dominantly secular as were their student populations. In that year the town council of the city of Basel, trying to decide whether to invest in the establishment of a university, appointed a commission of experts to give advice on the matter. The commission's report was strongly in the affirmative and presented a list of reasons why having a university would be advantageous to the city. Above all it stressed material advantages: A university would ensure a greater number not only of learned men and priests but also of lawyers and doctors; it would permit sons of local families to pursue higher studies in Basel; and, above all, it would ameliorate the city's economic situation by bringing in the buying power of foreign students. In addition to taking this practical line, designed to convince hardheaded, tightfisted burghers, the report played on their Christian sensibilities by arguing that a university would strengthen the faith against heresy and appealed to their concern for prestige by recalling how celebrated schools had earned enduring recognition from humanity. Among these it listed not only Christian universities like Paris, Oxford, and Bologna but also the heathen schools of Athens and the Jewish schools of Spain. Thus, even while it talked of strengthening the faith, it implicitly conceded that great learning had no religious boundaries and stressed earthly intellectual achievement rather than the Augustinian justification of learning as a preparation for knowing the Bible and God. Basel was to be, in the intent of its proponents, not a seminary for priests but a school that would unashamedly teach a variety of secular subjects and hope to rank with the greatest institutions of learning whether nominally Christian or pagan. This justification for study was not yet fully secular, but to put it beside Saint Augustine's *On Christian Doctrine* shows the change in attitudes toward learning that had taken place over one thousand years.

Conclusion

Looking back on the thousand years of educational ideas and realities that we have treated here so briskly, we may say in summary that by defending learning as a prerequisite for biblical studies, Saint Augustine and those he influenced ensured that Christianity would not become rabidly anti-intellectual. This defense had a delayed impact in the early medieval period because of the turbulent condition of Europe following the fall of Rome. Learning was at first passed on most tenuously in certain monasteries, but with the advent of Charlemagne and a few generations of peace the triumph of Augustine's views led to the strengthening of church schools throughout western Europe and the formation of a cultural tradition based on uniform religious texts, handwriting, and language. A wave of invasions from 850 to 950 threatened to cancel previous gains, but Carolingian institutions and traditions endured. Literacy, however, was a near-monopoly of the clergy, and learning was unoriginal and strictly subordinated to purposes of the faith.

A new epoch opened with the Renaissance of the Twelfth Century, when greatly changed material conditions allowed for great improvement in the quantity and quality of education. Schools grew and multiplied, teaching and scholarship became recognized as legitimate vocations, and inquiry became more and more independent. In the thirteenth century the burgeoning of education culminated in the founding of universities, and in the course of the twelfth and thirteenth centuries clerical monopolies became broken as more laymen became educated and lay schools were founded. Again new trials threatened to cancel previous gains, but in the later Middle Ages, despite turbulence and widespread anti-intellectualism, learning continued to spread. By 1500 education was available in European vernaculars as well as in Latin, more than just the wealthy were going to schools, and much learning was unashamedly secular.

Of course in 1500 Europe had just begun to traverse the road to full literacy. Most landed aristocrats were still stubbornly averse to education. According to a contemporary couplet, "noblemen born, to learn they have scorn," and only the educational revolution that began in the sixteenth century would change that situation in most western European countries. At the other end of the social spectrum, although some poor people were gaining literacy, their number was still pitifully low. This was particularly true of the rural poor: One estimate for a southern French area late in the sixteenth century is that 90 per cent of the merchants and 65 per cent of the urban artisans were literate, but only from 10 to 30 per cent of the rural population was so. Since most Europeans lived in the countryside until the nineteenth century, it is probably true that most were illiterate until that time.

Similarly, education was by no means fully secularized, and the spread of Lutheranism and Calvinism in the sixteenth century brought back in many areas the Augustinian attitude that learning should be subordinated to religion. Even Shakespeare justified education in religious terms when he made one of his characters say in *Henry VI,* Part 2, that "ignorance is the curse of

God, knowledge the wing wherewith we fly to heaven." Nonetheless, Europe was a world leader in learning and literacy, and progress would continue. Shakespeare's defender of education in *Henry VI* speaks against a villain who attacks the establishment of grammar schools as a traitorous corruption of youth and complains that talk of nouns and verbs is so abominable that it offends Christian ears, but by that time such villains were to be found in few places except on the stage.

A Critical Bibliography

Bibliographical essays of this sort customarily begin with mention of standard general works in English, but none will be made here because no such works dealing with the major topics treated in the foregoing essay exist. The title of Carlo M. Cipolla's *Literacy and Development in the West* (Harmondsworth, 1969) promises much, but Cipolla's work unfortunately is a very brief essay, particularly sketchy and derivative for the medieval period. James Westfall Thompson, *The Literacy of the Laity in the Middle Ages* (Berkeley, 1939), on the other hand, is detailed and extremely useful, but it is limited, as its title indicates, to the laity; it also stops at the year 1300 and lacks the findings of contemporary research. Thompson's study may be supplemented by V. H. Galbraith, "The Literacy of the Medieval English Kings," *Proceedings of the British Academy* 21 (1935): 202–38, which is reprinted in *Studies in History, British Academy Lectures,* ed. Lucy S. Sutherland (London, 1966), pp. 78–111, an informative and entertainingly written study but even more limited in its scope than Thompson's. Even when one proceeds to foreign languages there are no treatments of medieval education as a whole worth recommending. Mention must be made only of Herbert Grundmann, "Literatus-Illiteratus. Der Wandel einer Bildungsnorme vom Altertum zum Mittelalter," *Archiv für Kulturgeschichte* 40 (1958): 1–65, a tour de force by the late dean of German medieval intellectual historians, which, though only an essay, is a mine of information on the subjects of attitudes toward learning and the extent of literacy. Fortunately, excellent surveys of the great achievements of medieval thought, as opposed to the prosaic subject of elementary learning, are plentiful. Here it will suffice to mention a fine one that also treats educational institutions: David Knowles, *The Evolution of Medieval Thought* (New York, 1962).

In moving to particular studies, it is most efficient to proceed chronologically. The standard work on education in the ancient world, which ends with some illuminating material about transitions to the Middle Ages, is Henri

Marrou, *A History of Education in Antiquity* (New York, 1956). A delightful, even breezy, but wonderfully learned introduction to the thought of the Latin Fathers about pagan learning and education is Edward K. Rand, *Founders of the Middle Ages* (Cambridge, Mass., 1928). A lively introductory biography of Saint Augustine is Vernon J. Bourke, *Augustine's Quest of Wisdom* (Milwaukee, 1945). Peter Brown, *Augustine of Hippo* (London, 1967), a masterful intellectual biography that concentrates on the often subtle shifts of Augustine's interests and ideas over the years, blazed its way rapidly into the firmament of regularly cited titles, but the beginning student is warned that even seasoned scholars find it difficult. On Augustine's attitudes toward culture and education Brown and I have been greatly influenced by Henri Marrou, *Saint Augustin et la fin de la culture antique* (Paris, 1938), and the student who can negotiate French will find this basic study extremely rewarding. Less exciting than the previous works but useful for reference are Harald Hagendahl, *Augustine and the Latin Classics* (Göteborg, 1967)—an exhaustive tome—and George Howie, *Educational Theory and Practice in St. Augustine* (London, 1969). Howie has also selected and translated passages from Augustine on education in *St. Augustine on Education* (Chicago, 1969), but the student interested in Augustine's ideas on learning is still encouraged to read all of *On Christian Doctrine,* especially since it is easily available in the translation by D. W. Robertson (New York, 1958).

A milestone in the study of education in the barbarian West is the meticulous treatment of Pierre Riché, *Education et culture dans l'occident barbare, VIe–VIIIe siècles,* 3d ed. (Paris, 1972). Subsequent work in the field will be indebted to Riché, for a surer guide to the complicated history of education over several centuries and in several countries can hardly be imagined. Students who cannot read French may consult Riché's "Centers of Culture in Frankish Gaul Between the Sixth and the Ninth Centuries" in Sylvia L. Thrupp, *Early Medieval Society* (New York, 1967), pp. 221–36; unfortunately while this essay sets forth some of Riché's most important ideas it conveys practically none of his marvelous ability to turn gold out of the sludge of the sources, and there is no real substitute for this most impressive product of recent French historiography short of a complete translation into English. A useful introduction to Boethius is Gerald Vann, *The Wisdom of Boethius,* Aquinas Papers, 20 (London, 1952). Several editions of *The Consolation of Philosophy* are available. Best on Cassiodorus beyond the treatment in Riché is the edition of his *Introduction to Divine and Human Readings* by Leslie Webber Jones (New York, 1946), which has an extensive introduction.

Highly recommended on the Carolingian Renaissance is the first third of Philippe Wolff, *The Awakening of Europe* (Harmondsworth, 1968), to which the foregoing account is greatly indebted. More technical is Luitpold Wallach, *Alcuin and Charlemagne* (Ithaca, 1959). Basic documents pertaining to the

Carolingian revival of learning are edited in Stewart C. Easton and Helene Wieruszowski, *The Era of Charlemagne* (Princeton, 1961). The standard, indispensable treatments of the history of education in France and Germany from the Carolingian age to the High Middle Ages are respectively Emile Lesne, *Les Ecoles de la fin du VIIIe siècle à la fin du XIIe siècle* (Lille, 1940; volume 5 of Lesne's *Histoire de la propriété ecclésiastique en France*), and Franz Anton Specht, *Geschichte des Unterrichtswesens in Deutschland von den ältesten Zeiten bis zur Mitte des dreizehnten Jahrhunderts* (Stuttgart, 1885). Unsurpassable on monastic attitudes toward learning is Jean Leclercq, *The Love of Learning and the Desire for God* (New York, 1961).

Admirable on the tenth century is the second third of Wolff, *The Awakening of Europe,* already cited. This may be supplemented with Luitpold Wallach, "Education and Culture in the Tenth Century," *Medievalia et Humanistica* 9 (1955): 18–22; with a few pertinent pages in Pierre Riché, *De l'éducation antique à l'éducation chevaleresque* (Paris, 1968); and with Oscar G. Darlington, "Gerbert the Teacher," *American Historical Review* 52 (1947): 456–76 (the gushing of the last need cause no great concern).

The bulk of good work on medieval education deals with the High Middle Ages, and the following short list is perforce highly selective. Excellent introductions to the period may be found in the last third of Wolff, *The Awakening of Europe,* and also in John W. Baldwin, *The Scholastic Culture of the Middle Ages* (Lexington, Mass., 1971). More controversial but unquestionably among the most brilliant considerations of high medieval education and thought in English are two essays of R. W. Southern entitled "Medieval Humanism" and "Humanism and the School of Chartres" in his *Medieval Humanism and Other Studies* (New York, 1970). Also controversial but less convincing is the chapter entitled "Statecraft and Learning" in H. G. Richardson and G. O. Sayles, *The Governance of Mediaeval England* (Edinburgh, 1963), which argues for more extensive lay literacy in twelfth-century England than is generally thought to have been the case. On attitudes toward learning and educational practices in late twelfth-century Paris there is an invaluable store of information in part 2 of John W. Baldwin, *Masters, Princes, and Merchants,* 2 vols. (Princeton, 1970).

Beyond the last-mentioned title one must proceed to works in foreign languages for monographic detail about twelfth-century education. The two most detailed treatments of the institutions of twelfth-century learning (in addition to the studies of Lesne and Specht previously cited) are Gérard Paré, A. Brunet, and P. Tremblay, *La Renaissance du XIIe siècle: les écoles et l'enseignement* (Paris, 1933), and Philippe Delhaye, "L'Organization scolaire au XIIe siècle," *Traditio* 5 (1947): 211–68. On the sociology of twelfth-century learning see the highly suggestive article of Jacques Le Goff, "Quelle conscience l'université médiévale a-t-elle eu d'elle-même?" in *Beiträge zum*

Berufsbewusstsein des mittelalterlichen Menschen, ed. Paul Wilpert (Berlin, 1964), pp. 15–29, as well as the same author's *Les Intellectuels au moyen âge* (Paris, 1957) (announced for English translation but perhaps somewhat overrated in the current American vogue for things French), and, best of all, Peter Classen, "Die Hohen Schulen und die Gesellschaft im 12. Jahrhundert," *Archiv für Kulturgeschichte* 47 (1966) : 155–80, an outstanding treatment that has not yet received the attention it deserves in the English-speaking scholarly world. Abelard's autobiography is highly readable and available in several English translations.

On the history of universities there is a plethora of literature in all Western languages, and this is one field in which American scholars have made many basic contributions. For bibliographical orientation up to the year 1947 see Gray C. Boyce, "American Studies in Medieval Education," *Progress of Medieval and Renaissance Studies* 19 (1947) : 6–30. Good short accounts are Helene Wieruszowski, *The Medieval University* (Princeton, 1966)—which includes a useful collection of basic documents—and the more technical and ill-written but still informative treatment of Gordon Leff, *Paris and Oxford Universities in the Thirteenth and Fourteenth Centuries* (New York, 1968). The standard exhaustive work is Hastings Rashdall, *The Universities of Europe in the Middle Ages,* ed. F. M. Powicke and A. B. Emden, 3 vols. (Oxford, 1936). In addition, I have found extremely useful and provocative Herbert Grundmann, *Vom Ursprung der Universität im Mittelalter,* 2d ed. (Darmstadt, 1964).

Once one retreats from the history of universities the amount of good secondary literature dwindles. On thirteenth-century urban schools and growing lay literacy one must resort to scattered articles such as Gray C. Boyce, "Erfurt Schools and Scholars in the Thirteenth Century," *Speculum* 24 (1949) : 1–18; Charles T. Davis, "Education in Dante's Florence," *Speculum* 40 (1965) : 415–35; and Helene Wieruszowski, "Arezzo as a Center of Learning and Letters in the Thirteenth Century," *Traditio* 9 (1953) : 321–91. Those who can negotiate French and German should consult the basic articles of Henri Pirenne, "L'Instruction des marchands au Moyen Age," *Annales d'histoire économique et sociale* 1 (1929) : 13–28, and Fritz Rörig, "Mittelalter und Schriftlichkeit," *Die Welt als Geschichte* 13 (1953) : 29–41.

Much research remains to be done in the history of education in the later Middle Ages. The only brief treatment of a general nature in English that is to be recommended is the now somewhat out-of-date summary of G. R. Potter, "Education in the Fourteenth and Fifteenth Centuries," in the *Cambridge Medieval History,* vol. 8 (1936), pp. 688–717. Some information can also be garnered from the chapter on education in Bede Jarrett, *Social Theories of the Middle Ages, 1200–1500* (London, 1926), and there are interesting sociological insights in J. M. Fletcher, "Wealth and Poverty in the Medieval Ger-

man Universities with Particular Reference to the University of Freiburg,"
in *Europe in the Late Middle Ages,* ed. John R. Hale et al. (Evanston, 1965),
pp. 410–36. The literature in foreign languages is almost as scanty as that in
English, but the serious student would do well to consult *Les Universités
européennes du XIVe au XVIIIe siècle,* ed. Sven Stelling-Michaud (Geneva,
1967), and Friedrich Wilhelm Oediger, *Über die Bildung der Geistlichen im
späten Mittelalter* (Cologne, 1953). For an introduction to Petrarch's writings
see the anthology of David Thompson entitled *Petrarch* (New York, 1971).

The word "asculta" (listen), from a German manuscript of the second half of the thirteenth century. In the upper part of the "A," the Madonna is enthroned. In the lower part, Saint Benedict reads his Rule to some monks.

5.

Varieties of Christian Experience

JEFFREY BURTON RUSSELL

R ELIGION IS a human phenomenon affecting and affected by society, and the historian may, as does R. W. Southern in *Church and Society in the Middle Ages*, treat medieval Christianity as a function of society. But to understand merely its externals is to understand it incompletely, for historically Christianity has not emphasized its social functions. Its founder insisted, "My Kingdom is not of this world," preaching that material security is unreal and that the door to reality—to the Kingdom of God—stands before Christians as a challenge and a choice. The choice is whether to pass through the door to the Kingdom of God or to withdraw one's hand from the latch.

In a 1971 symposium, Sanctions for Evil, psychologists and sociologists examined man's rationalizations of crime: We use violence to achieve a noble end; we refrain from opposing evil until we have "enough" power; we assume that our side is morally good and incapable of evil and that those we oppose are subhuman. To what extent did medieval Christianity yield to such temptations to rationalize? To what extent was it true to itself? The historian is incapable of judging an institution by absolute standards, but he should not fail to ask the most internal and humanly most important question: To what extent did the institution prove consistent with its own principles? The question regarding medieval Christianity must be, To what extent and with what vigor did its members knock upon the door of the Kingdom and to what extent did they withdraw their hands from the latch?

In medieval Christianity, as in the history of Christianity as a whole, there were two powerful traditions of how the door to the Kingdom could best be opened. The tradition of prophecy urged men not to compromise with this world but to take the Kingdom of God alone and, if need be, with spiritual violence. The tradition of order, starting from the premise that this world, though less real than the other, is good and made by God, urged the building of a society on earth in accordance with the will of God. This essay will examine the lives of eight medieval Christians who sought the Kingdom through prophecy or through order.

The faith of Christians has always been tested from within as much as from without. It would be ingenuous to imagine that pristine Christianity was as golden as it seemed to later writers; yet the chief threats to Christians of the first three hundred years were external—the often active hostility of non-Christians, especially the Roman government and people. Worldly considerations must be of limited importance to men whose persistence in their faith often gained them torture or a cruel death. The peace of the Church—the toleration decreed early in the fourth century by Constantine and the establishment later in that century of Christianity as the state religion by Theodosius —marked the increase of internal temptations. For the first time, being a Christian was of worldly advantage. Gradually the church amassed wealth, land, and political power. As expectations of the second coming of Christ receded into the indefinite future, one sanction for evil—postponement of responsibility—became ever more tempting. Christians continued to prepare for the Kingdom of God, but the emphasis was upon the time given to prepare. Rather than lifting the latch of the door today, taking no thought for the morrow, they stored up their resources for the future. By acquiring power and prestige, the church planned to obtain the means of and the time for perfecting itself and bringing the Good News to others. Christians began to regard the lilies of the field as objects for gilding.

What occurred in the first three centuries of Christianity, gradually and undramatically and therefore the more perniciously, was what Max Weber has called the "routinization of charisma" and what Rudolf Sohm termed the conversion of the church from sacrament to corporation. As the second coming of Christ delayed, the sense that the Kingdom was going to be thrust upon the world immediately gradually faded. The channels to the Kingdom became silted up by complacency. Gone, for example, were men like the prophets who in the first century had wandered about in the manner of Paul and Barnabas, speaking as the spirit moved them. Gone was the possibility of martyrdom in the arena. Gone were most of the small communities in which bread and love and life were intensely shared, and infrequent was the meal of love called agape. The old saying "They must be Christians: See how they love one another" was less frequently heard in the land. The intense personal anguish of becoming a Christian by taking on a new life was replaced by routine baptism and confirmation or by the kind of mass political conversion that Clovis imposed upon the Frankish people late in the fifth century. The sacraments, especially baptism and the eucharist, continued to pierce the opacity of the door, but even the sacraments were routinized as clergy and laity became increasingly separated and the orders and ranks of clergy became more defined and discrete.

One of the most fervent protests against the routinization of charisma and the postponement of the Kingdom was the eremitical and monastic movement. From the third century in Egypt the Desert Fathers, as Helen Waddell calls them, bore uncompromising witness to a more immediate religion. In Palestine, where Saint Jerome was for a long while a hermit in the fourth century, throughout the Near East, in southern Gaul, in Ireland, and in southern Italy, centers of eremitical and monastic life appeared. One of these, Monte Cassino in Italy, produced a variety of monasticism that is still important and that for almost five centuries was one of the most pervasive forces in Western Christianity.

Saint Benedict

The chief founder of Western monasticism was Saint Benedict of Nursia (480?–543?). Little is known of his life. Born in Nursia in the Sabine hills, like many monastic leaders he came from a well-to-do family. After studying the liberal arts at Rome, he determined to emulate the hermits of the eastern deserts and retreat into seclusion. We do not know for certain what made him decide to leave the comforts of home and the benefits of education, but we may guess. In Rome Benedict would have seen a precarious world. The Roman Empire in the West had fallen; Italy was under the insecure rule of the Ostrogoths, whose power would soon be demolished by Byzantine reconquest and Lombard incursions. The church of central and southern Italy was almost completely disorganized. The civil service career open in the later empire to a man of Benedict's background and education could no longer seem either desirable or entirely useful. A mind as creative as Benedict's was probably repulsed by the sterile and pedantic teaching of the Roman schools.

Leaving Rome, the young Benedict went to live alone in a cave in the side of a cliff at Subiaco, his intention as a hermit being to devote his attention to God. There he was tempted, if any credence may be placed in the hagiographies, by lust, restlessness, and accidie (spiritual lassitude). He was lured back to the world of action by a group of men who asked him to teach them to live as he did, in holiness and peace. Reluctantly Benedict agreed and organized a monastic community. Although the community proved refractory and the experience unrewarding, it seems to have turned his mind from an eremitical to a cenobitic life. Quitting the deserted environs of Subiaco, he moved to Monte Cassino, which, on the high road between Naples and Rome, was scarcely out of the way. There in about 525 he founded a monastic community. The Rule Benedict wrote for this community was derived in part from the anonymous, contemporary Rule of the Master and was influenced by the rules of the Eastern monks Basil and Cassian. It became the basis of the Benedictine Order, which dominated the monastic life of Europe for half a millennium.

What could have induced a man of wealth and background to abandon his worldly advantages for a life of deprivation? The answer, holy zeal, may be found in chapter 72 of the Rule that Benedict wrote: "Just as there is an evil spirit or bitterness that seperates a man from God and leads him to hell, there is also a zeal that is good, one that separates a man from his vices and leads him to God and eternal life." For the love of God, one must give up all worldly things to which one is attached. In this Benedict was doing no more than following the message of the gospel. But why would a man who has determined to lead a hermit's life and devote himself to the contemplation of God let himself be persuaded to direct a monastic community? The need of those who implored him may have moved him. Benedict was not satisfied with saving his own soul; he felt responsibility for the welfare of others. He had observed the spiritual desolation of leaderless monks, "who call holy whatever they choose" (Rule, chapter 1). Nowhere in church or state in sixth-century Italy was there order or discipline: All was in pieces, all coherence gone. In a world of anarchy that was rendering anarchic even the lives of those who denied themselves the pleasures of the world in order to serve Christ, Benedict resolved that Monte Cassino would become a center of ordr.

Like earlier monastic rules, that of Benedict sought to provide a routine that would enable men to separate themselves from worldly things and devote their lives to the love of God without going to extremes of idleness or asceticism that would turn them from their quest. By voluntary and common consent these monks had come together and chosen Benedict their abbot; the abbot's duty as "father" of the house was to give them the instructions they needed. If they failed to follow the rule that bound them, the monastery would degenerate into a microcosm of the anarchic world beyond its walls.

The first duty of the monk was obedience—primarily to the abbot but also to the reasonable commands of his fellow monks. This obedience was to be rendered with joy in the knowledge that it brought one into closer communion with one's fellows and with God. Closely linked with obedience was humility, the willingness to accept legitimate criticism and the refusal to exalt oneself. In the monastery of Saint Benedict there was no hierarchy of wealth, power, or even learning. The equality of poverty was preserved. If a powerful or wealthy man wished to become one of the brothers, he had first to abandon all his worldly goods. If a wealthy man wished to place his son in the care of the monastery, he had to agree to leave no part of his estate to his child. The house as a whole might possess property, but nothing, not even pen or book, was allowed to the individual monk. In the beginning there seem to have been few if any ordained priests among the brothers. Chapters 60, 61, and 62 of the Rule grant that priests may be admitted to the society, though only on condition that they live like the other brothers. Provision is made for the ordination of worthy brothers to the priesthood, if that should prove desirable. Distribution was made to each according to his need (following Acts 4:35), and in this way the purity of the monastic community approached that of the early Christian communities in the days of persecution before the Peace of the Church.

The voluntary association of the brothers was itself a notable virtue. The technological feats made since the end of the Neolithic period had been based primarily upon slave labor. Only cruel exploitation had made possible the pyramids of Egypt and the Colosseum of Rome. The voluntary banding together of men into a unit that was economic as well as religious meant that great projects could be accomplished without slavery or coercion. Arguing that spiritual laziness was the enemy of the soul, Benedict ordained that a great part of the monks' waking day should be spent in manual labor. For most, this was work in the fields and gardens. For those who were craftsmen, it meant plying their trade, the products of which they might sell, providing the proceeds went not to themselves but to the community as a whole. The economic enterprises to which monasticism could thus lend itself reached their height in the twelfth and thirteenth centuries, when Cistercian monks settled and cultivated vast wilderness areas.

The essential work of the monastery was the worship of God. The monk was to offer each action of his life to God with a prayer, but communal worship was the center of monastic life. This was ordained in the Rule by the establishment of the monastic Office—the liturgy of prayers, responses, and readings that all monks were required to attend every three hours throughout the twenty-four-hour day (though two of the offices were sometimes combined to allow for six hours of uninterrupted sleep). In words and song the monks rendered love and thanks for their share in the haven of order and joy in an increasingly ruined and barbarous world. Whatever may have been the noteworthy intellectual, charitable, and economic by-products of monasticism, prayer—specifically communal prayer in the Office—was the essential activity of the monastic community.

Unlike the canons and friars of the twelfth and thirteenth centuries, Benedict had no thought of going out in the world to perform charitable acts. He ordained that guests would always be welcome at the monastery, particularly the poor, who would be accepted out of love and without hope of pecuniary reward. The intellectual pursuits Saint Benedict provided for were limited.

Periods of rest from manual labor and from the Office were to be used for reading, but the saint seems to have envisaged no more than the Scriptures, the Institutes of Cassian, the Rule of Basil, his own Rule, and a few other works. Intellectual labor for its own sake had no value. The Benedictine abbeys would become centers of learning and the chief preservers and transmitters of classical knowledge, though Saint Benedict had not had this in mind.

So that the monks might turn completely away from the things of this world and toward the love of God, they were enjoined not only to poverty, chastity, and obedience—the prime monastic virtues since the fourth century, the time of Saint Pachomius—but also to a moderation in food and drink that was almost a perpetual limited fast, and to silence. Aware that idle talk is harmful to minds that are cultivated or devout, Benedict forbade all chatter. The vice most frequently mentioned in the Rule is "murmuring"—the kind of talk, more corrupting than chatter, that criticizes, complains, and denigrates. Peace, order, stability, mutual love, gentleness, and generosity—these were Benedict's goals.

Where then was the worm in the rose? Why did not everyone accept a way of life that promised peace and joy? The problem was not primarily the indifference or hostility of the external world. Indeed, monasticism—as practiced by the Benedictines as well as by their Celtic rivals from Ireland—spread quickly through Italy and Gaul. By the middle of the seventh century Benedictine missionaries from Gaul had established houses throughout most of western Europe. Eventually, owing to the persuasiveness of Benedict's namesake, Saint Benedict of Aniane, the Frankish Church decided at the synod of Aachen in 817 to establish the Benedictine Rule in monasteries throughout the Frankish domains. From that time until just before 1100, almost all Catholic monasteries in the West were Benedictine.

Yet there were dangers even in the Rule itself. The power of the abbot was almost unlimited. He was to be elected by the brothers on the basis of his wisdom and holiness, but once elected, his power was nearly unchallengeable, for "he is held to act as Christ's vicar in the monastery" (Rule, chapter 2). The abbot was supposed to be gentle, but when necessary he could reprove and rebuke. He could isolate a recalcitrant brother from the community and in the worst instances chastise him with the whip. Only the vesting of such powers in the abbot could have brought order and tranquillity to the Benedictine monastery. Only such powers, extended in the tenth and eleventh centuries not to one but to hundreds of houses, could have made the abbots of Cluny almost equal in power to the pope. Not only the vices of incompetent abbots, but the very power and majesty of the most capable, marked an attention to the things of this world not wholly compatible with witness to the kingdom.

Another problem was celibacy. If one is to turn one's thoughts toward God, it is well to avoid the pleasures of the flesh, but the virtue of celibacy has been known to lead to a lack of understanding of the problems of those in whose lives sex has a legitimate place. Indeed, the whole concept of withdrawal from the world is ambivalent. One does not have to be a spiritual philistine or a secularist to understand the dangers of such a course. To create an island of stability and love in the midst of an anarchic universe is an archetypal urge. The history of Benedictine monasticism, however, indicates that withdrawal may mean not only turning one's face toward God but turning one's back toward one's fellow men.

In the eighth century, and again in the tenth, the Benedictines succumbed to this temptation. As the order spread and obtained land and wealth from men who believed that supporting a monastery was an act pleasing to God, the Benedictines grew rich and self-satisfied. Abbots grew lax in enforcing the Rule. The abbots of the monastery of Cluny, founded in 909 for the purpose of restoring strict obedience to the Rule, invited splendid guests who would have amazed, if not outraged, Saint Benedict. Dukes, counts, and bishops were lavishly entertained in exchange for opulent gifts and promises of worldly aid and comfort. The abbey of Cluny and those of some of her daughter houses were adorned with gold and precious stones, a luxury loudly denounced in the twelfth century by Saint Bernard, to whom the Benedictine Order seemed hopelessly corrupted.

Even in the sixth century Benedict's insistence upon the equality of all members of the monastery was ignored. A distinction in status came to be drawn between priests, whose numbers were increasing, and unordained brothers. Indeed, both priests and brothers gradually curtailed the amount of manual labor that they did themselves. With the vast estates they were granted, they also obtained, according to the law and custom of the early Middle Ages, the serfs who worked them. Manual labor could be left to the serfs, freeing the monks for other activities. Because of their labors in the *scriptoria* ("writing rooms"), Latin classics, both pagan and Christian, were preserved, beautiful illuminated manuscripts were produced, and intricate liturgical ritual and music were developed. The literary output of the period before the eleventh century was almost exclusively the work of monks. Had they not exploited the labor of the serfs, European culture would be poorer today. But important as these activities were, they meant that the Benedictines had become too busy with the things of this world. They had withdrawn their hands from the latch in order to furnish the antechamber.

Saint Boniface

In spite of the efforts of Benedictine and Celtic monks and the labors of a few outstanding popes like Gregory the Great (590–604), the church in the seventh century remained in difficult straits. Only if some force could be found to convert and organize northern Europe into a working part of the church could ruin be averted. Out of Devon, in England, the northwesternmost outpost of the Roman Church, came Winfrith, later called Saint Boniface, whose reforms became the base upon which the ordered Christian society of the next centuries would rest.

Winfrith (672?–754) was raised in the Celtic monasteries of Wessex, where the missionary spirit was strong. In the sixth and seventh centuries Celtic and Frankish missionaries had labored to bring the gospel to the pagan Teutons on the continent. Celtic missionaries from Ireland had been remarkably vigorous, founding great monasteries at Luxeuil in eastern France, Bobbio in north-central Italy, and St. Gall in Switzerland, and penetrating as far east as present-day Austria, Poland, and perhaps even Russia. English missionaries were influenced by the Celtic ideal of *peregrinatio* ("pilgrimage" or "wandering"). To the Irish zeal for conversion, the English—themselves converted to Roman Christianity in the seventh century—added a special devotion to Rome. The great English Saint Wilfrid of York (634–709?), who had evangelized Frisia (the modern Netherlands), rejected Celtic rites and insisted that the Roman liturgy be used in England. Because of his efforts a close relationship between the English clergy and the papacy developed. Saint Willibrord (658–739), Winfrith's most successful predecessor as missionary to the continent, had obtained support for his mission to the Frisians from the Carolingian mayors of the palace and from the pope. The double purpose of Willibrord and Winfrith was to convert the pagans to Christianity and to secure their obedience to the see of Peter.

Winfrith undertook his first mission to Frisia in 716, an unsuccessful venture from which he came back to England convinced of the need for organization and close cooperation between the secular and ecclesiastical powers. In 718 he returned to the continent and secured the support of Charles Martel and of the papacy for his conversion efforts. In 722 Pope Gregory II, one of the most important figures in the formation of the Western Church, gave him the name Boniface and consecrated him as missionary bishop. From that time on Boniface devoted himself to three tasks: converting pagan Frisia, Hesse, and Thuringia; organizing ecclesiastical institutions in the areas east of the Rhine; and reorganizing and reforming the Frankish Church. A life of hard work, honor, and achievement was capped by the crown of martyrdom when in 754 the "Apostle of the Germans" was murdered by a plundering band of Frisian pagans.

Saint Boniface's work has sometimes been taken for granted by those who assume that western Christendom would necessarily have developed into a coherent unit with Rome at its center. But when Boniface landed on the continent, there were few indications of such a future. Muslims were threatening the South; most of the people in the North were unconverted; and Gaul and

Italy were suffering from recurrent wars. Byzantine power in the West was fading rapidly, and the popes in both East and West were bereft of imperial support and, until the election of Gregory II, unable to establish their own prestige. Frankish military efforts eventually preserved Christian Europe from the Muslims, but that victory did not guarantee a united Christendom. France, Germany, and the British Isles might have developed self-sufficient national churches, which undoubtedly would have recognized Rome's primacy in theory but ignored it in fact. In subsequent centuries rulers challenged the idea of a united Christian society with varying degrees of success, but until the fifteenth and sixteenth centuries the idea of unity, for which Boniface was as responsible as any man, retained its allure.

Boniface's mission was timely. Pope Gregory II (715–731) and his successor Gregory III (731–741) were shaking off the control of the Byzantine emperor. Faced with hostility not only from that quarter but from the Lombards, the popes needed support from the North. In the past, papal policy toward the North (with the brief and consequential exception of Gregory the Great's interest in the conversion of England) had been passive nearly to the point of lacking interest. Now it could no longer afford to be. The Gregorys and Pope Zachary (741–752), who followed them, were eager to give Boniface their support. So also were the Carolingian mayors of the palace, who were determined to repress the anarchy of late Merovingian rule and secure the fortunes of their own dynasty.

Charles Martel, mayor of all the Frankish kingdoms, and his son Pepin III, who succeeded him as mayor and became the first Carolingian king, gave Boniface every support in his efforts to reform the Frankish Church. For about five years, from the succession of Pepin in 741, Boniface enjoyed a golden period, establishing new dioceses, reorganizing old ones according to the custom of the Roman Church, founding schools and monasteries, imposing the Rule of Saint Benedict and the Roman liturgy, disciplining clergy whose lives were immoral or whose obedience to Rome was imperfect, and recreating the institution of metropolitans. These papally appointed prelates (similar to later archbishops) obtained the *pallium* (a collar and attenuated robe symbolizing their authority) directly from the pope and were in charge of supervising the bishops placed under their authority. Pepin supported the great missionary's effort to secure Christian order, for he hoped to use Boniface's work to bring the Frankish Church under his own control. After 747, relations between them seem to have cooled. As Pepin's power grew, he wanted to limit papal prestige and began to regard Boniface's work as a mixed blessing. But in 751, when Pepin obtained his highest goal, the deposition of the last Merovingian king and his own coronation as king of the Franks, he devoted himself to continuing and even enhancing a close alliance with the papacy. The foundation of a unified Roman Church in western Europe had been constructed.

Of the political implications of his activities Boniface had little grasp. His own sense of his mission was to convert the pagans and to bring all Christians, new and old, to obedience to Rome, which, he believed, could alone provide the order and stability amidst which Christ's message could bring men to salvation. In a sense, Boniface's goal was to bring to the West the creative order that Saint Benedict had achieved in monastic communities. Through preaching, persuasion, and logical arguments, he believed that with the help of the Frankish rulers he could bring thousands of pagans to Christianity.

Conversion was supplemented by the moral reform of both clergy and laity. Boniface ordered the establishment or reaffirmation of the Benedictine Rule in monasteries where laxity had set in, and he himself founded houses like Fulda, in Germany, which were to become models of moral probity, intellectual light —and obedience to Rome. Pope Zachary in his charter for the foundation of Fulda forbade "any priest of any Church save that of the Apostolic See to exercise any rights at all over the monastery." The purpose of this papal exemption was to protect the monastery from interference by worldly bishops and laymen and to bind it in close obedience to Rome.

Such schools were to make possible the education of the clergy, whose members often had not been able to pronounce the words of baptism. Ignorance seems to have been the least of their vices. Boniface had constant difficulty with priests and nuns who were fornicators, blasphemers, drunkards, and murderers. Whole dioceses, he wrote Pope Zachary in 742, "have been put into the hands of greedy laymen or else corrupted by unworthy and fornicating priests." Boniface was no less concerned with the moral welfare of the laity. His attention to detail in the care of his vast flock rivaled that which Saint Benedict had given to one monastic house. In all things Boniface tried to instill in his people obedience to Christian morality and to Roman procedures. Marital problems were frequently complicated. For example, Boniface approved the marriage of a woman and her godfather, an acceptable union in the North. Finding later that Rome condemned it, he wrote to the pope in order to relieve his conscience.

Yet Boniface was by no means servile in his relations with the papacy. Burning with prophetic zeal, he more than once admonished the popes to take care that the Roman clergy were purged of gross sins. How could he, he asked, guarantee the loyalty of the northern people when pilgrims to Rome returned with tales of clergy sunk in crime and avarice? Nor did Boniface respect the person of a monarch beyond his moral deserts: He called King Ethelbald of Mercia to task for "wallowing in the filth of adultery and [being] submerged in an ocean of lechery . . . stealing the revenues of churches and monasteries . . . and oppressing monks and priests." He warned: "The wealth of this world cannot help you on the day of judgment . . . when after the death of the body the sinner's soul shall pass on to hell."

Unlike Benedict, Boniface clearly did not believe in retreating from the world. Even more than the founder of the Benedictine Rule, he had to deal with external enemies and hidden temptations. "All," he complained, "is in external conflict and internal anxiety." Successful though he was, his life bred frustrations. When a man goes out to impose his idea of order upon the world, he finds that the world resists him, or that it seems to accept and then turns away, or that it distorts his meaning. Wise and gentle as Boniface could be, as when he exhorted a young man Nithard to concentrate on his books if he felt the longing to write, his internal anxiety drove him sometimes to act as though he could compel men to pass through the door to the Kingdom in the way he believed right.

The zeal that made his successes possible pressed Boniface, when his will was thwarted, to violate the rules of charity. He realized that the Irish had done much to convert Germany; yet he resented their opposition to his efforts to bring the Bavarian Church closer to Rome. For all clergy and laity who resisted his efforts to impose Roman order, Boniface was without patience. He persuaded and reprimanded; when things grew bad, as when the heretics Aldebert and Clement found followers among the people, he prosecuted. But at no time in his life, so far as we know, did Boniface attempt to use physical force to bring anyone to Christianity or under the authority of the pope.

The use of political power as well as moral and intellectual suasion may have prompted others to use less nice techniques. At the end of the eighth century Charlemagne, successor of Pepin III, completed the conversion of Germany by invading and conquering Saxony and commanding its inhabitants to accept the Prince of Peace on pain of death. This, the seventh-century holy war of the Byzantine emperor Heraclius against the Persians, and the *Reconquista* (1085–1212) against the Muslims in Spain set precedents for the Crusades, the pogroms against the Jews, and the execution of heretics. To pound at the door unceasingly is one thing; to hew it down with a battleax is quite another.

The alliance that Boniface made with the Carolingians was not without other dangers. Sincere though Pepin III and Charlemagne were in their desire for an ordered church, their motives were not unmixed. As Christians they desired an uncorrupted clergy and an upright laity. But what was more to the point politically, they wanted obedience. They realized that in rebuilding the Frankish monarchy from the rubble in which the Merovingians had left it religion was a useful mortar. They claimed for themselves the right to issue ecclesiastical as well as secular legislation. Their measures usually improved the moral and educational level of the Christian people, but they took pains to establish their own political control over the church and to limit strictly the obedience to Rome that Boniface had wished. Indeed, in 794 Charlemagne called a synod at Frankfurt, where at his behest the Frankish bishops declared heretical a position on iconoclasm that the pope had already approved. Carolingian control over the Frankish Church set a precedent for later French and German kings in their controversies with the papacy.

Even apart from secular interference there were dangers in the ecclesiastical order that Boniface helped to create. It is not unlikely that the loyalty to Rome inculcated by Boniface entailed certain disadvantages for the church. Later conflicts between popes and secular rulers might have been avoided were it not for the claims of spiritual (and later even temporal) overlordship made by the popes. It is also possible that the Eastern and Western Churches could have avoided permanent schism if the Western Church had developed as more of a confederation of regional churches. This is speculation. But the powers placed in the hands of bishops and archbishops by Boniface's reforms in fact not only rendered the church more competent for good but also sowed seeds of contention. Popes, emperors, kings, and nobles would vie with one another to enlist the power of the bishops for their own political purposes, and the bishops disputed among themselves over their rights, prerogatives, lands, and authority. In Boniface's lifetime the archbishops of Mainz and Cologne contested control of the diocese of Utrecht. This behavior would be repeated frequently, with prelates sometimes even going to war with one another.

To achieve the salvation of Christian men and women, order was needed. To achieve order, organization was necessary, and organization required power. This dilemma was realized even more acutely in the eleventh century during the career of Pope Gregory VII.

Pope Gregory VII

As long as the Carolingian Empire remained strong, secular and clerical officials worked together relatively amicably for the peace, well-being, and integrity of the Christian people. With the collapse of the Carolingian Empire in the middle of the ninth century under the twin blows of internal dissension and external aggression by Magyars, Muslims, and Vikings, the church also deteriorated. Once again the monasteries, like Cluny, became centers of peace on the violence-torn continent, though even they were no refuge from the pagan and bloodthirsty Vikings. When in the tenth century order gradually began to reappear, the weakened and demoralized clergy could only follow the lead of the secular rulers. Finding ignorance, debauchery, and incompetence in almost every corner of the church, rulers like Otto the Great (936–973) in Germany and Edgar (959–975) in England attempted, for political as well as for spiritual reasons, to reestablish order in the clergies of their countries. The dignity of the papacy, also a victim of moral decay, was gradually restored through the efforts of the German rulers, who restrained the power of the Roman families that for a century had made the papacy a political football. The culmination of the age of royal reform was the reign of Henry III (1039–1056). A determined proponent of order, he in 1046 deposed three squabbling claimants to the papacy and put a German on the throne of Peter. In 1048, another German, Bruno of Toul in the duchy of Lorraine, was elected pope with Henry's approval. He took the name Leo IX.

Leo's reign opened a new era in the history of the church—the era in which reform was led by neither king nor monk but by the pope himself. Leo brought with him from Lorraine, a center of monastic reform and intellectual innovation as well as one of the most socially and economically advanced regions of Europe, a brain trust of able and devoted reformers, including the monk Hildebrand, who later became Pope Gregory VII.

Hildebrand was born to impecunious parents in Tuscany sometime between 1015 and 1020. He probably became a monk while still a young man. A friend and relation of Gregory VI (1045–1046), one of the popes deposed by Henry III, he accompanied that exiled prelate to Lorraine. There he met some of the leading reformers, including Bruno of Toul, with whom he returned to Rome when Bruno was elected Pope Leo IX. Hildebrand's influence increased steadily. A legate under Leo IX, he became archdeacon (almost "prime minister") under Pope Nicholas II (1059–1061) and was the chief adviser of Pope Alexander II (1061–1073). When Alexander died in 1073, Hildebrand was acclaimed as Pope Gregory VII by the Roman people, a choice affirmed the next day by the cardinals. "I am placed here," he wrote the Lombards in his first months in office, "to announce to all the nations justice and truth." Never wavering in this goal, Gregory VII was driven into exile by the victorious armies of King Henry IV and died at Salerno in 1085, where he is said to have uttered his own famous epitaph: "I have loved justice and hated iniquity; therefore I die in exile."

Gregory—"that holy Satan" as Saint Peter Damian called him—was never congenial to those who opposed him; his policies exalted the power of the papacy to an unprecedented degree. But it would be a mistake to imagine that the man was moved primarily by personal pride or ambition. No one is wholly free of such motivation, but the driving force behind Gregory was holy zeal to realize the Kingdom of God on earth at whatever cost to his own personal comfort. He was never under the illusion that he was popular. His letters are full of barely repressed anguish at his responsibilities: "We are," he wrote, "carrying alone at this critical time a ponderous load not only of spiritual but also of secular affairs." He had no wish to be placed in authority at Rome, "where, as God knows, I have lived under compulsion for the last twenty years" and where he was "led even to long for death" and suffered "a living death."

Gregory's program was to create, legislate, and enforce a rational order in Christian society. Saint Paul had taught that Christians form the mystical body of Christ. Subsequent theologians added that the visible manifestation of the mystical body was the church—the community of Christians. The reform papacy went further, identifying the church with the Roman Church, which by virtue of its authority represented Christian society as a whole. Gregory VII was the first to use the term "Christian society" to mean, precisely, the body of Christians in communion with Rome.

It would be too easy to be cynical and interpret this theory as the result of a drive for power on the part of Hildebrand or the papal reformers in general. Their concern was for reform. They believed that Christian society should not continue to drift in the anarchy and immorality that had so often characterized it in the past and that their duty was to build on earth a society that resembled the Kingdom of God. Gregory acknowledged that ultimate reality exists beyond the door in another world, but unlike some monks, who insisted that escape from this world was the only way to the Kingdom, Gregory proposed that an "image" of the Kingdom could be built on earth. He maintained that man's salvation lies in the more real, otherworldly Kingdom. But, he argued, if God's purpose were to draw us all immediately into that heavenly Kingdom, he would come again now to judge the living and the dead. That he does not indicates that he wishes men to use the time he has given them on earth to some purpose. The purpose was the construction of a society conforming as closely as possible to the ideal of the Kingdom and therefore leading Christian people to the paths of salvation. That Gregory thought that the charge on him and on all secular and ecclesiastical rulers was to lead men to salvation is clear from his correspondence: "He who does not oppose evil men out of regard for his station gives his consent"; consenting to an evil deed is tantamount to performing the deed.

The principles upon which the Christian society was to be built were justice and liberty. The Gregorian idea of justice has its roots in a tradition of natural law stretching back to Cicero and beyond. Justice is the state of society in which the laws of men (both secular and ecclesiastical) correspond most closely with the laws that exist in the mind of God and that revelation and reason have shown to man.

The Gregorian idea of liberty was the opposite of license. It consisted of the rights and duties inherent in one's appointed place in life. Nor was it egalitarian. Each person, noble and serf, has his place, and to attempt to change or improve it is to be prideful and destructive. Gregory believed the proper place of the clergy was above the laity (a position later popes made explicit by their tactless insistence that the greatest king must stand below the meanest priest). He wrote: "Divine providence ordained that there should be diverse grades and orders, that in the reverence of the lower for the higher and the affectionate care of the higher for the lower, there should be concord in diversity." Such sentiments are not congenial to the ideals of our own age; yet societies, whatever their ideologies, have divisions of labor and develop diverse grades and orders. Gregory recognized this fact and insisted that this situation be regulated by liberty. Each serf, for example, has certain duties he must render his master; and each serf has certain rights his master must preserve for him. If either defaults, he violates justice and must rectify his wrongdoing. The Gregorian idea of liberty is no respecter of persons. Bishops and kings must do their duty in accordance with the principles of justice just as the poorest peasant must, and because their responsibilities are greater their chastisement for failing will be harsher. Discord and war occur when liberty is ignored, and they impede the establishment of justice.

For such a system to work, there must be in—or rather above—society an organ that establishes and proclaims what is just and what is in accordance with liberty. Christ is the head and ruler of a Christian society, but there must be a means of making his voice heard on earth. The kings and emperors, even those who most sincerely and earnestly supported the church, had been unable to cope with corruption. The alternative to their power was papal authority, which not only seemed more practical at the time but had scriptural and patristic foundations that royalty lacked. Christ had entrusted the care of his flock to Peter and the other apostles, not to any king.

The papacy had other claims to pre-eminence. For centuries an ecumenical council had not been called, and grave difficulties with the Eastern Church made calling a new one seem futile. In addition, for two hundred years an increasing number of theorists had been considering papal duties and prerogatives. Not a conscious decision for change but a strong belief that he was following the best traditions of the church led Gregory and his advisers to declare that the pope, as the head of the Roman Church, was the monarch of all the church. He had *plenitudo potestatis* ("fullness of power") over both the ecclesiastical and the secular worlds, and every Christian was his subject: "We are so placed that, whether we will or no, we are bound to proclaim truth and righteousness to all peoples." Few rulers have proclaimed, and then tried to realize, principles as legitimate in Christian terms.

It is generally recognized that the theories of the Hildebrandine papacy were in most respects not a radical departure from the papal theories of the past. What was novel was Gregory's determination to put the theories into practice. Vicar of Peter, he took the title "bishop of bishops" as well. Previous popes had claimed the independence of the clerical from the secular order; Gregory argued that he ruled both, the clerical directly and the secular indirectly: "The Roman Church was founded by God alone. Only the Roman pontiff is by right called universal. He alone may depose or restore bishops. No synod may be considered a general council unless he has ordered it. The more important manifesto composed of chapter headings from earlier collections of canon law err. Whoever is not in conformity with the Roman Church is not a Catholic." These uncompromising statements, drawn from the *Dictatus Papae,* a papal cases under adjudication in every diocese should be submitted to the holy see. The Roman Church has never erred nor, as the Scriptures testify, will it ever inserted into the Papal Register under the year 1075, indicate the breadth of Gregory's view of his powers over affairs spiritual.

This authority was implemented in many ways. The activity of the curia, the papal court, rapidly increased. The volume of correspondence issued by the popes grew enormously during the eleventh century. The papal treasury both incurred new responsibilities and obtained income from new sources. The bureaucracy needed to maintain an expanding government expanded. Specialized departments appeared in the curia—the chancery, headed by the chancellor, responsible for the issuance of letters, decrees, charters, and other documents; the chamberlain; and a host of minor officers. The most important offices in the curia were beginning to be occupied by cardinals, clergy whose chief function was as bureaucrats in the papal government. So that the pope's rule might be felt in lands far from Rome, Gregory increased the use of papal representatives called legates, who during the period of their jurisdiction took precedence over the local clergy. The legates might be sent out on a limited assignment—for example, to spend a few months at Lyon to judge a dispute in that see—or they might be given full powers for a year or more over a whole kingdom. Charters of "liberty" were issued to monasteries throughout Europe, releasing them from obedience to anyone, layman or bishop, and placing them under the sole protection of the pope. Each of these measures was designed to draw the structure of spiritual order in Christian society more and more closely under the control of the pope. Another measure, totally consistent with Gregory's view of society, caused great difficulty with the secular authorities. This was the effort to remove the power to appoint bishops from the laity and to secure instead their free election by the clergy and people of a diocese. Later popes would claim the right to "papal provisions," appointing the bishops themselves.

Gregory believed that he ruled the secular order no less directly than he ruled the spiritual. As bishops were the pope's subordinates in the spiritual order, so emperors and kings were his servants in the secular. All must work together under Christ's vicar to assure the victory of Christ's justice on earth. "The pope alone may use imperial insignia," states the *Dictatus Papae.* "All princes are to kiss the feet of the pope, and his alone. He may depose emperors. He can be judged by no one. He may absolve subjects from the duty of obedience to rulers who are unjust." Gregory did not intend these statements as empty posturing. When King Philip I of France proved both adulterous and unwilling to restrain his lords from plundering pilgrims, Gregory excommunicated him. When Henry IV, whose power rested heavily upon the unswerving loyalty of his bishops, resisted Gregory's efforts to remove his control of their appointments, and when efforts at reconciliation failed, Gregory both excommunicated and deposed the emperor, entering into an armed alliance with the restive German nobility in an effort to make his deposition effective. That Gregory failed in this effort in no way limits its daring scope. In taking these actions, which caused him grief and trouble and eventually ended in his defeat and exile, he seems to have been moved by a deep sense of the responsibility of his office and a corollary fear that God would punish him for shirking his duty. "I am bound to reprove you," he wrote, "lest your blood be required at my hand and lest I be punished . . . by God." The most frequent phrase in his correspondence is "Cursed be he who holds back his sword from blood." He always explained that he meant from unpleasant responsibility, but it was an unfortunate phrase, to which more literal interpretations would soon be applied.

The holy zeal of Pope Gregory VII can scarcely be questioned, and the ideal of a united Christian society, under God, devoted to the principles of justice and liberty as they were then understood, is one of the noblest conceptions of human society ever enunciated. It was to become the keystone of papal policy. Yet the worm was working also in this rose. To grasp the ring of power even when one is a Hildebrand is to incur deadly peril, and Gregory's sweeping policies had a number of ill effects.

In the first place, the claim to papal monarchy ensured that the schism with the Eastern Church, which had been growing since the eighth century and had reached its climax in 1054, would persist. Relying upon ancient tradition and the dignity of their own imperial see, the patriarchs of Constantinople could never endure the Hildebrandine order. In the second, Gregory's insistence that bishops be loyal to him rather than to secular rulers ignored the political needs of those rulers and led not merely to the bitter struggle between Gregory and Henry IV but to three centuries of conflict with the kings of Germany, France, and England. The consequence was the engagement of the vicar of Christ in political and even military alliances and counteralliances. Thus Gregory's policies encouraged divisions in the Christian society he wished so strongly and so vainly to unify.

In the *Dictatus Papae* can be seen the unmistakable signs of hubris. The members of Gregory's curia did not lift the latch of the door. They imperiously commanded it to open. The immense powers claimed by the Hildebrandine papacy have seemed to some modern scholars as well as to medieval contemporaries such as the monk Sigebert of Gembloux a threat to Christian tradition. Always previously the church had been guided by tradition, the decisions of earlier popes, councils, and the slow accretions of canon law. Gregory claimed direct authority from God to dispense with the canons and to alter tradition.

"Jesus said, I am the way, the truth, and the life, not I am custom," he was fond of quoting. This is a fine sentiment when one is dealing with corrupt and decadent customs but dangerous when one tampers with legitimate mores. Sigebert of Gembloux, a supporter of the imperial position, saw in this threat to tradition not only the danger of disunity in the church but also an active encouragement to heresy. It was no coincidence, he argued, that heresies were spreading while the reform popes ruled at Rome, and he was right. Much as the popes deplored heresy their willingness to depart suddenly from tradition encouraged others to depart far more radically. The modern writer most sensitive to the tension between authority and tradition, Karl Morrison, has noted the tendency to totalitarianism inherent in such a doctrine of authority. A papal monarch absolute under God over Christian society needs in that great responsibility to enjoy freedom from error in judgment and from ill will. Such is not human nature, and a person with such authority could because of his reliance upon divine sanctions become cruel and ruthless.

The papal monarchs of the Middle Ages, with their great potential for evil, were never nearly so totalitarian or ruthless as other rulers, from Ashurnasirpal to Stalin. The popes were sincere in modeling their view of the Kingdom on that of Christ, and their actions were checked by the power exercised by other prelates and princes who did not recognize papal plenitude of power. In addition the reform popes always remained and probably always intended to remain—whatever pronouncements about papal authority they might issue—subject to tradition. Even the most imperious medieval popes—Innocent III; Innocent IV, and Boniface VIII—were inspired and limited by tradition.

Nevertheless, certain sinister implications of the Gregorian reform program transcended tradition. Gregory's willingness to enter political and military alliances with the German princes and the Normans was a natural consequence of his claim to power. One cannot claim universal dominion without being at least occasionally called upon to use force to maintain it. Force had been used before, in Charlemagne's bloody conversion of the Saxons, for example, but in the eleventh century it became almost a formal instrument of ecclesiastical policy. Gregory proclaimed the *Reconquista* against the Muslims in Spain a just war and called upon Christian knights to participate. On numerous occasions he implored Christian princes to take up arms in order to protect Constantinople from the Muslims, a call that was finally heeded under Pope Urban II when the first crusade was launched in 1095. Once the sword had been drawn against the infidel abroad, it could not fail to smite him at home. Papal policies were indirectly responsible for pogroms against the Jews, occurring from the 1090s onward. The first execution for heresy in the West occurred in 1022, long before Gregory's time, but under Gregory's successors prosecution and execution for heresy became institutionalized. Papally sponsored wars against heretics were followed in the middle of the thirteenth century by the establishment of the papal inquisition. The growth of an enormous bureaucracy around the papacy created a powerful establishment that required and justified its own defense.

Such abuses were not evident in the time of Pope Gregory VII, but they were latent in his policies, a fact that did not escape some of his contemporaries. Saint Peter Damian, one of the great prophetic voices of the mid-eleventh century, stated the monastic view of the struggle for control of Christian society. It did not matter to him whether pope or emperor was supreme ruler. Both the ecclesiastical and the secular hierarchies were orders of this world. The only true order and hierarchy was that arising from retirement from this world and devotion to the Kingdom, which is of the other world. There was perhaps too much secularization of charisma in Gregory's polity. In his *Agony of Christianity*, Miguel de Unamuno expressed concern that this might be true in our own day: " 'Christianity' has come to serve as designation for the Christian quality of a supposed body of Christians, a Christian society. But this is obviously an absurdity, since society kills Christianity, which is always an affair of solitary individuals."

Saint Bernard

The twelfth century, perhaps the most exciting time in the Middle Ages, witnessed three movements of great importance. The first was the sometimes swift, sometimes temporarily checked, rise of papal power and ecclesiastical organization along the lines sketched by Gregory VII. The second was the greening of Europe in an intellectual and artistic spring known as the Renaissance of the Twelfth Century. The third was an almost equally astonishing efflorescence of spiritual activity and fervor, both clerical and lay, that Giles Constable has termed the Reformation of the Twelfth Century.

The most striking manifestation of this Reformation was the rise of new monastic orders, breaking for the first time in almost three centuries the virtual monopoly of the Benedictine Order in the Western Church. The change had already begun in the eleventh century, when men like Saint Romuald and Saint Peter Damian sought a return to the earlier, more severe forms of monastic life. At the end of that century and at the beginning of the twelfth there was a virtual spate of reform movements—the Carthusians, dedicated to a total, almost eremitical retreat from the world; the orders of regular canons such as the Premonstratensians, Augustinians, and Victorines; the military orders such as the Templars and Hospitalers; and, most important of all, the Cistercians, upon whose rule those of the Premonstratensians and Templars were based. None of these represented a radical break from the Rule of Saint

Benedict, which was their inspiration, but they were a response to changed social conditions. As society became more settled, the need for monasteries as islands of peace and culture declined. Intellectual activity moved into the cities and centered on the episcopal schools, some of which developed into universities during the thirteenth century. Power, wealth, and even the leadership of reform in the church had under the influence of the reform papacy passed from the monasteries to the secular clergy. Yet the monks saw that as its power and organization increased the papacy was becoming more worldly. As they were required less and less frequently to act as scribes, schoolmasters, and dispensers of hospitality and remedies, the monks were able to revive their zeal for the other world and their prophetic function of calling the institutions of society, lay and clerical alike, to the bar of divine judgment. In carrying out this activity no order was more influential than the Cistercian.

A Benedictine monk, Robert, moved by the desire to return to strict obedience to the Benedictine Rule, left the monastery of which he was the abbot and with a group of hermits in 1075 went to found a new abbey at Molesme in Burgundy. The brothers of Molesme grew lax, and Robert left in disgust at least twice, each time being persuaded to return. On his second departure he took a few brothers faithful to his ideals with him and founded a new monastery at Cîteaux in 1098. After serving briefly as abbot, he returned to Molesme, leaving Cîteaux under the leadership of one of his followers, Alberic, who obtained a charter of liberty from the pope and thus gave Cîteaux full opportunity to develop its program of reform. He was succeeded in 1108 by Stephen Harding, an Englishman whose piety and organizational skills equaled or surpassed those of his predecessors. Alberic had drawn up a strict rule for the government of Cîteaux.

The Cistercian Rule was similar in most respects to the Benedictine, but it was stricter. It moved radically away from the intellectual emphasis that had become the hallmark of Benedictine houses and ordained less time for study. There was less time too for the liturgy, which had become increasingly ornate among the Cluniacs. The Cistercians returned to an emphasis upon personal manual labor, rejecting the serfs that the Benedictines had employed to do the heavy work, though they made extensive use of *conversi*, men who voluntarily attached themselves to the monastery as laborers without becoming brothers in the full sense. The Cistercians rejected all grants of any feudal honors, manors, or any land or possessions not needed to sustain life for the essential task of contemplation. Their churches contained no rich ornaments; their clothes were simple; and their ordinary diet consisted of black bread, water, and stewed vegetables. Devoted to chastising the flesh in order to nurture the spirit, the order enjoyed phenomenally rapid growth and influence through its first century and a half, testimony to the popular religious fervor of the twelfth-century reformation. Under Stephen Harding, a new monastic rule, the

Charter of Love, combining the strict discipline of Cîteaux with a plan of organization (much more decentralized than that of Cluny) for Cîteaux's daughter houses, was established.

The most important Cistercian leader, indeed probably the most influential European of his generation, was Saint Bernard (1090?–1153). Born in Burgundy of a family of the petty nobility, Bernard early learned the social assurance that allowed him later to consort with the rulers of Europe. It is not easy to categorize a man of such diverse activities. Like all great figures, he abounds in contradictions: A man of unyielding determination, he was filled with burning love and could move congregations to a degree unequaled by any other preacher of his time. A man of action whose activities carried him on numerous journeys through France, Germany, and Italy, he was a mystic for whom the most important activity was prayer. Few men have synthesized Martha and Mary, action and contemplation, as successfully as Saint Bernard. If one were looking for the trait common to all his activities, it would be prophetic zeal, an uncompromising devotion to the service of Christ and an equally unhesitating conviction that the voice of God spoke in his own breast.

In 1112, during a period of hard weather and disease that almost forced the abandonment of Cîteaux, Saint Bernard, attracted by reports of the abbey's severity, arrived with about thirty followers. The story, possibly apocryphal but nonetheless revealing of his character, is that four of these thirty were his brothers, whom he had persuaded to follow him over the protests of their parents and wives. It was said that the fifth brother, left alone to inherit all that his brothers had left, exclaimed, "What, this land for me, and the Kingdom of Heaven for you: It is not a fair trade." Finding even Cîteaux not stern enough for his taste, Bernard obtained Stephen Harding's permission to set out in 1115 with a few companions for the Valley of Wormwood, where they founded a daughter house called Clairvaux in which they lived in semi-eremitical asceticism. In the years before his death in 1153, Bernard helped the Cistercians grow into one of the most popular and influential orders in Europe.

Bernard's most striking exploits were in politics, but he was always at heart the monk and mystic of Clairvaux. Influenced by the Greek mystical tradition of Pseudo-Dionysius but even more by the work of Saint Augustine, Bernard argued that reason could lead one only so far toward God; one eventually had to abandon oneself to love of God. On the mystical way to God, one begins with humility, which is knowledge of self, proceeds to charity (love), which is knowledge of others, and ends with contemplation, which is knowledge of God. It is impossible to understand Saint Bernard's strenuous activities without grasping that he believed that contemplation of God is the proper activity of all Christians and that the purpose of a Christian society is to prepare men for that contemplation. His treatise *The Steps of Humility* was designed to help monks prepare themselves for a mystical life through the purgation of pride and attachment to things of this world. It describes the twelve steps (frivolity, boastfulness, arrogance, etc.) by which one might descend to the root sin of pride. With characteristic humility, this fierce but never egotistical zealot wrote, "I am more experienced in climbing down than I am in ascending."

To come to God one must leave the world behind. All pleasures must be abandoned for the joy and love that are the fulfillment of man's real nature and that, as C. S. Lewis said in *Surprised by Joy,* is "more desirable than any other satisfaction. I call it Joy, which is here a technical term and must be sharply distinguished both from Happiness and from Pleasure." Joy, perhaps, is the freedom and exaltation and longing and peace that come when one is grasped by God. Bernard was confident that men could be prepared for that joy by ascetic discipline.

Consequently all frivolity had to be banished from the monastery. Saint Bernard was even known to administer the discipline to a brother who had laughed or smiled, and he himself did humiliating penance when once he missed his evening prayers. His letters are full of severe criticism of people of all stations, from popes to prostitutes, enjoining them to abandon immorality; his treatise *De Conversione* was aimed particularly at the moral regeneration of the clergy. Bernard despised not only sin but all that turned men's minds away from God toward worldly vanities. Avarice was to his mind a vice almost as dangerous as pride. Bernard reflected and encouraged a change of values taking place in the twelfth century. Europe rapidly grew prosperous, finally recovering from the long era of relative stagnation. Lester Little has shown that as wealth began to abound moralists began to suggest that the sin of avarice was more dangerous than pride, which theretofore had been considered the root of all evil. The reform movements of the twelfth and thirteenth centuries, both orthodox and heretical, stressed poverty as the chief of the virtues that a Christian should embrace. Thus Bernard had supreme contempt for Cluny and for the other monastic houses that gloried in the rich beauty of their ornaments and furnishings and liturgy. That the poor should starve while churches were bedecked like courtesans was outrageous. For the love of Christ, wealth should be shared so that all would have enough to be clothed and fed; for the love of Christ, no man or church should have more. In this dour asceticism Bernard was not unlike a modern radical save that his emphasis was different: He feared the destruction of souls by riches more than the destruction of bodies by poverty.

For intellectual ornamentation he had hardly less contempt. Though his own work—the *Sermons on the Canticle* are only one example—showed great intellectual power and complexity, Bernard spoke as a prophet against the philosophers. "The learning of this world teaches us only vanity," he remarked.

"The apostles do not teach us to read Plato or follow his complicated thought; they teach us to live. Do you think this unimportant? To know how to live is the greatest of things." What Bernard feared was the tendency of rationalists like Peter Abelard to claim for the new scholastic dialectic a special, almost exclusive road to truth (like that natural science would claim for its own methodologies in the nineteenth century), arguing that that which is not susceptible to rational discovery is not real. Bernard had reason to fear this idea, for it was implicit in the ideas of Peter Abelard (1079–1142) and later explicit in some fourteenth-century philosophies.

Like Pope Gregory VII, Bernard was no respecter of persons. His belief that he spoke as a prophet enjoined upon him the responsibility and duty of correcting faults and chastising all the children of God. To Abbot Suger of St. Denis, the most powerful minister of the king of France, he wrote: "Two unheard-of and detestable improprieties have arisen in the Church lately. If you will pardon my saying so, one of these is the arrogance of your way of life." Later in the same letter he lamented that another minister "should against the Gospel serve God as deacon and Mammon as minister of state." The same zeal led him to accept the call by Pope Eugenius III and King Louis VII of France to proclaim the second crusade at Vézelay in 1146 and to intervene again and again in the politics of popes and kings.

As early as 1119, Bernard attacked the Gregorian papacy for having betrayed its ideals. It had amassed wealth, political power, and a vast bureaucracy, all of which impeded its mission to bear witness to the Kingdom. In 1130, on the death of Pope Honorius II, a minority of the cardinals, young men influenced by Bernard's ideas of reform, elected Innocent II pope. The Gregorian establishment, the older cardinals, greater both in number and in age, elected Anacletus II. There followed a schism, during which Bernard devoted his energies and persuasive powers to bringing the rulers of Europe to Innocent's side, an effort in which he was finally successful. Once secure on his throne, Innocent himself had to be taught not to stray from the way of truth. In 1139, disappointed by the pope's imperfections, Bernard wrote him, "Who will do justice to you for me? The tribunal of Christ stands there." The pope is answerable to Christ and to the prophet who speaks with the voice of Christ.

The extraordinary basis, unprecedented in ecclesiastical history, on which Bernard sought the confirmation of a pope, the canonicity of whose election was to say the least open to question, was Innocent's moral superiority. In 1145 Bernard wrote in his treatise *De Consideratione,* addressed to Pope Eugenius III: "The pope ought to be a model of piety, the champion of truth, the defender of the faith, the teacher of nations, the terror of the wicked, the glory of the good, the hammer of tyrants, the light of the world, the anointed of the lord."

Bernard's policies toward the pope had two striking implications. The first is the notion that the pontiff should be chosen not for his administrative or political skills, his intellectual abilities, or even his qualities as a peacemaker, but solely on the basis of his holiness. The argument is curiously ambivalent. On the one hand it is reminiscent of the old monastic position of Saint Peter Damian, who refused to judge between the papal and imperial hierarchies because he believed that the proper concern of Christians is not secular power. Saint Bernard not only agreed but took the amazing position that the primary concern of the rulers of this world is not with this world. In other words, Bernard imposed monastic otherworldliness upon the Christian society of the Gregorians. The kernel of both systems is the same: The function of Christian society is to save souls. But the fruit has a different taste altogether. According to Bernard, the primary concern of rulers is not to build a society whose structure reflects the will of God so that when the door of the Kingdom opens mankind will be in good order to receive him; rather the duty of rulers is to recognize that the Kingdom is at hand and that it requires not the building of a satisfactory society on earth but the immediate thrusting of the Christian people through the door into the other world. Many contemporary heretics shared these views of the great champion of orthodoxy.

The second implication is that the supreme judge of society is not the pope but the prophet, the man who has the spirit of God. The prophet goes forth to the people not in robes of state but in rags as did John the Baptist or naked as did Isaiah. The voice of the seer is the voice of God.

What is there to say of this monk who started a crusade, crowned a pope, and chastised kings? Of his zeal for the Kingdom there can be no doubt. But dangers were inherent in his position. The principle that the man with prophetic charisma has a right to rule may produce a Hitler as well as a Gandhi. The man who is responsible only to God (or to some other superhuman principle) is bound neither by tradition nor by law. Both tradition and law limited the dangers of authoritarianism in the Gregorian program. The prospects for the tyranny of antinomianism in Bernard's position are limitless. Who is to judge when the prophet speaks with the tongue of Christ and when he speaks with that of madness? And how, when the prophet dies, are we to choose his successor?

Dangers of other sorts lurked in Bernard's zeal. He preached sternly against anyone's daring to harm the Jews, but his feelings toward Muslims and heretics were less benevolent. If the crusades, with their effort to win Christ's battles by the sword, are less than perfect expressions of Christian love, Saint Bernard's responsibility for the second crusade is culpable. The source of his attacks upon the Reformist and Catharist heretics of France was moral rather than spiritual outrage, but they bespoke his refusal to recognize that the spirit of prophecy might take forms other than that manifested in himself. Bernard's unrelenting persecution of the philosophers Abelard and Gilbert de la Porrée are the best known examples of the lack of charity and anti-intellectualism that were among the least attractive products of his holy zeal.

Indeed, even Bernard's mysticism was curiously limited. He was unresponsive—it seems almost completely so—to beauty in either nature or art. The story is told of his day-long journey on the shores of the Lake of Geneva, at the end of which he could not remember having seen the lake at all. Augustinian mysticism requires one to look into the world of nature to find God, but to Bernard nature was a "book" in which one sought allegories of the divine dispensation. In this frame of mind one categorizes nature, dissecting it and using it. To take a rose and make it a symbol of the Virgin and to pluck a rose, slice it, and put it on a slide under a microscope are not dissimilar actions, and they are both to be contrasted with the religious experience of letting oneself be grasped by the rose. For Bernard, nature's only other value was in its possibilities for mortification. He withdrew into the wilderness to mortify his flesh, not to lift up his spirit. His contempt for art is clear in his condemnation of the Cluniac way of life and in his single-minded defense of poverty. He considered the arches, windows, statues, and reliquaries of Cluny manifestations of avarice and luxury. That they could be other than that or more than that did not seem to have occurred to him. It would be absurd to criticize Saint Bernard for lacking the aesthetic sensibilities of an eighteenth-century Romantic, for too much insensitivity to art and nature was built into the Judaeo-Christian theological tradition. Yet other men of his day were sensitive to beauty. One has only to read the hymns of the twelfth century and look at its cathedrals to realize that a man of Bernard's brilliance could have opened his mind to this experience. But to "sum up" Saint Bernard would be to presume. A lesser mind does not dispose of a greater one by forcing it into categories. If his zeal was not without its limitations, if it was too single-minded, it was nonetheless directed toward opening the door of the Kingdom with all the vast powers of intellect and energy that the man possessed.

Valdes

The prophetic spirit of the twelfth century touched the laity as well as the clergy. Peasants and even children went on crusade, and the efforts of the monastic orders and regular canons to recruit lay brothers were enormously successful. The enthusiasm for reform could not all be retained within the bounds of the church. It demanded all, brooked no limitations, and impatiently cast aside the restrictions of the principles of order when they stood in its way. From the twelfth century onward through the Middle Ages, the zeal of the laity tended to express itself most often in love of poverty.

It is no accident that most of the leaders of both orthodox and heretical prophetic movements were men of wealth. The evangelical statement of Christ that "You cannot serve both God and Mammon" was taken less as a moral injunction than as a statement of fact. The search for security in wealth was considered the meanest and most corrupting of sins. If a man commits murder, rape, or larceny, he will probably not be pleased with himself, and there is hope of revival as long as there is hope of repentance. But if he devotes his life to the acquisition of money and is successful, he is likely to be very pleased with himself indeed. Then, because there is little hope of repentance, there is little hope of salvation. In an age as devoted as our own to the notion that material improvement is desirable, the medieval belief in the virtue of poverty is scarcely comprehensible. But it permeated all society. When during the Peasants' Revolt of 1381, for example, the rebels sacked the houses of the wealthy, they did not loot, they destroyed, what they found. They believed that no one should enjoy an inordinate amount of wealth; all men should have equal access to the goods of this world to provide themselves with the necessities of life. The possession of wealth was regarded as a violation of justice, the implication being that one gained it only by depriving others. The wealthy appeared to be trapped in sin not only because their wealth causes them to look down upon the poor but also because constant care and concern for worldly success grows like scar tissue over their eyes, blotting out the light of life.

One of the most important, and certainly the longest lived, of medieval heresies was founded by a rich merchant of Lyon. The unsubstantiated story of the conversion of this merchant, Valdes (often erroneously called Peter Waldo), is that around 1173 he heard a sermon relating an old story about a rich saint who had abandoned all for God. The story struck him vividly with the vanity of his worldly life. Immediately he determined to distribute his goods to the poor and to wander barefoot around town and countryside preaching the gospel. Not learned in Latin, Valdes prevailed upon a couple sympathetic clerics to translate the New Testament and the writings of some of the Fathers into the vernacular so that he might increase his eloquence as a preacher by committing them to memory. Increased literacy in the vernacular, particularly among townsmen engaged in manufacture and trade, had prepared a large audience for such translations and for the dissatisfaction with the church that proceeded from the realization that the clergy did not often live as the apostles had done.

Valdes' behavior was condemned by the clergy for two reasons. First, translating the Scriptures was forbidden because the people, unequipped with understanding of theology and canon law, might fall into heresy. Second, preaching without a license from the bishop was also forbidden. These prohibitions sprang from the earnest efforts of the reform papacy to end the ignorant, erratic, and sometimes grossly deceitful practices that had characterized all too many clergy and preachers early in the Middle Ages. The reasons for routinizing charisma in this way were therefore both sensible and spiritual, but they failed to take into account the possibility of a true prophetic spirit's arising outside the regularly ordained clergy. Such a spirit simply could not tolerate such restraints.

Valdes continued to preach without a license and attracted a large number of disciples. No idea of separating himself from the church entered his mind at this time, if indeed it ever did. He appealed to Pope Alexander III for permission to preach and was summoned to Rome to address his request in 1179 to the Third Lateran Council. Many of the prelates there assembled, led by the brilliant but acerbic and arrogant Walter Map, made fun of Valdes' theological simplicity and lack of Latin. Although the pope sympathetically approved Valdes' decision to embrace a life of poverty for the love of Christ, he refused to intervene between Valdes and the authority of the archbishop of Lyon. The pope, aware of the extremes to which some popular lay preachers had gone and faced with a choice between allowing a prophetic enthusiast to preach and upholding the principles of ecclesiastical order, chose the latter course.

Valdes continued to refuse to yield to a prohibition he believed contrary to the will of God. The voice of God within him, he began to feel, was greater than the authority of any prelate, whether bishop or pope. At a synod held at Lyon in 1180 by the legate Cardinal Henry of Albano, Valdes voluntarily appeared and set his name to a confession of faith that was impeccably orthodox. This again obtained for him the approbation of the papacy, in the person of the cardinal, who praised his life of abstinence. It is not known whether the cardinal gave Valdes license to preach, but in any event the prophet continued to do so and authorized his followers, even women, to do the same. Whatever the cardinal's decision on Valdes himself, he never would have approved preaching by women. Therefore, at about this time Valdes was moved to take a more independent stand against ecclesiastical order. The forces of order replied. In 1182, Jean Belles-Mains, archbishop of Lyon, expelled Valdes and his followers from his diocese. They spread throughout southern France and northern Italy, winning numerous converts and provoking appeals to the curia from outraged prelates. The effect was that in 1184 Pope Lucius III and the Council of Verona declared that the "Poor Men of Lyon," as they called them, were heretical.

The irony that has often been noted is that a generation later, another rich merchant whose conversion led him to a wandering, barefoot life of poverty, was received by another pope with open arms and swiftly canonized after his death. This was Francis of Assisi. Even then the forces of order were unable to cope with the demands of the prophetic spirit, for both the papacy and the

Franciscan Order itself soon rejected Francis' doctrine of apostolic poverty. The forces of prophecy—represented by the Franciscan Order—were co-opted by the forces of order and conservatism. In the years following the condemnation of the Valdesians (Waldensians), many reconverted; some joined the more extreme heretical sect of the Catharists; others merged with other Reformist sects like that of the Humiliati; others retained their beliefs, which have continued to find followers to the present day.

The orthodox Alan of Lille, writing at the end of the twelfth century about the Valdesians, argued that Valdes was "led by his emotions, not sent by God." Yet in some respects Valdesian principles resemble not only those of Saint Francis but even those of Saint Bernard. It is difficult to define these doctrines because the Valdesians often merged with other heretics or were accused of adopting their ideas and because their principles became more radical as Valdes' alienation from the ecclesiastical establishment increased. Most of their ideas could have been accommodated within the framework of orthodoxy —the abandonment of personal wealth; a life devoted to wandering and preaching, supported by begging; the prohibition of oaths; and the insistence that nothing could justify the taking of human life. Some of their doctrines, probably formulated after the disappointing experiences of 1179–1184, went much farther: Man is justified not by external authority, office, or order, but solely by the voice of God speaking within. The just are the successors of the apostles and have no need of bishops or priests; thus there is no reason to have churches. Every man who is justified by the spirit within has the right to preach, to absolve from sin, and to consecrate the Eucharist. The vanity and worldliness of most of the clergy demonstrates the falsity of their claim to apostolic justification. An unworthy priest could not consecrate the Eucharist; a just priest had that power, but no more than did any just man. Not order, not office, not external authority and appointment, but merit alone gave a man priestly powers over the Eucharist and license to preach.

This argument and that of Saint Bernard regarding the papacy have some features in common. Bernard and Valdes both insisted not only on internal justification by illumination but on an ordering of the church and society as a whole by authority conferred by prophetic charisma. The widely enthusiastic response to both Bernard and Valdes (different though they were in many respects) indicates that a Christian people roused by the spiritual enthusiasm of the century felt that the well-ordered *societas christiana* of Pope Gregory VII was not enough. It is to the great spiritual and political credit of Pope Innocent III that a generation later he was able to accommodate some of the potentiality of similar movements of enthusiasm—the Franciscans and the Dominicans—within the ecclesiastical order. The short-sightedness of the earlier generation lost the church a saint in Valdes.

The career of Valdes poignantly exposed the dilemma of the church. Was it possible to found order upon the rejection of order, the antinomianism implicit in the Valdesian position? If every man who felt the spirit moving within him and declared himself a prophet was accorded the sanction, or even the toleration, of the church, how was the church to protect itself from extremists? In the twelfth century the "prophet" Tanchelm distributed his bathwater as a holy relic; the "prophet" Eudo of Brittany brandished a forked stick at a synod to prove that he was the Christ returned to earth. In those days, says the Book of Judges, referring to the period of instability preceding the establishment of the kingdom of Israel, every man did that which seemed right in his own eyes, and disorder and immorality reigned over the land. How, without order, could people be protected from the immorality urged by the unscrupulous? The organization of the church was necessary. Yet that very organization, that very order, the inertia conferred by timidity and tradition, permitted dullness of sensitivity that could fail to discern the knock of prophecy on the door.

King Louis IX

The thirteenth century was calmer than the twelfth. The papacy continued to advance its monarchical claims over Christian society and to increase the size and complexity of the vast structure that upheld the Christian order. Prophets were either incorporated into the church, as were friars, or stilled, by force if necessary, as were Catharists. Europe, growing more populous and wealthy, had the upper hand over Islam. Great cathedrals and great theologies rose, intricate and shining. The forces that were to disturb this order, such as the national state, were forming but not yet a serious threat. It was possible in the thirteenth century for a great king to be a great defender of ecclesiastical order.

Louis IX of France (1226–1270), canonized by the church, was such a ruler. Testimonies to his personal holiness are manifold and convincing. He built religious houses, schools, hospitals, and gave generously from his own purse. In 1246–1248 he was responsible for building that confection of light and color known as the Sainte-Chapelle. He personally visited and tended the sick, even those with the most loathsome diseases. On one occasion he asked his friend Jean de Joinville (later his biographer) whether he would prefer to have leprosy or to have committed a mortal sin. Joinville replied with understandable honesty that he would rather have committed thirty mortal sins than to suffer from leprosy. The king was shocked, as befitted a man who on another occasion vowed that he would gladly have himself branded with a red-hot iron if his subjects would give up the use of profane language. Branding he never had to endure, but he did have himself scourged with small chains to mortify his flesh. Devoted in prayer, he taught his children every night at bedtime, and sometimes he arranged sermons for his court.

Like the zeal of Bernard, the piety of Saint Louis was not that of a milque-toast. He not only led his troops in two crusades but plunged unhesitatingly into the midst of battle when the safety of a comrade was threatened. Nervous, driving, and imperious, he was totally devoted to the service of Christ and intolerant of all who did not share his enthusiasm. For the lukewarm, he had stern reprimands; for those who refused to accept the order of the Catholic Church, he did not shrink from the sentence of death. One has on the whole an impression of the simple, almost single-willed determination of a man who is incapable of, and intolerant of, subtleties. There could be no hesitation about accepting Christ and his cross. Saint Louis died of a wasting disease while on crusade near Tunis in 1270. Near the end he was heard to cry out, "Jerusalem, Jerusalem!"

Louis was only twelve when he succeeded to the throne in 1226. For the first eight years of his reign the country was ruled by his almost equally pious and certainly equally determined mother, Queen Blanche of Castile. Even after Louis attained majority, Blanche had immense influence and was responsible for many of the firm and judicious policies of the reign. She told the young king that a ruler who tolerates sin among his subjects is himself guilty of the sin, a precept that Louis always observed, though he had little success in passing it on to his descendants.

Louis was the grandson of Philip II Augustus (1180–1223) and the grandfather of Philip IV the Fair, (1285–1314), the two kings who did most to expand royal territories and administration, making France the most important power in Europe for virtually five centuries. Louis' policies were in many respects similar to those of the two Philips. He was neither a utopian nor a prophet. He curbed the power of the nobles, forbidding the construction of private castles. He encouraged the prosperity of the towns by establishing general peace throughout the realm, and he secured the royal appointment of mayors, thus making of the burghers a reliable source of revenue and political support. He increased royal power markedly by issuing *ordonnances* without troubling to obtain the consent of his barons. He sent out royally appointed *enquêteurs,* usually friars, to ensure that the *baillis* and *sénéchaux,* the local officials upon whom royal control of the provinces had rested since the time of Philip II, were doing their duty and defrauding neither king nor people. Only in territorial acquisition did Louis lag behind the rest of his family. Though he obtained some lands and worked hard and well to pacify the areas of the Midi lately acquired by his father Louis VIII (1223–1226), he voluntarily relinquished other territories by treaty to the kings of England and Aragon. Some modern historians have pointed out that this was not wholly an ingenuous policy, for Louis did succeed in wresting from Henry III of England in return for Poitou that monarch's recognition that he held his French lands as a vassal of the Capetian king. Yet it is inconsistent with Louis' character to see in this action a subtle stroke of policy. Louis was not given to subtlety. Whether he lost more than he gained in these exchanges, his motivation was the procurement of peace and justice. To judge otherwise is to forget that Louis' belief in the superior reality of the Kingdom of God to that of the kingdom of France was absolute.

The reign of the secular monarch Louis IX was as much an exercise in the art of constructing a Christian society as that of the spiritual monarch Gregory VII. A fourteenth-century prayer in the mass of Saint Louis says that "He founded the throne on justice." Justice was the keystone of his policy as it had been of Gregory's. He believed that his consecration as king had granted him spiritual powers. In his mind there was no distinction between church and state, between secular and spiritual policy. God had conferred royal authority upon him so that he might secure the salvation of the souls of the people entrusted to his care. His position toward the papacy seems to have been one of practical parallelism. He recognized the necessity of a unified Christian order and accepted the position of the pope as head of that Christian society. But as king he had absolute power over his segment of Christian society. Louis was the spiritual leader of his bishops as much as he was the temporal suzerain of his barons.

Though Louis respected the papal dignity, he was unwilling to allow the pope to take any action infringing upon the rights of the French kingdom and the French Church. In 1247 the French bishops (following the example set by the English in 1245) issued a document entitled *Complaints of the French Church,* protesting undue papal taxation and papal provisions—that is, papal appointment of bishops. Louis agreed with them. As long as the pope upheld venerable tradition he would have the loyalty of France, but if he introduced "new and unheard of" exactions, they would be rebuffed. This willingness to challenge papal authority was in the background of the attack upon Pope Boniface VIII by Louis' grandson Philip the Fair.

Justice, strict and equal, was the uncompromising demand of the king. He attempted to repress feudal war and the right of vendetta, commiserating with the lot of the peasants whose persons and lands suffered in such wars and condemning all disorder in a kingdom whose watchword was to be harmony. Not only bishops and nobles but his own family could expect no more than strict justice from him. On one occasion when his brother had imprisoned a knight, the king heard the case, freed the knight, and rebuked his brother for violating the principle of justice. In the written instructions that he personally drew up for his son, Louis admonished him to defend the rights of others even, if need be, against his own, and in judgment always to prefer a poor man against a rich man unless and until the case be proved against the former. He enjoined upon his son the policy that he himself had always followed: Never make war against fellow Christians unless war is forced upon you by an intolerable violation of your own rights. Louis' reputation for impartial judgment was so great that rulers of other countries submitted their disputes to him. The English king and barons in 1264 sought his judgment of whether the Provisions of Oxford, which the nobles had forced Henry III to accept, were valid. In the Mise of Amiens Louis annulled the Provisions, whose limitations of royal power he judged an infringement upon the right of a monarch to care for his subjects' welfare as he saw fit. That there were kings less selfless than himself Louis did not seem to realize; the English barons were of another opinion and set aside the Mise.

Fierce devotion to justice and to Christian order was not, in either Gregory VII or Louis IX, a blessing unmarred by intolerance. Both men felt deeply their absolute responsibility before God for their subjects. If the Christian people were to be protected in their faith and prepared for salvation, what of those who resisted? Resistance could be interpreted not only as unwillingness to cooperate with the civil authority, as it would be today in most countries, but also as a rupture of God's justice. As Christ is head of the mystical body, so the pope under Christ is head of the church, and so the king under Christ is head of his kingdom on earth. Therefore, those who resist the authority of the king of France resist the authority of God. They are cut off from the mystical body of Christ and are as rotten fruit to be cut from the tree.

The attitude of the saintly king toward heretics and infidels was not mild. On two occasions he undertook crusades against the Muslims that were costly in treasure and life and in addition wholly unsuccessful. Reasoning correctly that crusades to Palestine were futile as long as the center of Muslim power lay in Egypt, Louis invaded that country in 1249. At the end of his life he undertook a second crusade against Egypt, but circumstances diverted it to Tunis, where the king died in 1270. The displacement of the crusades farther and farther from Jerusalem is not without pathos; but no displacement, defeat, or death could have shaken Louis' conviction that it was God's will that he war against the Saracen.

His attitude toward the Jews was no more friendly, though it was restrained by self-interest. Louis was shocked that so many "perfidious" Jews were allowed to live and prosper in the midst of a Christian society. On the recommendation of the pope and with the vigorous assistance of the friars, Louis had copies of the Talmud and other Jewish books seized and burned. He would have expelled the Jews from France altogether had he not been persuaded by his advisers that their skill as traders made them an indispensable financial asset. His grandson Philip the Fair would resolve the dilemma by seizing the property of the Jews and then expelling them. It is important to notice that in this instance what separated the behavior of the saint from that of the reprobate was a different economic judgment, not a Christian conscience.

Toward heretics Louis was less restrained. Most of the heretics were in the

Midi, where Catharism had flourished until the Albigensian crusade of Louis VIII and the northern barons. Large numbers of Catharists and other heretics still remained to be converted or killed. With the double purpose of pacifying a recently annexed territory and ridding the kingdom of those who, cut off from the body of Christ, had become limbs of Satan, Louis welcomed the papal inquisition into his kingdom. The activity of the inquisitors (friars for the most part) was not limited to the Midi—a testimony to the pre-eminence of Christian over political motives in Louis' mind—but ranged over the whole kingdom. The most notorious of the French inquisitors, Robert le Bougre, was active in Flanders and in the North. The king not only gave the inquisitors a virtually free hand in the prosecution of heretics; he aided them with money and military assistance. By the time Louis died in 1270 Catharism was no longer a serious problem in the kingdom of France.

The ferocity of Louis' attitudes toward dissenters was not wholly a product of the Christian spirit of order. In part it derived from feudal values, which the simple mind of Louis, like that of most of his noble contemporaries, was unable to separate from those of Christianity. One of the perennial problems of religion is that it not only influences society but to a large extent takes on the color of its social context. The Christianity of feudal noblemen was different from that of monks, burghers, and peasants. Courage and loyalty, the virtues uppermost in Louis' mind, are compatible with Christianity, but their taproot extends into the primitive loyalties of man to man that lay at the foundations of feudalism. In the ideal feudal relationship each man would be bound by strict loyalty to his lord above him and to his vassal beneath him: hence Louis' courage in war and willingness to risk his life in battle for his friends; hence his openness and honesty in diplomacy, his insistence upon strict justice for those placed beneath him. To violate these principles would be a blot upon his chivalry as well as upon his Christianity, and to Joinville and other contemporaries Louis was not only the model of the Christian king but of the *prud'homme,* the "verray, parfit gentil knyght," a Roland and a Charlemagne incarnate in one flesh. Christ was not only Saint Louis' God but also his feudal seigneur. This explains Louis' incomprehension of those who did not follow Christ as loyally as he. That Joinville should have preferred sin to leprosy seemed not only bad religion but a breach of feudal loyalty and chivalric courtesy. That heretics should deny the authority of king and pope, who were under Christ's suzerainty seigneurs of the Christian people, was an act of treason. As Ganélon the traitor is the most evil villain of the *Chanson de Roland,* so the heretics were the most evil villains of the kingdom of France. Any man who sought his own gain at the expense of his men was dishonored. A nobleman disloyal to his vassal was a disgrace to chivalry as well as to Christianity.

Like most simple worlds, that of Saint Louis is both attractive and frightening. It raises the question whether single-minded determination to force the door of the Kingdom by physical battle against those who seem to stand in the way is altogether satisfactory. A ruler's assumption that he is the anointed of God can be a sanction for evil: Convinced of the righteousness of his own position, he must be equally convinced of the evil of those who oppose him. Heretics, Jews, Muslims, and pagans stood outside the bounds of the society Louis felt himself bound to protect. (Some Christian writers, such as Saint Bernard, did insist that respect be shown the Jews, the people of the old covenant, and that they be converted only by peaceful persuasion.) He showed the most scrupulous care to the humblest of loyal Christians but had no compunction about killing those he considered cut off from the body of Christ. To suggest that Louis IX was totalitarian would be an absurdity: He was neither an Ashurnasirpal nor a Stalin, but a man limited in power and devoted to justice. Yet Louis shared with these tyrants something with which the world of the twentieth century is especially familiar—the classification of certain groups, whether nations, classes, races, or religions, as less than fully entitled to membership in the human community and the consequent willingness, even sense of duty, to exterminate them.

Saint Thomas Aquinas

From the time of Justin Martyr in the second century, Christianity had wed reason to revelation, Greek to Jewish modes of thought. Late in the fourth and early in the fifth centuries Saint Augustine, perhaps Christianity's most original thinker, created a powerful body of thought based on Platonic as well as Pauline patterns. Yet Augustine's unparalleled genius never attempted to create a formally organized philosophical or theological system. His mode of thought was allusive and peripatetic, wandering from one topic to another, here and there illuminating the landscape of the mind with brilliant insights. For seven centuries after Augustine, Western Christianity produced few original philosophers—the only exception in the early Middle Ages being John Scotus Eriugena. The intellectual life of Europe quickened during the eleventh and early twelfth centuries. Efforts were made to think consecutively, moving from one logical point to the next and gradually building up a systematic structure of knowledge. Saint Anselm (1033–1109) was one of the first to employ this approach. Another great figure famous for using it was Peter Abelard. By midcentury it was entrenched in the schools of western Europe and ever since has been known as the scholastic method.

This method at first permitted the schoolmen to organize previously existing thought into logical patterns, pursuing logical details through dialectical method until the original ideas were drained of their sap, leaving brittle and arid stalks. In the second half of the eleventh century, however, schoolmen began to turn their attention to the metaphysical works of Aristotle, which were being newly translated. It is difficult for us to imagine, now that Aristotle is taken for granted, the excitement and warmth generated in the schools by the infusion of these new ideas, a warmth that melted the icy rigidity into which logic had been frozen. Like the ideas of Darwin, Freud, and Einstein in modern times, Aristotle's ideas opened up new worlds of thought. The implications of Aristotelian metaphysics, especially when accompanied by Arabic Neoplatonic commentaries, were too radical for many of the schoolmen, whose rigid systems had no place for new ideas. For a century conservatives put up a running battle against them, insisting that it was impossible to reconcile Aristotle with what they understood to be truly Christian thought.

Those who did not reject the new ideas but rather attempted to incorporate them into existing forms of thought found themselves with the rare opportunity of creating a new synthesis. Alexander of Hales and Albertus Magnus, one a Franciscan and the other a Dominican, began not only to explore the intricacies of Aristotelian thought but to reconcile it with Christianity. Of the new synthetic thinkers the most original, brilliant, and productive was Saint Thomas Aquinas (1225–1274), called the "angelic doctor" because of the clarity of his vision. Thomas was born in Italy, a younger son of a noble family. Like many intellectuals, he had a life externally lacking in excitement, although at least one lurid story about his youth is recounted. His family wished him to pursue a career of power and influence in the church. In order to turn his attention away from the world of God, his brothers challenged his chastity by bringing a prostitute to his chamber. They hid to watch, but were chagrined when Thomas indignantly drove her out. It was clear that he would not be the kind of churchman interested in worldly vanities.

Sent as a child by his family to study at the great Benedictine abbey of Monte Cassino, Thomas went from there to the University of Naples, became a Dominican, studied at Paris and at Cologne, where he was a pupil of Albertus Magnus, and then returned to Paris as professor of theology. Learning both the old systems of thought and the new Aristotelian ideas, Thomas synthesized them into a system of philosophy and theology that manages to be both complex and lucid and has been compared for its intricacy, balance, and combination of lightness with bulk to the great Gothic cathedrals then being constructed.

Aquinas drew upon Augustine, Aristotle, Maimonides, Neoplatonism, and the early scholastics, but he went beyond them all. He not only "baptized" Aristotle but extended and developed Aristotelian thought along Christian lines, creating a new body of material, called by Dom David Knowles in *The Evolution of Medieval Thought* "a wholly new and original Christian philosophy." The author of treatises on numerous topics, Aquinas is most noted for his three great monuments of synthesis—the *Commentary on the Sentences* of Peter Lombard, the *Summa Contra Gentiles,* and the final and greatest work, the *Summa Theologiae* (1266–1273). The subtleties of Aquinas never fail to astound, but the ease with which one can follow his thought is even more amazing in view of its intricate complexity. The *Summa Theologiae* is so utterly lucid and logical that its perfection has in some ways put people off: One misses the sudden flashes of brilliance, the personal fervor, the human excitement, that touches the work of Saint Augustine, for example. Yet to suppose Thomas a dry pedant lacking warmth would be to misjudge the man badly. His clear and logical method prohibited the introduction of much personal fervor. But even in the *Summae,* and more often in some of his minor works, the feeling breaks through, especially in the poetry attributed to him. In any event, we know that a few months before his death he left Part Three of the *Summa Theologiae* unfinished because his mystical life had become so warm and immediate that he had no more patience with or confidence in his intellectual work. The experience of God in which he lived for those months before he died in the spring of 1274 was so complete that he said all he had written was as nothing "in comparison with the things I have seen and which have been revealed to me."

Though Aquinas used Augustine and other sources, his thought is best grasped opposite to that of Aristotle, *"The* Philosopher," as Thomas called him. Like Aristotle's epistemology, Thomas' is sensual—"Nothing is in the intellect unless it got there through the senses"—and he rejects Augustine's Platonic assumption of innate ideas. Though Aquinas mentions some "self-evident principles"—for example, that something cannot at once be and not be—most of his arguments, including even his proofs of the existence of God, are based upon sense data. Because the mind is not a passive receptacle, we must organize our sensual experience through reason. In this belief Aquinas has more in common with empiricism than with Augustine's inner illumination, and it allows him to make a clear distinction between "natural theology," which he sometimes terms "philosophy," and "revealed theology." The former deals with things that right reason acting upon empirical data can grasp. The latter has to do with things that we can know only through revelation. For example, God is Three Persons is a theological proposition to which, unlike the existence of God, we would never come by way of reason and experience.

But though Thomas revered Aristotle, he went beyond him. Frequently in the *Summa Theologiae* Aristotle's opinions are placed among those to be refuted. The differences between the two philosophers are many but can be reduced to two of fundamental importance. First, Aristotle's universe is wholly natural, with a deity that is merely a logical postulate; whereas Thomas' universe pulses with the living God. Second, Aquinas distinguishes between essence and existence, a distinction that some have deemed the hallmark of his thought and that enables the understanding to penetrate past the natural world into the world above nature. In the words of the great hymn attributed to Thomas, "Praestet fides supplementum sensuum defectui" ("Faith will go on where the senses leave off"). Christians had always argued that the walls barring them from the Kingdom could be scaled by faith; mystics identified this faith with love. Particularly at the end of his life Thomas would not have argued that philosophy was a better way to God than was mystical love. Yet philosophy can be a way among others, he argued, if the distinction between essence and existence is kept in mind.

The distinction is this: Each material thing possesses both existence and essence. Its existence is its own, and it possesses reality as an individual substance (Aquinas was not a Platonist). But its essence is both in itself and in God. Only in God is existence equivalent to essence. For example, an individual tree exists in this world in its own right. In addition it possesses an essence of "treeness," which it shares with other trees and whose origin is in the mind of God. In a sense the world is a projection of the mind of God. This argument allowed Thomas to formulate an analogical theology of essential analysis. Through analysis of the essences of things we will find in individual beings analogies to the mind of God. The beauty of a tree helps us get toward an understanding of God's beauty. The method has its limitations, Thomas admitted, for the boundaries of the human mind prevent it from ever grasping the infinite and the eternal, but we can at least see by analogy what we shall see face to face when illuminated by the glory of God. The scholastic method was perfect for carrying out essential analysis, which, though empirically based, differs from natural science in its concentration upon the internal essence of things rather than upon their physical characteristics.

A related, important point about Aquinas' epistemology is that he believed that things are more or less what they seem to be. Kant would object to this assumption, but had Thomas known of Kant's distinction between noumena and phenomena he would doubtless have rejected the notion that phenomena do not generally reflect noumena accurately. He considered the statements we make about external things and about their analogies to God valid.

It is difficult to select and isolate an example of Thomas' thought because his system is so closely knit and each section of the *Summa Theologiae* draws, like a geometrical proposition, upon preceding sections. Yet not to do so would leave us with vague generalizations. In the first part of the second part of the *Summa,* questions 18 through 21, Thomas considers the basic principles of morality. Here, as throughout the *Summa,* each question deals with a broad subject, Question 18, for example, being on "Good and Evil in Human Acts in General." Each question is divided into a number of articles posing subsidiary problems. Article 1 of Question 18 asks, "Are All Acts Good or Can Some Be Bad?" In each article Thomas follows the scholastic method, first citing objections against his position, then countering with an opposite statement, usually from an ancient authority, subsequently proceeding to a major statement of his own opinion based on all the evidence, and concluding with replies to each of the objections.

Hundreds of volumes of commentary and elucidation have been written on these four questions of the *Summa* alone, and what follows does not pretend to be more than a brief discussion of some of the principles used by Thomas in constructing his moral philosophy. Those accustomed to view Saint Thomas Aquinas as a legalistic representative of an authoritarian church are always surprised at how seldom he puts verbs in the imperative mood. Relativists for whom morality consists solely of personal preference are baffled by his method of eschewing hortatory declarations and constructing a philosophy of ethics upon facts and logic. Beginning with empirically observed facts about people, Thomas goes on to use reason to construct a *scientia* of human behavior. One does not need to be a Thomist to be impressed with the result: the construction of a rational, coherent statement of the principles of morality based not upon authority, not upon legalism, not upon tradition, and not upon personal whim, but upon human reason.

Indeed the emphasis upon reason places an enormous value upon the individual human being. We are slaves neither to the will of others nor to our own feelings, for any intelligent person can use his reason to understand the principles of morality. Among other things, this doctrine is a sophisticated defense of liberty, for if man does not have the rational power to understand the choice he makes in any given situation, he does not have true freedom.

Thomas' argument begins on the same ground as Aristotle's *Nicomachean Ethics:* The end-purpose of any being is happiness, which is defined as the complete fulfillment of its nature. Everything in the universe seeks its proper place through the workings of the laws of nature. Man, having intelligence and will as well as a physical body, differs from irrational creatures in possessing the ability to seek this end consciously. For Aristotle, the happiness of man consisted of *eudaimonia,* the rest and well-being one finds by fulfilling his nature in terms of the *polis.* Aquinas puts human happiness in a broader context: For him it is *beatitudo,* repose and fulfillment in the living God. God is the end-purpose in which alone we can achieve fulfillment of our human nature.

In the construction of his ethics, Thomas does not pause long with God. His purpose is not to describe some kind of sacred utopia or to urge us to saintly transports. God wills for us that which is possible, and though he is our supreme end and good, there are many subsidiary, wholly natural, and wholly proper ends, such as good health. Thomas' moral philosophy is not rooted in some world unrelated to human experience: On the contrary it grows in the deep and fertile soil of that experience. In that sense it is truly an existential more than an essential morality. Yet Thomas consistently avoids two extremes. On the one hand his ethics are not wholly situational, for there are abstract principles discoverable by reason; on the other hand he rejects the notion that moral ideas can exist in a world other than that of the experience of individual thought and action. His ethics are not wholly utilitarian, based solely upon natural appetites; neither are they, like Kant's, based upon the categorical imperative of an abstract good that one does for its own sake. Abstract though his analysis sometimes becomes, Aquinas always has in mind the individual making choices in real and particular matters.

As moral good is the fulfillment of man's nature, evil is lack of fulfillment. For Thomas as for most of the scholastics, evil is privation—the lack of perfection in a being. Privation can be purely ontological: A dog's lack of wings is not an evil, for it is no defect in its canine nature; if a dog lacks eyes, however, that is a privation and an evil. Moral evil consists of a privation of the proper order and harmony in human affairs, as when a man chooses to commit adultery with his neighbor's wife.

How does moral evil occur? If each agent seeks its own happiness and good, why does a man commit adultery? Evil is a defect in the principles of his action. It may come from a deliberate act of will to do what he knows is wrong; more frequently it arises from a defect in reason, which misleads the will. Thomas eschews voluntarism (emphasis upon the independence of the will) as firmly as he would have eschewed modern behaviorism. The basis of human behavior is reason and logic. Right reason will lead us to good; defects in reason will bring about a defective action.

Any defect renders an act evil.[1] In order to perform a good action, a man must will something (1) that is good in itself (*bonum ex genere*) (for example, giving food to a hungry person is always good; torturing someone is always bad); (2) with the right intention—that is, with the proper end and goal in mind; (3) with the right objective (means to the end); and (4) in the right circumstances. For example, a sculptor may carve statues (*bonum ex genere*) to get money to buy a house (objective) with the intention of sheltering his family, and he carves them with tools he has purchased fairly, and so on.

Thomas' emphasis upon the importance of circumstances absolves him from any suspicion of abstract rigorism, and his understanding of principles removes him from the camp of situation ethics. His morality occupies a middle ground, where both principles and situations are important. It also occupies a high

---

[1] Thomas' view is that we proceed from discernment of our intent by reason followed by an interior act of will, which produces an external deed.

ground, for a defect in any of the four categories renders an act imperfect and to that degree evil. There are relatively few perfectly good actions. But there are degrees of imperfection and evil: The imperfection in failing to walk back to the shop to return an extra dime received in change is quite different from the imperfection in sneaking into a neighbor's house to remove his furniture while he is on vacation.

Sometimes, indeed, we are faced with a choice of imperfections, or evils. In fact this is the basis of Thomas' argument regarding the presence of ontological evil in the universe. He admits that no one can fully explain the presence of pain or defects in nature that do not proceed from the ill will of creatures. As evil is not a thing in itself but only a privation, it is fair to say that God did not create this kind of evil. But it must be admitted that God permits it. In some way that we cannot grasp, the greater perfection of the universe requires the diverse and subsidiary imperfections that exist within it. God chooses the greater good in spite of its entailing lesser evil, just as we would choose to remove a cancerous eye from a child in order to accomplish the greater good of saving its life. Human beings face an even more difficult choice between evils, for unlike God we can be misled by reason.

This raises the question of conscience, where Aquinas again affirms both the validity of principles on the one hand and human freedom on the other. Conscience is defined as the dictate of reason in a moral matter. Conscience is not a special moral sense but a rational judgment followed by an act of will, these functions together constituting free will. In asking whether he should will X or Y, a man consults his reason, and its answer is his conscience. It is never right to act against conscience, for that would constitute an imperfection of intention. If, for example, a man believes he is obliged to take money from Mr. Jones in order to give it to Mr. Green, and he fails to act according to this obligation, he has failed to intend that which he believes to be good, and this is in itself a defect.

On the other hand, obedience to conscience does not exclude evil, since reason—conscience—may be misled. If a man's conscience tells him to kill someone and he follows it, he has avoided doing evil by violating his conscience but has done a very serious *malum ex genere,* a deed bad in itself no matter how noble the intention. In order to be fully good, an action must be free from imperfection in all categories.

Nor is a badly formed conscience, or the ignorance that causes it, usually to be excused. Ignorance of what is good is not to be excused, for example, if a man adopts that ignorance in order to do what he pleases. (The current word for this process is *rationalization.*) Neither is a defect of reason excused if it results from a bad habit that a man has allowed himself to get into. If he steals while his reason is distorted by the influence of drugs or because of need for drugs to which he has become addicted, he is culpable for having created that habit. These are examples of voluntary, willed ignorance. Some ignorance, like of a child or an idiot or of an intelligent man whose judgment had been distorted by illness, fear, or something else beyond his control, is not culpable. The individual who signs a false statement under fear of torture, for example, may not be morally culpable; however, the intrinsic evil of the deed, the *malum ex genere,* remains. Evil is thus not the same as guilt, but most of us are responsible most of the time for a badly formed conscience.

The ideas of Thomas, after overcoming initial resistance, eventually became for centuries almost the only accepted Catholic system of theology. At the Council of Trent in the sixteenth century his *Summa Theologiae* lay open with the Bible for the reference of the assembled fathers; in the seventeenth century most Catholic theological activity was bent on categorizing and commenting on him. In spite of a few really creative Thomists like Suarez, Thomism (the term was first used about 1340) finally became as arid and logic-bound as the scholastic systems before Aquinas. The thought of all great men becomes rigid in the hearts of their less great followers. One cannot understand Aquinas without realizing that these ideas were in his time tremendously original, exciting, and based upon a profound understanding of man and openness to God. Aquinas was not an arrogant intellectualist who assumed that he could lay hold of the universe and cut it into categories to fit his own mind; he was a sensitive, humane, and mystically attentive man. To understand Aquinas one must read the *Summae* less as an ageless system to be defended or attacked than as the living work of an intellectually excited and creative man.

Even those sympathetic to Aquinas tend to apologize for the abstraction of his moral thought. His almost mathematical reasoning seems to respond insufficiently to the human thirst for answers to questions of guilt, freedom, death, fear, and love. Such criticism could be made of many modern systems of thought, and Aquinas was aware that the most powerful communication among men (or between man and God) occurs when "heart speaks to heart." Finally, it may be argued that in the long run eloquence is less effective in speaking to the eternal problems of human existence than Thomas' dispassionate investigation of moral principles without rhetoric, special pleading, or antinomian defeatism. If to long for the truth is also in some way to long for the Kingdom, then Thomas pierced the door with his peerless lucidity.

Julian of Norwich

The fourteenth and fifteenth centuries were a period of far-reaching social changes. From the tenth century onward the population of Europe had been rapidly increasing. Large areas of the countryside were brought under cultivation, and towns grew in size and number. From the beginning of the fourteenth century a series of disastrous famines and plagues, of which the Black Death is the most famous, reduced the population. At the same time, increased commercial activity encouraged the growth of industry and drew people from the countryside to work in the towns. As a result, from the middle of the fourteenth century the rural population declined considerably while some cities continued to grow. These economic changes produced a multitude of social consequences. The urban bourgeoisie grew in number and power; the feudal and manorial arrangements of earlier medieval Europe fell increasingly into desuetude. Political, ecclesiastical, and intellectual ideas also underwent striking transformation. The Great Schism of the late fourteenth and early fifteenth centuries, together with the growth of conciliarism and nationalism, gravely weakened the power of the papacy and undermined the ideal of Christian unity. In the intellectual world, from the beginning of the fourteenth century the era of scholastic synthesis began yielding before a wave of skepticism about the powers of reason to perceive truth.

Most of these changes were only dimly understood at the time, but their results produced a strange and widespread sense of uneasiness. A series of violent peasants' revolts struck England, France, and other areas of western Europe. Movements of prophetic reform swept the laity, who demanded a more spiritual clergy. Some of these movements moved beyond the limits of orthodoxy, such as the Lollards and the Hussites, who relied for their authority not upon the visible church but upon what they felt was the dwelling of the Spirit within. Other popular religious manifestations were even more bizarre —the movement of the flagellants, the dance mania, witchcraft, and demonolatry. These were phenomena that appeared repeatedly in various areas of Europe and in every social group from nobility to peasantry.

One of the most widespread and impressive phenomena of the time was mysticism. It is not proper to speak of mysticism as a movement, because its manifestations were varied and relatively independent of one another. From the late thirteenth century the Rhineland and the Low Countries produced a number of mystics, among them Meister Eckhart (1260–1327), Ruysbroeck (1293–1381), and Thomas à Kempis (1379–1471). Though the majority of the famous mystics were clergy or religious, they attracted a wide and enthusiastic following among the laity. The mysticism of the Low Countries and the Rhineland became corporate. Groups of laymen and laywomen formed societies like the Brethren of the Common Life, devoted to the practice of what was called the *devotio moderna,* "the new devotion," a fervent search for a more direct experience of God and an impatience with conventional liturgical practices that sometimes brought them to the verge of heresy. In other areas mysticism, though also increasingly widespread, tended to be more individual in its expression, as in Sweden, which produced Saint Bridget (1303–1373), and in Italy, which produced Saint Catherine of Siena (1347–1380), whose combination of an ascetic and intense mystical life with energetic action in public affairs is the best parallel in the late Middle Ages to Saint Bernard's earlier prophetic spirit.

In England, the fourteenth and fifteenth centuries produced a succession of extraordinarily eloquent mystics, including Richard Rolle the hermit (d. 1349), Walter Hilton (d. 1396), the anonymous author of the *Cloud of Unknowing,* and the anchoress Julian of Norwich (b. 1342?).

It is not useful to attempt a definition of mysticism here, for it is really not one phenomenon but a collection of similar phenomena. We shall here consider mysticism a variety of the spirit of prophecy in the Christian Church. Though usually the result of asceticism, meditation, and prayer, mysticism goes beyond all these. Many Christians have led ascetic, prayerful, and meditative lives without becoming mystics. Mysticism is the sense of an advanced state of union with God, where the individual seems drawn out of himself by the deity. The intensity of this communion impedes its communication to others. Mystics seem agreed that it is impossible to put the experience adequately into words. Yet mysticism is by no means devoid of intellectual content. Though there have doubtless been great numbers of people who have had mystical experiences without having been able or willing to make the attempt to report or analyze them, most mystical writing was done by mystics who have tried to elucidate and explain their experiences for the benefit of others. When one reads a mystical writer—and, much more, when one reads about mysticism— one must be aware that he is seeing through a glass darkly something that appeared in the original experience dazzlingly bright and clear.

In both semi-eremitical and corporate mysticism, as well as in other lay movements ranging from reform to witchcraft, women had a part disproportionately larger than that which they played in most other social contexts in the Middle Ages. No wholly convincing explanation has yet been made for this, though reasonable hypotheses have been put forward. For whatever reasons, in these groups women might attain more personal independence and influence than in other segments of society. One certainly is not obliged to believe the clerical anti-feminists of the Middle Ages and the psychoanalytical anti-feminists among modern scholars who have both suggested that the reason lay in the hysterical susceptibility of females. The most personally warm and eloquent of the English mystics was Julian of Norwich. It is possible to speculate in psychoanalytical terms on the circumstances and content of her revelations. But there is not one truth about human beings, but many; and there is not one way to understand them, but many.

It seems most useful to examine Julian's mind in the religious framework in which she and those for whom she wrote understood the world. Julian's *Revelations of Divine Love* is a work of intellectual prophecy, an attempt to express and elucidate an intense and moving mystical experience.

Very little is known of the external aspects of Julian's life. She was born about 1342. Early in her life she had asked God for three gifts—that she might experience Christ's passion as fully as if she had been there with the Marys; that she might be seriously ill while still young, the better to learn from suffering; and that she might receive the three "wounds" of contrition, compassion, and longing for God. At one time or another she may have been a Benedictine nun. It is certain that later she became an anchoress and most probably remained one until her death. An anchorite (female: anchoress) was one who withdrew (Gr. *anachôrein*) from the world for a life of prayer. Some were nuns and monks; others were laymen and laywomen. Instead of living in convents, they shut themselves up in rooms or apartments, the size and comforts of which varied considerably, from which they never emerged. They led a life of prayer and meditation in seclusion, although they might receive visitors or talk through a window to people in the street. This was not only a salutary modification of an eremitical life that might have proved too much of a strain for many but also allowed the anchorites to serve as spiritual counselors for others.

We know the date of Julian's revelation, but we do not know whether at that time she was living at home or whether she had become an anchoress. On May 8, 1373, having been granted her second wish—sickness unto death at age thirty—she had received the last rites and, unable to move, was gazing upon a crucifix that her confessor was holding before her eyes. It was four o'clock in the morning. In the five hours that followed she received fifteen showings, the sixteenth and last coming the following night.

Julian wrote two accounts of her experience. The first and shorter account seems to have been composed shortly after the revelation. It is less speculative and less confident. The second and more eloquent version, written about twenty years after the vision, contains the products of her long meditations about the revelation. At first she had been unsure about the meaning of the visions: Were they delirium, she wondered. If they were from God, what did they mean? Twenty years later she knew: " 'What, wouldst thou know thy Lord's meaning in this thing? Know it well. Love was his meaning. Who sheweth it thee? Love. Wherefore sheweth he it thee? For love. Hold thee therein. Thou shalt know more in the same, but thou shalt never know other therein, without end.' Thus was I learned that love is our Lord's meaning. And I saw full surely in this, and in all, that before God made us, he loved us. Which love was never slaked, nor ever shall be. And in this love he hath done all his works. . . . In our making we had beginning: but the love wherein he made us was in him from without-beginning. In which love we have our beginning. And all this shall we see in God without end."[2]

[2] All quotations from Julian's second account of her experience are from James Welsh's eloquent translation of *The Revelations of Divine Love of Julian of Norwich* (New York: Harper and Row, 1962), copyright © 1961 by James Welsh.

Julian's theology in the longer version is learned and relatively sophisticated without being original, the one striking exception being her perception of Christ as the *mother* as well as the Savior to his people. Scholars have debated to what extent she was influenced by Augustinian Platonism, by the Rhenish mystics, by Pseudo-Dionysius, by the Ancrene Riwle, and by the Bible. All are possible influences; only the last is certain. But such debates are of limited utility. The strength and power of Julian's revelations come not from her theology but from what Evelyn Underhill in *Essentials of Mysticism* called "that mixture of gaiety and awe, that balanced understanding of the natural and the divine," that characterizes them.

Julian's writing is personal, and however little we may know of her external life we come to understand her internal life, her personality, directly. It is her joy that impresses us most. The sins she warns us against most strongly are lack of hope and lack of zest—the uncongenial sins of dour despair. We should be full of joy and mirth as we approach our Lord, who is courteous, good, and merry. Christ, our kindly and forgiving mother, in his courtesy forgets our sins when we repent, and he wills that we also forget them, discarding all our heaviness and doubtful dreads. Though Julian's revelations were at one time circulated by well-meaning preceptors as "words of comfort," they are scarcely bland. She was a woman who had known suffering and sore pain in body and soul. Her joy is that she found at the core of suffering a point that is God and a love that is at the true heart of the matter.

Julian is in a sense more typical of the medieval religious spirit than are some of the other figures we have discussed precisely because she was more obscure. Her lack of political, economic, even intellectual influence in her own time made her appear irrelevant to most historians until the last half-century. It may be that the incipient breakdown of so many medieval ideas and institutions encouraged the reassertion of the individual in the late fourteenth and fifteenth centuries. Perhaps the intensity of her individual devotion to Christ makes her typical of the Christian individualism too often forgotten by those who study movements on the large scale.

The showings came to Julian as she lay sick unto death. When she fixed her eyes upon the crucifix, she recalled, "My sight began to fail; and the chamber around me grew as dark as if it had been night, except about the image of the cross where the daylight remained (I knew not how)." Suddenly then, "I saw the red blood running down from under the garland, hot and fresh, plenteous and life-like, just as it was in the time that the garland of thorns was pressed down upon his blessed head." This first showing, like those that followed, consisted of a vivid sense impression accompanied by intense feeling: "suddenly the Trinity filled full my heart with the utmost joy."

God's love sustains the universe: God "shewed a little thing, the size of a hazel-nut, which seemed to lie in the palm of my hand; and it was as round as any ball. I looked upon it with the eye of my understanding, and thought, 'What may this be?' I was answered in a general way, thus: 'It is all that is made.' . . . And this little thing that is made—it seemed as though it would fade away to nothing, it was so small." From this we learn that "no soul can be in rest until it is naughted of everything that is made," for nothing that is made has importance or meaning to us but God alone.

Though the universe is nothing in itself, it is real and full of meaning because God sustains it and loves it: "See, I am God: see, I am in all things: see, I do all things: see, I never lift my hands off my works, nor ever shall, without end: see, I lead all things to the end that I ordain it to, from without-beginning, by the same might, wisdom and love that I made it with. How should anything be amiss?"

Julian keenly feels the problem of pain and the problem of sin. Many of her showings are of the Passion of Christ, the pain of God, which is the pain of the world, and "there was no pain that could be suffered like to the sorrow I had, to see him in pain." "Here I saw, in my understanding, a great oneing between Christ and us. For when he was in pain, we were in pain; and all creatures that could suffer pain, suffered with him. . . . Thus was our lord Jesus pained for us; and we all stand in this way of pain, with him."

Into this pain Christ brings love, for his love induced him to suffer for us. " 'Behold and see that I loved thee so much (before ever I died for thee) that I would die for thee. . . . And now is all my bitter pain and all my hard travail turned to my everlasting joy and bliss.' . . . This shewed our good Lord to make us glad and merry, his countenance full of . . . mirth and joy." For "I may make all things well: and I can make all things well: and I shall make all things well: and I will make all things well: and thou shalt see thyself that all manner of things shall be well."

"Sin is the sharpest scourge that any chosen soul can be smitten with." But God does not abandon the sinner, for "This is the sovereign friendship of our courteous Lord, that he keepeth us so tenderly whilst we are in our sins." Indeed the worst sin is to forget this love and to abandon ourselves to despair. When troubled we must pray, no matter how little we may feel at the time that God can hear us. "Pray inwardly, though thou feelest naught, though thou seest naught, yea though it seemeth thou canst not pray for dryness and barrenness." For "the brightness and the clearness of truth and wisdom maketh [a person] to see and to know that he is made for love; in which love God endlessly keepeth him."

How deep is the love of God for man in his misery appears in the fifty-first chapter, which describes another showing: A "lord sitteth in solemn state, in rest and in peace. The servant standeth before his lord reverently, ready to do his lord's will. The lord turneth upon his servant a look full of love, sweet and meek. He sendeth him into a certain place, to do his will. The servant not only goeth, but starteth out suddenly, and runneth in great haste, for love, to do his lord's will. But straightway he falleth down into a ravine, and taketh full great hurt . . . but he cannot rise or help himself in any manner. In all this, the most misfortune that I saw him in was failing of comfort; for he could not turn his face to look upon his loving lord, in whom is full comfort; though he was very close to him. . . . And I beheld with deliberation to discover if I could perceive in him any fault; or whether the lord would assign to him any blame. And truly there was none seen; for his good will and his great desire were the only cause of his falling." One is reminded of Graham Greene's Major Scobie, in *The Heart of the Matter,* whose misdirected efforts to help others led to their ruin and his, yet sprang from his love and pity for them. For "Love and dread are brethren."

The difficulties with mysticism are many. There is the impossibility of knowing whether the experience comes from God or is delusion. Moreover, there are false prophets, cynical charlatans or self-deluded maniacs, who, in the words of the *Cloud of Unknowing,* "experience a spurious warmth [that] they imagine to be the fire of love," and from this comes much "hypocrisy and error." Yet hearing Julian, one feels that she was not mistaken in sensing, as did Father Paneloux in Camus' *The Plague,* "a light which glows, a small still flame, in the dark core of human suffering."

Conclusion

The shortness of this essay has made it necessary to omit discussion of the rich religious history of the Jews, the Muslims, and the Eastern Orthodox. The pattern of medieval Christianity itself was more intricate than we have shown, for there were as many threads in the pattern as there were individuals in Christian society. To understand medieval Christianity more fully, it would be necessary to explore its antecedents in the Near East, among the Greco-Romans, and in the Bible and the Church Fathers. It would be necessary to consider theology and the way Christians developed some of the perennial questions of human existence, such as the source of evil and the idea of justice, and it would be necessary to study in detail ecclesiastical institutions such as the episcopate, the papacy, and canon law. The problem of church and state and the history of mass religious movements have also scarcely been touched. The diversity of interpretations of these complexities is also much greater than has been described here. Historians who have been able to use the insights of psychology, social psychology, and sociology to good effect have in the past few decades greatly broadened understanding of medieval religion.

The purpose of this essay has been to get inside the phenomena of medieval religion. The two traditions of prophecy and order were equally concerned with opening the door to the Kingdom, and, having the same goal, they often worked together in the same individual. They are nearly always distinguishable, nonetheless, and frequently they are in tension with one another. Each of the eight individuals we have considered, though living in different chronological times and in various social circumstances and though diverging in their emphasis upon prophecy or order, manifested a burning desire to achieve the Kingdom.

A Critical Bibliography

This listing of books for further reading is very select. With a few exceptions, these works are readily obtainable in English.

The best church history in English will be *The Christian Centuries,* of which the first two volumes have appeared: Jean Daniélou and Henri Marrou, *The First Six Hundred Years* (London, 1964), and David Knowles and Dimitri Obolensky, *The Middle Ages* (London, 1969). A detailed series of volumes in French, now nearly completed, is Augustin Fliche and Emile Martin, *Histoire de l'église* (Paris, 1935–). Two short summaries of medieval church history have recently appeared: Richard W. Southern, *Western Society and the Church in the Middle Ages* (Harmondsworth, 1970), and Jeffrey B. Russell, *A History of Medieval Christianity: Prophecy and Order* (New York, 1968). An excellent comparative study of the English and the Italian churches is Robert Brentano, *The Two Churches* (Princeton, 1968). An anthology of fine selections is Marshall W. Baldwin, *Christianity Through the Thirteenth Century* (New York, 1970).

The history of Christianity at the time of Constantine and the Peace of the Church is the subject of a volume of essays edited by Arnaldo Momigliano, *The Conflict Between Paganism and Christianity in the Fourth Century* (Oxford, 1963). On the same topic see also A. H. M. Jones, *The Decline of the Ancient World* (New York, 1966); Jones, *Constantine and the Conversion of Europe* (London, 1948); and Andrew Alföldi, *The Conversion of Constantine and Pagan Rome* (Oxford, 1948). A good comparative study of the Latin and Byzantine Churches is Deno J. Geanakoplos, *Byzantine East and Latin West: Two Worlds of Christendom in Middle Ages and Renaissance* (New York, 1966).

On church and state in the West see Gerd Tellenbach, *Church, State and Christian Society at the Time of the Investiture Conflict* (Oxford, 1940); Norman F. Cantor, *Church, Kingship, and Lay Investiture in England, 1089–*

1135 (Princeton, 1958); T. R. S. Boase, *Boniface VIII* (London, 1933); the classic by Ernst Kantorowicz, *Laudes Regiae: A Study in Liturgical Acclamations and Mediaeval Ruler Worship* (Berkeley, 1946); and a number of recent and good collections: Bennett D. Hill, *Church and State in the Middle Ages* (New York, 1970); Brian Tierney, *The Crisis of Church and State 1050–1300* (Englewood Cliffs, 1964); Thomas M. Jones, *The Becket Controversy* (New York, 1970); Schafer Williams, *The Gregorian Epoch: Reformation, Revolution, Reaction?* (Boston, 1964).

On mysticism in general Evelyn Underhill's books *Mysticism* (London, 1911) and *The Essentials of Mysticism* (London, 1920) have not been surpassed. David Knowles, *The English Mystical Tradition* (London, 1961), has a good chapter on Julian. On Bernard's mysticism there is Etienne Gilson, *The Mystical Theology of Saint Bernard* (London, 1940).

David Knowles' *Christian Monasticism* (New York, 1969) is an excellent survey of the history of the subject by one of the greatest monastic historians. Other standard or recent books on aspects of monasticism are Herbert Workman, *The Evolution of the Monastic Ideal* (London, 1913; reprinted Boston, 1962); Jean Décarreaux, *Monks and Civilization* (London, 1964); R. B. Brooke, *Early Franciscan Government* (Cambridge, 1959); W. A. Hinnebusch, *History of the Order of Preachers* (New York, 1966–).

The best general history of the medieval papacy is Geoffrey Barraclough, *The Medieval Papacy* (New York, 1968). A recent brilliant study of medieval Christian political theory with emphasis upon the papacy is Karl F. Morrison, *Tradition and Authority in the Western Church 300–1140* (Princeton, 1969). Equally brilliant and already a classic is Walter Ullmann, *The Growth of Papal Government in the Middle Ages,* 2d ed. (London, 1962). On canon law, the best short book in English is Robert C. Mortimer, *Western Canon Law* (Berkeley, 1953).

On religious dissent, see Norman Cohn, *The Pursuit of the Millennium,* 3d ed. (London, 1970); Walter Wakefield and Austin P. Evans, *Heresies of the High Middle Ages* (New York, 1969); Gordon Leff, *Heresy in the Later Middle Ages,* 2 vols. (Manchester, 1967); Jeffrey B. Russell, *Dissent and Reform in the Early Middle Ages* (Berkeley and Los Angeles, 1965); Russell, *Religious Dissent in the Middle Ages* (New York, 1971); Robert Lerner, *The Heresy of the Free Spirit in the Later Middle Ages* (Berkeley and Los Angeles, 1972).

Books on other aspects of medieval thought particularly relevant to this essay are F. C. Copleston's clear introduction to the thought of Saint Thomas, *Aquinas* (Harmondsworth, 1955), and Gerhart Ladner's brilliant monograph, *The Idea of Reform* (Cambridge, Mass., 1959).

The Contributors

RICHARD L. DeMOLEN received his Ph.D. in history from the University of Michigan in 1969. Since 1970 he has been engaged in research at the Folger Shakespeare Library. His principal publications are *Erasmus of Rotterdam: A Quincentennial Symposium, Richard Mulcaster's "Positions," Desiderius Erasmus, The Meaning of the Renaissance and Reformation,* and *Printing and the Renaissance.* He is presently editing the correspondence of William Camden for the Royal Historical Society.

DAVID HERLIHY is professor of history at Harvard University. He earned his Ph.D. in history from Yale University in 1955. He has authored *Pisa in the Early Renaissance: A Study of Urban Growth* and *Medieval and Renaissance Pistoia: The Social History of an Italian Town* and has edited *Medieval Culture and Society* and *The History of Feudalism.* Professor Herlihy has received fellowships from the Fulbright Commission, the Guggenheim Foundation, the American Council of Learned Societies, and the Center for Advanced Study in the Behavioral Sciences.

DAVID NICHOLAS, an associate professor of history at the University of Nebraska, received his Ph.D. in history from Brown University in 1967. His major publications are *Town and Countryside: Social, Economic, and Political Tensions in Fourteenth-Century Flanders, Stad en Platteland in de Middeleeuwen,* and *The Medieval West: An Agrarian Society.* Dr. Nicholas has held fellowships from the Woodrow Wilson Foundation, the Social Science Research Council, the American Council of Learned Societies, the Fulbright Commission, and the National Endowment for the Humanities.

DONALD E. QUELLER earned his Ph.D. in history from the University of Wisconsin in 1954. In 1968 he became a professor of history at the University of Illinois. He is the author of *The Office of the Ambassador in the Middle Ages* and *Early Venetian Legislation on Ambassadors* and the editor of *The Latin Conquest of Constantinople.* Professor Queller has received fellowships from the Fulbright Commission, the Rockefeller Foundation, and the Guggenheim Foundation.

ROBERT E. LERNER received his Ph.D. in history from Princeton University in 1964. At present he is an associate professor of history at Northwestern University. Dr. Lerner has published *The Heresy of the Free Spirit in the Later Middle Ages* and *The Age of Adversity: The Fourteenth Century* and has been awarded fellowships by the Woodrow Wilson Foundation, the Germanistic Society of America, and the Fulbright Commission.

Jeffrey Burton Russell was awarded his Ph.D. in history from Emory University in 1960. He is presently professor of history at the University of California at Riverside. He has published *Dissent and Reform in the Early Middle Ages, Medieval Civilization, Prophecy and Order: A History of Medieval Christianity, Religious Dissent in the Middle Ages,* and *Witchcraft in the Middle Ages.* Professor Russell has also been awarded a Fulbright Scholarship, Harvard Junior Fellowship, a Guggenheim Fellowship, and a National Endowment for the Humanities Senior Fellowship.

Art Credits

Index